BABY FOOD UNIVERSE

RAISE ADVENTUROUS EATERS WITH A WHOLE WORLD OF FLAVORFUL PURÉES AND TODDLER FOODS

KAWN AL-JABBOURI, WITH GEMMA BISCHOFF, R.D.

FAIR WINDS

Brimming with creative inspiration, how-to projects, and useful information to enrich your everyday life, Quarto Knows is a favorite destination for those pursing their interests and passions. Visit our site and dig deeper with our books into your area of interest: Quarto Creates, Quarto Cooks, Quarto Homes, Quarto Lives, Quarto Drives, Quarto Explores, Quarto Gifts, or Quarto Kids.

First Published in 2017 by Fair Winds Press, an imprint of The Quarto Group,
100 Cummings Center, Suite 265-D, Beverly, MA 01915, USA.
T (978) 282-9590 F (978) 283-2742 QuartoKnows.com

21 20 19 18 17   1 2 3 4 5

ISBN: 978-1-59233-747-7

Digital edition published in 2017

Library of Congress Cataloging-in-Publication Data

Names: Al-Jabbouri, Kawn, author. | Bischoff, Gemma, author.
Title: Baby food universe : raise adventurous eaters with a whole world of
   flavorful purees and toddler foods / Kawn Al-Jabbouri with Gemma Bischoff,
   R.D.
Description: Beverly, Massachusetts : Fair Winds Press, 2017.
Identifiers: LCCN 2017018609 | ISBN 9781592337477 (paperback)
Subjects: LCSH: Infants—Nutrition. | Baby foods. | Quick and easy cooking. |
   BISAC: COOKING / Baby Food. | COOKING / Methods / Quick & Easy.
Classification: LCC RJ216 .A464 2017 | DDC 641.5/6222--dc23 LC record available at https://lccn.loc.gov/2017018609

Design: Kathie Alexander
Page Layout: *tabula rasa* graphic design
Illustration: Shutterstock
Photography: Kelly Pfeiffer

The information in this book is for educational purposes only. It is not intended to replace the advice of a physician or medical practitioner. Please see your health-care provider before beginning any new health program.

Printed in China

MIX
Paper from
responsible sources
FSC® C018479

CONTENTS

INTRODUCTION

HELLO, MY NAME IS KAWN, AND I AM MOM TO A BEAUTIFUL, SMALL FAMILY BASED IN DENMARK, AS WELL AS FOUNDER OF THE WEBSITE KIDS FOOD UNIVERSE. I AM VERY EXCITED TO INTRODUCE YOU TO THE EXCITING WORLD OF WEANING (INTRODUCING BABY FOOD), WHERE COLORS AND FLAVORS BURST OVER YOUR BABY'S TASTE BUDS ON A DAILY BASIS. INTRODUCING YOUR LITTLE ONE TO AMAZING TASTES AND TEXTURES AT AN EARLY AGE IS THE BEST WAY TO RAISE HEALTHY, ADVENTUROUS EATERS.

There are so many benefits of cooking your own baby food, and I am honored to guide you along this journey and share all that I have learned with my babies. Homemade baby food made from fresh foods you eat yourself is a far healthier, more nutritious choice than premade baby food. It gives you the chance to control what your baby eats while avoiding unnecessary sweeteners, food additives, and processing, which all compromise food's nutritional value.

Real, quality food does not have a six-month shelf life, but that is not something you will have to worry about when you make the food using fresh, trustworthy ingredients. Plus, believe it or not, this is the most economical way, by far, to feed your children. It is also a great way to instill healthy eating habits in your children for life. With all these benefits, be assured that your efforts to enhance your baby's diet and health are very wise ones, indeed.

When you first start feeding your baby food other than breast milk or formula (a stage known as weaning), you'll feed whole foods puréed for easy eating, which is exactly what most people think of when they think "baby food." But contrary to popular belief, puréed food does not have to be plain and distasteful. Just think of what you like to eat, and you'll realize a lot of it is great for your baby, too. And making these purées does not have to be difficult. I started my website to show parents that making homemade baby food is a much easier process than they might think! I was a first-time mom myself once, and if I could do it, so can you!

In the beginning, I spent every one of my first child's nap times studying nutritional facts and techniques on how to introduce solid food. For me, it was never an option to leave my son's diet up to someone else and pick jars from a supermarket's shelves. Over the course of my journey, I met and talked to many parents. None of the ones who make their own baby foods have ever regretted the time they spent in the kitchen (when they could have been resting) creating delicious, wholesome food for their children. While it can be hard finding the time, I love cooking, and I love to experiment with different types of food—exotic foods and superfoods—and I am on a mission to spice up the traditional bland baby-food experience with a more adventurous approach, while still following the guidelines for optimal nutrition.

Through my time, research, and kitchen experiments, I have come up with tons of easy-to-make, kid-approved recipes, and I'm thrilled to share them with you. This book is a collection of all my efforts, which, I think, will make it easier for you to discover the joy of cooking for your children. I hope you and your little one enjoy this journey just as much as my husband and I have.

ALWAYS CONSULT YOUR HEALTH PROFESSIONAL

The recommended age to start the weaning process is six months; please consult your child's health care provider if you wish to start earlier than this. Babies are different, and so are their needs. Some babies have a sensitive stomach (especially if born prematurely) and, therefore, need more time before they can start weaning. You will have to wait longer before you can introduce certain foods.

This book was examined by a dietitian and follows the global recommendations for nutrition, but if your health professional's advice conflicts with information in this book, follow her advice, as recommendations can change over time and your health professional has knowledge of any specific needs relating to your child's health and nutrition. Please let your doctor know if you have any concerns.

GETTING STARTED

Getting ready to start solids is less time consuming if you own the right tools and plan ahead. There is no need to buy expensive, fancy kitchen gadgets; you probably already have most of what you need. Of course, online websites are a great place to look if you need something, but do not forget your friends with older babies!

COOKING UTENSILS

FOLLOWING IS A BASIC LIST OF ESSENTIAL
AND OPTIONAL TOOLS TO KEEP ON HAND.

COOKING EQUIPMENT

- Paring knife and two cutting boards
- Saucepan or pot
- Steamer attachment, such as a steamer basket or a sieve, or steamer machine
- Immersion blender, food processor, or countertop blender
- Masher or just a fork
- Ovenproof baking dish
- Baby food freezer trays and single-portion containers or an ice cube tray

You might like owning these, too:

- Apple divider to core fruits like apples and pears
- Reusable pouches for meals on the go or for toddlers who like smoothies—I have made good use of reusable pouches and know many other parents who loved them as well. Search "reusable pouches" online and you will find hundreds of brands.

ESSENTIAL EQUIPMENT FOR BABY

- High chair
- Feeding spoons (not made of metal to begin with, as metal spoons can hurt your baby's gums)
- Bib
- Bowl and plate (made from nontoxic silicone)

THE BEST COOKING METHODS

HOMEMADE BABY FOOD ALWAYS TASTES BETTER WHEN YOU USE SEASONAL FRESH PRODUCE, AND IF YOU PREPARE IT THE RIGHT WAY, THERE WILL BE MINIMAL LOSS OF NUTRIENTS AND FLAVOR.

This section teaches you about the best cooking methods—steaming, roasting, and baking—to help keep your baby's food as nutritious and tasty as possible. Eating raw fruits and veggies is thought to be the best way to retain most nutrients, but raw foods require considerably more chewing than cooked food, especially for babies, which can increase the workload on the digestive system, so it's recommended to cook baby's food gently until his digestive system is well developed.

COOKING AND NUTRIENT LOSS

Temperature: Most fruits and vegetables are heat sensitive, which can lead to the damage and loss of significant amounts of nutrients when they're cooked. If you buy processed baby foods, look for those enriched or fortified—such as cereal fortified with iron—to make up for any nutritional losses during processing.

Water: Some fruits and vegetables lose nutrients, such as vitamins C and B, when exposed to water. The longer the produce is submerged in water, the more nutrients will wash out. A combination of heat and water submersion means an increased risk of nutrient loss.

DIETITIAN TIP

Cooking some vegetables actually increases the availability of certain nutrients our bodies use. Examples of this are lycopene in tomatoes and carotenoids (antioxidants) in carrots.

APPROXIMATE STEAMING TIMES

Vegetable	Cook Time	Vegetable	Cook Time
Asparagus	9 to 12 minutes	Okra	8 to 10 minutes
Broccoli florets	5 to 7 minutes	Parsnips	8 to 10 minutes
Brussels sprouts	10 to 15 minutes	Peas	2 to 4 minutes
Carrots, diced	5 to 7 minutes	Potato	10 to 20 minutes
Cauliflower florets	5 to 7 minutes	Spinach	2 to 4 minutes
Green beans	6 to 8 minutes	Sweet potato	8 to 12 minutes
Greens	5 to 10 minutes	Turnips	8 to 12 minutes
Kale	7 to 10 minutes	Zucchini	5 to 8 minutes

STEAMING

Steaming is a very gentle cooking method. It is one of the best methods for cooking baby food as it prevents nutrients from washing away in the water. Any type of steamer equipment will work, such as a steamer pot, steamer basket, a sieve, strainer, or colander.

If you use a bit too much water when steaming, you might notice the water changes color. This is because it had contact with the vegetables and some of the water-soluble nutrients have leached out. In this case, the best thing to do is use this water to thin purées or create broth to use for other meals, such as soups.

ROASTING AND BAKING

These methods are the easiest and, at the same time, some of the best ways to preserve the food's nutrients and flavor. Be wary of roasting in oil, however, as this significantly increases the calories in your child's meal.

BOILING

Boiling has a big disadvantage when it comes to cooking your baby's food—nutrient loss into the cooking water. However, this can be drastically decreased by using a small amount of water that only covers the bottom of the pot. You can also take advantage of the leftover boiled water, as it contains lots of nutrients and can be used to cook pasta or rice or to add flavor to purées.

KITCHEN HYGIENE

PROPER KITCHEN HYGIENE IS A VERY IMPORTANT PART OF MAKING HOME-COOKED BABY FOOD. WHILE IT IS NOT POSSIBLE TO CREATE A COMPLETELY STERILIZED OR GERM-FREE ENVIRONMENT, FOLLOWING THESE SIMPLE STEPS WILL HELP PREVENT BACTERIAL GROWTH.

1. Wash your hands with soap and water.

2. Wash kitchen utensils properly.

3. Wash all produce thoroughly.

4. Use different cutting boards for different types of food. Never cut produce and meat on the same cutting board.

5. Change kitchen towels often.

6. It is best to store the meal in the refrigerator or freezer immediately after it cools to avoid bacterial growth. (Bacteria grow fast at room temperature.) You can freeze baby food that has been refrigerated for 24 hours, but do not freeze it if it has been in the fridge for longer than that.

7. Do not reheat a meal more than once.

8. Never refreeze food that has been defrosted or reheated.

9. Leftovers from a meal should be thrown away, as food that has been in contact with saliva might be contaminated with bacteria.

PREPPING BABY FOOD

MAKING HOMEMADE BABY FOOD IS SO MUCH EASIER THAN MOST PEOPLE THINK—ESPECIALLY WHEN YOU PLAN AHEAD. BEING PREPARED HELPS MAKE COOKING NOT JUST A LOW-STRESS AFFAIR, BUT ALSO AN ENJOYABLE EXPERIENCE.

Batch cooking and prepping one to two weeks ahead will save you a lot of time and ensure a good, nutritious meal is always on hand.

1. Schedule a couple of hours in your calendar to do the cooking—maybe during your baby's nap time.

2. Choose a few recipes and write down the ingredients.

3. Shop for all the ingredients one day in advance.

4. Prepare the ingredients by peeling, cutting, pitting, and coring everything at once.

5. Cook as instructed in the recipes. Take it one recipe at a time.

6. Blend the ingredients and leave them to cool to room temperature.

7. Pour the mixture into clean baby food containers sized for individual meals. Do not overfill the containers, as the food expands when frozen. For younger babies that are just beginning the weaning process, freeze the meal in ice cube trays.

8. Seal the containers and label them with the date and the type of purée.

9. Reheat whenever you want to serve the meal (see page 14 for reheating methods).

These simple steps make it easy to keep a supply of healthy, delicious baby food that will last a few months in the freezer.

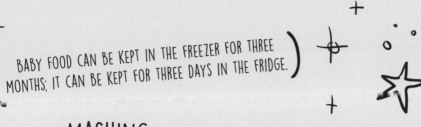

BABY FOOD CAN BE KEPT IN THE FREEZER FOR THREE MONTHS; IT CAN BE KEPT FOR THREE DAYS IN THE FRIDGE.

MASHING

When preparing your baby's meal, make sure the cooked produce is soft and easy to blend or mash—it should cut easily when stuck with a fork or knife. Blend the food according to your baby's ability to chew; if your baby can handle more than fluids, then try and mash the food with a fork or with a food masher, that way, you will give your little one something to chew on so they can practice the chewing motions.

FREEZING

Frozen baby food portions are the best way to ensure you always have nutritious meals on hand. When you cook a big batch of something and freeze it into small portions, you will be able to mix it with other vegetables you've prepared the same way. That way, you can mix, match, and vary the food your baby eats throughout the day, so your little one gets all the vitamins that different types of produce offer.

HOMEMADE BABY FOOD STORAGE GUIDELINES

Baby food meals can be kept frozen for three to six months. For optimal quality and nutrient retention, keep baby food cubes in the freezer no longer than three months. If you store your baby food in freezer bags, make sure the air is completely emptied from the bag so that it does not crystallize.

Keep in mind that some produce, such as pears, apples, bananas, and avocados, can change color once frozen.

⇨ DIETITIAN TIP

Submerging hot, just-cooked vegetables in cold water before puréeing is a process called "blanching and chilling." This inactivates enzymes (proteins involved in processes that result in food browning, mushiness, and off flavors) and helps ensure a better result when storing or freezing.

INCLUDING BREAST MILK AND INFANT FORMULA IN HOMEMADE BABY FOOD

When you start making purées, you will quickly discover that certain fruits and vegetables need a little more help than others to blend smoothly. Many recipes suggest adding plain water to make blending easier. I recommend using something much more nutritious, such as breast milk, formula, or a homemade broth for savory meals because it adds flavor to your baby's food as well as vital nutrients. Adding breast milk or formula also gives food a familiar flavor, so baby may be more tempted to try it.

USING FROZEN BREAST MILK AND FORMULA

Breast milk cannot be frozen twice. If you want to use it in a batch of food you intend to freeze, it has to be freshly expressed and only refrigerated before you use it in the recipe. Then, once mixed into your recipe, you can freeze it and defrost when required.

Most infant formula brands state they are not suitable for freezing as the formula separates in its frozen state. It is safe, it just changes texture when frozen. If you wish to add formula to your baby's meals, do so at the very end, after you defrost the food and just before you serve it.

REHEATING METHODS

There are several ways to reheat frozen home-cooked baby food—some better than others for retaining nutrients.

THAWING

Thawing is the best way to preserve the nutritional content. Simply thaw the desired portion overnight in the refrigerator. Always use the fridge because thawing at room temperature can cause bacterial growth. It will take about twelve to twenty-four hours for a baby purée to thaw in the fridge, depending on the portion size.

STOVETOP

This is a quicker way to thaw baby food. Place the frozen baby-food cube in a saucepan and reheat it slowly over low heat while stirring until it is completely defrosted and comfortably warmed. Let it cool a bit and serve.

MICROWAVING

Healthy microwaving practices are important. Always use microwave-safe containers to reheat food, and never cover with plastic wrap unless the package states it is microwave safe. If you want to steam something in the microwave, use minimal water and ensure the food is covered well.

When you microwave a food to thaw it, be sure to stir the food after it's heated and leave it to cool. Microwaving can leave hot spots in places and cold spots in others. The time it takes to thaw a food in the microwave varies depending on your microwave and the serving size.

LILLYPOTS

Lillypots are a unique product, specifically designed for heating baby food without compromising the nutrition. They are small easy-to-use pans, with separate compartments, that fit on top of a typical saucepan. It simply uses the heat from the simmering water below to defrost your small frozen portions of food safely and easily.

SHOPPING SMARTLY

MAKING HEARTY HOME COOKED MEALS FOR YOUR BUNDLE OF JOY ISN'T JUST HEALTHIER, IT'S LESS COSTLY IF YOU JUST KNOW HOW TO SHOP. HERE ARE SOME GREAT TIPS TO GET YOU STARTED.

SEASONAL PRODUCE

There are several benefits to buying seasonal produce: It tastes better, has a minimum loss of nutrients, and is usually less expensive. Produce that is frozen immediately after harvest retains its nutritional value, so buy fruits and veggies while in season and freeze them for later use.

CHOOSE ORGANIC

Babies eat much more food in relation to their body weight compared to adults, and, for that reason alone, it is best to introduce food that is free from harmful chemicals such as synthetic pesticides, GMOs (genetically modified organisms), synthetic hormones, artificial fertilizers, and antibiotics to provide the best nourishment for their fragile, developing brains and bodies.

There are some serious concerns about pesticides as many scientists have suggested links to a variety of long-term health problems, including hormone disruptions, cancer, and brain toxicity. Pesticides can be particularly damaging for babies' sensitive brains and body development because children's systems do not process toxins the same way adults do.

The Environmental Working Group (ewg.org) creates the "Dirty Dozen" and "Clean 15" lists to show consumers which produce is highly exposed to pesticides and should, preferably, be purchased organic, and which fruits and veggies are least likely to hold pesticides.

DIRTY DOZEN (PLUS A COUPLE)

1. Strawberries
2. Grapes
3. Apples
4. Celery
5. Peaches
6. Leafy vegetables such as spinach, kale, and salad greens
7. Sweet bell peppers
8. Nectarines
9. Cherries
10. Blueberries
11. Cherry tomatoes
12. Root vegetables such as potatoes, carrots, etc.
13. Pears
14. Cucumbers

CLEAN 15

1. Onions
2. Avocados
3. Pineapples
4. Mangos
5. Asparagus
6. Sweet peas (frozen)
7. Kiwi
8. Bananas
9. Cabbage
10. Broccoli
11. Papaya
12. Eggplant
13. Cantaloupes
14. Sweet potatoes
15. Watermelon

⇨ DIETITIAN TIP

You must still scrub and wash organic fruits and vegetables well to remove any soil or dirt, which can contain harmful bacteria.

INTRODUCING SOLID FOOD

YOUR LITTLE ONE WILL GET MOST OF HER NOURISHMENT FROM BREAST MILK OR INFANT FORMULA FOR THE FIRST YEAR. INTRODUCING SOLID FOOD IS TO SUPPLEMENT THAT.

When your infant turns six months, the iron reserve your baby is born with starts to decrease. (If your baby was born prematurely, then his doctor may have prescribed an iron supplement. This shouldn't be stopped when he begins on solids. Please follow the advice of your health care provider.) It's at this point that breast milk and infant formula can no longer provide your baby's developing brain and body with the energy and nutrients required, and you should, therefore, supplement his diet.

Another important reason to introduce solid food when your baby turns six months old is that postponing the introduction can make it harder for your baby to accept new foods.

IRON-RICH FOODS

- Red meats such as beef
- Chicken thighs
- Turkey meat
- Legumes
- Kale, spinach, and leafy greens

You can also mix in foods rich in vitamin C, as they help with the absorption of iron. Broccoli, red and yellow bell peppers, berries, and tomatoes are all high in vitamin C.

 DIETITIAN TIP

If your baby wakes up at night and you think it is due to hunger, you can start weaning by offering just a little baby cereal as a supper before bedtime. This will keep him fuller longer than milk alone.

8 SIGNS YOUR BABY IS READY FOR SOLID FOOD

YOUR BABY ...

- Can hold her head up—Your baby needs to be able to maintain a steady, upright position to take her first mouthfuls.

- Can sit up supported—Not all babies can sit by themselves by the time they are ready to wean. In that case, it would be fine if your baby sits on your lap while eating. The high chair can be introduced when your baby is sitting up completely unsupported.

- Makes chewing motions and is able to move chewed food to the back of his mouth and swallow it—If all the food is ending up around his face, you may need to wait a little longer.

- Demands feedings more frequently

- Seems less satisfied after a milk feed

- Has good coordination of the eyes, hands, and mouth—She can see a food, hold it, and put it in her mouth all by herself.

- Seems interested in food you eat and tries to reach for it

- Grabs the food and feeds himself with it

There are also signs that some people *mistake* for being signs of readiness. These include the following:

- Chewing on fists (can also be a sign of wanting to feel safe or comforted or of teething)

- Waking up during the night when baby has previously slept through the night (very common during growth spurts)

- Wanting extra milk feeds

FIRST MOUTHFULS

The World Health Organization recommendations say you should breastfeed or bottle-feed your baby exclusively for the first six months of his life. After that, you can start introducing solid food into the diet. However, every baby is different, and some babies need solid food before then. For example, if she is not satisfied with milk supplies only; has certain health issues; is not gaining weight as she should; or shows early signs of readiness and acceptance of solid food. If you think your baby is ready for solid food before six months, ask a health professional for the green light to start.

CHOOSE THE RIGHT TIME

It does not matter what time of day you offer the meal, but it is important that your baby is well rested and not too hungry when trying something new. Choosing the right time to introduce solid food is important for making the experience a positive one for both of you. A good time for your first try with solids is when your baby seems receptive and not cranky—after a naptime or 30 to 40 minutes before her usual feed time works well.

LIMIT DISTRACTIONS

Choose a place with limited distractions and make your baby feel comfortable. Try not to show signs of frustration, even if your baby refuses to eat the first mouthfuls. Babies tend to pick up on your feelings, and it can affect how they think and feel about the experience.

➪ DIETITIAN TIP

Remember the saying "food before one is just for fun!" Let your baby feel the food—yes, it gets messy, but understanding first with touch and sight enables her to familiarize herself with different food colors and textures. Plus, you can take some great photos to document this milestone!

THE TRANSITION

All babies are different—and so are their reactions to solid food. It is completely normal if your baby eats only a couple spoonfuls at feedings for the first couple of weeks. Your baby needs to adjust to the idea of eating something solid and to practice the chewing and swallowing motions. Your baby might rather play, poke, and smear the food instead of eating it—that is very common! He is exploring the new textures. Your little one loves to sense the food—not just through tasting it—and should be allowed to do so as it stimulates a number of senses in so many ways. Some babies get used to the idea of solid food immediately and already eat one-quarter to one-half cup (55 to 115 g) of food from the very first feeding.

The point is that there is no right or wrong way for your little one to eat. She will tell you the amount she wants and when she has had enough by turning her head to the side or by simply closing her mouth tightly. It is important that you respect their appetite and not force-feed. Babies pushed to clean the plate or to eat one more bite tend to ignore their own body signals, which can lead to overeating and weight problems in the future. If your baby does not finish his food most of the time, scale back the portions and just add more to the plate as he eats. As long as your baby is thriving and gaining weight according to his curve, rest assured that everything is fine.

Begin by feeding solid food at one meal a day. Nurse or bottle-feed your baby before or after serving the solid food; however, be aware that if you serve a bottle before the meal, your little one might not eat much solid food. As your baby gets used to her new diet, increase the amount of food according to your baby's appetite. Remember that teething and colds can also affect appetite. That is fine as long as her needs are met through milk feeds. When she is ready to try solids again, she will.

ALLERGENIC FOODS

SOME OF THE TOP ALLERGENIC FOODS ARE VALUABLE PARTS OF A HEALTHY DIET, AND THE NEW RECOMMENDATIONS DO ENCOURAGE PARENTS WITHOUT A FAMILY HISTORY OF FOOD ALLERGIES TO INTRODUCE THESE FOODS AT AN EARLIER AGE THAN PREVIOUSLY THOUGHT.

Eggs, fish, shellfish, peanuts, tree nuts, wheat, and gluten can be introduced as early as six months of age if you are careful—some of these foods can be choking hazards. For example, nuts should be ground or milled and peanut butter spread very thinly. Don't give whole nuts to a child under the age of five, due to the risk of choking.

TOP EIGHT ALLERGENIC FOODS

These eight allergenic foods make up 90 percent of children's food allergies. Unless otherwise noted, you can try introducing these foods as early as six months of age.

1. Cow's milk: not recommended until after twelve months of age

2. Eggs: especially the egg whites; the egg yolk rarely causes allergies

3. Peanuts and peanut butter, sesame seeds, and tahini

4. Tree nuts, such as almonds, cashews, hazelnuts, and walnuts

5. Soy

6. Wheat and gluten

7. Fish

8. Shellfish

COW'S MILK

The recommendation to wait to introduce cow's milk is not related to the risk of an allergic response; it is because as a main drink, cow's milk doesn't provide the nutrition your baby needs at a young age. However, dairy foods can be enjoyed as part of the weaning experience, such as full-fat natural or Greek yogurt, pasteurized cheeses, and whole cow's milk used in cooking.

INTRODUCING ONE INGREDIENT AT A TIME

When you introduce a new ingredient, wait four to seven days before you introduce another one. Once you are sure your baby is not allergic to a specific food, the coast is clear to include it with other ingredients you have also tested or are testing.

Children with a family history of allergies might be at higher risk of developing allergies themselves. If this is the case with your little one, it is better to wait until your baby gets older than the standard recommended age to introduce the top allergenic foods (see page 22). If your baby does have an allergy, do not be disheartened; most allergies are outgrown during early childhood. Your pediatrician will let you know when the time is right and safely guide you through the reintroduction to see if the allergy remains.

Myth alert! Eating nuts while pregnant or breastfeeding does not increase the risk of a child developing a nut allergy.

⇨ DIETITIAN TIP

If a child (or his immediate family) has been diagnosed with a food allergy, eczema, or asthma, there is a higher chance of that child having a peanut allergy. If you are concerned about this, speak to your child's doctor before introducing foods containing peanuts.

ALLERGIC REACTIONS

Signs of allergic reactions can include the following:

- Nausea and vomiting

- Diarrhea

- Hives (red spots like mosquito bites)

- Flushed skin or rash

- Swelling, especially of the lips, tongue, or face

- Difficulty breathing

- Loss of consciousness

These symptoms can be serious and **require immediate medical attention.** If you feel your baby may have a food allergy, inform her doctor and write down all foods your baby has eaten prior to the symptoms appearing. This will help the doctor recognize any patterns.

COW'S MILK ALLERGIES AND BREASTFEEDING

If your baby is diagnosed with a cow's milk allergy and you use infant formula, you will be prescribed a new, special formula. If your baby is breastfed, the mother will have to avoid all dairy food and switch to a milk alternative. There are many different plant and nut milks available. The most important thing to look for is a milk alternative that has been calcium enriched; otherwise, a supplement will be required for the breastfeeding mother.

As with introducing all new foods, the best practices for introducing allergenic foods are similar:

1. Introduce only one allergenic food at a time.

2. Introduce the food early in the day, so you can detect any symptoms during the child's waking hours.

NON-ALLERGENIC REACTIONS

SOME FOODS DON'T TRIGGER ALLERGIC REACTIONS BUT CAN CAUSE DISCOMFORT DUE TO SENSITIVITY TO CERTAIN FOODS, MANIFESTING IN THE FORM OF RASHES, CONSTIPATION, OR DIARRHEA. IF YOUR BABY HAS A REACTION TO A PARTICULAR FOOD THEN IT IS BETTER TO HOLD OFF WITH THIS FOOD UNTIL HIS DIGESTIVE SYSTEM IS WELL DEVELOPED.

DIAPER RASHES

Apart from teething periods, some food types do trigger diaper rash, especially acidic foods like citrus fruits. So, if your little one has a bout of diaper rash, avoid these foods:

- Kiwi
- Tomatoes and tomato-based foods
- Citrus fruits and juices
- Watermelon
- Strawberries
- Pineapple
- Sour apples, plums, and peaches
- Grapes

CONSTIPATION

Constipation in babies can be caused by several things. First, babies who are exclusively breast-fed can undergo a phase of constipation when first being introduced to solid foods. A diet low in fiber contributes to constipation as well. This is a big part of why it is important to vary your baby's diet.

Some other reasons can be the following:

- Diets low in fiber (as noted)
- Diets high in fiber but low in fluids
- Calcium-rich diets (yogurt, cheeses, and milk)
- Bananas, apple purée, and starchy foods such as breads, pasta, and white potatoes can also cause constipation.

If your baby is constipated, try to stimulate his bowels by "bicycling" his legs around while he lies on his back or gently massage his tummy. If older children suffer with constipation, give them more whole-grain foods to increase their fiber intake.

Foods that can help relieve constipation and act as a natural laxative include the following:

- Apples
- Apricots
- Flaxseed/flax oil
- Grapes
- Prunes, peaches, plums, and pears
- Raspberries
- Strawberries

DIARRHEA

If your baby experiences diarrhea, probiotic yogurts and starchy foods like bananas can help regulate that. During this time, make sure that he gets enough fluids (especially in hot weather).

IMPORTANT!

It is essential to watch for dehydration in babies and children who have persistent diarrhea. Keep offering their milk feeds as usual—focus on fluids rather than solids if they lose interest in eating. Don't dilute formula, but you can offer sips of water between feeds.

If you are worried that your baby is getting dehydrated (signs include sunken eyes, a sunken soft spot on a young baby's head, a dry mouth, fewer wet diapers, or dark yellow urine), contact the doctor. You can also consider an oral rehydration solution to help rehydrate baby (available from most pharmacies).

FOODS THAT CAN CAUSE BLOATING AND GAS

Some foods may cause gas and be a bit hard for your baby's tiny tummy to digest. If you find that's the case with certain foods, cut them from baby's diet for now and reintroduce them in a couple of months. If your baby has persistently painful or extreme gassiness, consult a pediatrician, as it might be a food intolerance. Here are some foods that can cause gas and bloating:

- Artichokes
- Beans and legumes
- Bran
- Broccoli
- Brussels sprouts
- Cabbage
- Cauliflower
- Garlic
- Onions
- Prunes and plums

Sometimes, mixing spices and herbs with gas-producing foods can ease the effects of bloating or help get rid of them. For instance, ground cumin is often added to meals that contain beans and legumes, as it can help reduce indigestion.

FOODS TO AVOID IN THE FIRST YEAR

- **Honey** can contain bacteria that cause botulism in babies under the age of twelve months.

- **Whole milk as a drink**—Babies cannot get the nutrition they need from cow's milk; breast milk or infant formula should remain the main drink until the age of one. When you introduce milk, offer whole milk, not reduced-fat milks, as your baby will need the extra calories and nutrients.

    - At the age of two, slowly switch to semi-skimmed milk if your baby is eating a balanced diet and is growing well.

    - Between ages one and three, your baby/toddler will need around 350 milligrams of calcium per day. This is equal to about 9½ ounces (280 ml) of whole milk. If you also offer cheese or yogurt during the day, this also contributes to calcium intake.

    - Don't offer one-percent milk until after five years of age, as it doesn't contain enough calories or vitamin A.

- **Salt** should be avoided. Babies' kidneys do not process salt well and it can harm their kidneys.

    - Between one and three years of age, your baby/toddler should consume no more than 2 grams of salt per day (or 800 mg sodium). To ensure your baby doesn't consume too much salt, do not offer processed meats, takeout meals, chips, packet soups and sauces, or add stock cubes or bouillon to meals.

- **Whole nuts** should not be introduced until five years of age, as they pose a choking hazard.

- **Soft/blue cheeses**—Gorgonzola, Brie, Camembert, and other mold-ripened soft cheeses are best avoided for the first year, as they are usually made with unpasteurized milk.

- **Liver pâté**—Liver can be introduced after six months, but it is recommended that infants and young children do not have liver or liver products more than once a week for the first year, and, when they do have them, it should only be in limited amounts. Liver is very high in vitamin A, which can be harmful if eaten in excess.

- **Caffeinated drinks**—Tea and coffee are not suitable for babies or children. Even if you feel tempted to add tea to your baby's milk bottle to warm the milk, do not do it as tea may prevent the absorption of iron. However, some herbal drinks, such as those containing fennel but no caffeine, can have a calming effect if your baby is having tummy aches or gas and are fine in small quantities.

- **Sugar**—Avoid using sugar or any artificial sweeteners. They are not nutritious and are not good for your baby. Always check food labels for these hidden sugars: white sugar, honey, glucose/maple/corn syrups, fructose, unrefined brown sugar, cane sugar, nectar, fruit juices, and smoothies. Instead, use natural sources to sweeten purées, like dates, stewed or dried figs, apricots, prunes, or mashed ripe banana. You can even sweeten purées with infant formula and breast milk, as they have a naturally sweet taste. Babies under two years of age should consume no more than 2 grams (about ½ teaspoon, or 3 cubes) of sugar per day.

- **Certain additives**—The additives E102, E104, E110, E122, E124, E129, and E211, often found in sweets such as lollipops, cakes, juice drinks, baked goods, biscuits, and some canned food and yogurts, have been linked to an increase in hyperactive behavior and should be avoided.

- **Raisins**—These should be avoided for the first year, and children under the age of three years should not have more than 50 grams (about 2 ounces) of raisins a week. Raisins can have an increased amount of ochratoxin, which can be carcinogenic.

CHOKING HAZARDS—ALWAYS BE PRESENT

A golden rule when serving your little one a meal is that you should ALWAYS be present during mealtime, even throughout toddlerhood. In case your child chokes, you need to be there to help. Avoid letting your little one run, walk, or lie down while eating. A further caution is to avoid giving your little one food in the car seat while you cannot supervise. Teach your baby or toddler to sit down during mealtimes—it can reduce the risks of choking.

When an infant or toddler chokes, it happens silently—even if you are next to him but on the phone, you could very easily not notice. Coughing or gagging is not a sign of choking. If your baby is choking—he won't be able to cry or make much noise.

Choking-hazard foods include the following:

- Hot dogs and sausages—cut these into long noodle-like strips until your child is four years old. (I avoid them completely, as they aren't very healthy—or buy the nitrite-free types.)

- Popcorn—not until three years of age

- Whole nuts or chopped nuts—not until the age of five. (Ground nuts are fine from six months on.)

- Whole grapes—cut lengthwise until your child is four years old.

- Sticky, soft foods such as peanut butter in *large* dollops—make sure to thin out these foods when using as a spread; it can stick to the roof of a child's mouth and form a glob.

- Marshmallows, chewing gum, and hard candies

- Large chunks of meats and cheese—shred or cut these up. Cut meats no larger than your fingertip or slow cook them until very tender.

- Produce that is hard and solid, such as apples, carrots, and celery—either shred or cook them and cut them up. Raw apples can be given at two years old and raw carrots after the age of three.

BE A GOOD ROLE MODEL

FAMILY MEALS TOGETHER ARE A GREAT TIME TO MODEL GOOD EATING HABITS BY PUTTING PHONES, LAPTOPS, AND EVERYTHING ELSE ASIDE AND CONNECTING WITH EACH OTHER. IN FACT, KIDS WHO EAT FAMILY MEALS TOGETHER PICK UP BETTER EATING HABITS THAN THOSE WHO DO NOT SIT TOGETHER AT MEALTIMES.

If your little one sees the adults in the home eating a varied and healthy diet, they will most likely follow your lead—maybe not straight away, but eventually! Therefore, be present and eat at least one meal every day with your little one to teach the values and enjoyment of eating together at the family table.

OFFER A DIVERSITY OF FOOD

Your baby might not like the taste of cauliflower or other foods the first couple of times, but do not get discouraged. This is completely normal. Your baby needs to adjust to the new flavors he is exposed to. Keep offering the food for eight to ten weeks as part of a varied diet, and your little munchkin will eventually learn to accept and like that food. Do not force it; it can easily become a control game.

A good way to entice your little one to accept new foods is to eat that food yourself. Show him you like eating greens by saying things like, "Mmmm. This Brussels sprout is delicious!" This creates curiosity and tempts him to try it. Letting your baby eat with children the same age or older can also help him become more adventurous with foods. Weaning is a new experience, and it takes time, so do not get frustrated—it is all part of the journey.

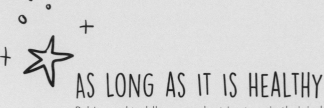

AS LONG AS IT IS HEALTHY

Babies and toddlers eagerly strive to gain their independence, and may be insistent about which foods they want to eat. It's great to ask your child for his input on what he wants to eat (he'll be more than happy to eat something he chooses himself), but open-ended questions like "What do you want for breakfast?" can lead your little one to become demanding at mealtimes. Instead, try offering a couple of healthy options: "Do you want scrambled eggs or oatmeal for breakfast?" This allows your little one to satisfy his need for control while still nourishing his small, developing body.

TEXTURES

Always encourage your little one to try different textures. Once he masters thin purées and cereals, gradually thicken their consistencies by reducing the amount of liquid added. It will help your baby practice the chewing motion (also essential for speech development) so he can transition to increasingly solid food, and then table food, which is our main goal.

There are several ways to introduce solid food, but most infants go through these stages in this order:

1. Thin or runny purées the consistency of yogurt

2. Semi-liquid purées that contain some small lumps

3. Mashed foods

4. Small finger foods

In the beginning, make sure the meals don't contain any large pieces of food. Blend ingredients well, at least until your little one masters the chewing motion and can handle bigger chunks or lumps of food. When your baby gets used to one texture, move to the next stage. We want the end result to be table food, but always offer the food according to your little one's readiness.

TEETH FOR SOLID FOOD

THE NUMBER OF TEETH YOUR BABY HAS IS NOT A FACTOR WHEN DEALING WITH SOLID FOOD—YOU MIGHT BE SURPRISED BY HOW WELL BABIES CAN CHEW SOLID FOOD USING THEIR GUMS!

Many babies are ready to eat more substantial food than just purées around seven to eight months of age and should not be stopped if they do not yet have any teeth. As long you make sure the food is soft finger food—like hard-boiled eggs, steamed carrots, or ripe fruit—they can chew on it and it will dissolve easily.

Delaying the introduction of finger foods into toddlerhood can make toddlers develop an aversion to whole pieces of food and textured food, which may make them fussier and selective toward whole foods. A one-year-old should be able to handle soft, cut-up table food regardless of the number of teeth she has. If you are still uncomfortable serving finger food by that time, I suggest consulting a health professional to guide you through moving to more solid foods or even be present when you serve the food if choking hazards are your concern.

INTRODUCING FOOD:
FOUR TO SIX MONTHS

AS ALREADY NOTED, IT IS BEST TO WAIT UNTIL YOUR BABY TURNS SIX MONTHS OLD TO INTRODUCE SOLID FOODS. ONE REASON IS THAT YOUR SIX–MONTH–OLD'S IMMUNE SYSTEM WILL BE STRONGER AND MORE RESISTANT TO FOOD–BORNE INFECTIONS.

Not all food is suitable for babies that young, though, as their digestive systems cannot process certain kinds of food. Most babies younger than four to six months will also push food out of their mouths due to the tongue-thrust reflex. However, it often only takes a few spoonfuls for babies to learn to keep the food in their mouths, but a six-month-old baby will do it with more ease as she is more developed.

If your health care professional suggests introducing solid foods earlier than six months, it is important to know which foods are not suitable at that age. The following foods **should be avoided for four- to five-month-old babies:**

- Foods containing wheat and gluten: bread, pasta, breakfast cereals, etc.

- Eggs

- Fish and shellfish

- Meats

- Citrus fruits

- Nuts and seeds (The small pieces can irritate their delicate gut lining.)

- Liver

- Soy products (tofu, soy milk)

- Dairy foods, especially soft and unpasteurized cheeses and cow's milk

- Honey

Take the introduction of solid foods slowly. Use simple ingredients and wait at least four days between the introductions of each food, so you can check for allergies along the way.

BABY-LED WEANING

Baby-led weaning essentially skips the traditional purée stage and immediately starts with soft finger foods that babies can handle themselves. This way, you give your baby full control of what she eats and how much she wants to eat, while experiencing food in its original form. You can find recipes that are great for baby-led weaning in chapter 5.

Parents typically start baby-led weaning around the age of six months; before then, baby simply will not have developed the necessary motor skills to feed himself. In the very early stages, baby is given steamed stick pieces of food, typically about the size of a large chip. They need to be this size so baby can easily pick them up and get them to his mouth. The softness of the finger food can vary, but, generally, you should be able to squish the pieces between your thumb and forefinger easily, much like, say, a slightly overripe avocado.

While this technique suits some babies more than others, there is no right or wrong way of introducing solid food as long as the food is healthy, varied, and age appropriate. Many parents do a mixture of both baby led weaning and purées.

Parents can often be undecided about baby led weaning due to the worries about choking. However, if food is prepared correctly and baby is well supervised, then the choking hazard is no greater than if your baby eats purées.

It is important to follow baby's lead and not be too disappointed if it does not go according to plan. Weaning of all varieties is a messy, but very fun, affair and should be treated as such.

FOODS FOR FOUR+ MONTHS

Fruit

Apples
Banana*
Peach*
Pears*

Vegetables

Avocado*
Butternut squash
Hokkaido pumpkin
Sweet potato

Cereals and Grains

Buckwheat
Cornmeal
Millet
Oats
Rice (once per week)

May be served raw if very ripe

FOUR TO SIX MONTHS:
GOOD FIRST FOODS FOR EARLY WEANING

Babies who are introduced to solid food at four to six months should usually be served easily digested food that is thin and puréed and ranked very low on the allergy scale. More solid, chunkier foods, like soft, cooked bits of age-appropriate foods, can be eaten by most babies at six months. Follow your baby's lead; see what he is ready for when it comes to textures.

Babies can start food as early as four months if they no longer seem satisfied by just milk alone. If this is the case with your baby, then follow the guidance of your pediatrician for early weaning. At four months old, your baby only has a very small stomach, so he will only be able to eat small amounts of food at a time (try Baby's First Apple Purée on page 60, Sweet Potato Purée on page 65, or Butternut Squash Purée on page 66). Milk should remain the primary source of nutrition, and your baby should be consuming around 2 to 3 ounces (60 to 90 ml) of milk per pound (455 g) in weight. (This is a guide; if your baby takes much more or less than this, please speak to your health care provider.)

When your baby starts on solid food at six months, some good first foods can be grain porridges and vegetable purées with a little meat. Fruit purées are great as snacks between meals or as toppings to breakfast cereals. You can use fruit pulp to sweeten the porridge and vary the taste, or give fruit purées as dessert after a savory meal. The content of vitamin C in fruits and vegetables makes it easier for the body to absorb iron from other foods.

Avoid using fruit purées as a main meal, though. They are usually very light and do not satisfy for as long as vegetables and proteins do. Also, fruit does not contain enough calories to support your baby's needs—and babies tend to prefer sweet flavors over vegetable purées. Do not focus on fruits until vegetables are an established part of your baby's diet, just in case the sweet flavors make them turn his nose up at healthier, heartier veggies.

If your baby is under six months of age, avoid serving grain porridges that contain gluten. This can, potentially, lead to a gluten intolerance. When you cook porridges, vary the grain types, and once you do introduce porridges with gluten at six months, continue varying the porridges, serving ones with and without gluten. Cornmeal, millet, rice, buckwheat and amaranth are all gluten-free options, while rye and wheat contain gluten. Oats are naturally gluten-free but are often contaminated with gluten during production, so be sure to look for a gluten-free label on the packaging. Also avoid using too much high-fiber food, like brown rice and cereals with a lot of bran, as they can cause diarrhea.

MEAL PLAN FOR FOUR TO SIX MONTHS

Breakfast
- Breast milk or infant formula
- Baby cereal or cooked and puréed apple or mashed banana or mashed avocado

Lunch
- Breast milk or infant formula

Dinner
- Breast milk or infant formula

Before bed
- Millet or oat porridge made with breast or formula milk
- Breast milk or infant formula

LIMIT RICE: ALL TYPES

Rice contains inorganic arsenic, which has been linked to long-term health effects.

- Limit rice-based porridges.

- Only serve two or three servings per week, especially for infants.

- Cook rice in a large volume of water, using the ratio of 1 part rice to 6 parts water.

- Rice milk should not be given to children under the age of three years old.

⇨ DIETITIAN TIP

Leave oat porridge to soak overnight in the milk, and then it can just be gently warmed in the morning. You can also serve it cold if you like, which is great for the summer.

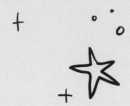

FOODS TO LIMIT OR AVOID

Certain foods, while very nutritious, should be offered only sparingly because they contain high amounts of nitrates, a chemical that occurs naturally in vegetables but may cause a rare but serious blood disorder called *methemoglobinemia* (a type of anemia, also known as "blue baby," that inhibits the blood's absorption of oxygen) in infants.

VEGETABLES HIGH IN NITRATES

It is recommended that you not feed your baby green beans, squash, spinach, beets, fennel, celery root, or carrots under the age of six months. After six months, you can feed these veggies to your baby, but spinach, beets, fennel, and celery root should still not make up more than one-tenth of a meal and should only be served a few times a month.

FISH WITH HIGH LEVELS OF MERCURY

Fresh tuna and other oily fish with high levels of mercury, such as swordfish, king mackerel, shark, and tilefish, have many nutritional benefits, but, due to environmental toxins like methylmercury, they should be limited or completely avoided for babies and toddlers under the age of three years. The content of methylmercury is easily absorbed by the body and can affect babies' and toddlers' brain development and nerve system.

Salmon is good for babies, but buy wild salmon rather than farmed salmon. Even frozen wild Alaskan salmon is a healthier option than salmon bred in fish farms, as wild-caught salmon contains fewer toxins and are less polluted because they live and eat in the open water of their natural environments.

APRICOTS DRIED WITH SULFUR DIOXIDE

Most dried fruits are chemically treated with sulfur dioxide to prevent spoiling and to preserve their color. It is an air pollutant and can cause severe health problems. Buy the ugly brown organic dried apricots; these are untreated and natural.

IMPORTANT PARTS
OF YOUR CHILD'S DIET

CHILDREN NEED A BALANCED DIET THAT WILL HELP THEM MAINTAIN A HEALTHY WEIGHT AND NORMAL DEVELOPMENT. ENCOURAGING YOUR CHILDREN TO EAT FROM THE DIFFERENT FOOD GROUPS IS A GREAT WAY TO MAKE SURE THEY GET ALL THE NOURISHMENT THEY NEED. PROTEINS, CARBOHYDRATES, AND FAT ARE JUST AS IMPORTANT TO YOUR CHILD'S DIET AS FRUITS AND VEGETABLES.

PROTEINS

Proteins are important for your little one's growth and development. Do not just offer red meats, though; offer a variety of lean meats, like fish and skinless chicken and turkey. Also, protein does not only mean meat. You can also get it through dairy, legumes, meat alternatives (tofu/soy), eggs, and some plants.

CARBOHYDRATES

Carbohydrates provide your little one's cells with energy and are your baby's main source of energy. Starch is the most important part of carbohydrates, which you find in bread, dried beans and lentils, grains, pasta, potatoes, white rice and brown rice, and sweet potatoes.

⇨ DIETITIAN TIP

Take great care in ensuring all bones are removed when serving fish. Also, where possible, buy responsibly caught fish. Look for the blue Marine Stewardship Council label on packaged fish for assurance the fish comes from a certified sustainable fishery.

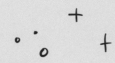

DAIRY

When it comes to drinking milk, stick to breast milk or formula until your little one turns one. Cow's milk does not contain the essential nutrients your baby needs in the first year. However, it is completely fine to cook your baby's food with cow's milk from six months of age on. It adds a creamy, familiar flavor and calcium to porridges and provides more nutrients than water. Remember to always offer your baby the full-fat version, as she needs the calories. Do not feed low-calorie spreads, yogurts, and reduced-fat cheeses to baby.

Milk Substitutes

Plant and nut milks (soy, almond, rice, and coconut) should not be given to babies or toddlers (unless advised by a health care professional) as a substitute for drinking milk, as they do not contain anywhere near the nutrients required to grow and develop properly. These can, however, be used for cooking and in smoothies if no allergies are present.

IRON

Iron affects brain development and is also important for the blood and muscles. Anemia, which is iron deficiency, is one of the most common nutritional diseases and can cause weakness and tiredness in your infant. Great sources are oily fish, red meats, turkey and chicken thighs (dark meat), apricots, egg yolks, leafy greens, and legumes like lentils and beans.

⇒ DIETITIAN TIP

It is recommended that babies not be given soy-based formula or soy milk due to the phytoestrogen content of these milks. Phytoestrogens mimic female sex hormones, and there are concerns that exposure to phytoestrogens can affect the development of male reproductive organs in young babies.

For older children consuming a balanced diet, the amount of phytoestrogens is significantly lower in relation to their body size.

KEY FACTORS FOR RAISING VEGAN AND VEGETARIAN BABIES

If you are vegetarian or vegan and want to raise your baby using the same diet, then there are several important nutritional factors to consider. Here are a few keys for raising robust vegan or vegetarian babies:

- While breastfeeding, a vegan mom should continue to take vitamin B_{12} and vitamin D supplements, as she did during pregnancy.

- Then during late weaning, vegetarian and vegan children even more so need special attention paid to their iron and calcium Intake.

- Also pay close attention to your baby's energy level. Diets that rely heavily on plant-based foods tend to be much higher in fiber and lower in energy than diets that contain animal proteins, so it is essential that vegan and vegetarian babies are offered foods rich in healthy fats and plant proteins and that they consume fortified cereals (for iron and vitamin B_{12}) as well as calcium-enriched plant milks. (Babies who are given formula milk do not require additional vitamin supplements as the formula milk is already enriched.)

FAT

Fat plays a very important role in a child's diet and should be incorporated into meals to help fuel rapid growth—not to mention fat helps the absorption of vitamins A, D, E, and K.

Breast milk and infant formula both contain lots of fat, and, for the first twelve months, these should be your baby's primary fat source. According to pediatricians, babies and toddlers under the age of two years should get 50 percent of their total energy (calories) from a variety of fat types. As you prepare food for your baby or toddler, incorporate healthy fats into the diet. It is recommended to focus on omega-3 fats that are found in salmon, flaxseed, cold-pressed canola oil (also known as rapeseed oil), kale, and eggs.

A generous helping (about ½ teaspoon, or 3 g) of fat should be added to each meal that does not contain infant formula, breast milk, or meat. Do this starting with the very first home-cooked meal you prepare for your baby. You will find most of my recipes say to add a fat of choice. Here are examples of what I like to use:

- Cold-pressed canola oil (non-GMO)
- Grass-fed dairy butter (It contains more nutrients.)
- Extra-virgin olive oil
- Coconut oil
- Avocado oil (or just avocado)
- Nut butters (from six months if no allergies present themselves)

HERBS AND SPICES

Once your little one is introduced to each food separately to determine whether there are any allergies, you do not need to create a special menu for him. Just cook food that the whole family eats and set a portion aside before adding any seasonings. Most pediatricians recommend introducing spices at eight months of age, not because of allergies, but because they can cause tummy aches and heartburn.

Herbs, on the other hand, can be added to baby's meals as early as six months.

⟹ DIETITIAN TIP

Certain oils don't respond well when heated due to their chemical makeup. For example, extra-virgin olive oil, melted coconut oil, and avocado oil should be added to your baby's food after it is cooked because if heated to a high temperature, they start to break down and release toxins called free radicals that can attack our body's cells.

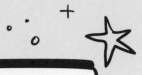

HERBS, SPICES, AND THEIR POSSIBLE BENEFITS

HERBS AND THEIR BENEFITS

Start introducing herbs at six months.

Basil: has antibacterial properties, calms the stomach, and helps with loss of appetite and gas

Dill: boosts digestive health; gives relief from insomnia, hiccups, and diarrhea; and has high amounts of vitamins A and C

Oregano: helps with coughs, asthma, croup, and bronchitis; also used for stomach disorders such as heartburn and bloating

Rosemary: helps with loss of appetite and digestive problems including heartburn and intestinal gas; also used for coughs

Thyme: is an appetite stimulant; helps with cough, sore throat, colic, upset stomach, gas, diarrhea, bedwetting, dyspraxia (a movement disorder in children), and parasitic worm infections

SPICES AND THEIR BENEFITS

Start introducing spices at eight months.

Cinnamon: aids digestion and is a good antioxidant; helps with muscle and stomach spasms; prevents nausea and vomiting, diarrhea, infections, colds, and loss of appetite

Cumin: effective against diarrhea and gas problems in babies and children; a pinch in gassy food like legumes will help your baby get rid of gassiness more easily; helps treat colic and bowel spasms; and is also used to increase urine flow to relieve bloating

Curry (a mixture of other ingredients): boosts bone health and protects the immune system from bacterial growth; increases our liver's ability to remove toxins from the body

Nutmeg: helps babies sleep better and aids easy digestion; treats stomach problems like gas

SIX TO SEVEN MONTHS

AFTER THE FIRST TASTES OF SOLID FOOD, YOUR BABY WILL BE READY FOR MORE
FLAVORFUL COMBINATIONS AS WELL AS THICKER CONSISTENCIES. YOUR BABY'S
DIGESTIVE SYSTEM IS NOW READY FOR MORE SUBSTANTIAL AND APPETIZING FOODS.

After doing a four- to seven-day test for allergies, you can start combining more foods that your little one has not shown any reaction to, such as millet with mashed banana or cooked egg yolk or sweet potato and kale.

At six months you can now introduce the following:

• eggs

• fish

• gluten (wheat and rye)

• lean meat

• nuts (ground)

• small amounts of dairy products (cottage cheese, cheeses, and full-fat yogurt as well as other dairy products)—For children under the age of three, avoid curd and quark because they contain high amounts of protein that can be difficult for small children to digest.

MEAL PLAN FOR SIX TO SEVEN MONTHS

Breakfast
• Breast milk or infant formula
• Buckwheat porridge topped with date purée
• Fruit/vegetable purée, such as carrot and banana

Lunch
• Breast milk or infant formula

Dinner
• Savory meal such as mashed broccoli and white potato purée
• Breast milk or infant formula

Before bed
• Breast milk or infant formula

SEVEN TO NINE MONTHS

BY NOW, YOUR BABY WILL LIKELY HAVE STARTED ON A RANGE OF PURÉED AND MASHED FOODS, AND MAYBE EVEN SOME FINGER FOODS. SHE WILL BE GETTING NECESSARY FATS AND CARBOHYDRATES FROM THESE FOODS AND HER BREAST MILK OR FORMULA FEEDINGS.

Your seven- to nine-month old baby will now need approximately four hundred calories from the food she eats each day, which should also provide the following:

- 6 grams of protein
- 200 milligrams of calcium
- 3.5 milligrams of iron
- 2 milligrams of zinc

MASHED FOOD AND FINGER BITES

Most babies are ready for soft finger foods at this age as their hand-to-eye coordination is more developed. Some babies master this earlier; follow your baby's lead. His appetite is likely to have increased by now, and he likely eats bigger portions of solid food. Interest in self-feeding has probably grown, which is a step toward independence and eating table food—encourage this behavior. Most babies' digestive systems are ready for spices at this age, which means you have more opportunity for adventurous cooking—and eating.

Some examples of finger foods suitable for this age are soft ripe fruits (such as melon, mango, kiwi, banana, peach, or steamed apples), cooked vegetables (such as carrot, parsnip, green beans, broccoli, cauliflower, bell pepper), raw but ripe avocado, bread, potato, or pasta. Read more about finger foods on page 146.

MEAL PLAN FOR SEVEN TO NINE MONTHS

Breakfast
- Cereal, such as Oatmeal Porridge (page 54), with cow's milk
- Fruit, such as mango, pear, and steamed apple, as a finger food
- Breast milk or infant formula

Lunch
- Savory course, such as Creamy Tomato Soup (page 168) with grilled cheese sticks
- Breast milk or infant formula

Dessert
- Cut-up ripe figs

Dinner
- Savory meal, such as Pasta with Pesto and Cherry Tomatoes (page 156)
- Breast milk or infant formula

Before bed
- Breast milk or infant formula

TEN TO TWELVE MONTHS

BY THIS AGE, MOST BABIES MASTER THE CHEWING MOTIONS AS WELL AS SELF–FEED FINGER FOODS AND CHUNKIER FOOD BITES. THEY SHOULD BE EATING THREE MEALS A DAY THAT INCLUDE A VARIETY OF MINCED AND CHOPPED FOODS.

Each meal should contain about 4 to 6 tablespoons (60 to 90 g) of these foods. They should also have a small nutritious snack between meals, as well as at least three feedings of breast milk or infant formula.

DINING WITH THE FAMILY

Most ten- to-twelve-month-old babies can eat what the rest of the family is eating, but baby's food should be cut into small bite-size chunks. She may be enjoying a wide range of flavors and several textures at each meal, though some can be fussy eaters. Even if that's the case, fear not—more on that later (see page 48).

Make sure the food you offer is suitable for self-feeding and that baby can pick it up with his tiny hands or start practicing with a spoon. Allow your child to practice as much as he wants using cutlery; this helps him use these tools properly later on. It is messy, but that is the best way to practice and learn. Slippery foods like avocado can be cut with a special cutter that forms a zigzag pattern so it gives a better grip.

Continue breastfeeding or bottle-feeding on demand or give your baby his usual milk feeds per day. For a balanced diet, a ten- to twelve-month-old baby should get at least 14 ounces (425 ml) of infant formula or breast milk and about six hundred calories each day from the foods he eats, which should also provide the following:

- 9 grams of protein
- 300 milligrams of calcium
- 5 milligrams of iron
- 3 milligrams of zinc

Babies at this age also continue to need fat, carbohydrates, and other vitamins and minerals from their diet.

MEAL PLAN FOR TEN TO TWELVE MONTHS

Breakfast

- Cereal, such as Creamy Millet Porridge (page 57) with chopped banana topping

- Fruit, such as kiwi and raspberries, as finger food

- Breast milk or infant formula

Lunch

- Savory meal with finger foods, such as bread spread with Humble Egg Mash (page 59) with avocado and some sliced cucumber and corn bites

Dessert

- Sautéed pears

- Water in a cup

Dinner

- Savory meal with finger foods, such as Salmon Patties (page 155) with Root Vegetable Mash (page 121)

Dessert

- Watermelon and blackberry bites

- Breast milk or infant formula

Before bed

- Breast milk or infant formula

⇒ DIETITIAN TIP

It is recommended that babies from six months to five years old are given vitamin D supplements (except babies receiving more than 17 ounces, or 500 ml, of infant formula per day, as this is fortified with vitamins).

TODDLERS:
TWELVE MONTHS TO TWENTY-FOUR MONTHS

BY THE AGE OF TWELVE MONTHS, YOUR LITTLE ONE OFFICIALLY BECOMES A TODDLER! SHE WILL ONLY NEED ABOUT 12 OUNCES (355 ML) OF MILK A DAY NOW. THIS CAN BE VARIOUS TYPES OF MILK, SUCH AS BREAST MILK, FORMULA, COW'S MILK, GOAT'S MILK, OR SHEEP'S MILK.

As exciting as toddlerhood sounds, it also brings challenges. Toddler mealtimes differ a lot from baby mealtimes. Finger food is still a very important part of feeding, but when your toddler reaches the age of eighteen months, his hand-eye coordination will likely be developed well enough for him to spoon-feed himself carefully. Be forewarned: He might just discover those utensils also work well as a food catapult.

While your toddler's growing mobility leads to asserting more desire for independence, this, of course, means he is much more active. One of the most challenging aspects of having a toddler is getting her to sit still, especially at mealtimes. For anyone who has never seen the personification of the phrase "ants in your pants," look no further than your friendly toddler.

At this age, her appetite might change as well. Unlike babies, toddlers do not gain weight quite so quickly because, by now, they are very mobile and burning off lots of the energy that your wonderful food has provided!

"FUSSY EATING"

"Fussy eating" is basically a term made up especially for toddlers. While it can be frustrating to continually throw uneaten food into the trash can, it is normal for your toddler to love a certain food one week, only to refuse it the next or hurl it over his shoulder if it's not to his satisfaction. All you can do is try again in a couple days or weeks. Your little one's taste buds change all the time and so does his love for certain foods. Fussy eating is simply a phase most toddlers go through, typically in their second year.

Picky eating is also a way for your toddler to show independence. She might be testing how far she can push your limits of authority by controlling what comes in and out of her mouth. Try not to get all worked up if she refuses to eat. Just accept it and give her as much control as possible over her own appetite. Your job is to provide a variety of healthy foods to choose from every time. If your toddler is more likely to eat something she chooses herself, let her pick from a small selection of healthy foods that includes at least one thing she likes, instead of overwhelming her with too many choices.

Your toddler may often refuse lunch and eat nothing much at all for dinner. If that is the case, give him a healthy snack between his main meals. That way, he will have eaten something. And if he doesn't eat the entire plateful for dinner, so be it. If allowed to do so, most toddlers are generally pretty good at regulating their food intake. Do not worry, your toddler will not starve to death if he skips a meal; he'll generally eat just enough to meet his needs. Focus on the bigger picture and evaluate how he has eaten during the week instead of each day. If he has been eating well-balanced meals for a couple of days and has a "purple patch" of not eating, it is probably nothing to worry about. So long as he is hydrated and taking snacks, these periods often sort themselves out over time. If you are concerned about your child's appetite or weight, please speak to his pediatrician.

However, more important than what your toddler eats is the environment she eats it in. I cannot emphasize enough about how important it is to keep stress out of mealtimes. Toddlers absorb and react to stress in a way that can affect them over their formative years and into later life. If you, the parent, place a ton of importance on—and are really stressed over—broccoli, your toddler will grow up associating broccoli with that experience, which could lead to a lifelong aversion. This scenario doesn't just apply to traditionally "unwanted" foods like broccoli; it can be true of any food. So please, whatever you do, try not to make mealtimes a heated affair. Offer and re-offer foods. As you will discover, it is not possible to reason with a toddler (if you do find a method that works, please write to me and tell me how!). So keep it simple and look at the bigger picture when it comes to mealtimes with your toddler. Rome wasn't built in a day, nor was a plate of greens eaten in one either.

I hope you and your bundle of joy enjoy the recipes in this book!

WHEN CAN I INTRODUCE...?

Following are general guidelines for when it's okay to start introducing baby to certain foods.

Fruit	Months
Apple	4–6 months
Apricot	6–8 months
Avocado	4–6 months
Banana	4–6 months
Blueberry	6–8 months
Cherry	6–8 months
Citrus	8–12 months
Coconut	6–8 months
Cranberry	6–8 months
Fig	6–10 months
Grapes	6–10 months
Guava	6–8 months
Kiwi	8–10 months
Mango	6–8 months
Melon	8–10 months
Nectarine	4–6 months
Papaya	4–8 months
Peach	4–8 months
Pears	4–6 months
Persimmon	6–10 months
Plum	6–8 months

	Months
Pomegranate	7–8 months
Prune	6 months
Pumpkin	4–6 months
Strawberry	7–12 months

Vegetables	Months
Asparagus	6–8 months
Beans	6–12 months
Beet	7–10 months
Broccoli	6–10 months
Carrot	6–8 months
Cauliflower	6–8 months
Corn	6 months
Cucumber	8–10 months
Eggplant	8–10 months
Green beans	6 months
Kale	6–10 months
Leek	6–10 months
Onion	6–10 months
Parsnip	6–8 months
Peas	6–8 months
Peppers, bell	6–10 months

Potato, white	6–10 months
Spinach	7–12 months
Squash, butternut	4–6 months
Sweet Potato	4–6 months
Tomato	6–8 months
Turnip	6–10 months

Meats & Proteins	Months
Beef	6–8 months
Chicken	6–8 months
Eggs	6–12 months
Fish	6–12 months
Tofu	8 months
Turkey	6–8 months

Grains	Months
Barley	6 months
Buckwheat/kasha	4 months
Flax	8 months
Kamut	6 months
Millet	4–6 months
Oatmeal	4–6 months
Pasta	6 months
Rye	6 months
Rice	4–6 months
Quinoa	8 months
Wheat germ	8 months

Dairy	Months
Cheese	6 months
Cottage cheese	6 months
Cow's milk	12 months as a drink, 6 months in food
Cream cheese	6 months
Greek yogurt	6 months, limited amounts
Quark	3 years old
Ricotta cheese	6 months
Yogurt, natural	6 months

BASIC PURÉES
ONE-INGREDIENT RECIPES

YIELD

Each recipe includes an approximate yield for how many meals it will make, and most recipes make a few. You may find you get more or less depending on how much liquid you use to reach the consistency you like and how hearty your little one's appetite is. The recipes also tell you how long they keep in the fridge or freezer, which will help you keep nutritious meals on hand.

USING BREAST MILK AND FORMULA

For most recipes in this book, you can use a little breast milk or formula to create the consistency you want. Either will help smooth a purée and give food a little more creaminess and nutrition. It is important to remember that *breast milk can only be frozen once*, so if you are going to freeze a recipe after you cook it, use freshly expressed breast milk. Formula can be frozen but the texture will change; it's best to add formula at the very end, after you defrost the food and just before you serve it.

STEAMING AND MASHING OR BLENDING

Many recipes call for steaming and mashing or blending the ingredients. It's a good rule of thumb to steam all ingredients until they are soft and you can cut into them easily (see page 9).

You can also reserve the steamer water to thin the consistency of a purée when you mash or blend it while giving it a little vitamin/flavor kick. You can use a fork, food processor, blender, or other method to blend the food—there is no "one way" to do it. The goal is to make the consistency of the purée as thin or as chunky as your little eater is able to eat and enjoy.

PRODUCE

It is very important to wash all produce. Regardless of how you cook the ingredients, and even if you peel the produce, everything should be cleaned thoroughly to make sure it is hygienic and safe for little bellies. Though most recipes instruct you to peel fruits, once your baby gets used to eating lumps, start to leave peels on foods you normally eat with peels. I recommend buying organic and cleaning with a produce scrubber.

CHOOSING FATS

Many recipes call for a fat of choice. I recommend the following:

- Grass-fed dairy butter (It contains more nutrients than non-grass-fed.)
- Olive oil
- Coconut oil
- Avocado oil (or just avocado)
- Cold-pressed canola oil (non-GMO)
- Nut butters (for six months and older if no allergies present themselves)

OATMEAL PORRIDGE

 6 months and older   **2 to 3 meals**   **Keeps in the fridge for 24 hours**

Oats are a wholesome food high in calcium, soluble fiber, and iron—and perfect for little growing bodies. They aid digestion, can improve the immune system, and are rich in vitamins and minerals. They are also much easier to digest than rice and are one of the least likely grains to cause an allergic reaction in babies.

Not all babies can handle a coarse porridge, especially if they are under six months of age. For a smoother texture, grind the oats to a fine powder in a blender. Cow's milk adds a sweet, creamy flavor, but you can also add infant formula for a similar flavor.

Add Simple Pear Purée (page 72) or mashed banana to sweeten the porridge, or top it with applesauce or berry sauce (pictured). It is also delicious on its own with just a bit of unsalted butter.

INGREDIENTS

½ cup (40 g) oats

1½ cups (355 ml) water, milk, or formula

1 teaspoon (5 g) unsalted butter

1. MIX.
In a small or medium saucepan, stir together the oats and liquid. Break up any lumps.

2. COOK.
Heat on medium heat while stirring until it reaches a thick consistency and large bubbles form.

3. SERVE WITH BUTTER FOR YUMS!
You can also top the porridge with a fruit purée, as mentioned above.

⟶ DIETITIAN TIPS

- Overnight oats are a great way to prepare oats without cooking. Soak your oats in milk or, even better, breast milk, and refrigerate overnight. In the morning, you will have a cold, hearty porridge. Gently heat the oats if you prefer; it just cooks much faster!

- Leftover oatmeal can also be spread one-half inch (1.5 cm) thick on a lined baking sheet and baked at 350°F (180°C, or gas mark 4) for 20 minutes. Slice it, let cool, and you have handy snacks! Refrigerate in a sealed container for 24 to 48 hours.

CORN PORRIDGE

 6 months and older   2 to 3 meals   Keeps in the fridge for 24 hours

One of the great things about corn porridge is that it ranks low on the allergy scale and is gluten free, which makes it a good first food for your little one. It satisfies and can be added to lots of purées to make them more filling.

INGREDIENTS

½ cup (70 g) cornmeal

2 cups (475 ml) water, or milk

1 teaspoon (5 g) fat of choice

Small amount breast milk or formula (optional)

1. **BOIL THE CORNMEAL AND WATER.**
   In a saucepan over medium heat, bring the cornmeal and water to a boil, stirring continually.

2. **SIMMER.**
   Once it boils, reduce the heat to low and simmer for 2 minutes while stirring.

3. **ONCE THICK, ADD THE FAT AND BREAST MILK (IF USING).**
   If needed, add breast milk or formula to thin the porridge until it is the consistency of a creamy soup.

4. **COOL AND SERVE.**

CREAMY MILLET PORRIDGE

Millet has a high protein content similar to rice and wheat that, therefore, satisfies a baby's appetite well into the morning. It is also one of the least allergenic grains, which makes it a great first food, especially if your baby is ready for solid food before the age of six months, because it is gluten free, nutritious, easily digested, and versatile.

INGREDIENTS

½ cup (100 g) millet, ground in the blender for a softer texture

1½ cups (355 ml) water, or milk

1 teaspoon (5 g) unsalted butter

1. BOIL THE MILLET AND WATER.
Stir for about 7 minutes until it reaches a porridge-like consistency and large bubbles form.

2. ADD THE BUTTER.
Remove from the heat and add the butter.

3. COOL AND SERVE.

 TIP

Top this porridge with applesauce for more flavor and added nutrients.

COZY SEMOLINA PORRIDGE

 6 months and older   2 to 3 meals   Keeps in the fridge for 24 hours

The comforting texture and mild taste of semolina is easy on the stomach and, as it is made from durum wheat, it's digested slowly, making it a great comfort food. It will help your child feel full for a long time and is a great meal to sleep on if he tends to wake up hungry in the night.

Semolina can improve kidney function and is a good source of vitamins E and B, which are essential for good immunity. It also contains minerals beneficial for the health of your baby's bones and nervous system.

INGREDIENTS

½ cup (38 g) semolina

1½ cups (355 ml) water, or milk

1 teaspoon (5 g) unsalted butter

 TIP

You can also top this porridge with applesauce or a mashed banana for more flavor and added nutrients.

1. BOIL THE SEMOLINA AND WATER.
In a saucepan over medium heat, bring the semolina and water to a boil while stirring continually.

2. KEEP STIRRING!
Stir for 5 to 7 minutes until it reaches a porridge-like consistency and large bubbles form.

3. ADD THE BUTTER.
Remove from the heat and add the butter.

4. COOL AND SERVE.

HUMBLE EGG MASH

 6 months and older (if no egg allergies in the family)

 1 to 2 meals

❄ Keeps in the fridge for 24 hours

Egg protein contains all the essential amino acids, which are the building blocks for hormones, skin, tissues, and more. They are considered an essential part of any diet because our bodies cannot make them on their own. Eggs, especially the yolks, are filled with essential vitamins such as vitamins D, A, E, and B_{12}. They contain nutrients like choline and cholesterol, essential for babies' brain development. You can also buy eggs that contain omega-3 fatty acids, depending on what the hens are fed.

If you are worried about allergies, use just the yolk, as it rarely causes any reactions—it is usually the egg whites that do that.

INGREDIENTS

1 free-range egg

1 to 2 teaspoons (5 to 10 ml) breast milk or infant formula

 TIP

Add a pureed vegetable to the mash for extra nutrients.

1. HARD—BOIL THE EGG.
Bring a pot of water to a boil and then slowly add the egg and boil for 10 to 12 minutes.

2. COOL, PEEL.

3. MASH IT ALL.

4. COOL AND SERVE.

BABY'S FIRST APPLE PURÉE

 6 months and older   6 to 8 meals   Freeze for up to 3 months

Apple purée is nutritious, easy on baby's tummy, and helps guard against constipation as it is filled with fiber. Apples rarely cause allergic reactions and make a wonderful base for many other purées. While the bulk of the apple's nutrition is in the peel, until your little one is used to a lumpier consistency, it is safer to remove it. If you want to leave the peel on, blend the cooked apples in a food processor to ensure no large, fibrous bits of peel remain.

INGREDIENTS

6 sweet apples

1 tablespoon (15 g) fat of choice

⇒ TIP

Add frozen apple-purée cubes to your toddler's or baby's hot morning porridge to help cool it quickly and add nutrients and flavor. You can also use the frozen apple cubes with other fruit or vegetables prepared the same way. Apple goes with many flavors, which means you can mix and vary the purées.

1. PEEL, CORE, AND CHOP THE APPLES.

2. STEAM.
   Place the chopped apples into a steamer pot or a saucepan with just enough water to cover. Steam or boil for 10 to 15 minutes or until soft. Add more water if the pot begins to dry out.

3. BLEND IT ALL!
   Use the leftover steamer water or breast milk to thin the consistency, if desired. Or, add baby cereal to thicken the purée and make it a more satisfying meal. A food processor or blender works best here.

4. COOL AND YUM!

AVOCADO MASH

 6 months and older   1 meal   Eat immediately

Avocado contains healthy fats and vitamins such as C, K, E, and folate, and it does not require cooking! The healthy monoun-saturated fats are a great energy source for your rapidly growing baby. If that's not enough, avocado helps with the absorption of other nutrients!

As avocado contains a lot of healthy fat, you do not need to add fat, breast milk, or infant formula to this dish. However, you can add breast milk or formula for extra softness and creaminess. Serve this in small amounts with a main meal as it is very energy dense and filling for your baby's small stomach—which also makes it a great choice if your baby needs to gain a little weight!

INGREDIENTS

1 ripe avocado

DIETITIAN TIP

Avocado is best served ripe, especially for reducing the chance of indigestion in babies. To check the ripeness of an avocado, flick off the small, round stem on top. If you see a lovely green color it is perfect (yellow means it is underripe and brown is overripe). If the avocado is not ripe, place it in a paper bag with an overripe banana. The chemical reaction between the two will ripen the avocado much faster. I've tried this, and it really works!

1. SLICE THE AVOCADO. REMOVE AND DISCARD THE PIT.

2. SCOOP OUT THE FLESH.

3. MASH!
You can purée the mixture with a blender if your baby cannot handle small lumps yet.

4. SERVE AND ENJOY!

HOKKAIDO PUMPKIN PURÉE

 6 months and older   6 meals   Freeze for up to 3 months

The easy-to-work-with Hokkaido pumpkin is creamy and naturally sweet. Its vibrant color makes it a great first food for babies. It is a real vitamin bomb, rich in calcium, magnesium, beta-carotene, and vitamins A, B, and C. It can even help with stomach, kidney, and heart problems. The skin is edible and becomes wonderfully soft when baked. I recommend buying organic Hokkaido pumpkins so you can use the whole squash with confidence.

INGREDIENTS

1 medium-size Hokkaido pumpkin
(substitute acorn squash If unavailable)

1 teaspoon (5 g) fat of choice

Small amount breast milk or formula,
for blending (optional)

⇨ TIP

Steam the Hokkaido pumpkin to retain the maximum amount of nutrients (though baking enhances color and flavor). To steam, prepare the pumpkin the same way as in step 2, but slice it into smaller parts and steam for 15 minutes, or until soft.

1. **PREHEAT THE OVEN TO 400°F (200°C, OR GAS MARK 6).**

2. **HALVE THE PUMPKIN. REMOVE THE SEEDS AND STRINGS.**

3. **BAKE.**
   Place both halves face down in a baking dish. Add just enough water to cover the bottom of the dish. Bake for 40 to 45 minutes until the pumpkin is soft and tender.

4. **PEEL.**
   Note: Peeling is difficult and not necessary if you use organic pumpkin.

5. **BLEND IT ALL.**
   A food processor or blender works best here.

6. **COOL AND SERVE.**

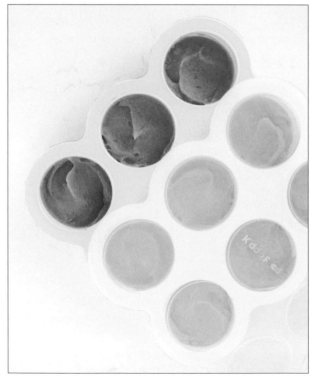

SWEET POTATO PURÉE

 6 months and older   6 meals   Freeze for up to 3 months

Sweet potato is one of those tastes babies rarely reject. It is an excellent first food because it's easy to digest and rarely causes any allergic reaction. It is filling, high in fiber—which helps prevent constipation—and promotes regularity for a good digestive system. It is also filled with nutrients such as beta-carotene, vitamin C, phosphorous, magnesium, and calcium, to name a few.

INGREDIENTS

2 medium-size sweet potatoes

1 teaspoon (5 g) fat of choice

⇒ DIETITIAN TIPS

- As your baby gets used to lumps, leave the skins on to increase fiber intake. Just make sure the sweet potatoes are thoroughly washed and diced into small pieces before cooking.

- Use frozen cubes of sweet potato purée in your baby's or toddler's hot purées, porridges, or pasta sauces to add nutrients and flavor. It will also cool the meal faster.

- Instead of baking, steam sweet potatoes to retain the maximum amount of nutrients. However, baking enhances the sweet flavor and creamy texture.

1. **PREHEAT THE OVEN TO 400°F (200°C, OR GAS MARK 6).**

2. **POKE.**
With a fork, poke holes all over the sweet potatoes' skin

3. **BAKE.**
Place on a baking sheet or in a baking dish and bake for 40 to 45 minutes or until the flesh turns soft and tender when pierced with a fork.

4. **COOL.**

5. **SKIN.**
You can remove the skin with your fingers or halve the sweet potato and scoop out the flesh with a spoon.

6. **MASH!**
Add in fat and mash with a fork or immersion blender.

7. **COOL AND SERVE.**

BUTTERNUT SQUASH PURÉE

 6 months and older   6 to 8 meals   Freeze for up to 3 months

Butternut squash doesn't just taste great, but is also good news for babies' vitamin and mineral intake as it's filled with vitamins A and C and other nutritious goodies such as beta-carotene. Baking winter squashes, like acorn squash and Hokkaido pumpkin, enhances their naturally sweet flavor.

INGREDIENTS

1 medium butternut squash

1 tablespoon (15 g) fat of choice

Small amount breast milk or formula, for blending (optional)

 TIP

Picking a ripe butternut squash: Visually, the squash should be beige all over—the darker, the better, with no green patches. The skin should be matte, not shiny, and free of cuts and blemishes. Feel the squash; it should feel heavy for its size. Tap it gently with your knuckles. You'll hear a hollow sound if it's ripe.

1. PREHEAT THE OVEN TO 400°F (200°C, OR GAS MARK 6).

2. HALVE THE SQUASH. REMOVE THE SEEDS AND PULP.

3. BAKE.
Place both halves face down in a baking dish. Add just enough water to cover the bottom of the dish. Bake for 40 to 45 minutes until the squash is soft and tender.

4. COOL AND PEEL.

5. BLEND IT ALL.
A food processor or blender works best here.

6. EAT AND LOVE!

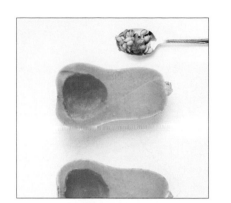  

BROCCOLI PURÉE

 6 months and older 6 to 8 meals Freeze for up to 3 months

INGREDIENTS

1 head broccoli

1 teaspoon (5 g) unsalted butter

Small amount breast milk or formula, for blending (optional)

 TIP

For older kids, add a little grated cheese to boost the flavor as well as add calcium, protein, and healthy fats.

1. CHOP THE BROCCOLI.

2. STEAM.
Place the chopped broccoli into a steamer pot. Steam for 10 minutes or until you can cut through it easily with a knife.

3. BLEND IT ALL.
A food processor or blender works best here.

4. COOL AND SERVE.
Serve a little and freeze the rest to mix with other vegetables to vary the flavor.

DATE PURÉE

 6 months and older 3 to 4 small meals Freeze for up to 3 months

INGREDIENTS

10 pitted dates

½ cup (120 ml) water

1 teaspoon (5 g) fat of choice

Small amount breast milk or formula, for blending (optional)

1. BOIL THE DATES.
Place the dates in a saucepan with the water and boil for a couple of minutes.

2. BLEND IT ALL.
A food processor or blender works best here.

3. MIX A LITTLE INTO OATMEAL OR PORRIDGE.
Use only 1 to 2 teaspoons (5 to 10 g). Freeze the rest in ice cube trays.

CARROT PURÉE

 6 months and older   6 to 8 meals   Freeze for up to 3 months

Carrots are rich in beta-carotene, which is converted into vitamin A in the liver. Carrots also boost the immune system, improve digestion, and are rich in pantothenic acid, folate, potassium, iron, copper, manganese, and vitamins A, C, K, and B6. Half-steamed carrots are ideal for babies to gnaw on and can be very helpful in easing the discomfort of teething. They also make a super tasty purée. Once your little one moves on to snack foods, cooked carrots are ideal snacks for between meals.

INGREDIENTS

6 large carrots

1 tablespoon (15 g) fat of choice

Small amount breast milk or formula, for blending (optional)

⇒ DIETITIAN TIPS

- Unlike other vegetables, carrots increase their nutritional value when they're cooked. Though babies can get constipated from too much carrot—don't let that deter you from trying them. Just be aware of changes in digestion and have some prune purée at the ready!

- Avoid using baby carrots, as they are just regular carrots cut by a machine into smaller pieces and cleaned with chlorine so the color doesn't change during packaging.

1. **PEEL, TRIM THE ENDS, AND SLICE THE CARROTS.**

2. **BOIL.**
Place the sliced carrots in a saucepan with just enough water to cover. Boil for 20 to 30 minutes or until you can easily cut through the carrots with a knife. Add more water to the pot if needed.

3. **BLEND IT ALL.**
A food processor or blender works best here.

4. **COOL AND ENJOY!**

EASY-PEASY PEA PURÉE

 6 months and older   3 to 4 meals   Freeze for up to 3 months

Peas go with just about anything, and they are super healthy considering their tiny size. They are a good source of vegetable protein and calcium, vitamins A, B$_6$, and C, and iron.

The skins can be difficult to blend completely smooth. If you run into that issue and your baby is not used to textures yet, run the blended peas through a strainer or sieve to remove the skins.

INGREDIENTS

1 cup (130 g) frozen peas

1 teaspoon (5 g) fat of choice

Small amount breast milk or formula, for blending (optional)

1. STEAM.
Place the peas into a steamer pot. Steam for 4 to 5 minutes.

2. BLEND IT ALL.
A food processor or blender works best here.

3. COOL AND SERVE.

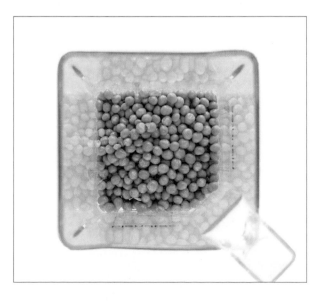

SIMPLE PEAR PURÉE

 6 months and older 4 to 6 meals Freeze for up to 3 months

Pears rarely cause allergic reactions, are easily digested, and rich in soluble fiber that can help prevent constipation. They are a source of vitamin C, which helps with iron absorption, so they pair well with iron-rich grains such as oatmeal.

INGREDIENTS

6 ripe pears

1 tablespoon (15 g) fat of choice

1. **PEEL, CORE, AND CHOP THE PEARS.**

2. **STEAM.**
   Place the chopped pears into a steamer pot. Steam for about 5 minutes or until soft. Add more water if the pot begins to dry out.

3. **MASH!**

4. **COOL AND ENJOY.**

MASHED POTATOES

 6 months and older 2 to 3 meals Does not freeze well

The iron, phosphorous, calcium, magnesium, and zinc in potatoes contribute to building and maintaining your baby's bone structure and strength. Try blending them with carrots, parsnips, broccoli, sweet potatoes, winter squashes, spinach, or beef.

INGREDIENTS

2 cups (220 g) peeled and diced potato

1 teaspoon (5 g) butter

Breast milk or formula, for blending (optional)

1. **BOIL.**
   Place the diced potatoes over medium heat with enough water to cover. Boil the potatoes for about 20 minutes (time can vary depending on the type of potato) or until soft and easily mashed with a fork. Drain the water.

2. **MASH IT ALL.**
   When you blend potatoes, they can get a gluey consistency. Stick to mashing and use plenty of milk.

3. **COOL AND SERVE.**

COMBO PURÉES
TWO— AND THREE—INGREDIENT RECIPES

After doing simple purées and testing for allergies by introducing one food at a time (see page 23), it is time to get creative with baby food combinations! The mix-and-match concept comes in handy to ensure your baby has a varied diet and with the different nutrients produce offers. These recipes give you total control over what your little one eats, and you can make sure her nutritional needs are met by combining things like iron-rich recipes that include meat, spinach, or kale with vitamin C–containing ingredients like broccoli and red bell pepper, which maximize iron absorption.

Combining foods is really where the fun begins! Get adventurous and try combinations you normally wouldn't think of. Just make sure the combinations are age appropriate for your little one.

CREAMY AVOCADO AND BANANA PURÉE

 6 months and older   2 meals   Keeps in the fridge for 24 hours
(The purée will brown but is still edible.)

This easy, quick, no-cook recipe is totally portable! All that's required is to mash the ingredients with a fork—and you can do that just about anywhere. This one is an easy win. Trust me.

INGREDIENTS

1 ripe banana

1 ripe avocado

> ⇨ **TIP**
>
> This is a good meal to use up a ripe banana, and it makes a great toddler smoothie if you just add some coconut water or milk and mix in some baby spinach. It's so delicious, both of you can enjoy it!

1. PEEL AND SLICE THE BANANA.

2. SLICE THE AVOCADO IN HALF.
Remove and discard the pit.

3. PEEL AND CHOP THE AVOCADO.

4. BLEND IT ALL.
A food processor or blender works best here.

5. SERVE.

APPLE AND PEAR PURÉE

 6 months and older   6 to 8 meals   Freeze for up to 3 months

Jarred food just does not taste this fresh and good. This combination is soft, easy to make, and filled with fiber. You can serve this light fruit purée as is or use it as a topping to add flavor and nutrients to baby's morning porridge. Given that pears and apples very common in older kids' diets, it makes sense to introduce them early and offer them at least a few times a week.

INGREDIENTS

4 apples

4 pears

1 tablespoon (15 g) fat of choice

Small amount breast milk or formula, for blending (optional)

1. PEEL, CORE, AND CHOP THE FRUITS.

2. STEAM.
Place the chopped apples and pears into a steamer pot. Steam for 10 minutes or until soft.

3. BLEND IT ALL.
A food processor or blender works best here.

4. COOL AND SERVE.

SWEET POTATO AND PEAR PURÉE

 6 months and older   4 meals   Freeze for up to 3 months

Both sweet potatoes and pears are on the low end of the allergen scale, so this combo makes a great first food. You'd be hard pressed to find a baby who won't get into this with some enthusiasm, and I hope it becomes one of your go-to dishes in the first stages of weaning.

INGREDIENTS

2 ripe pears

1 medium-size sweet potato

1 teaspoon (5 g) fat of choice (coconut butter adds a delicious aromatic flavor)

Small amount breast milk or formula, for blending (optional)

 TIP

You can peel the sweet potato, cut it, and steam it with the pears for less work. I prefer baking, as that enhances the sweet flavor.

1. **PREHEAT THE OVEN TO 450°F (230°C, OR GAS MARK 8).**

2. **PEEL, CORE, AND CHOP THE PEARS.**

3. **POKE.**
   With a fork, poke holes all over the sweet potato's skin.

4. **BAKE.**
   Place the sweet potato on a baking sheet or in a baking dish and bake for 40 to 45 minutes or until the flesh turns soft and tender when pierced with a fork.

5. **COOL AND PEEL THE SWEET POTATO.**

6. **STEAM THE PEARS.**
   Place the chopped pears into a steamer pot. Steam for about 5 minutes or until soft.

7. **BLEND IT ALL.**
   A food processor or blender works best here.

8. **COOL, ENJOY!**

BUTTERNUT SQUASH RISOTTO

 6 months and older   4 meals   Freeze for up to 3 months

This super creamy and delicious baby meal is also filling and nutritious. If your experiences are anything like mine, there will be little need for washing up after this lip-smacking combo.

INGREDIENTS

½ cup (100 g) arborio rice, or other risotto rice

1 cup (235 ml) Homemade Broth (page 116), or water

1 teaspoon (5 g) unsalted butter

1 cup (245 g) butternut squash purée (page 66)

1. COOK THE RICE.
   Cook the rice in the broth according to the package directions. Stir occasionally so it does not stick together.

2. STIR IN THE BUTTER.

3. ADD THE SQUASH PURÉE AND COMBINE.

4. COOL AND ENJOY!

BUCKWHEAT AND FIG PORRIDGE

 6 months and older   2 meals   Keeps in the fridge for 24 hours

INGREDIENTS

1 dried fig, chopped

¾ cup (175 ml) water, or milk

¼ cup (43 g) buckwheat

½ teaspoon (2.5 g) fat of choice

1. BOIL.
   Place the chopped fig in a saucepan with the water and boil until soft.

2. STIR IN THE BUCKWHEAT.
   Keep stirring while the buckwheat and fig cook for 5 minutes. Reduce the heat to low and cook for 2 minutes more and continue stirring.

3. REMOVE FROM THE HEAT.

4. MIX IT ALL.

5. SERVE.

PEAR WITH RYE BREAD PURÉE

 6 months and older   4 to 6 meals   Freeze for up to 3 months

This is a satisfying fiber-packed baby meal. The rye bread contains the highest level of bran and provides the most satiety of any bread. It improves digestion and relieves constipation as it is rich in fiber. Just be sure to look for a loaf that has only natural ingredients. Add infant formula or breast milk to the purée for a creamier flavor.

INGREDIENTS

1 slice seedless rye bread (or with seeds, but blend it well)

2 cups (475 ml) water, or milk

4 ripe pears

1 teaspoon (5 g) butter

1. **SOAK THE BREAD.**
Soak the rye bread in the water for 15 minutes. Break it apart with a fork.

2. **PEEL, CORE, AND CHOP THE PEARS.**

3. **STEAM.**
Place the chopped pears into a steamer pot. Steam for 5 to 7 minutes or until soft.

4. **BLEND IT ALL.**
Blend everything—including the boiling water—until you reached the desired consistency. A food processor or blender works best here.

5. **COOL AND ENJOY!**

APPLE AND SWEET POTATO PURÉE

 6 months and older 4 meals Freeze for up to 3 months

This super delicious beginner purée—sweet and vibrant in color—is a big hit with babies. Adding some infant formula or breast milk gives it a creamier flavor that many babies like.

INGREDIENTS

2 small sweet potatoes

1 apple

1 teaspoon (5 g) fat of choice

Small amount breast milk or formula, for blending (optional)

1. PEEL AND CHOP THE SWEET POTATOES.

2. PEEL, CORE, AND CHOP THE APPLE.

3. STEAM.

Place the chopped sweet potatoes into a steamer pot. Steam for 5 minutes. Add the apple and continue to steam for another 5 to 10 minutes or until soft.

4. BLEND IT ALL.

A food processor or blender works best here.

5. COOL AND ENJOY!

SWEET POTATO AND KALE

 6 months and older   6 to 8 meals   Freeze for up to 3 months

Kale is known as the king of greens for a good reason—it is one of the healthiest vegetables around. Even spinach cannot compare to the number of nutrients that kale provides. To maintain the maximum amount of nutrients, it is recommended that you steam it for 5 minutes.

You can sneak any veggie your little one is refusing to eat, including bitter kale, into his diet if you mask it with sweet potato. This creamy, tasty combo is filled with nutrients and is an excellent source of vitamins A and C, as well as iron.

INGREDIENTS

2 large kale leaves

3 small sweet potatoes

1 teaspoon (5 g) fat of choice

Small amount breast milk or formula, for blending (optional)

1. **PREHEAT THE OVEN TO 450°F (230°C, OR GAS MARK 8).**

2. **REMOVE AND DISCARD THE KALE STEMS. CHOP.**

3. **STEAM.**
   Place the chopped kale into a steamer pot. Steam for about 5 minutes or until soft.

4. **POKE.**
   With a fork, poke holes all over the sweet potatoes' skin.

5. **BAKE.**
   Place the sweet potatoes on a baking sheet or in a baking dish and bake for 40 to 45 minutes or until the flesh turns soft and tender when pierced with a fork.

6. **COOL AND PEEL THE SWEET POTATO.**

7. **BLEND IT ALL.**
   A food processor or blender works best here.

8. **COOL AND SERVE.**

SWEET POTATO AND BLACK BEAN PURÉE

 6 months and older   4 meals   Freeze for up to 3 months

Protein sources do not always have to be meat. Adding beans to your baby's diet provides variety while ensuring she gets some needed protein. This, though, should not be one of the first purées you feed baby, as the protein in the black beans can be harder to digest than other foods.

Organic canned black beans are equally yummy, and make for a quicker option. If you use dried beans, soak them for at least 10 to 12 hours before boiling in fresh water.

Sweet potatoes are filled with vitamin A and fiber. Their creamy, sweet, natural taste is highly appealing to most babies.

INGREDIENTS

1 large sweet potato

½ cup (125 g) dried black beans soaked overnight in water, or (120 g) organic canned black beans

1 teaspoon (5 g) fat of choice

Small amount breast milk or formula, for blending (optional)

1. PEEL AND CHOP THE SWEET POTATO.

2. STEAM.

Place the chopped sweet potatoes into a steamer pot. Steam for about 15 minutes or until soft. Reserve the cooking water to use for thinning the purée, if needed.

3. BOIL THE BLACK BEANS.

If using dried, soaked beans, boil them for at least 30 minutes or until soft. Drain the beans and discard their cooking water.

4. BLEND IT ALL.

A food processor or blender works best here.

5. COOL AND ENJOY!

➢ DIETITIAN TIP

Including plant-based protein sources such as beans and lentils in your weekly diet has many health benefits. Plant proteins contain fiber and are significantly lower in fat (in particular saturated fats) and cholesterol, unlike animal protein sources. You should, however, continue to offer animal protein sources as they provide key nutrients in forms that are far more readily available to our body (for example, iron and the protein "building blocks" called amino acids).

ZUCCHINI, CARROT, AND FIG PURÉE

 6 months and older   4 to 6 meals   Freeze for up to 3 months

This summer purée bursts with flavor and color. Figs have many health benefits for infants, such as boosting the immune system, aiding digestion, and protecting the liver. They are also a good source of vitamins A, E, and K, as well as the minerals calcium, potassium, and manganese, and they are a great source of dietary fiber.

INGREDIENTS

3 ripe fresh figs

3 carrots

½ zucchini

1 teaspoon (5 g) fat of choice

Small amount breast milk or formula, for blending (optional)

 TIP

If your baby is eight months or older, add a pinch of cinnamon to give this purée a boost of flavor.

1. PEEL AND CHOP THE FIGS, CARROTS, AND ZUCCHINI.

2. STEAM THE VEGETABLES.

Place the chopped zucchini and carrots into a steamer pot. Steam for about 15 minutes or until soft. You might want to add the zucchini 5 minutes after the carrots, as they cook faster.

3. BLEND IT ALL.

A food processor or blender works best here.

4. COOL AND SERVE.

CHICKEN AND APPLE PURÉE

 6 months and older   4 meals   Freeze for up to 3 months

Chicken can be hard to introduce on its own, as many babies, initially, dislike the flavor. If you gradually introduce it in combinations like this, which give it a bit more of a moist texture, your little one will love it in no time.

Chicken goes equally well with fruits or vegetables, giving you endless serving possibilities. While I always recommend using organic produce when possible, I know that sometimes it is easier said than done. For chicken, though, I must insist there is a world of difference between the taste of your standard supermarket bird and a quality organic one. Some things are just worth the extra money, and you will be doing your baby so much good by choosing the tastier, cleaner option.

INGREDIENTS

1 apple

¼ small organic boneless, skinless chicken breast

1 teaspoon (5 g) fat of choice

½ cup (120 ml) water

1. PEEL, CORE, AND DICE THE APPLE.

2. CHOP THE CHICKEN.

3. SAUTÉ.
In a saucepan over medium heat, heat the fat and sauté the chicken breast for 5 minutes or until it is no longer pink.

4. ADD THE DICED APPLE AND WATER.

5. BOIL.
Boil for 10 minutes until everything is cooked.

6. BLEND IT ALL.
A food processor or blender works best here.

7. COOL AND SERVE.

DIETITIAN TIP

The darker thigh and leg meat is richer in iron, so if your baby was born prematurely or suffers with low iron, these are good to use instead of breast or wing meat.

HOKKAIDO PUMPKIN AND MANGO PURÉE

 6 months and older   6 to 8 meals   Freeze for up to 3 months

It's nice to experiment with different fruits and vegetables, such as the Hokkaido pumpkin here, as they all have slightly different flavors—and who doesn't want a baby with a well-developed palate? Hokkaido pumpkin is a great first food as its sweet, creamy taste and texture make it a favorite among babies. It is a wonderful source of calcium, magnesium, phosphorus, potassium, beta-carotene, and vitamins A, B, and C. The peel is edible and delicious once cooked.

INGREDIENTS

1 small Hokkaido pumpkin (Substitute acorn squash if unavailable.)

1 ripe mango

1 teaspoon (5 g) fat of choice

Small amount breast milk or formula, for blending (optional)

 TIP

Instead of steaming the Hokkaido, you can bake it, which enhances its naturally sweet flavor. Steaming retains the maximum nutrients.

1. HALVE THE PUMPKIN. REMOVE THE SEEDS AND STRINGS AND CHOP.

2. PEEL, PIT, AND CHOP THE MANGO.

3. STEAM THE PUMPKIN.
   Place the chopped pumpkin into a steamer pot. Steam for 15 minutes or until soft. Once cooled, peel it or if it's organic leave the peel on as it is edible.

4. BLEND IT ALL.
   A food processor or blender works best here.

5. SERVE. DELICIOUS!

ASPARAGUS, CHICKPEA, AND SWEET POTATO PURÉE

 6 months and older    6 meals   Freeze for up to 3 months

This makes a protein-rich, creamy, satisfying baby meal. Asparagus adds a nutty taste, and the chickpeas create the sustenance, which is rounded out nicely with the sweetness of the sweet potato.

I have noticed that, from time to time, asparagus can cause little ones to have a little extra wind. It's generally nothing to worry about, but make a mental note in case you notice some unwanted side effects.

INGREDIENTS

1 large sweet potato

1 handful asparagus, fresh or frozen

1 to 2 tablespoons (10 to 20 g) cooked chickpeas, or (15 to 30 g) canned organic unsalted

➥ DIETITIAN TIP

I LOVE chickpeas! Not only are they a source of protein, but as a legume, they also contain fiber, so they are filling and nutritious. If there are chickpeas leftover after making this recipe, make Homemade Hummus Dip (page 181).

1. PREHEAT THE OVEN TO 400°F (200°C, OR GAS MARK 6).

2. POKE.
With a fork, poke holes all over the sweet potato's skin.

3. BAKE.
Place the sweet potato on a baking sheet in a baking dish and bake for 40 to 45 minutes or until the flesh turns soft and tender when pierced with a fork.

4. COOL AND PEEL THE SWEET POTATO.

5. REMOVE AND DISCARD THE WOODY ENDS OF THE ASPARAGUS.
Chop the asparagus into 1-inch (2.5 cm) lengths.

6. STEAM.
Place the chopped asparagus into a steamer pot. Steam for about 15 minutes or until soft.

7. BLEND IT ALL.
A food processor or blender works best here.

8. COOL AND ENJOY!

BUTTERNUT SQUASH AND QUINOA

 8 months and older   6 to 8 meals   Freeze for up to 3 months

Quinoa (keen-wa) may be introduced after eight months because it can be difficult for a six- or seven-month-old baby to digest, although many babies can tolerate it prior to eight months. The chance of quinoa causing an allergic reaction is low. It is a nutritious grain that acts as a natural laxative (like brown rice) and makes a great addition to your little one's diet. It is a source of protein and a great source of vitamins and minerals.

INGREDIENTS

1 small butternut squash

½ cup (87 g) quinoa

1 tablespoon (15 g) fat of choice

Small amount breast milk or formula, for blending (optional)

1. PREHEAT THE OVEN TO 400°F (200°C, OR GAS MARK 6).

2. HALVE THE BUTTERNUT SQUASH. REMOVE THE SEEDS AND PULP.

3. BAKE.
Place both halves face down in a baking dish. Add just enough water to cover the bottom of the dish. Bake for 40 to 45 minutes until the squash is soft and tender.

4. WASH AND COOK THE QUINOA
Quinoa needs a thorough rinse under running water or a soak so its bitterness is washed away. Rub the seeds between your fingers while rinsing. Cook according to the package directions.

5. COOL THE SQUASH AND PEEL.

6. BLEND IT ALL.
A food processor or blender works best here.

7. COOL AND SERVE. YUM!

APPLES, ZUCCHINI, AND PRUNES

 6 months and older   6 to 8 meals   Freeze for up to 3 months

INGREDIENTS

½ zucchini

3 apples

2 or 3 dried prunes

1 tablespoon (15 g) fat of choice

Small amount breast milk or formula,
for blending (optional)

1. PEEL AND SLICE THE ZUCCHINI.

2. PEEL, CORE, AND DICE THE APPLES.

3. CHOP THE PRUNES.

4. STEAM.
Place the sliced zucchini, diced apples, and chopped prunes into a steamer pot or a saucepan. Steam or boil for 10 to 15 minutes or until soft.

5. BLEND IT ALL.
A food processor or blender works best here.

6. COOL AND SERVE. AMAZING!

PEAR, BANANA, AND NECTARINE PURÉE

 6 months and older   4 to 6 meals   Freeze for up to 3 months

INGREDIENTS

2 ripe pears

1 ripe nectarine

1 ripe banana

1 teaspoon (5 g) fat of choice

Small amount breast milk or formula,
for blending (optional)

1. PEEL, CORE, AND CHOP THE PEARS.

2. PEEL, PIT, AND CHOP THE NECTARINE.

3. PEEL AND SLICE THE BANANA.

4. BLEND IT ALL.
A food processor or blender works best here.

5. ENJOY!

GREEN BEANS, BUTTER BEANS, AND PEAR PURÉE

 6 months and older   4 meals   Freeze for up to 3 months

Butter, or lima, beans and other legumes contain certain sugars our bodies can't break down and can often cause gassiness. If your baby has a sensitive tummy, you might want to use only half the amount of beans or wait until your little one is eight months or older to introduce this recipe.

INGREDIENTS

2 pears

1 handful green beans

¼ cup (47 g) cooked butter (lima) beans, or (60 g) canned organic unsalted

1 teaspoon (5 g) fat of choice

Small amount breast milk or formula, for blending (optional)

1. PEEL, CORE, AND CHOP THE PEARS.

2. TRIM AND CHOP THE GREEN BEANS.

3. STEAM.
Place the chopped pears and green beans into a steamer pot. Steam for 10 to 12 minutes or until soft.

4. BLEND IT ALL.
Place all the ingredients in a blender, or use an immersion blender, and blend.

5. COOL AND SERVE. YUM!

PUMPKIN, APRICOT, AND DATE PURÉE

 6 months and older   6 to 8 meals   Freeze for up to 3 months

This creamy, vibrant purée is nutritious and full of fiber. It is also perfect for babies who prefer sweet over savory. Babies are different, and their tastes change like the wind. I see many parents worry that their babies only seem interested in sweet tastes, but this is nothing to fret about so long as you keep your eye on the bigger picture. They say even adults taste buds change every seven years, so don't worry if your six-month-old doesn't love veggies yet.

INGREDIENTS

2 ripe apricots (not sour)

½ Hokkaido pumpkin (Substitute acorn squash if unavailable.)

7 soft pitted dates

1 tablespoon (15 ml) plant-based fat

Small amount breast milk or formula, for blending (optional)

⇒ DIETITIAN TIP

As your baby gets older, the best way for him to become more accepting of certain foods (usually vegetables) is to let him eat with other children his age. When he sees his peers eating something new, I guarantee he will try some, or at least show interest. This works best if the vegetables are left in the middle of the table as a "help yourself" option.

1. **BOIL THE APRICOTS.**
Place the apricots in a sauce pan with water and boil for 1 minute.

2. **COOL, PEEL, PIT, AND CHOP THE APRICOTS.**

3. **REMOVE THE SEEDS AND STRINGS FROM THE PUMPKIN AND CHOP.**

4. **STEAM THE PUMPKIN.**
Place the chopped pumpkin into a steamer pot. Steam for about 15 minutes or until soft. Once cooled, you can peel it or leave the skin on if you use organic, as it is edible.

5. **BLEND IT ALL.**
A food processor or blender works best here.

6. **COOL AND SERVE.**

BUTTERNUT SQUASH, CAULIFLOWER, AND KALE PURÉE

 6 months and older   8 meals   Freeze for up to 3 months

Rest assured your baby has munched on a very nourishing meal with this vegetable purée. A simple purée with a very hearty texture is great for batch cooking and leaves plenty of room to add different types of protein. Beef, chicken, turkey, or even fish (such as salmon) can be added to make this into a more satisfying meal.

INGREDIENTS

1 small butternut squash

1 large kale leaf

¼ head cauliflower

1 tablespoon (15 g) fat of choice

Small amount breast milk or formula, for blending (optional)

➡ DIETITIAN TIP

When your baby begins to eat larger amounts of purée, it is time to ensure he gets regular sources of protein, too. This means as he progresses from just one small meal to, perhaps, two and consumes less milk, he will benefit from more fish, meat, lentils, chicken, cheese, and eggs. Offer different sources of protein during the day to ensure your baby gets a good mix of amino acids (protein building blocks)—this advice goes for the whole family!

1. **HALVE THE BUTTERNUT SQUASH. REMOVE THE SEEDS AND PULP AND CHOP.**

2. **REMOVE AND DISCARD THE KALE STEM AND CHOP.**

3. **REMOVE THE CAULIFLOWER LEAVES AND CHOP.**

4. **STEAM.**
   Place the chopped squash, kale, and cauliflower into a steamer pot. Steam for 15 minutes or until soft.

5. **COOL AND PEEL THE SQUASH.**

6. **BLEND IT ALL.**
   A food processor or blender works best here.

7. **SERVE AND ENJOY!**

SWEET CORN, KALE, AND CARROT PURÉE

 6 months and older   **4 meals**   **Freeze for up to 3 months**

Using fresh produce brings your purées to a higher level of freshness and taste. If fresh is not handy, organic canned or frozen corn is a good option here. Cooking time for the corn will vary depending on the type of corn and how mature it is, but fresh sweet corn usually cooks faster.

INGREDIENTS

2 carrots

1 kale leaf

1 ear sweet corn

1 teaspoon (5 g) fat of choice

Small amount breast milk or formula, for blending (optional)

⇒ DIETITIAN TIP

Using canned corn is fine as long as you rinse the corn under running water to remove the salt it is packed in. Look for canned corn that is low salt.

---

1. **PEEL AND CHOP THE CARROTS.**

2. **REMOVE AND DISCARD THE KALE'S STEM. CHOP.**

3. **REMOVE THE CORN'S STEM, HUSK, AND SILK.**

4. **BOIL THE CORN.**
   In a saucepan over high heat, cover the corn with water and boil for about 10 minutes or until tender.

5. **STEAM THE CARROTS AND KALE.**
   Place the chopped carrots and corn into a steamer pot. Steam for about 10 to 15 minutes or until soft.

6. **COOL THE CORN. CUT OFF THE KERNELS.**

7. **BLEND IT ALL.**
   A food processor or blender works best here.

8. **COOL AND SERVE.**

RED LENTIL, APPLE, AND SWEET POTATO PURÉE

 6 months and older   4 to 6 meals   Freeze for up to 3 months

Lentils are a great source of protein and iron, and they are high in fiber. They are especially good if you decide not to feed your baby a lot of meat or if she does not like the taste of meat and you need a substitute. However, if you desire to add meat, chicken and turkey go well with this combo.

There are different types of lentils; some cook faster and smoother than others, so read the package directions. Split red lentils cook much faster than whole ones, for example.

INGREDIENTS

2 apples

1 large sweet potato

¼ cup (48 g) red lentils, rinsed

1 tablespoon (15 g) fat of choice

Small amount breast milk or formula, for blending (optional)

 TIP
If you want to add meat to this meal, chicken or turkey would be a great fit.

1. PEEL, CORE, AND CHOP THE APPLES.

2. PEEL AND CHOP THE SWEET POTATO.

3. STEAM.
Place the chopped sweet potato into a steamer pot. Steam for 10 minutes. Add the apple and steam for 5 minutes more or until soft.

4. COOK THE LENTILS.
Follow the directions on the lentils' package.

5. BLEND IT ALL.
A food processor or blender works best here.

6. COOL AND SERVE.

RED CABBAGE, APPLE, AND BANANA PURÉE

 6 months and older   4 to 6 meals   Freeze for up to 3 months

Have you ever heard of red cabbage in a purée? While it is not an obvious choice, it certainly adds a distinct flavor and a beautiful purple color that I am sure your little one will enjoy. If you want to raise an adventurous eater, be brave and try a few twists and turns along the way—and this turn is absolutely great. This makes another great topping for porridge.

INGREDIENTS

2 sweet apples

1 cup (90 g) chopped red cabbage

1 banana

1 teaspoon (5 g) fat of choice

Small amount breast milk or formula, for blending (optional)

1. **PEEL, CORE , AND CHOP THE APPLES.**

2. **STEAM.**
   Place the chopped red cabbage and apples into a steamer pot. Steam for about 10 minutes or until soft.

3. **PEEL, SLICE, AND ADD THE BANANA.**
   Strain the steamed red cabbage and apples into a bowl. Add the banana.

4. **BLEND IT ALL.**
   A food processor or blender works best here.

5. **COOL AND SERVE. DELICIOUS!**

⤳ DIETITIAN TIP

While green cabbage is the variety most commonly eaten, it is actually red cabbage that comes out on top regarding nutrition. Its vibrant color indicates its rich abundance of antioxidants.

CHICKPEA, BANANA, AND MILLET PURÉE

 6 months and older  2 to 3 meals Keeps in the fridge for 24 hours
(The purée will brown but is edible)

This is like a baby version of hummus! The chickpeas provide a great, slow-release energy and the millet gives a kick of carbs, which are rounded off nicely with the sweetness of banana.

INGREDIENTS

2 tablespoons (25 g) millet

¾ cup (175 ml) water

2 tablespoons (20 g) cooked chickpeas, or (30 g) canned organic unsalted

1 large ripe banana

Small amount breast milk or formula, for blending (optional)

1. COOK THE MILLET.
   In a saucepan over medium high heat, bring the millet and the water to a boil. Stir for about 7 minutes until it reaches a porridge-like consistency and large bubbles form.

2. PEEL AND SLICE THE BANANA.

3. BLEND IT ALL.
   A food processor or blender works best here.

4. COOL AND ENJOY!

KIWI, BANANA, AND AVOCADO PURÉE

 7 months and older 3 to 4 meals Keeps in the fridge for 24 hours
(The purée will brown but is edible)

Kiwi can be an unusual taste for some babies, so add it sparingly the first few times it's introduced. It is also acidic; if your baby has a sensitive tummy and a tendency to get diaper rashes, you may want to wait until ten to twelve months to serve this fruit.

INGREDIENTS

1 large banana

1 ripe kiwi

1 ripe avocado

1. PEEL AND SLICE THE BANANA AND KIWI.

2. PIT THE AVOCADO. PEEL AND CHOP.

3. BLEND IT ALL.
   A food processor or blender works best here.

4. AMAZING!

GREEN BEANS, RED BELL PEPPER, AND POTATO PURÉE

 6 months and older   4 meals   Keeps in the fridge for 24 hours

Potatoes are a perfect vehicle to deliver all sorts of other fabulous tastes in a mashed and merry bundle. While this purée does call for steaming, feel free to roast the potatoes and bell peppers in the oven instead.

INGREDIENTS

3 medium potatoes

¼ red bell pepper, seeded

1 large handful green beans

1 tablespoon (15 g) fat of choice

Small amount breast milk or formula, for blending (optional)

1. PEEL AND CHOP THE POTATOES.

2. TRIM AND CHOP THE GREEN BEANS.

3. SEED AND CHOP THE RED BELL PEPPER.

4. STEAM.
Place the chopped potatoes, green beans, and red bell pepper into a steamer pot. Steam for about 15 minutes or until soft. Green beans cook faster, so add them to the steamer 5 minutes after the potatoes and bell pepper.

5. BLEND IT ALL.
A food processor or blender works best here.

6. COOL AND ENJOY!

WALNUT, EGG YOLK, AND SWEET POTATO PURÉE

 6 months and older (if no egg or nut allergies in the family)　　 2 to 3 meals　　 Keeps in the fridge for 24 hours

This purée is wonderful for neurological and nerve development, and the unusual combination really gives it that wildcard taste factor. YES, it isn't ordinary to use egg yolks or walnuts in a baby purée, but isn't it a shame these super omega-3 foods are forgotten? If there are no allergies in the family, explore different foods for your adventurous eater.

INGREDIENTS

2 organic or free-range eggs

1 medium-size sweet potato

3 walnuts

Small amount breast milk or formula, for blending (optional)

DIETITIAN TIP

Buy omega-enriched eggs if you can find them to ensure your eggs have good omega-3 content. Regular eggs can have significantly different levels depending on the feed the hens are given.

1. HARD-BOIL THE EGGS.
Bring a pot of water to a boil and then slowly add eggs and boil for 10 to 12 minutes.

2. PEEL, CHOP, AND BOIL THE SWEET POTATO.
Place the chopped sweet potato in a sauce pan with water. Boil for about 15 minutes until tender.

3. GRIND THE WALNUTS.
Use your blender, or crush them, and be sure to blend all ingredients very well at the end.

4. PEEL THE EGGS.

5. REMOVE THE WHITES AND SAVE FOR ANOTHER USE.

6. BLEND IT ALL (EXCEPT EGG WHITES).
Blend it very well to make sure the walnuts are completely ground to avoid choking hazards. A food processor or blender works best here.

7. COOL AND SERVE.

WHITEFISH, SWEET POTATO, AND GREEN BEAN PURÉE

 6 months and older 4 meals Freeze for up to 3 months

Fish can sometimes be a hit-or-miss affair with little eaters. What you have to remember is, even though they turn their noses up at certain foods today, nine times out of ten, with gentle persuasion, over time, most babies learn to love most foods—or at least tolerate the ones they do not quite want to marry.

Use your choice of whitefish, fresh or frozen, in this recipe. Make sure it is good quality and does not smell too fishy.

INGREDIENTS

1 medium-size sweet potato
1 handful green beans
1 small boneless whitefish fillet
Small amount breast milk or formula, for blending (optional)

1. PEEL AND CHOP THE SWEET POTATO.

2. TRIM AND CHOP THE GREEN BEANS.

3. RINSE THE WHITEFISH FILLET AND CHOP.

4. STEAM.
Place the chopped sweet potato, green beans, and chopped whitefish into a steamer pot. Steam for 15 to 20 minutes or until the fish is cooked through and the vegetables are soft. You might want to add the green beans 10 minutes after starting the other ingredients, as they cook faster.

5. BLEND IT ALL.
A food processor or blender works best here.

6. COOL AND SERVE.

CHICKEN, APRICOT, AND RED LENTILS

 6 months and older   6 meals   Freeze for up to 3 months

Meat and vegetable combos can be a tricky affair. However, one tried-and-true combo beloved the world over is chicken and apricot. It is also a double whammy for protein, as both chicken and lentils are rich in this nutrient.

INGREDIENTS

½ organic boneless, skinless chicken breast

5 dried organic apricots, unsulfured

1 teaspoon (5 ml) oil of choice

½ cup (96 g) red lentils, rinsed

1 cup (235 ml) water

 TIP

To make this meal even more delicious, use coconut milk instead of water.

1. CHOP THE CHICKEN.

2. CHOP THE APRICOTS.

3. COOK.

In a medium pot over medium heat, heat the oil and sauté the chicken until it is cooked through, about 10 minutes. Add the lentils, apricots, and water. Boil for about 15 minutes, stirring occasionally. Add more water if necessary.

4. BLEND IT ALL.

A food processor or blender works best here.

5. COOL AND SERVE. DELICIOUS!

APPLE, CHICKPEA, AND FLAXSEED PURÉE

 8 months and older (if you omit the flaxseeds, suitable for 6 months)

6 meals

 Freeze for up to 3 months

Flaxseeds are a superfood filled with omega-3 essential fatty acids—the "good" fats we want more of. They are also filled with fiber, which aids digestion and prevents constipation. However, babies do not benefit unless the flaxseed is finely ground. Use milled or ground flaxseed for this purée.

INGREDIENTS

3 apples

½ cup (82 g) cooked chickpeas, or (120 g) canned organic unsalted

¼ teaspoon ground flaxseed

1 tablespoon (15 g) fat of choice

Small amount breast milk or formula, for blending (optional)

1. PEEL, CORE, AND CHOP THE APPLES.

2. STEAM.
Place the chopped apples in a steamer pot. Steam for about 10 minutes or until soft.

3. BLEND IT ALL.
A food processor or blender works best here.

4. COOL AND SERVE.

BEET, CARROT, AND CHICKPEA PURÉE

 7 months and older   4 to 6 meals   Freeze for up to 3 months

This purée is so nutritious, delicious, and colorful. However, the beet component, though a great source of iron, folate, and antioxidants, will have you beaten if it gets on clothes. Have wipes at the ready and definitely leave that white onesie in the dresser. Beef goes well with this combo if you want to add some protein.

INGREDIENTS

3 carrots

¼ small beetroot

½ cup (82 g) cooked chickpeas, or (120 g) canned organic unsalted

1 teaspoon (5 g) fat of choice

Small amount breast milk or formula, for blending (optional)

1. **PEEL AND CHOP THE CARROTS.**

2. **PEEL AND CHOP THE BEET.**

3. **COOK.**
Place the chopped carrots and beets in a saucepan with water or into a steamer pot. Boil or steam for 15 to 20 minutes or until soft.

4. **BLEND IT ALL.**
A food processor or blender works best here.

5. **COOL AND SERVE. YUM!**

CARROT, APPLE, AND POMEGRANATE PURÉE

 7 months and older   3 to 4 meals   Freeze for up to 3 months

Pomegranate is a super healthy and delicious fruit with tons of antioxidants, vitamins like A, C, E, and K, and folic acids. It also helps the body absorb iron, and that is just to name a few of its benefits.

The seeds are hard and can become sharp when blended, so pass the purée through a sieve to strain any remaining seeds and seed bits, making it completely fine for your baby to enjoy.

INGREDIENTS

1 sweet apple

4 small carrots

½ cup (187 g) pomegranate seeds

1 teaspoon (5 ml) plant-based oil

Small amount breast milk or formula, for blending (optional)

⟿ DIETITIAN TIP

If using a whole pomegranate (instead of purchasing just the seeds), here is a speedy (and therapeutic) way to deseed a pomegranate:

1. Cut the fruit in half widthwise.

2. Hold one half and gently try to pop the seeds out a little by pushing underneath and, at the same, time pulling back the edge of the pomegranate (like turning it inside out).

3. Hold it over a mixing bowl (with the seeds facing down to the bowl) and bash the pomegranate with a wooden spoon until all the seeds fall out—I said it was therapeutic!

1. PEEL, CORE, AND CHOP THE APPLE.

2. PEEL AND CHOP THE CARROTS.

3. STEAM.
Place the chopped carrots into a steamer pot. Steam for 5 minutes. Add the apple and steam for 10 minutes more or until soft.

4. BLEND IT ALL.
A food processor or blender works best here.

5. STRAIN.
Pour the purée through a sieve and make sure there are no pomegranate seeds left in the purée.

6. COOL AND ENJOY!

COMPLETE MEAL PURÉES
RECIPES WITH THREE–PLUS INGREDIENTS

Is your little one ready for a full meal? The recipes in this chapter are as delicious as they are filling and nutritious! You'll discover how you can start experimenting with more exotic flavors and spices to raise adventurous eaters who love healthy, hearty foods.

ADDING FORMULA OR BREAST MILK

Just as you did in the previous chapters, you can add a bit of breast milk, formula, fresh water, or the steamer water to thin a purée to the desired consistency for these recipes. **Formula and breast milk are no longer listed in the ingredients lists**, though, as they can be omitted for older kids who can eat lumpier foods.

GETTING ENOUGH IRON

Having red meat twice a week, along with meals containing other iron-rich meats (dark chicken meat and salmon) should be enough to provide a good amount of iron. Where possible use lean, fresh meat rather than highly processed meats like sausages, cold cuts, or burgers. You can also get iron from non-animal sources such as fortified breakfast cereals, dark green vegetables, whole grains, and beans.

ALTERNATIVE BINDERS FOR EGGS

Many parents deal with trying to find alternative binders when their little ones can't have eggs. Here are some healthy substitutes:

• Egg replacer products   • Flaxseed   • Chia seeds   • Psyllium husk   • Mashed banana

CHICKEN, ASPARAGUS, AND GREEN BEAN PURÉE

 6 months and older   4 meals   Freeze for up to 3 months

This is a delicious, savory, and filling meal. The consistency of this purée becomes a bit gluey when puréed because of the potato, but that does not seem to bother little eaters. Spice it up with a seasoning of choice if your baby is over eight months of age.

INGREDIENTS

½ organic boneless, skinless chicken breast

3 asparagus spears

1 handful green beans

2 medium-size white potatoes

 TIP

Add 1 tablespoon (15 ml) cream, powdered formula, or breast milk for a creamy consistency. If you have a food processor with a "K-beater" attachment, you can make soft mashed potatoes and add that separately to the purée, instead of puréeing it altogether. Add a little milk and butter to the potatoes to get a nice creamy texture and remove any lumps.

1. DICE THE CHICKEN.

2. REMOVE AND DISCARD THE WOODY ENDS OF THE ASPARAGUS. CHOP.

3. TRIM AND CHOP THE GREEN BEANS..

4. PEEL AND CHOP THE POTATOES.

5. STEAM.
Place the diced chicken and chopped asparagus, green beans, and potatoes into a steamer pot. Steam for about 15 minutes or until the chicken is thoroughly cooked and the vegetables are soft.

6. BLEND IT ALL.
A food processor or blender works best here.

7. COOL AND SERVE.

HOMEMADE CHICKEN BROTH

 6 months and older   3 quarts (2.9 L)   Freeze for up to 3 months

In any recipe that calls for water, you can use broth instead to add flavor and nutrients. Broth is also an excellent replacement for salts and spices, and it is a flavorful idea to use it to cook rice, bulgur, quinoa, pasta, or any other grain. It also great in purées, soups, and stews.

There are many ways to make homemade broths. Vary the ingredients to your liking, as they do not have to be exactly as in this recipe. You can make a version with just vegetables, for example. Open your fridge and you may find you have most of the items you need. And remember, you can freeze broths for later use.

INGREDIENTS

3 carrots

3 stalks celery

1 onion

1 leek

3 quarts (2.9 L) plus ¾ cup (175 ml) water

2 bay leaves

1 free-range or organic chicken

1 bunch fresh parsley

➢ DIETITIAN TIP

Using broth has many advantages. It is rich in minerals that can support a healthy immune system (so it's great to use if your family starts to get a cold), and it contains collagen and glutamine, which can help reduce inflammation and help maintain a healthy digestive system. Always use organic chicken or beef when making your own broth.

1. PEEL AND CHOP THE CARROTS, CELERY, ONION, AND LEEK.

2. BOIL.
In a large pot over medium heat, bring everything—except the parsley—to a boil. Remove any scum that rises to the surface.

3. SIMMER.
Reduce the heat to low and simmer for at least 2 hours. Add the parsley 10 minutes before you turn off the heat. The "skin" on top is packed with tons of nutrients, so stir it right back into the pot from time to time.

4. STRAIN.

5. COOL AND FREEZE.
Once cooled, freeze the broth in baby food containers (ideally, ice cube trays) and use whenever you want to flavor your little one's meals by adding the broth to whatever you're cooking.

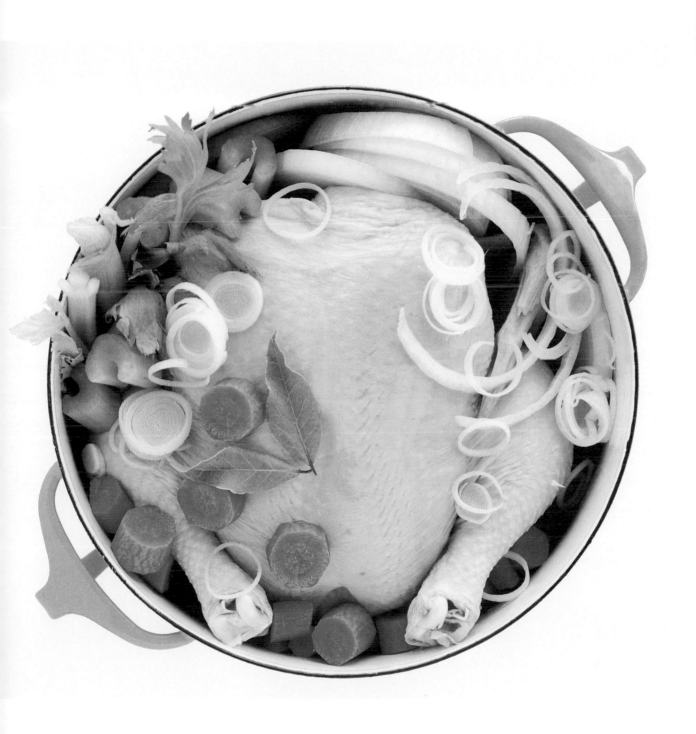

CHICKEN AND RED LENTIL CURRY PURÉE

 8 months and older, or 6 months and older if you omit the curry powder   8 to 10 meals   Freeze for up to 3 months

This meal is all about the benefits of blending your little one's food. You can add plenty of nutritious ingredients, and your baby will love it! This is a wonderful meal for your baby to sleep on.

INGREDIENTS

2 carrots

1 small zucchini

½ organic boneless, skinless chicken breast

Olive oil, for sautéing

1 teaspoon (2 g) salt-free curry powder

½ cup (96 g) red lentils, rinsed

1 ear corn, kernels removed, or ½ cup (82 g) frozen or (105 g) canned organic low-salt

1 scallion, chopped

½ cup (65 g) frozen peas

 TIP

Add ½ cup rice (97.5 g) or quinoa (92 g) to make this recipe more filling. If you use canned corn, buy a low-salt version and rinse the corn well before cooking.

1. **PEEL AND DICE THE CARROTS AND ZUCCHINI.**

2. **DICE THE CHICKEN.**

3. **SAUTÉ THE CARROTS AND ZUCCHINI.**
   In a large pot over medium heat, heat the olive oil and sauté the carrots and zucchini for 7 minutes.

4. **STIR IN THE CURRY POWDER. SAUTÉ FOR 1 MINUTE MORE.**

5. **ADD THE CHICKEN, LENTILS, CORN, AND SCALLION. KEEP COOKING!**
   Add enough water to cover by about 1/2 inch (1 cm). If the pot begins to dry out, add more water as needed. Boil for 25 minutes.

6. **ADD THE PEAS. BOIL FOR 5 MINUTES MORE.**

7. **BLEND IT ALL.**
   A food processor or blender works best here.

8. **SERVE AND ENJOY!**

CHICKEN, VEGGIES, AND LENTILS

 6 months and older   8 to 10 meals   Freeze for up to 3 months

This super healthy purée meets all your baby's daily needs for protein, vitamins, and minerals. Great for batch cooking, this is a great winter or fall purée to kick start your little one's immune system into gear to fight colds. It is so hearty, almost a stew, and the double protein kick from the lentils and chicken give your baby that slow energy release she needs.

INGREDIENTS

1 small Hokkaido pumpkin
(Substitute acorn squash if unavailable.)

⅓ onion

2 small sweet potatoes

1 parsnip

½ organic boneless, skinless chicken breast

1 tablespoon (15 ml) olive oil

2 cups (475 ml) Homemade Chicken Broth (page 116), or water

½ cup (96 g) red lentils, rinsed

 TIP

Using Homemade Broth (page 120) in this recipe is not just about the taste (although it is decidedly more delicious this way). Broth is packed with vitamins and minerals as well as amino acids, glucosamine, gelatin, and collagen. It is a powerhouse of goodness for the whole family.

1. HALVE THE PUMPKIN. REMOVE THE SEEDS AND STRINGS AND CHOP.
   If you bought organic, you do not need to peel the Hokkaido, as the skin is edible.

2. PEEL THE ONIONS, SWEET POTATOES, AND PARSNIP AND CHOP.

3. DICE THE CHICKEN.

4. SAUTÉ.
   On a saucepan over medium heat, heat the oil. Sauté the chicken and vegetables for about 10 minutes. Cook the chicken until it is white and no longer pink.

5. ADD THE CHICKEN BROTH AND BOIL FOR 10 MINUTES.

6. ADD THE LENTILS AND BOIL FOR 10 TO 15 MINUTES.

7. BLEND IT ALL.
   A food processor or blender works best here.

8. SERVE AND ENJOY!

ROOT VEGETABLE MASH

 6 months and older   6 servings   Keeps in the fridge for 24 hours

As great variation of plain old mashed potatoes, this recipe includes plenty of nutrients and flavor. It is hearty and its soft texture and lightly sweet flavor make it a big favorite among kids.

INGREDIENTS

4 or 5 white potatoes (approximately 1 pound, or 400 g)

3 broccoli florets

2 parsnips

1 large carrot

1 sprig fresh rosemary or thyme (optional)

3 cups (705 ml) water, or Homemade Chicken Broth (page 116)

1 teaspoon (5 g) butter

⇨ **TIP**

Add some beef to this meal for an iron boost.

1. PEEL AND DICE THE POTATOES, PARSNIPS, AND CARROT.

2. CHOP THE BROCCOLI.

3. BOIL THE POTATOES, PARSNIPS, AND CARROT. In a medium pot over high heat, combine the diced potatoes, parsnips, carrot, rosemary (if using), and water. Boil, covered, for about 10 minutes or until all the produce is soft enough to mash easily with a fork.

4. ADD THE BROCCOLI AND BOIL 10 MINUTES MORE.

5. ADD BUTTER AND MASH!

6. SERVE WARM.

BROCCOLI, KALE, COCONUT, AND COUSCOUS

 6 months and older   3 meals   Freeze for up to 3 months

INGREDIENTS

1 kale leaf, stem removed

4 broccoli florets

½ cup (88 g) couscous

½ teaspoon (2.5 g) coconut butter

1. **CHOP THE KALE AND BROCCOLI.**

2. **STEAM.**
   Place the chopped kale and broccoli into a steamer pot. Steam for about 10 minutes or until soft.

3. **COOK THE COUSCOUS.**
   Cook the couscous in water according to the package directions.

4. **BLEND IT ALL.**
   A food processor or blender works best here.

5. **SERVE.**

MINTY QUINOA, RASPBERRY, AND COCONUT PORRIDGE

 8 months and older   3 portions   Freeze for up to 3 months

INGREDIENTS

2 tablespoons (22 g) quinoa

1 cup (235 ml) water

10 fresh raspberries

½ ripe banana

4 or 5 fresh mint leaves (optional)

¼ cup (60 ml) coconut milk

1. **WASH AND COOK THE QUINOA.**
   Quinoa needs a thorough rinse or a soak so its bitterness is washed away. Rub the seeds between your fingers while rinsing. Cook according to the package directions.

2. **PEEL AND SLICE THE BANANA.**

3. **BLEND IT ALL.**
   A food processor or blender works best here.

4. **SERVE.**

THYME, BEEF, CARROT, AND WHITE POTATO PURÉE

 6 months and older   4 meals   Keeps in the fridge for 24 hours

The beef in this meal is a rich source of iron and protein. Offering your baby meats earlier rather than later helps her maintain proper levels of iron, as the stores she was born with start to run out when she turns six months old. Use lean beef—the less marbling, the leaner the cut.

INGREDIENTS

3 small carrots

2 medium-size white potatoes

1 clove garlic

½ onion

4 lean beef cubes (about 3 ounces, or 85 g)

1 sprig fresh thyme, or pinch ground thyme (optional)

1. PEEL AND CHOP THE CARROTS, POTATOES, GARLIC, AND ONION.

2. CHOP THE BEEF.

3. BOIL.
In a medium pot over high heat, combine all the ingredients. Cover them halfway with water. Boil for about 30 minutes or until the beef is cooked. Cut into a piece of beef to make sure there is no red or pink left inside.

4. REMOVE AND DISCARD THE THYME SPRIG.

5. BLEND IT ALL.
A food processor or blender works best here.

6. SERVE AND ENJOY.

KIDNEY BEANS, PARSNIP, BEETS, AND BEEF

  7 months and older   **4 meals**   **Keeps in the fridge for 24 hours**

Beans are a terrific alternative to grains to make a purée more filling. They are also a great source of protein, making them a great alternative to meat as well. They can, however, give babies a little gas, so cumin is added here to help baby's digestion.

INGREDIENTS

1 apple

1 large parsnip

1 small white potato

¼ of a beet

½ cup (92 g) dried kidney beans soaked overnight in water, or (128 g) canned organic unsalted

1 tablespoon (15 g) minced beef or diced beef cubes

½ teaspoon ground cumin

1. PEEL, CORE, AND CHOP THE APPLE.

2. PEEL AND CHOP THE PARSNIP, POTATO, AND BEET.

3. BOIL THE BEANS.
If you are not using canned beans, place the soaked kidney beans in a saucepan with water and boil for 30 to 40 minutes until soft.

4. STEAM.
Place the chopped apple, chopped vegetables, and beef into a steamer pot. Steam until the meat is cooked through and no red or pink remains when you cut into it.

5. BLEND IT ALL.
A food processor or blender works best here.

6. SERVE.

SUPER VEGETABLE AND FISH MEAL

 6 months and older   6 meals   Freeze for up to 3 months

You cannot go wrong with this super-tasty superfood meal!

INGREDIENTS

1 kale leaf

2 carrots

½ whitefish fillet (about 2 ½ ounces, or 70 g), fresh or frozen

1 tablespoon (15 ml) olive oil

¼ cup (60 ml) water

½ cup (77 g) fresh sweet corn, or canned low-salt, or (140 g) frozen

½ cup (65 g) frozen peas

½ teaspoon (1.25 g) ground cumin

1. REMOVE AND DISCARD THE KALE STEM AND CHOP.

2. PEEL THE CARROTS AND CHOP.

3. DICE THE WHITEFISH FILLET.

4. SAUTÉ THE CARROTS AND KALE.
   In a medium pot over medium heat, heat the olive oil and sauté the carrots and kale.

5. ADD THE WATER AND BOIL FOR 10 MINUTES.

6. ADD EVERYTHING ELSE. SIMMER FOR 15 MINUTES.
   Add a little more water if needed.

7. BLEND IT ALL.
   A food processor or blender works best here.

8. SERVE.

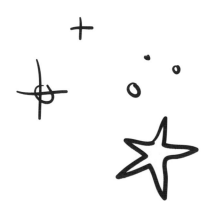

FISH AND PUMPKIN PURÉE

 6 months and older   6 to 8 meals   Freeze for up to 3 months

Many parents ask me how old their baby needs to be before they can introduce fish. While I highly recommend using it once or twice in your weekly rotation from six months on, many parents choose to wait a bit longer because they're afraid their little ones will dislike the taste.

INGREDIENTS

4 medium-size parsnips

½ Hokkaido pumpkin (Substitute acorn squash if unavailable.)

1 tablespoon (15 ml) oil

1 small whitefish fillet of choice, frozen is fine if it is good quality and thawed before use

½ teaspoon ground cumin

½ teaspoon ground thyme

1½ cups (355 ml) water, or Homemade Chicken Broth (page 116)

½ cup (65 g) frozen peas

⇨ DIETITIAN TIP

When consuming freshwater fish, it is important to know where it came from because of contamination levels in certain areas. You can find out more through your state's health department or Department of Environmental Conservation websites.

1. PREHEAT THE OVEN TO 400°F (200°C, OR GAS MARK 6).

2. PEEL THE PARSNIPS AND CHOP.

3. REMOVE THE SEEDS AND STRINGS FROM THE PUMPKIN AND CHOP.

If you bought organic, you do not need to peel the Hokkaido, as the skin is edible.

4. SPRINKLE THE WHITEFISH FILLET WITH THE SPICES AND BAKE.

Place the fish in a baking dish and season with cumin and thyme. Bake for 20 minutes or until cooked.

5. MEANWHILE, SAUTÉ.

In a large pot over medium heat, heat the oil and sauté the chopped parsnips and pumpkin for about 2 minutes.

6. ADD THE WATER. BOIL FOR 15 MINUTES.

7. ADD THE PEAS. BOIL FOR 5 MINUTES MORE.

8. BLEND IT ALL.

A food processor or blender works best here.

9. SERVE AND ENJOY!

FISH, ZUCCHINI, PEAS, AND MINT

 8 months and older, or 6 months and older if you omit the curry powder 4 meals Freeze for up to 3 months

Nutrition guidelines say two servings of fish a week are ideal, and this is a delicious way to get in one of those servings. Fish is always talked about for aiding brain development, and considering babies' brains grow rapidly, it makes sense to incorporate some fish into their diet. This is also of particular importance during pregnancy. If you, as a pregnant mother, don't like fish, you can take a good EPA/DHA supplement with your regular prenatal vitamin.

INGREDIENTS

½ whitefish fillet (about 2½ ounces, or 70 g), frozen or fresh (I use boneless flounder)

½ zucchini

1 small handful chopped fresh mint (optional)

1 tablespoon (15 ml) oil of choice

½ cup (82 g) cooked fresh sweet corn, or (105 g) canned low-salt, or (140 g) frozen

1 teaspoon (2 g) mild salt-free curry powder

½ cup (120 ml) water

¼ cup (33 g) frozen peas

1. DICE THE WHITEFISH FILLET.

2. PEEL AND CHOP THE ZUCCHINI.

3. SAUTÉ THE WHITEFISH, ZUCCHINI, AND MINT.
In a medium pot over medium heat, heat the oil and sauté the diced whitefish, chopped zucchini, and mint for about 5 minutes.

4. ADD THE CORN, CURRY POWDER, AND WATER. SIMMER FOR 10 MINUTES.

5. ADD THE PEAS. SIMMER FOR 5 MINUTES MORE.

6. BLEND IT ALL.
A food processor or blender works best here.

7. SERVE.

BAKED SALMON, TOMATO, AND SQUASH PURÉE

 6 months and older if seasonings are omitted; 8 months and older with seasonings

 4 meals

 Freeze for up to 3 months

This is the perfect fall purée. Salmon is rich in omega-3 fatty acids, which are the essential for baby's brain, eye, and nerve development. It is very important to make sure all bones are removed from the fish! Run your fingers over the fillet before cooking to remove any remaining bones and check again after cooking.

INGREDIENTS

½ butternut squash

6 cherry tomatoes

2 cauliflower florets

1 small (2½ ounces, or 55 g) salmon fillet (wild-caught if possible; if frozen, thaw before use)

1 clove garlic, minced

Small pinch ground thyme

Small pinch ground dill

 TIP

Make sure the fish is thoroughly cooked to kill any foodborne bacteria and viruses.

1. PREHEAT THE OVEN TO 400°F (200°C, OR GAS MARK 6).

2. REMOVE THE SEEDS AND PULP FROM THE SQUASH. PEEL AND CHOP.

3. CHOP THE TOMATOES AND CAULIFLOWER.

4. SKIN THE SALMON. REMOVE ALL THE BONES. SEASON AND CHOP.
   I use garlic, thyme, and dill to season this dish, but use different spices if you prefer.

5. BAKE.
   Place the salmon in a baking dish and bake for 15 to 20 minutes. Cut into the salmon to check for doneness. It will be firm when done. Also double check for bones before blending.

6. BLEND IT ALL.
   A food processor or blender works best here.

7. SERVE.

PASTA, ZUCCHINI, SWEET POTATO, AND CARROT PURÉE

 6 months   6 meals   Freeze for up to 3 months

This yummy, colorful purée is packed with vegetables and is very satisfying, which makes it a great meal for your baby to sleep on—especially if your little one tends to wake up hungry during the night. You can also add some protein like beef or chicken to the meal, which gives it an iron kick, too.

INGREDIENTS

3 small carrots

1 large sweet potato

½ zucchini

½ cup (53 g) dry whole-grain pasta

1 teaspoon (5 ml) oil plus 1 teaspoon (5 g) additional fat of choice

1. PEEL AND CHOP THE CARROTS, SWEET POTATO, AND ZUCCHINI.

2. STEAM.
Place the chopped carrots, sweet potato, and zucchini into a steamer pot. Steam for 15 minutes or until soft.

3. COOK THE PASTA.
In a small pot over high heat, bring water to a boil and then cook the pasta for about 8 to 9 minutes or until soft. Drain.

4. BLEND IT ALL.
A food processor or blender works best here.

5. SERVE.

CAULIFLOWER, SWEET POTATO, AND GREENS PURÉE

 6 months and older   4 meals   Freeze for up to 3 months

All kind of vegetables can be masked by the flavor of sweet potatoes!

INGREDIENTS

2 kale leaves

2 small sweet potatoes

2 cauliflower florets

1 handful green beans

1 teaspoon (5 g) fat of choice

➥ DIETITIAN TIP

Add 2 teaspoons (10 ml) cream, powdered infant formula, or breast milk for a creamier flavor and texture. You can also add a little cheese, if you like, for a boost of protein and calcium as well as fat and flavor. Be aware of the salt content, though, and use only a small pinch of grated (pasteurized) cheese.

1. REMOVE AND DISCARD THE KALE STEMS AND CHOP.

2. PEEL AND CHOP THE SWEET POTATO.

3. TRIM AND CHOP THE GREEN BEANS.

4. CHOP THE CAULIFLOWER.

5. STEAM.
Place the chopped kale, sweet potatoes, and cauliflower into a steamer pot. Steam for 15 minutes or until soft. You might want to add the kale 5 minutes into steaming, as it cooks faster.

6. BLEND IT ALL.
A food processor or blender works best here.

7. EAT AND LOVE.

FIBER-RICH VEGGIE AND RICE PURÉE

 6 months and older   6 meals   Freeze for up to 3 months

It is important to be aware, right from the start, that, at some point, your baby is going to suffer from periods of constipation. It's nothing to worry too much about, and this very hearty and tasty purée is perfect for helping reverse that issue.

INGREDIENTS

3 carrots

2 cauliflower florets

2 broccoli florets

½ cup (77 g) fresh sweet corn, or (105 g) canned low-salt, or (140 g) frozen and thawed

½ cup (95 g) brown rice

2 cups (475 ml) Homemade Chicken Broth (page 116), or water

½ cup (30 g) chopped fresh parsley

1 teaspoon (5 g) fat of choice

1. PEEL THE CARROTS.

2. CHOP ALL THE VEGETABLES.

3. STEAM.
Place all the vegetables into a steamer pot. Steam for 10 minutes or until soft.

4. COOK THE RICE.
Cook the rice with the broth according to the package directions.

5. BLEND IT ALL.
A food processor or blender works best here.

6. SERVE.

⇒ DIETITIAN TIP

As you reduce your baby's milk feeds, you need to ensure he gets enough fluid to counterbalance the fiber he now eats, as a high-fiber diet without enough fluid can lead to constipation. Little sips of water or milk throughout the day are ideal. Take extra care if you live in a hot climate.

PLUM, APPLE, MINT, AND TOFU PURÉE

 8 months and older   3 meals   Freeze for up to 3 months

It is suggested to wait until baby is eight months old before introducing tofu because soy products have a high allergen potential, and they are only recommended in moderate amounts as part of a varied diet. This is a very light purée, so adding something like oatmeal or millet to thicken it is a good idea.

INGREDIENTS

1 sweet apple

3 very ripe plums

4 fresh mint leaves

1 tablespoon (15 g) organic (non-GMO) tofu or Greek yogurt

1. PEEL, CORE, AND CHOP THE APPLE.

2. STEAM.
   Place the chopped apple into a steamer pot. Steam for 10 minutes or until soft.

3. BOIL THE PLUMS FOR 1 MINUTE.

4. COOL THE PLUMS; REMOVE THE PEEL AND PIT.

5. BLEND IT ALL.
   A food processor or blender works best here.

6. SERVE.

VANILLA, STRAWBERRY, AND BROWN RICE PURÉE

 7 months and older   6 to 8 meals   Freeze for up to 3 months

Strawberries are rich in vitamin C, and they are a very good source of dietary fiber.

INGREDIENTS

2 large carrots

5 fresh strawberries

1 tablespoon (12 g) cooked brown rice, or (10 g) white rice

¼ teaspoon (1 g) vanilla powder, or 1 vanilla bean split and scraped

1 teaspoon (5 g) fat of choice

1. PEEL AND CHOP THE CARROTS.

2. STEAM
Place the chopped carrots into a steamer pot. Steam for 15 minutes or until soft.

3. BLEND IT ALL.
A food processor or blender works best here.

4. SERVE AND ENJOY!

⇨ DIETITIAN TIP

Vanilla can be purchased in many forms, but there are only two you should use for baby foods:

- **Vanilla bean**: This whole food is the best way to buy vanilla as it is unprocessed and can be stored for years.

- **Vanilla powder**: This is made by drying and grinding whole vanilla beans. It saves you the job of splitting and scraping the bean, but it can be expensive.

VANILLA, CHERRY, BANANA, AND OAT PURÉE

 6 months and older   4 meals   Keeps in the fridge for 24 hours (The color will change but the purée is edible.)

Cherries are a favorite summer fruit filled with powerful antioxidants that have anticancer properties. They also contain natural melatonin, an antioxidant that helps with sleep and bodily regeneration. If you, as a sleep-deprived parent, want the benefit of cherries even when they are out of season, try tart cherry juice.

INGREDIENTS

3 tablespoons (15 g) oatmeal

½ cup (120 ml) milk

1 large ripe banana

½ cup (77 g) sweet cherries, pitted

½ teaspoon (2 g) vanilla powder, or 1 vanilla bean split and scraped

½ teaspoon (2.5 g) fat of choice

1. COOK THE OATMEAL.

2. PEEL AND SLICE THE BANANA.

3. BLEND IT ALL.
A food processor or blender works best here.

4. SERVE AND ENJOY!

⟹ TIP

No-cook recipes save tons of time on busy mornings. You can let the uncooked oatmeal in this recipe soak in the fruit purée overnight and serve as it as a super-easy breakfast that will need a little chewing. You can also blend the oatmeal porridge and fruit purée together for a smooth consistency.

MILD COCONUT AND PAPAYA CURRY PURÉE

 8 months and older, or 6 months and older if you omit the curry

 3 to 4 meals

 Freeze for up to 3 months

I really hope this recipe will convince more parents to be more adventurous with spices in baby food. After the initial stage of weaning is done and baby is eating happily, it is the perfect time to look into spicing things up. The coconut butter here gives it a boost of flavor.

INGREDIENTS

2 small sweet potatoes

¼ ripe papaya, sliced (no seeds)

⅓ cup (80 ml) coconut milk

¼ teaspoon salt-free curry powder

1 teaspoon (5 ml) coconut butter, or other fat

1. PREHEAT THE OVEN TO 425°F (220°C, OR GAS MARK 7).

2. WASH, DRY, AND POKE THE SWEET POTATOES.
With a fork, poke holes all over the sweet potatoes' skin.

3. BAKE.
Place the sweet potatoes on a baking sheet or in a baking dish and bake for 40 to 45 minutes or until the flesh turns soft and tender when pierced with a fork.

4. COOL AND PEEL THE SWEET POTATOES.

5. BLEND IT ALL.
A food processor or blender works best here.

6. SERVE.

 **DIETITIAN TIP**

Once your baby is good at self-feeding, spread this purée on top of a whole-wheat wrap and slice it into little bite-size strips. Roll it up to make eating it even more interesting—babies eat with their eyes, too.

AVOCADO, CHICKPEA, PEAR, AND FLAXSEED PURÉE

 6 months and older   2 to 3 meals   ❄ Keeps in the fridge for 24 hours

"No-cook superfood purée" is what I call this meal! The avocado, chickpeas, and pear taste wonderful together, and the flaxseed gives this meal a kick of omega-3 fatty acids. Flaxseed is also a high-fiber superfood that works as a natural laxative. Make sure the flaxseed is ground or milled so your baby can benefit from its wonderful nutrients.

INGREDIENTS

3 ripe pears

½ ripe avocado

1 tablespoon (10 g) cooked chickpeas, or (15 g) canned organic unsalted

4 fresh basil leaves (optional)

½ teaspoon (1 g) ground flaxseed (optional)

1. PEEL, CORE, AND CHOP THE PEARS.

2. PIT THE AVOCADO. PEEL AND CHOP.

3. BLEND IT ALL.
A food processor or blender works best here.

4. SERVE.

 TIP

This makes a great smoothie for a toddler, too. Just add some milk to liquefy. If your baby has milk allergies, try it with coconut milk or almond milk.

QUINOA, APPLE, RAISINS, AND PEAR PURÉE

 8 months and older   4 meals   Freeze for up to 3 months

Quinoa is rich in protein and a great source of vitamins, minerals, and antioxidants. Its high fiber content acts as a natural laxative for your little one, which makes it a good meal for constipated babies. Add some coconut milk to turn this into a yummy toddler smoothie.

INGREDIENTS

½ cup (87 g) quinoa

3 ripe pears

2 sweet apples

¼ cup (35 g) raisins

2 cups (475 ml) water

Oil of choice, for drizzling

➥ DIETITIAN TIP

Quinoa is available in many forms. Keep an eye out for quinoa flakes that can be used as a cereal or oat substitute or the puffed quinoa "pops" that are great in baked goods as a more nutritious alternative to puffed rice.

1. WASH THE QUINOA.

Quinoa needs a thorough rinse under running water or a soak so its bitterness is washed away. Rub the seeds between your fingers while rinsing.

2. PEEL, CORE, AND CHOP THE PEARS AND APPLES.

3. BOIL.

Place the quinoa, pears, apples, and raisins in a saucepan with water. Cook over high heat, covered, until the quinoa is soft and you can see its strings, about 15 to 20 minutes.

4. BLEND IT ALL.

A food processor or blender works best here.

5. SERVE.

QUINOA, APPLE, DATES, AND CINNAMON PURÉE

 8 months and older   6 meals   Freeze for up to 3 months

This is a wonderful purée to start your day with, and your entire home will smell like cinnamon. This is a definite favorite superfood meal!

INGREDIENTS

¼ cup (43 g) quinoa

1 apple

4 to 6 soft pitted dates

1 ripe banana

½ teaspoon (1 g) ground cinnamon
(omit for babies under eight months)

1. COOK THE QUINOA.
Quinoa needs a thorough rinse under running water or a soak so its bitterness is washed away. Rub the seeds between your fingers while rinsing. Cook according to the package directions.

2. PEEL AND CORE THE APPLE. CHOP THE APPLE AND DATES.

3. ADD THE DATES AND APPLE TO THE QUINOA.
Boil for 15 to 20 minutes. Add more water if needed.

4. PEEL AND SLICE THE BANANA.

5. BLEND IT ALL.
A food processor or blender works best here.

6. SERVE AND ENJOY!

BABY'S SUNSHINE QUINOA MASH

 8 months and older   4 meals   Freeze for up to 3 months

The benefits of quinoa are endless! It's such a nutritious grain, packed with fiber calcium, iron, and folate.

INGREDIENTS

2 large carrots

2 small sweet potatoes

1 large parsnip

2 tablespoons (23 g) quinoa

1 teaspoon (5 g) fat of choice

 TIP

Spice this up a little with some curry powder or cinnamon. Do not overdo it, though, as quinoa can be a little bit bitter.

1. **PEEL AND CHOP THE CARROTS, SWEET POTATOES, AND PARSNIP.**

2. **STEAM.**
   Place the chopped carrots, sweet potatoes, and parsnip into a steamer pot. Steam until cooked halfway.

3. **COOK THE QUINOA.**
   Quinoa needs a thorough rinse under running water or a soak so its bitterness is washed away. Rub the seeds between your fingers while rinsing. Cook according to the package directions.

4. **BLEND IT ALL.**
   A food processor or blender works best here.

5. **SERVE.**

BEYOND PURÉES

FINGER FOOD AND TODDLER RECIPES

I was terrified of my child choking when I introduced finger foods, but not only did nothing bad happen, my child's first bites went very well. While solid food can cause concern, if you're careful, it's almost always a fun and rewarding experience.

BABY FINGER FOODS AND SELF-FEEDING

Finger foods and self-feeding are a very important step toward developing fine motor skills, like the pincer grasp, and hand–eye coordination. Your baby might start by "shoveling" food up to his mouth, but he will soon enough start using his thumb and forefinger to pick up the food. You'll marvel at how he can pick up something as tiny as a pea.

Learning to self-feed is a great step toward independence—she's feeding herself and learning to control how much she eats. In the early stages, more food ends up scattered around than actually in her mouth. Allowing your little one to explore solid food through her hands creates a building block for better future management skills. Just wait patiently and enjoy the messy view.

WHEN TO START

Babies are ready for finger foods usually between seven and nine months (some begin before and some begin after, all are fine). Your baby will let you know when he's ready to start with signs like trying to grab the spoon and feed himself or swiping food off your plate. Other essential signs include that your baby can hold her head up and sit unassisted. See page 19 for all essential signs.

Your baby may not have many teeth when you introduce finger foods, so start with those foods your baby can gum on and that will dissolve easily in his mouth.

It's important that vegetables and unripe fruit are cooked so they're soft enough to mush easily. Everything should be cut into tiny pieces at the beginning, no more than 1 inch (2.5 cm) long.

GENERAL FINGER-FOOD ADVICE

Your baby should always sit upright when being offered finger foods to minimize the possibility of choking. For early bloomers that like to self-feed but have not mastered the pincer grasp, cut soft foods into round pieces a little smaller than a quarter so baby can hold the food with her entire hand. Once she masters the pincer grasp, cut foods no more than 1 inch (2.5 cm) long.

Finger foods should not contain any seeds, tough skins, chewy bits, or bones. Peel fruits such as grapes or plums in the beginning, and once your little one is used to solids, leave the peels on.

Pick foods that are easy to hold and not too slippery. Use a wavy metal cutter to give foods like avocado and banana a better grip.

Apple chunks and whole grapes can be choking hazards—use a mandoline to cut them into thin slices. Cut grapes in half lengthwise.

Remember, your baby is learning all about the tastes, textures, and colors of foods. Offer a variety of finger foods with a variety of these traits.

GREAT FIRST FINGER FOODS

- Corn, canned (low salt) or fresh cooked
- Eggs, hardboiled cut into small bites, or scrambled
- Grapes, halved and cut lengthwise
- Hummus on soft flatbread
- Large beans cut in half, like butter (lima) beans and kidney beans
- Meatballs, quartered
- Peas
- Ripe avocado
- Ripe banana
- Ripe blueberries
- Ripe kiwi
- Ripe mango
- Ripe papaya

- Seedless rye bread with spread
- Slow-cooked meat cut into small bites
- Small whole beans, like black beans
- Soft-boiled pasta cut in small pieces
- Soft-boiled potato
- Soft-boiled sweet potato
- Soft dates, peeled and pitted
- Steamed apples
- Steamed broccoli florets
- Steamed cauliflower florets
- Steamed diced carrots
- Steamed fish cut into small bites
- Steamed zucchini
- Tofu, cooked

HOW TO START THE INTRODUCTION

Sit your baby in a high chair to eat. Whenever possible, sit down and eat with your baby at the same time. Never leave your baby unsupervised.

Adding an entire meal to the tray can be overwhelming, so keep it simple. Start by placing a couple finger food pieces onto your baby's tray and add more as your baby eats.

Let your baby discover for himself what to do with the food; demonstrate how you eat the food, but try not to correct him. Remember, it's a learning process, and he will get better. If you are feeding more than one baby at a time, or your baby really loves flinging foods, a removable plastic mat under your table can make a world of difference.

TODDLER EATING HABITS

Toddlers need a balanced diet to support their rapid growth and energy. A balanced diet means a variety of foods from the different food groups that will foster lifelong healthy eating habits. While this might sound easy, toddlers are famously fussy eaters and their food preferences change like the wind—they're becoming more independent and asserting their control through eating. Sometimes, they simply resist change or have sensitive taste buds and don't like food that has a strong flavor. All of this is normal behavior that they will likely outgrow. To help them (and you) through this phase, here are some suggestions.

No matter how tempting it is to only serve the foods your toddler likes, it is important to offer a variety of foods consistently. Offer fruit and vegetables as part of a normal daily meal—the more she sees greens on her plate, the more likely she'll be to eat them when she's ready. It is normal for your toddler not to try new foods until you have served them numerous times. She needs time to adjust to the new foods and you can help by making those foods accessible. Your child is not going to starve; don't feel like you need to serve less nutritious fare just to get her to eat.

Don't force the issue and show your frustration if foods are being rejected. Stick to your guns and meal plans as much as you can. Remember that as a parent you are solely responsible for what, when, and where your child eats, while your toddler is responsible for how much he eats and how fussy he is on any given day.

Respect your toddler's appetite by watching for signs such as the following:

- Slowing down his eating
- Playing with food
- Trying to leave the table

These signs usually mean your toddler is done eating. Try not to force him to stay at the table if he did not clean his plate. Instead, respect his appetite and allow him to leave if he wants to. Not causing battles around mealtimes is important.

TIPS FOR TODDLER MEALTIMES

For everyone's sanity (and dignity), keep the following in mind during mealtimes:

- **Keep your toddler interested:** Make their diet varied, and, from time to time, be adventurous and serve unusual foods, such as dragon fruit. However, don't be adventurous every day, as this might confuse your toddler and have adverse effects.

- **Do not bribe your toddler:** Do not bargain with your toddler to eat his meal with the promise of a dessert afterward. This will only make him think the dessert is more important than the savory course, and he will want the dessert more.

- **Keep portions small:** Toddlers can be overwhelmed by big platefuls and lose their appetites. You can always offer more once she finishes what she started with.

- **Shape it!** One way to entice eating is by shaping or arranging fruit and vegetables into shapes like fish, hearts, and faces or try to cut raw, colorful vegetables and place them in a rainbow.

- **Plate it!** Putting different types of food in the cups of a muffin tin or an ice cube tray can sometimes get toddlers to eat during fussy periods.

- **Change the setting:** A new environment might help redirect your toddler's focus from the meal to the new place and stave off mealtime battles.

- **Let your child choose:** Let your child choose between different healthy foods. He likes to feel in control of what he eats. This aids independence and helps during fussy periods.

- **Involve your toddler:** Your toddler is born with natural curiosity. Let them "help" in the kitchen when possible by washing ingredients, pouring ingredients into bowls, pressing the food processor button, and any other appropriate task. Your toddler will love being involved, and it also provides an opportunity to investigate new foods apart from what's on the dinner table. They're more likely to try things if they are familiar with them. Read more about toddler eating habits on page 48.

FINGER-FRIENDLY FRENCH TOAST STICKS

 8 months and older   8 sticks   Freeze for up to 3 months

French toast sticks are beloved by babies and toddlers, super easy to make, and keep nicely in the freezer. They are great on their own or dipped in applesauce or homemade jam.

INGREDIENTS

2 slices whole-grain bread

2 free-range eggs

¼ cup (60 ml) milk

Cinnamon, to sprinkle (optional)

1 to 2 tablespoons (14 to 28 g) unsalted butter

1. CUT EACH SLICE OF BREAD INTO 4 STICKS.

2. WHISK THE EGGS, MILK, AND CINNAMON (IF USING).

3. DIP THE BREAD STICKS INTO THE EGG MIXTURE, COATING ALL SIDES.

4. COOK UNTIL GOLDEN BROWN.

   In a skillet over medium heat, melt the butter. Add bread sticks and cook on one side. Flip and continue cooking until the sticks are golden brown and slightly crisped on the edges, about 5 minutes.

5. SERVE TO SMILES!

KALE OMELET ROLL

 8 months and older   4 servings   Keeps in the fridge for 24 hours

This omelet's shape makes it easy for your little one to eat it unassisted. It can be held whole with his hand, or you can cut it into squares to be picked up using the pincer grasp.

When it comes to eggs, choose free range. Studies have shown they are lower in cholesterol, lower in saturated fat, and higher in vitamins and omega-3s—and they just taste better.

INGREDIENTS

1 large kale leaf

2 tablespoons (28 ml) oil, such as coconut or non-GMO canola

3 small free-range eggs

Pinch of pepper

Pinch of ground paprika

¼ cup (30 g) shredded cheese, such as mozzarella or Cheddar (optional)

1. **REMOVE AND DISCARD THE KALE STEM AND CHOP.**

2. **SAUTÉ.**
   In a medium sauté pan over medium heat, heat the oil and cook the kale for 5 minutes or until soft.

3. **BEAT THE EGGS, PEPPER, AND PAPRIKA.**

4. **POUR THE EGGS OVER THE KALE. COOK FOR 5 MINUTES.**
   Cover the pan so the eggs cook on both sides until solid.

5. **SPRINKLE ON THE CHEESE.**

6. **FLIP, FOLD, AND ROLL.**
   Flip the omelet, fold it over the middle, and then fold it once again so it looks like a roll.

7. **CUT AND SERVE!**

CHICKEN MINI-BURGERS

 8 months and older   12 mini-burgers   Freeze for up to 3 months

These chicken burgers are a nice break from, and a healthier option than, store-bought breaded chicken patties that are loaded with unhealthy additives and preservatives. They also make wonderful finger food when cut into bite-size pieces, as they have a soft but firm texture.

INGREDIENTS

14 ounces (400 g) ground organic chicken meat

1 medium onion, roughly chopped

1 cup (60 g) chopped fresh parsley

½ red bell pepper

2 broccoli florets

1 free-range egg (optional)

1 tablespoon (11 g) chia seeds (optional)

Seasoning of choice, such as garlic, paprika, thyme, or coriander

2 tablespoons (28 ml) frying oil

1. BLEND EVERYTHING—EXCEPT THE OIL.

In a food processor, first blend the chicken and onion. Add the remaining ingredients—except the oil—and blend very well until dough-like and easily shaped.

2. MAKE 12 MINI-BURGERS.

Use a wet tablespoon to make the right size.

3. SAUTÉ.

In a large skillet or sauté pan over medium-high heat, heat the oil. Sauté the chicken burgers until they turn golden brown, about 7 to 10 minutes per side. They're ready when you can easily cut through them.

4. SERVE.

⇒ TIPS

- You can also bake or steam these patties. For young babies who have just started on finger food, I recommend steaming as they become very soft but firm.

- These seasonings go well with chicken:

  Herbs and spices: chili powder, cilantro, garam masala (spice blend), ginger, harissa (spice blend), *Herbes de Provence* (spice blend), marjoram, rosemary, sage, tarragon, and thyme

  Other: garlic, lemon, and pesto

SALMON PATTIES

 8 months and older　　　 14 patties　　　 Freeze for up to 3 months

Salmon, with its omega-3-fatty acids and vitamin D, is a wonderful brain-boosting food that makes a perfect toddler meal. It also makes great finger food, as it has a firm but soft consistency that is easy for babies to chew. If you cut the patties into small finger bites, they are ideal for baby-led weaning.

INGREDIENTS

14 ounces (100 g) salmon (wild caught if possible; if frozen, thaw before use)

2 scallions

¼ red bell pepper

1 clove garlic

1 large free-range egg (Omit if there are allergies.)

1 slice whole-grain bread

2 tablespoons (28 ml) fresh lemon juice (optional)

Pinch of pepper

Pinch of dried dill

Pinch of dried parsley

 TIP

Add chopped vegetables, like broccoli or green beans, for extra nutrients.

1. SKIN AND SLICE THE SALMON.

2. CHOP THE SCALLIONS, RED BELL PEPPER, AND GARLIC.

3. MIX THE SALMON AND EGG. ADD EVERYTHING ELSE AND BLEND.
   In a food processor, mix the salmon and egg. Add the remaining ingredients and process until a thick paste forms.

4. CHILL.
   Refrigerate the paste for 10 minutes.

5. MAKE THE SALMON PATTIES.
   Use a wet tablespoon to form 14 patties.

6. SAUTÉ OR STEAM.
   Sauté the patties over medium heat for about 7 to 8 minutes per side or until firm. Or place the patties into a steamer pot and steam until cooked through. Cut through the thickest part to see if it is thoroughly cooked.

7. SERVE AND ENJOY!

PASTA WITH PESTO AND CHERRY TOMATOES

 8 months and older

 4 meals

 Keeps in the fridge for 2 days in an airtight container

This meal is perfect if you're looking for something new to put in your preschooler's lunch box or serve at snack time. Use spiral pasta types to begin with, especially for babies, as that shape is less slippery and offers a better grip.

INGREDIENTS

1 cup (84 g) dry spiral pasta

½ teaspoon olive oil

1½ tablespoons (23 g) green pesto, such as basil

2½ chopped cherry tomatoes

½ cup (60 g) shredded mozzarella cheese

1. COOK THE PASTA.
Cook the pasta according to the package directions. Drain.

2. SAUTÉ.
Heat the olive oil in a skillet and sauté the cooked pasta.

3. STIR IN THE PESTO AND TOMATOES.

4. ADD THE MOZZARELLA CHEESE. LET IT MELT.

5. CUT INTO BITE—SIZE PIECES AND SERVE.

 TIP

Store-bought pesto often contains lots of salt; I recommend making your own. Better news on the pastas: There are several brands of dried pasta that contain about 25 percent puréed vegetables. These are a great for getting a little more nutrition into a meal.

PASTA WITH MEAT SAUCE

 8 months and older   6 meals   Freeze for up to 3 months

Get your toddler to eat more vegetables with this tasty pasta sauce packed with sneaky spoonfuls of vegetables.

INGREDIENTS

10½ ounces (295 g) lean ground beef

3 tablespoons (45 ml) vegetable oil

1 medium onion, chopped

1 stalk celery, chopped

1 clove garlic, minced

½ cup (65 g) chopped carrot

½ red bell pepper, chopped

Seasoning of choice, such as paprika, oregano, thyme, basil, or pepper

1½ cups (355 ml) canned organic tomato sauce

2 cups (about 200 g) dry pasta

½ cup (50 g) grated Parmesan cheese

1. SAUTÉ THE BEEF.
In a medium saucepan over medium heat, heat the oil and cook the beef until browned, about 7 to 8 minutes, breaking up the meat with a spatula.

2. ADD THE ONION, CELERY, AND GARLIC TO THE BEEF.
Sauté for 5 minutes.

3. ADD THE CARROT AND RED BELL PEPPER.
Sauté for 2 minutes more.

4. ADD THE HERBS AND SPICES.
Keep sautéing for about 2 minutes.

5. STIR IN THE TOMATO SAUCE AND COOK.
Cover the pan and boil for 15 minutes, stirring occasionally.

6. COOK THE PASTA
Cook the pasta according to the package directions. Drain.

7. MIX EVERYTHING—EXCEPT THE CHEESE!
Optionally, give it all a couple pulses with an immersion blender for a softer texture.

8. SPRINKLE WITH PARMESAN CHEESE. SERVE.

MASHED-POTATO PATTIES

 8 months and older   12 to 14 patties   Keeps in the fridge for 2 days in an airtight container

These patties are easy to make, and the ingredients are almost always on hand. They make wonderful finger foods and are ideal for baby-led weaning, as the patties are soft on the inside and easy to grasp.

INGREDIENTS

5 medium white potatoes

1 free-range egg

1 cup (60 g) chopped fresh herbs, or 1 chopped scallion

½ small carrot, grated

2 tablespoons (16 g) frozen peas

1 clove garlic, minced

Pepper to taste

1 tablespoon (15 ml) oil of choice

1. PEEL AND DICE THE POTATOES.

2. BOIL.
Place the diced potatoes in a pot over medium heat with enough water to cover. Boil the potatoes for about 20 minutes or until soft and easily mashed with a fork. Drain the water.

3. MASH THE POTATOES.

4. STIR TOGETHER EVERYTHING—EXCEPT THE OIL.

5. FORM THE PATTIES.
Use a wet tablespoon to form 12 to 14 patties.

6. SAUTÉ.
In a large skillet over medium heat, heat the oil and cook the patties until the surface turns golden brown, about 7 to 8 minutes. Flip and cook the other side until golden brown, about 4 to 5 minutes more.

7. SERVE.

"ANYTIME" MEATBALLS

 8 months and older   About 30 small meatballs   Freeze for up to 3 months

I call these "anytime" meatballs because they make a versatile meal and aren't (thankfully) governed by the hands of time—lunch or dinner, this is a very handy recipe. You can serve it as cut-up finger foods, add it to baby purées for a protein and iron kick, or serve with tomato sauce.

INGREDIENTS

12 ½ ounces (355 g) ground beef, turkey, or organic chicken

1 clove garlic, minced

1 small onion, chopped

½ carrot, finely chopped

½ cup (30 g) chopped fresh parsley

3 tablespoons (15 g) grated Parmesan cheese

1 medium free-range egg (Omit if there are allergies.)

Seasoning of choice, such as rosemary, paprika, thyme, cayenne pepper, or pepper

1. PREHEAT THE OVEN TO 400°F (200°C, OR GAS MARK 6).

2. MIX EVERYTHING.
In a food processor, blend everything into a dough-like mixture that is firm enough to hold its shape easily.

3. MAKE MINI MEATBALLS.
Use a tablespoon to make about 30 meatballs.

4. BAKE FOR 15 MINUTES.

5. SERVE WITH LOVE!

 TIP

You can boil or steam the meatballs instead of baking them. These methods should take 15 to 20 minutes. If you prepare them this way, freeze the cooking water and use it as broth or to cook your baby's pasta, quinoa, or rice in. That's a great way to add nutrients and flavor without using salt.

TURKEY MEATBALLS WITH SWEET POTATO SAUCE

 8 months and older   4 to 6 meals   Keeps in the fridge for 2 days

Turkey is a great alternative to red meat and is available year-round. It's also easily digested just like chicken, which makes it a good first food to tick off on the protein list.

INGREDIENTS

For Sweet Potato Sauce:

2 medium sweet potatoes

1 clove garlic, minced

1 cup (235 ml) water, or Homemade Chicken Broth (page 116)

2 tablespoons (30 ml) oil of choice

For Turkey Meatballs:

3.5 ounces (100 g) ground turkey

1 cup (60 g) chopped fresh parsley

1 clove garlic

1 free-range egg (Omit if there are allergies.)

2 tablespoons (14 g) bread crumbs

⇒ TIP

Serve this sauce on pasta or rice. Stand back and watch the beautiful mess your little explorer will make—one bite for me, one bite for the floor.

1. MAKE THE SWEET POTATO SAUCE.
Peel and dice the sweet potatoes. Boil them in the water until soft, about 15 minutes.

2. ADD THE GARLIC. BOIL FOR 5 MORE MINUTES.

3. BLEND UNTIL SMOOTH.
Add more liquid if needed.

4. MAKE THE TURKEY MEATBALLS.
In a food processor, blend the ingredients very well until dough-like and easily shaped.

5. MAKE 6 TO 8 MEATBALLS.
Use a wet tablespoon to make the right size.

6. MIX THE MEATBALLS WITH THE SWEET POTATO SAUCE.

7. COVER, SIMMER, AND STIR OCCASIONALLY.
Use the same pot you used to make the sauce. Add more liquid if needed. Cook over medium heat until the turkey meatballs are cooked through, about 10 minutes.

8. SERVE AND SMILE!

WHITEFISH PATTIES

 8 months and older   12 patties, depending on size   Freeze for up to 3 months

The idea your child might not like fish can make you skip the thought of it entirely. Maybe knowing that fish is a super-nutritious food filled with omega-3-fatty acids, low in saturated fats, high in proteins, vitamin D, and B vitamins will encourage you to try it! It is a brain-boosting food for your little one, and it would be a shame to omit it from the weekly menu rotation.

INGREDIENTS

14 ounces (400 g) fresh whitefish fillet of choice, or frozen and thawed

1 bunch fresh parsley, or cilantro

3 tablespoons (23 g) oat flour

1 free-range egg

Seasoning of choice, such as pepper, dill, or thyme

2 tablespoons (30 ml) oil of choice

1. BLEND IT ALL—EXCEPT THE OIL.
In a food processor, mix until a paste forms that you can shape easily.

2. CHILL, 5 TO 10 MINUTES.

3. MAKE THE PATTIES.
Use a wet tablespoon to make about 12 patties.

4. COOK THE PATTIES
Heat the oil in a skillet over medium heat and sauté the patties for about 10 minutes per side until golden brown.

5. SERVE AND ENJOY!

 TIPS

If the paste is too runny to form a shape, add some bread crumbs, oats, or oat flour to thicken it, or use any other binder of choice.

Seasonings that go well with fish include chervil, chives, cilantro, dill, ginger, tarragon, lemon, marjoram, miso paste, mustard, and pesto.

FRITTATAS

 8 months and older   8-10 meals   Freezes for up to 3 months

Eating eggs for breakfast helps kids feel satisfied longer, as the proteins take longer to burn than carbs. You can use all kinds of leftover ingredients to make frittatas, so feel free to change up the cheeses, veggies, and meats.

INGREDIENTS

2 medium white potatoes

6 cherry tomatoes

6 champignon (white button) mushrooms

2 broccoli florets

1 leek

9 or 10 large free-range eggs

1 cup (115 g) shredded mozzarella cheese

Seasonings of choice, such as thyme and pepper

1 clove garlic, minced (optional)

3 tablespoons (45 ml) of oil, plus 1 tablespoon (15 ml) for greasing the dish

1. PREHEAT THE OVEN TO 375°F (190°C, OR GAS MARK 5).

2. PEEL THE POTATOES. CHOP ALL THE VEGETABLES.

3. WHISK THE EGGS, CHEESE, AND SEASONINGS.

4. OVER MEDIUM HEAT, SAUTÉ THE VEGETABLES AND GARLIC.
Heat the oil in a skillet over medium heat and sauté the vegetables and garlic for 7 minutes.

5. BAKE.
Place the sautéed vegetables in a greased 8 x 12-inch (20 x 30 cm) baking dish. Pour the egg mixture over the vegetables. Bake for 20 to 25 minutes until you can stick a toothpick into the mixture and it comes out clean.

6. COOL AND THEN CUT INTO SQUARES AND SERVE.

⟹ TIP

If your toddler is going through a fussy eating period, you and your little one can use a cookie cutter to make interesting shapes out of the frittatas. It's a fun way to get your toddler engaged in the kitchen, and your toddler might be more open to eating foods he has helped prepare.

CRUNCHY FALAFEL

 10 months and older   About 20 pieces   Freezes for up to 3 months

This protein-packed meal makes great finger food that can be served on its own, with Fresh Tzatziki Dip (page 166) or Homemade Hummus Dip (page 181), stuffed into pita bread, topping a salad, or accompanied by homemade tabbouleh. Cut the falafels according to your baby's ability to chew.

Only used dried chickpeas soaked overnight for this recipe. If you use canned, your falafels will be sloppy and not hold their shape.

INGREDIENTS

1½ cups (300 g) dried chickpeas soaked overnight in water

1 bunch fresh parsley, or cilantro

1 onion

3 cloves garlic, minced

3 tablespoons (23 g) all-purpose flour

3 tablespoons (45 ml) olive oil

2 tablespoons (28 ml) fresh lemon juice

1 teaspoon ground cumin

1 teaspoon baking soda

1½ cups (355 ml) organic cold-pressed canola oil

1. BLEND IT ALL—EXCEPT THE CANOLA OIL!
Use a food processor to blend the ingredients into a coarse paste. The texture should be firm enough to hold its shape easily.

2. MAKE FLAT MINI PATTIES.
Use a tablespoon to make about 20 falafel patties. Don't make them too thick or they won't cook properly in the middle.

3. HEAT THE CANOLA OIL IN A SKILLET OVER HIGH HEAT. FRY THE PATTIES IN THE HOT OIL UNTIL CRISPY, ABOUT 5 MINUTES PER SIDE.

4. SERVE.

 TIP

If the mixture becomes too loose, add some bread crumbs or more flour. You can bake the falafels instead of frying them for a healthier option. Just oil the falafels and place them on a baking sheet. Bake in a preheated 375°F (190°C, or gas mark 5) oven for 30 to 40 minutes, flipping halfway. The longer you bake them, the firmer they get.

CHICKPEA VEGETABLE PATTIES

 8 months and older   10 patties   Freeze for up to 3 months

INGREDIENTS

½ cup (55 g) grated carrot

½ cup (60 g) grated zucchini

½ cup (30 g) chopped fresh parsley

3 medium free-range eggs

1 cup (240 g) canned organic unsalted chickpeas, drained

Seasoning of choice, such as curry, thyme, or garam masala

3 to 4 tablespoons (45 to 60 ml) frying oil

1. SQUEEZE THE ZUCCHINI.
This helps prevent the mixture from becoming watery.

2. BLEND THE CHICKPEAS.
A food processor or blender works best here.

3. MIX IT ALL—EXCEPT THE OIL—AND MAKE MINI PATTIES.
Use a tablespoon to make about 10 patties.

4. FRY THE PATTIES.
In a large skillet over medium heat, heat the oil. Fry the patties for about 5 minutes per side to a nice golden brown color. Cut through one patty to make sure it is cooked.

5. SERVE.

FRESH TZATZIKI DIP

 8 months and older   2 to 3 portions   Keeps in the fridge for up to 3 days in an airtight container

INGREDIENTS

¼ of a cucumber

½ cup (115 g) plain yogurt

1 tablespoon (15 g) full-fat Greek yogurt

2 tablespoons (28 ml) olive oil

5 fresh mint leaves (optional)

1 clove garlic, minced

Squeeze fresh lemon juice

Pepper to taste

1. GRATE THE CUCUMBER. SQUEEZE OUT THE MOISTURE.

2. MIX EVERYTHING.

3. SERVE CHILLED. SO COOL!

CHICKEN LENTIL SOUP

 8 months and older   6 to 8 meals   Freeze for up to 3 months

Soups make a quick, warm meal offering plenty of nutrients for growing bodies. Add any vegetables you like to this soup, as they add to the flavor and nutrition.

INGREDIENTS

6 cauliflower florets

4 broccoli florets

3 carrots

1 onion

1 whole organic boneless, skinless chicken breast

1 tablespoon (15 ml) olive oil

1 sprig fresh thyme (optional)

1 quart (1 L) water

½ cup (96 g) red lentils, rinsed

1 teaspoon (2 g) curry powder

1. CHOP ALL THE VEGETABLES.

2. CHOP THE CHICKEN.

3. SAUTÉ.
Heat the olive oil in a skillet over medium heat. Sauté the onion for 8 to 10 minutes.

4. ADD THE CHICKEN, CARROTS, THYME, AND WATER.

5. SIMMER FOR 10 MINUTES.

6. ADD THE CAULIFLOWER, BROCCOLI, AND LENTILS.
Increase the heat and boil for 10 to 15 minutes more.

7. SERVE. SO GOOD!

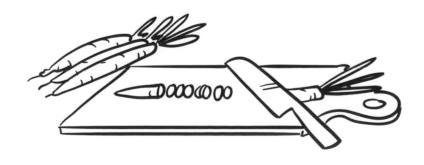

CREAMY TOMATO SOUP

 8 months and older   6 to 8 portions   Freeze for up to 3 months

For the cozy comfort accompaniment, I recommend using whole-grain bread to make a grilled cheese sandwich, and cutting it into sticks for your toddler. You can also use frozen portions of this soup as an "emergency" pasta sauce if you run out of time to prepare a meal from scratch. Avoid unripe or sour tomatoes; instead, use fresh, vine-ripened red tomatoes for the ultimate flavor. Plum or grape tomatoes are great options.

INGREDIENTS

2 small onions

2 stalks celery

1 clove garlic

1 cup (24 g) fresh basil leaves

2 tablespoons (28 ml) olive oil

2½ cups (270 g) chopped ripe tomatoes

1½ cups (355 ml) water, or Homemade Chicken Broth (page 116)

2 tablespoons (31 g) tomato purée, or canned tomato paste

½ teaspoon (3 g) salt (optional)

½ teaspoon (1 g) turmeric

½ cup (120 ml) heavy cream (optional)

1. CHOP THE VEGETABLES.

2. SAUTÉ.
Heat the olive oil in a sauce pan over medium heat and sauté the chopped onions and garlic.

3. ADD THE TOMATOES AND CELERY.
Sauté for 2 to 3 minutes more.

4. STIR IN THE WATER, TOMATO PURÉE, SALT, AND TURMERIC.

5. COVER AND COOK.
Boil for 15 minutes.

6. REMOVE FROM THE HEAT. BLEND IN THE BASIL.
In a blender, blend the soup (do not fill it all the way) to a very smooth consistency. Return to the pot.

7. STIR IN THE HEAVY CREAM. BOIL FOR 5 TO 7 MINUTES.

8. SERVE AND WATCH FOR SMILES!

➯ TIP
Avoid tomatoes if your little one has diaper rash, as tomatoes are acidic and can worsen the problem.

HEALTHY MAC AND CHEESE

 8 months and older   6 to 8 portions   Freeze for up to 3 months

This healthy mac and cheese recipe is 80 percent vegetables. It's also free from loads of flour and butter, but still creamy, comforting, and packed with nutrition for you and your little one to enjoy.

INGREDIENTS

½ medium butternut squash

½ small sweet potato (optional)

2 cups (about 200 g) dry pasta

½ cup (60 g) grated Cheddar cheese

¾ cup (175 ml) milk

1 kale leaf (optional)

1 to 2 tablespoons (5 to 10 g) grated Parmesan cheese (optional)

Seasonings of choice

1. PREHEAT THE OVEN TO 400°F (200°C, OR GAS MARK 6).

2. REMOVE THE SEEDS AND PULP FROM THE SQUASH.

3. POKE.
With a fork, poke holes all over the sweet potato's skin.

4. BAKE.
Place the squash face down in a baking dish. Add just enough water to cover the bottom of the dish. Place the sweet potato in a separate baking dish or on a baking sheet. Bake both for 40 to 45 minutes until soft and tender.

5. COOK THE PASTA.
Cook the pasta according to the package directions. Drain.

6. BLEND EVERYTHING—EXCEPT THE PASTA.
In a food processor or blender, blend the ingredients to a smooth consistency. Add some of the cooking water or more milk to smooth the sauce if necessary.

7. MIX THE COOKED PASTA WITH THE SAUCE AND SERVE WARM.

WHITE POTATO BITES WITH CHEESY BROCCOLI SAUCE

 8 months and older   6 meals   Keeps in the fridge for up to 2 days

Cheddar cheese is tasty but mild in flavor, and it is high in protein and calcium. It adds a creamy flavor to yummy, filling meals.

INGREDIENTS

1 large baking potato

1 tablespoon (14 g) unsalted butter

**½ white onion, very finely chopped,
or 1 tablespoon (7 g) onion powder**

**1 clove garlic, minced, or ⅛ teaspoon garlic
powder**

1 tablespoon (7 g) all-purpose flour

½ cup (120 ml) milk

Pepper to taste

¼ cup (30 g) shredded Cheddar cheese

4 steamed broccoli florets, finely chopped

➪ DIETITIAN TIP

If your toddler has an aversion to onion,
use onion powder instead.

1. PEEL AND DICE THE POTATO.

2. BOIL.
Place the diced potatoes in a pot over medium heat with enough water to cover. Boil the potatoes for about 20 minutes or until soft and easily mashed with a fork. Drain.

3. MELT THE BUTTER.
In a saucepan over medium heat, melt the butter.

4. ADD THE ONION, GARLIC, AND FLOUR.
Whisk constantly for 1 minute.

5. WHISK IN THE MILK AND PEPPER.

6. BOIL, STIRRING CONSTANTLY, FOR 7 MINUTES.

7. REDUCE THE HEAT TO LOW. STIR IN THE CHEDDAR CHEESE UNTIL MELTED.

8. ADD THE CHOPPED BROCCOLI.

9. POUR THE SAUCE OVER THE POTATO BITES.

10. SERVE. SMILE!

CHEESY ZUCCHINI RICE

 8 months and older   6 meals   Freeze for up to 3 months

Zucchini is amazing! It promotes eye health; has a high concentration of vitamin C; is full of carbohydrates, protein, and fiber, and contains large quantities of potassium, folate, and vitamin A. For this recipe, there is no need to cook the zucchini. Reheat any leftovers over high heat to prevent food poisoning.

INGREDIENTS

1 cup (235 ml) Homemade Chicken Broth (page 116), or water

½ cup (100 g) white rice, preferably Arborio rice

½ teaspoon turmeric

Sprinkle of salt (optional)

1 small zucchini, grated

½ cup (58 g) shredded Cheddar cheese

¼ cup (60 ml) milk, or nondairy substitute such as coconut milk or almond milk

1 or 2 tablespoons (5 to 10 g) grated Parmesan cheese (optional)

1 small clove garlic, minced, or ½ teaspoon garlic powder

Seasoning of choice, such as pepper, thyme, or curry

1. BRING THE CHICKEN BROTH AND RICE TO A BOIL.

2. REDUCE THE HEAT. SIMMER UNTIL SOME LIQUID IS ABSORBED.

3. STIR IN THE TURMERIC AND SALT (IF USING).

4. COVER AND COOK FOR ABOUT 15 MINUTES.
Cook until all the liquid is absorbed. The cooking time depends on the type of rice used. Follow the package directions for best results.

5. MIX EVERYTHING!

6. SERVE WARM.

➙ DIETITIAN TIP

Turmeric is the spice everyone is talking about, and for good reason. It is a powerful antioxidant with well-documented anti-inflammatory properties, and it has been seen to support the regulation of blood sugar.

PEA AND CHICKEN RISOTTO

 8 months and older   6 meals   Freeze for up to 3 months

The cheese gives this meal a hearty texture and contains a host of nutrients like protein, calcium, and vitamins A and B12, which are great for brain development.

INGREDIENTS

½ organic boneless, skinless chicken breast

1 tablespoon (15 ml) olive oil

½ cup (100 g) risotto rice

1½ cups (355 ml) Homemade Chicken Broth (page 116), or water

1 teaspoon (2 g) curry powder

1 small handful spinach

½ cup (65 g) frozen peas

1 cup (115 g) shredded mozzarella cheese

1. CHOP THE CHICKEN.

2. SAUTÉ.
Heat the olive oil in a skillet over medium heat and saute the chicken for 5 to 7 minutes.

3. ADD THE RICE, CHICKEN BROTH, CURRY, AND SPINACH.

4. COVER. BOIL FOR 15 MINUTES.
Cook until the rice is just about done. Cooking time depends on the type of rice you use. Follow the directions on the package for best results.

5. ADD THE PEAS. BOIL FOR 4 MORE MINUTES.
Add more broth if needed.

6. MIX REALLY WELL.

7. SERVE.

 TIP
If your baby can't chew yet, blend this into a purée.

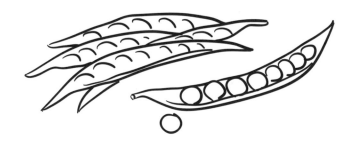

ROOT VEGETABLE CHIPS

 18 months and older; teeth are required for chewing

 A few snack times

Can be kept in a paper sack for a couple of days

This healthy snack is loaded with folate, vitamin C, beta-carotene, antioxidants, phytochemicals, and fiber. Keep these vegetable chips in a resealable plastic bag with a paper towel inside (to absorb moisture). These are great served with Homemade Hummus Dip (page 181), Avocado Guacamole (page 179), and Fresh Tzatziki Dip (page 166).

INGREDIENTS

1 sweet potato

1 beet

1 potato

1 parsnip

2 to 3 tablespoons (30 to 45 ml) olive oil

Ground cinnamon or thyme to taste

1. PREHEAT THE OVEN TO 350°F (180°C, OR GAS MARK 4).

2. THINLY SLICE THE VEGETABLES.

3. SPREAD THEM INTO A SINGLE LAYER ON A RIMMED BAKING SHEET.

4. BRUSH WITH OLIVE OIL.

5. SPRINKLE ON CINNAMON OR THYME.

6. BAKE FOR 10 MINUTES.

7. FLIP 'EM! KEEP BAKING.
   Bake for about 5 minutes more. Keep an eye on these chips because some of the thinner ones will begin to brown sooner than the rest. When they seem crispy, remove them from the oven.

8. SERVE WITH DIP.

FOUR-INGREDIENT BANANA PANCAKES

 8 months and older   8 small pancakes   Freeze for up to 3 months

These easy pancakes have no added refined sugar, and they're diary and gluten free. The pancakes are naturally sweetened by the ripe banana and are filled with antioxidants and fiber, plus the omega-3s and protein that chia seeds provide. Almond flour is a great source of vitamins E and B, has powerful antioxidants, and supports the immune system—not to mention it contains several essential minerals for bone health, including calcium, phosphorus, potassium, and zinc. Serve this treat completely guilt free.

INGREDIENTS

1 ripe banana

1 free-range egg

4 tablespoons (24 g) ground almond flour, or oat flour if there are nut allergies

1 teaspoon chia seeds (optional)

1 tablespoon (15 ml) frying oil

DIETITIAN TIP

Cooking with coconut oil is great; however, you must make sure you only gently heat this oil as it will break down (start to smoke) and create damaging free radicals if it goes above 350°F (180°C). Be aware of this for baked goods, too.

1. PEEL AND MASH THE BANANA. NO LUMPS ALLOWED!

2. WHISK THE EGG INTO THE BANANA.

3. WHISK IN THE ALMOND FLOUR.
You want a thick batter consistency. Add more flour if the mixture is too runny.

4. STIR IN THE CHIA SEEDS.

5. FRY THE PANCAKES IN OIL.
Add a little oil to a skillet over medium heat. Each pancake should equal about 1 tablespoon (15 g) of batter. Spread it just a little with a spoon. Cook for about 7 to 8 minutes and flip it as soon as it gets firm and golden brown. Cook for 5 minutes more.

6. SERVE. YUMMY!

CRISPY BAKED KALE CHIPS

 18 months and older; teeth are required for chewing   A few snack times   Eat immediately

Kale chips are a nutritious snack and one of the very few ways you can get your toddler to eat one of the world's healthiest superfoods! Even if you're not a fan of kale, these crispy chips might convert you.

INGREDIENTS

2 kale leaves

1 tablespoon (15 ml) olive oil

 TIP

Start with completely dry kale leaves (after washing). Otherwise the water can "steam" the chips while baking and lead to soggy kale chips. Not good.

1. PREHEAT THE OVEN TO 350°F (180°C, OR GAS MARK 4).

2. REMOVE AND DISCARD THE KALE'S STEMS. CHOP THE LEAVES INTO BITE–SIZE PIECES.

3. DRIZZLE WITH OLIVE OIL. MASSAGE THE LEAVES.

4. SPREAD OUT.
   Spread the leaves into a single layer on a baking sheet. It is very important that they don't overlap!

5. BAKE UNTIL A BIT BROWN, FLIP, AND KEEP BAKING.
   All in all, it takes 10 to 15 minutes to crisp, but every oven is different so keep an eye on the chips.

6. SERVE. SO DELICIOUS! (ADMIT IT.)

GUACAMOLE

Avocados brim with vitamins such as A, C and K. Their healthy monounsaturated fats make it easier for the body to absorb fat-soluble vitamins from other foods, which is why it is great to pair avocado with as many foods as possible.

1. HALVE AND PIT THE AVOCADOS. SCOOP OUT THE FLESH INTO A BOWL.

2. ADD THE GARLIC.

3. MASH!

4. STIR IN THE ONION, TOMATO (IF USING), CILANTRO, AND LIME JUICE.

5. SERVE AND ENJOY!

INGREDIENTS

2 ripe avocados

1 clove garlic, minced

¼ small onion, chopped

1 diced plum tomato (optional)

¼ cup (4 g) chopped fresh cilantro (optional)

1 teaspoon fresh lime juice

 TIP

Make some easy "cheat tortilla chips" by cutting tortillas into triangles and sprinkling with a little oil. Place them on a baking sheet so they don't overlap, and bake for 15 minutes in a preheated 350°F (180°C, or gas mark 4) oven.

HOMEMADE HUMMUS DIP

 8 months and older   3 to 4 servings   ❄ Freeze for up to 3 months

This Middle Eastern classic is easy to make and requires minimal preparation—it also doesn't hurt that it's highly nutritious. It's a fantastically versatile meal that can be served for breakfast, lunch, dinner, snack, or side.

INGREDIENTS

1 can (15 ounces, or 425 g) organic, unsalted chickpeas

¼ cup (60 ml) water

3 tablespoons (45 g) tahini

1 to 2 tablespoons (15 to 30 g) Greek yogurt

2 tablespoons (28 ml) fresh lemon juice

1 tablespoon (15 ml) extra-virgin olive oil

1 clove garlic, minced

1 teaspoon ground cumin

1 teaspoon ground paprika

½ teaspoon (3 g) salt

1. BLEND IT ALL.
A food processor or blender works best here.

2. SERVE AND THAT'S IT!

TIP

You can make this completely from scratch by soaking dried chickpeas overnight in water and boiling them the next day. Then just follow the recipe.

HEALTHY CHOCOLATE PUDDING

 8 months and older   4 to 6 servings   Freeze for up to 3 months

This quick no-cook chocolate pudding is a favorite of mine and a guilt-free one at that, as it contains only natural ingredients and is sweetened by fruit. Bonus: This recipe is freezable. Double the ingredients and freeze half so you have some on hand whenever you or little ones crave it.

INGREDIENTS

2 ripe bananas

1 large ripe avocado, pitted

8 soft pitted dates

1 tablespoon (5 g) raw cacao powder

1 teaspoon chia seeds (optional)

½ cup (120 ml) homemade orange juice, or other liquid

1. BLEND IT ALL.
   A food processor or blender works best here.

2. CHILL FOR 15 MINUTES.

3. SERVE AND ENJOY!

DIETITIAN TIP

What is the difference between cacao and cocoa?! In short: cacao powder hasn't been roasted and is cold-pressed to remove the fat (for cacao butter). This process means the enzymes remain active. Cocoa may look the same, but it has been roasted at high temperatures and usually contains added sugar.

FINGER FOOD FRUIT SALAD

 8 months and older   A couple of snack times   Keeps in the fridge for 24 hours

When it comes to finger foods, fruits are one of the most important snacks in your arsenal. They are filled with fiber and nutrients like vitamin C, which helps the body absorb iron. If storing leftovers, note that the banana might change color, but is edible—a squeeze of fresh lemon juice can help prevent discoloration.

INGREDIENTS

1 tablespoon (9 g) berries of choice, such as strawberries, blueberries, raspberries, or blackberries

4 grapes

1 apple, or pear

½ of a banana, or mango

¼ cup (60 g) plain yogurt

½ teaspoon vanilla powder, or 1 vanilla bean split and scraped

1. CUT THE FRUIT INTO BITE–SIZE PIECES.
Core and peel as necessary. Remember to cut the grapes lengthwise to avoid choking hazards.

2. MIX THE YOGURT AND VANILLA.

3. ARRANGE THE FRUIT ON A PLATE AND SERVE.
Serve the yogurt mixture on the side for dipping.

BLUEBERRY OAT MUFFINS

 8 months and older   12 to 14 muffins   Freeze for up to 3 months

I like to use natural sweeteners like coconut sugar, which is derived from the coconut palm tree and is touted as being more nutritious and lower on the glycemic index than refined sugar. Use all sugars sparingly, however, as your growing toddler needs nutrient-dense food, and even the best sweeteners are mostly empty calories.

INGREDIENTS

1 cup (145 g) ripe fresh blueberries

2 cups (250 g) plus 1 tablespoon (8 g) wheat flour, or (428 g) oat flour for a gluten-free option

½ cup (72 g) coconut sugar

2 teaspoons baking powder

1 teaspoon salt

3 free-range eggs

1 cup (230 g) Greek yogurt

½ cup (120 ml) melted butter

1 teaspoon vanilla powder, or
1 vanilla bean split and scraped

½ cup (40 g) oats

➯ TIPS

- Coconut sugar contains several minerals including iron and zinc, plus the prebiotic inulin that supports a healthy gut. However, it is made up of 70 percent sucrose (table sugar). Even so, it is still a better option than table sugar or agave nectar, as the fructose level is considerably lower.

- You can substitute ground nuts and seeds for a little of the wheat flour to boost the nutritional content.

1. PREHEAT THE OVEN TO 375°F (190°C, OR GAS MARK 5).

2. TOSS THE BLUEBERRIES WITH 1 TABLESPOON (8 G) OF FLOUR.
This keeps the blueberries from dropping to the bottom of the muffins.

3. STIR TOGETHER THE REMAINING FLOUR, COCONUT SUGAR, BAKING POWDER, AND SALT.

4. IN A SEPARATE BOWL, WHISK THE EGGS, YOGURT, BUTTER, AND VANILLA.

5. FOLD THE WET INGREDIENTS INTO THE DRY INGREDIENTS.

6. GENTLY STIR IN THE BLUEBERRIES AND OATS.

7. POUR THE BATTER INTO A MUFFIN TIN.

8. BAKE FOR 15 TO 25 MINUTES.
Baking time depends on your oven. Take them out when they turn golden brown and a toothpick inserted into the center of a muffin comes out clean.

9. COOL AND SERVE. SO GOOD!

DATE TRUFFLES

 8 months and older   12 truffles, depending on size   Freeze for up to 3 months

This tasty no-cook recipe is not only delicious but filled with nutritional goodness (though high and calories and should only be served as an occasional treat). The task of mixing is also perfect for little ones to help with, even if "helping" just means licking the bowl afterward. There's plenty of room to play with the coating, which is especially good with desiccated coconut, cacao powder, and crushed or ground sesame seeds and nuts like pistachios.

INGREDIENTS

1 cup (135 g) hazelnuts, or (145 g) mixed nuts

12 soft pitted dates

2 tablespoons (10 g) raw cacao powder

1⅔ cups (142 g) desiccated coconut, divided

➪ TIP

If the dough is too firm, add more soft dates. The stickier the dough, the better the coconut coating will adhere. Do not add too many dates because that can make the pastry too soft to form anything (plus they are very sweet). If it's too sticky, add more nuts or desiccated coconut. It is all about finding the right balance of ingredients.

1. GRIND THE NUTS IN FOOD PROCESSOR.

2. ADD THE DATES, CACAO POWDER, AND 2/3 CUP (57 G) COCONUT. MIX AGAIN.
   The ingredients should stick together almost like a dough. Do not blend too much—just give it a couple of pulses and check to see if the mixture is firm enough to hold its shape as a ball.

3. MAKE THE BALLS.
   Use your hands to form about 12 truffles.

4. ROLL THE BALLS TO COAT IN THE REMAINING CUP (85 G) OF COCONUT.

5. SERVE.
   If you are serving these later, say dessert time, keep them refrigerated until then.

ACKNOWLEDGMENTS

Over the course of my journey, I have met and talked to some wonderful people to whom I want to give a special thanks. Without them this book would not have been possible.

To my beloved husband and children for their love and undying support. It makes me proud to know that my passion for cooking has kept you all healthy and happy.

To my friend and mentor Tam Rodwell for being my biggest motivator and inspiring me to believe I could achieve everything I wanted to do.

To Margaret Mead and Pamela Rodwell for their advice and support on my writing. It made it so much easier knowing I could rely on you for help when I needed it.

Thanks also to Katherine Furman, Amanda Waddell, Marissa Giambrone, Gemma Bischoff, and the amazing team at Quarto Publishing for taking a chance on a first-time author. It has been an amazing experience, and I'm so grateful for the opportunity you have given me. A special thanks also to Kelly Pfeiffer, the very talented photographer behind the book's amazing images. I'm so happy I got to work with you to create this special book together.

I've also worked with some amazing brands over the last few years that I want to thank for contributing with their wonderful products to this book:

Done by Deer www.donebydeer.com

Kiddo Feedo www.kiddofeedo.com

Oogaa www.oogaa.com

Lillypots www.lillypots.co.uk

Finally, thanks to all the readers and supporters on my social media sites for your kind words and continuous support. This would not have been possible without you!

ABOUT THE AUTHORS

Kawn Al-jabbouri first started her Instagram, Baby Food Universe, as a way to record what she was feeding her first child. To her surprise, it rapidly grew into the most popular baby food page on social media. She now mixes her writing and promotional work while caring for her two sons in Denmark, where she lives with her husband. Her cooking draws its inspiration from her Middle Eastern heritage and she mixes that with modern day western fair. It provides her army of new parent followers all they need to raise healthy, happy, and adventurous eaters.

Gemma Bischoff is a registered dietitian, recipe developer, and mother of twin boys. She runs the website www.dietitianadvice.ch and has experience working in both hospitals and private practice. She currently lives and works in Switzerland as a health and nutrition consultant.

ABOUT THE PHOTOGRAPHER

Kelly Pfeiffer is a recipe developer, food stylist, photographer, and author of two cookbooks: *Superfoods at Every Meal* and *Superfood Weeknight Meals*. Her beautiful food photography and recipes can be found at www.noshandnourish.com.

INDEX

PowerPoint® 2013

Visual™

by William Wood

WILEY

John Wiley & Sons, Inc.

Teach Yourself VISUALLY™ PowerPoint® 2013

Published by
John Wiley & Sons, Inc.
10475 Crosspoint Boulevard
Indianapolis, IN 46256

www.wiley.com

Published simultaneously in Canada

Wiley publishes in a variety of print and electronic formats and by print-on-demand. Some material included with standard print versions of this book may not be included in e-books or in print-on-demand. If this book refers to media such as a CD or DVD that is not included in the version you purchased, you may download this material at http://booksupport.wiley.com. For more information about Wiley products, visit www.wiley.com.

Library of Congress Control Number: 2012956412

ISBN: 978-1-118-51042-1

Manufactured in the United States of America

10 9 8 7 6 5 4 3 2 1

Trademark Acknowledgments

Contact Us

For general information on our other products and services please contact our Customer Care Department within the U.S. at 877-762-2974, outside the U.S. at 317-572-3993 or fax 317-572-4002.

For technical support please visit www.wiley.com/techsupport.

WILEY   **Sales** | Contact Wiley at (877) 762-2974 or fax (317) 572-4002.

Credits

About the Author

William (Bill) Wood is a consultant who teaches the Microsoft Office Suite and develops programs with the VBA language. As a part-time writer, he has written books and classroom workbooks about Microsoft Access, Excel, and PowerPoint. He has a formal education as a Biomedical Engineer, a field in which he has worked for many years. He also continues his education in graduate studies at Milwaukee School of Engineering and Medical College of Wisconsin in the field of Medical Informatics. Bill also works as a volunteer member of the National Ski Patrol.

Author's Acknowledgments

Thank you to the entire Wiley team for helping me complete another book — you are all very friendly and helpful. Special thanks go to Aaron Black and Jade Williams, who gave me their undivided attention when I needed it.

Thank you to Technical Editor Vince Averello for doing a thorough and detailed job. Thanks to Copy Editor Marylouise Wiack for being thorough. I write like an engineer and Marylouise gave my writing eloquence with her recommendations.

Special thanks to my sweetheart and wife, Shane, who kept things together while I took the time to write this book — it would have been difficult to do it without her help and support.

These people had a direct influence on this book, but thank you also to my friends who took an interest in this book and listened to me talk about it while I wrote it.

How to Use This Book

Who This Book Is For

This book is for the reader who has never used this particular technology or software application. It is also for readers who want to expand their knowledge.

The Conventions in This Book

❶ Steps

This book uses a step-by-step format to guide you easily through each task. **Numbered steps** are actions you must do; **bulleted steps** clarify a point, step, or optional feature; and **indented steps** give you the result.

❷ Notes

Notes give additional information — special conditions that may occur during an operation, a situation that you want to avoid, or a cross-reference to a related area of the book.

❸ Icons and Buttons

Icons and buttons show you exactly what you need to click to perform a step.

❹ Tips

Tips offer additional information, including warnings and shortcuts.

❺ Bold

Bold type shows command names or options that you must click or text or numbers you must type.

❻ Italics

Italic type introduces and defines a new term.

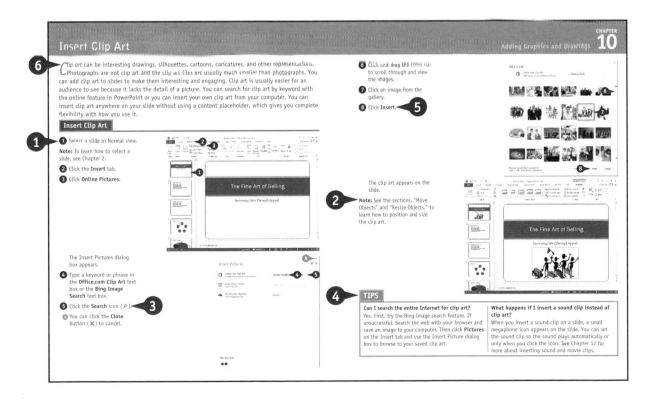

Table of Contents

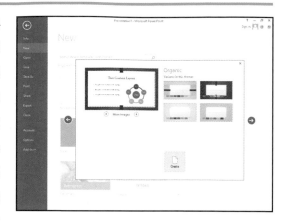

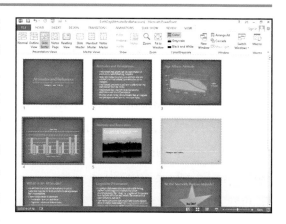

Chapter 3 Changing PowerPoint Options

Chapter 4 Writing and Formatting Text

Table of Contents

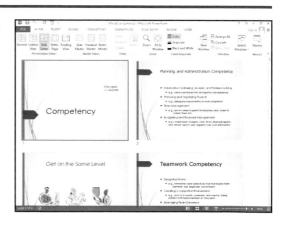

Chapter 7   Working with Outlines

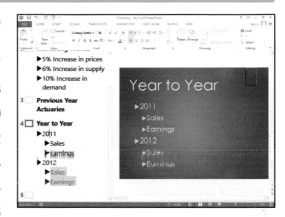

Chapter 8   Using Themes

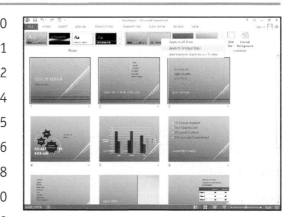

Table of Contents

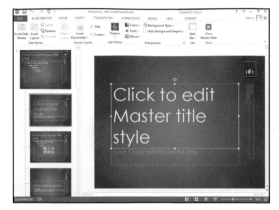

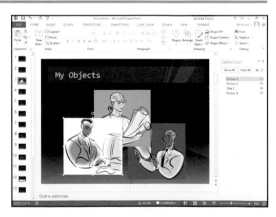

Chapter 11   Enhancing Slides with Action

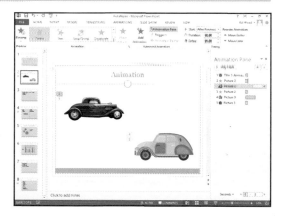

Table of Contents

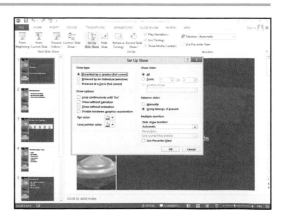

Chapter 14   Printing Presentations

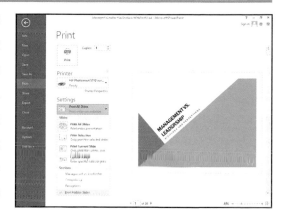

Chapter 15   Presenting a Slide Show

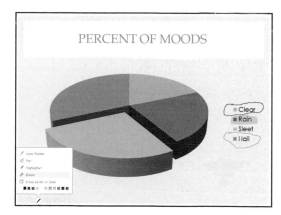

Table of Contents

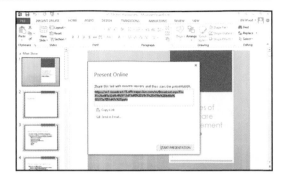

CHAPTER 1

Starting with PowerPoint Basics

Discover PowerPoint basics such as creating, saving, and closing a presentation. Each presentation you build exists in its own separate PowerPoint file. After showing you how to create a new presentation, this chapter teaches you how to find and open existing presentation files.

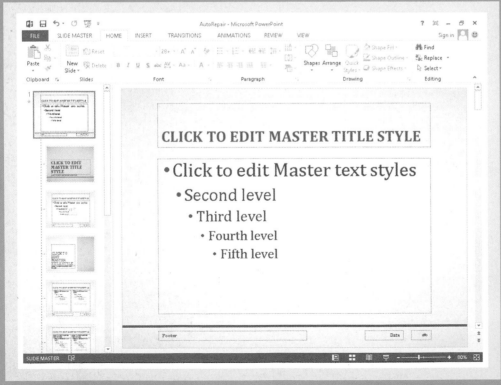

Introducing PowerPoint

With PowerPoint, you can create a professional-looking slide show. The PowerPoint program provides tools you can use to build presentations that include graphics, media, animations, and an assortment of ways to transition from slide to slide. It provides various views and user interfaces to suit your particular needs. These PowerPoint tools enable you to design and build a quality presentation. Many tasks start in Backstage view. To access this view, click the File tab on the ribbon.

Build an Outline

You can type text in outline form to build slides for your presentation. In the Outline view, an icon represents each slide, and each slide contains a slide title next to the icon. Second-level lines of text on the outline appear as bullet points on the slide. These bullets convey the main points you want to make about each topic.

5 ☐ **BUSINESS REVENUE**

6 ☐ **QUARTERLY SALES**
- 10 Clients Added
- 2 Clients Lost
- 20 Leads Called
- 5 Proposals Completed

Choose a Slide Design and Layout

A slide design applies preset design elements such as colors, background graphics, and text styles to a slide. A particular slide layout applied to a slide determines what type of information that slide includes. For example, a Title Slide layout has a title and subtitle. A Title and Content layout includes a title, plus a placeholder that holds a list of bullet points, a table, or other graphic elements.

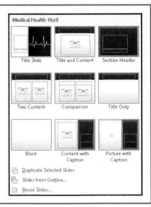

Add Content

You can add content such as text, charts, and pictures to the slide in the Slide pane of Normal view. You can also insert text boxes that enable you to add slide text that does not appear in the presentation outline.

Work with Masters

A set of slide designs and a slide theme combine to create a set of master slides. Masters enable you to add content that you want to appear in a particular location on slides. This saves you from having to add repeating content, such as your company logo, to each slide. For example, you can set up the master so an identical footer appears on every slide.

Organize Slides

After creating several slides, you may need to reorganize them to create the proper sequence for your presentation. You can reorder slides in Slide Sorter view. This view shows slide thumbnails that you can move, delete, duplicate, or hide. You can also perform these actions on the Slides Thumbnail pane in Normal view.

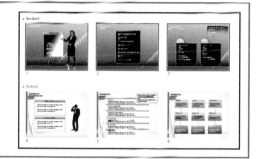

Set Up Your Show

You can add narration, animations, and transitions to your slides. You can record a narration that plays when you give your presentation. Use animation to move an element on-screen, such as a ball bouncing onto the screen. Transitions control how a new slide appears on-screen — for example, a slide can fade in over the previous slide.

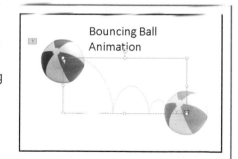

Run a Slide Show

After you add the content, choose slide designs, and add special effects, you are ready to run your slide show presentation. Tools appear on-screen during the slide show — they help you control your presentation and even enable you to make annotations on your slides as you present them. Presenter view shows your notes and provides a timer to ensure that your presentation is flawless.

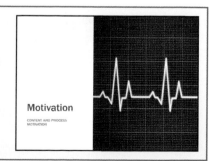

Start PowerPoint and Explore the Start Screen

You can start PowerPoint from the new Windows 8 Start screen so you can begin designing a presentation. When you open PowerPoint 2013, the redesigned start screen appears automatically. From the start screen, you can start a new presentation or open an existing one. The start screen lists recently opened presentations and allows you to create a presentation from templates on your computer, or search for PowerPoint templates on the Internet.

Start PowerPoint and Explore the Start Screen

1 Turn on your computer.

2 Press ⊞.

The Start screen appears.

3 Right-click the background on the Start screen.

The All apps button appears.

4 Click the **All apps** button.

6

All applications appear on the Start screen.

5 Position the mouse pointer (🔓) at the bottom of the Start screen.

Ⓐ A scroll bar appears.

6 Scroll across to find the PowerPoint 2013 icon.

7 Click the **PowerPoint 2013** icon.

PowerPoint opens and displays the start screen.

Ⓑ You can open a recently opened presentation.

Ⓒ You can open a file from your computer.

Ⓓ You can create a new presentation by clicking a template.

Ⓔ You can search for a template on the Internet.

TIP

Is there a quicker way to open PowerPoint?

1 Repeat Steps **1** to **6**.

2 Right-click **PowerPoint 2013**.

3 Click **Open file location**.

4 Click the **Home** tab.

5 Click **Copy** and the shortcut appears on your desktop.

Start a New Presentation

You can create a new presentation from the start screen when you start PowerPoint, or from the File tab on the ribbon *(also known as Backstage View)*. You can create a new presentation from scratch or by using a template. Creating a presentation from scratch allows you to design freely without preconceived notions, while working from a template saves time and promotes ideas by starting you off with a certain look and theme. You can find templates on your computer, as well as on the Internet for free or for a fee. Your computer needs an Internet connection to download online templates.

Start a New Presentation

1 Click the **File** tab to show Backstage view.

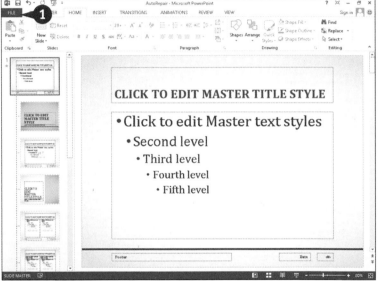

2 Click **New.**

Templates available on your computer appear.

A You can choose a blank presentation.

B You can click the **Pushpin** button (📌) to pin a template to this list (📌 changes to 📌).

3 Click the presentation template of your choice.

This example uses Organics.

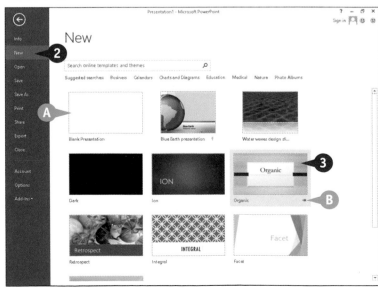

A dialog box appears, showing a preview of the template.

C You can click the **Close** button (✖) to cancel.

D You can click **Back** (◁) or **Forward** (▷) to view other slides from this template.

E You can click **Back** (◀) or **Forward** (▶) to view other templates from the list.

4 Click a color scheme.

The preview changes to reflect your preferences.

5 Click **Create**.

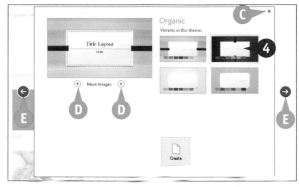

PowerPoint creates a presentation from the template.

TIPS

Is there another way to create a blank presentation?
Yes. When you launch PowerPoint from the Windows 8 Start screen, the start screen has an option to create a blank template. Simply click the **Blank Presentation** option.

Can I get templates from the Internet?
Yes. You can find many templates online, a lot of them free. Click the **File** tab, and then click **New**. At the top of the screen, click the **Search online templates and themes** text box to start the process. A dialog box appears that allows you to search online.

Search for Templates Online

The larger your choice of PowerPoint templates, the greater the chance you will find one that suits your needs. Fortunately, there are literally thousands of PowerPoint templates available online. You can search for an online template by using the PowerPoint search feature, or an Internet search engine.

The PowerPoint search feature allows you to search by a keyword and shows you online presentation templates associated with that keyword. The search feature shows you a preview of the template and the name of who provided it, and then downloads the template for you! Remember to download only files from websites that you trust.

Search for Templates Online

1 Click the **File** tab to show Backstage view.

2 Click **New**.

Templates available on your computer appear.

A You can search by clicking one of the suggested searches.

3 Type a keyword in the search text box and click (🔍).

This example uses Sports.

4 Click **Search** (🔍).

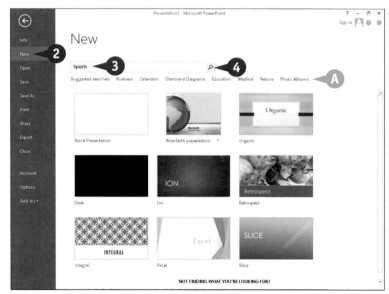

PowerPoint shows online templates that match the search text.

B Click the **Pushpin** button (📌) to pin a template to your list of templates (📌 changes to 📌).

5 Click the template of your choice.

A dialog box appears, showing a preview of the template.

Ⓒ You can click **Back** (Ⓒ) or **Forward** (Ⓓ) to view other slides from this template.

Ⓓ You can click **Back** (Ⓓ) or **Forward** (Ⓓ) to view other templates from the list.

Ⓔ You can click the **Close** button (✖) to leave Backstage view.

⑥ Click **Create**.

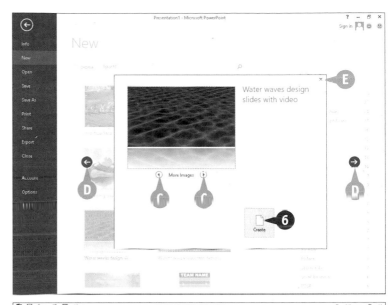

PowerPoint creates a presentation from the template.

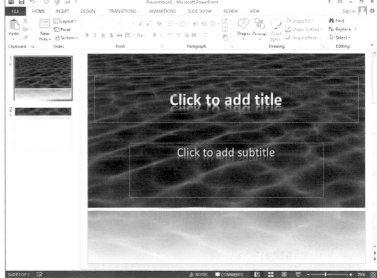

TIPS

Do templates come in different sizes?
Yes. Templates come in two slide sizes. The 16:9 aspect ratio is for widescreen, and the 4:3 aspect ratio is for conventional monitors. Your choice of template may require you to change the aspect ratio. See Chapter 6 to learn about changing aspect ratios.

I need more space to work. Can I hide the ribbon?
Yes. To hide the ribbon, simply double-click a tab and the ribbon disappears except for the tabs. Then click a tab and the ribbon appears temporarily so you can execute a command. Double-click a tab again to show the ribbon continuously.

Save a Presentation

After you create a presentation, you should save it for future use. You should also save the presentation often while working on it to avoid losing any changes. Saving a PowerPoint file works much like saving any other Microsoft Office program file: You need to specify the location in which to save the file and give the file a name. If you want to save a presentation that has previously been saved, you can click the Save icon in the upper-left corner of the PowerPoint window to quickly save it.

Save a Presentation

1 Click the **File** tab to show Backstage view.

2 Click **Save As**.

3 Click **Computer**.

4 Click **Browse**.

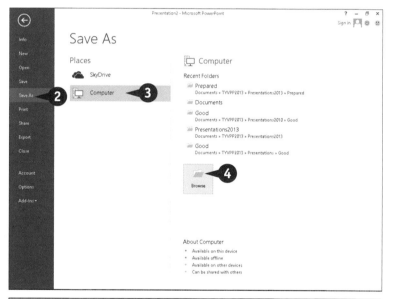

The Save As dialog box appears.

5 Click the folder where you want to save your file.

This example saves to My Documents.

6 Click in the **File name** text box to select the text and then type a filename.

A You can click and drag the scroll bar to find more folder locations.

B You can click **New folder** to create a new folder.

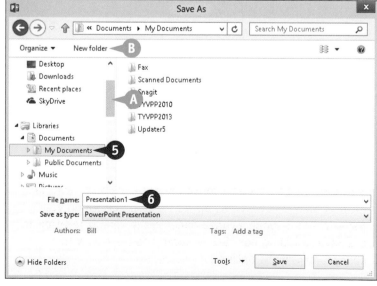

In this example, the filename is WaterWaves.

7 Click the **Save as Type** down arrow ( ) to change the file type from the default.

Note: If you choose a format other than the default PowerPoint format, you may see a prompt about an issue such as version compatibility. Respond to the prompt to continue saving.

8 Click **Save**.

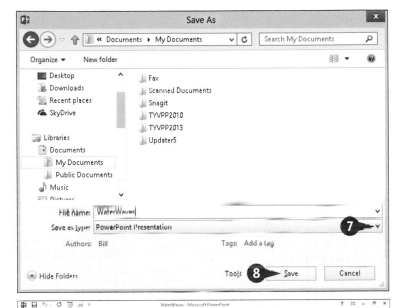

PowerPoint saves the presentation and the Save As dialog box closes.

C The new filename appears in the title bar.

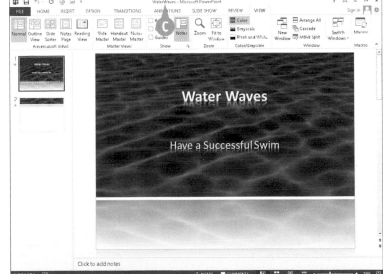

I save presentations in a specific folder all the time. Is there a quick way to locate that folder in the Save As dialog box?
Yes. You can make your favorite folder the default local file location in the PowerPoint Options dialog box. When you perform a save, your favorite folder is the default location in the Save As dialog box. See Chapter 3 to learn how to change PowerPoint options.

Must I always use the Save As dialog box?
No. You can click the **Save** icon (🖫) on the Quick Access Toolbar or press Ctrl + S. To save a copy of your presentation under a new name, click the **File** tab, click **Save As**, and then specify a new filename and save location.

Find a Presentation

Sometimes you want to open a presentation file but you forget what you named it or you forget which folder contains it. Finding that file is very important because you need it not only to design the presentation, but also to present the slide show. If it is not on the Recent Presentations list in Backstage view and browsing for it is unsuccessful, you can use the PowerPoint search feature to locate the file. You can also use the search feature on the Windows 8 Start screen to locate it.

Find a Presentation

Use the Open Dialog Box

1 Click the **File** tab to show Backstage view.

2 Click **Open**.

3 Click **Computer**.

4 Click **Browse**.

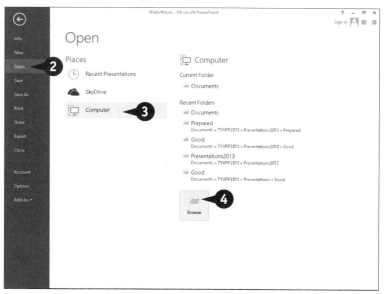

5 Click the parent folder that you think may hold the file, even if you think it is in a subfolder.

6 Type a keyword in the search text box.

Note: PowerPoint searches filenames and file contents.

This example searches for Water.

As you type, the Open dialog box shows files containing the keyword.

7 If PowerPoint finds your file, click it.

8 Click **Open**

The file opens.

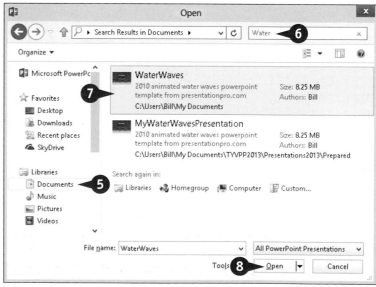

Use the Windows 8 Start Screen

1 Press ⊞ + F.

The Search screen appears.

2 Type a keyword in the text box.

3 Click the **Search** icon (🔍).

Files that contain the keyword appear in the search results.

4 If PowerPoint finds your file, click it.

A You can position your mouse pointer (🖑) over the file to see details about the file.

The file opens.

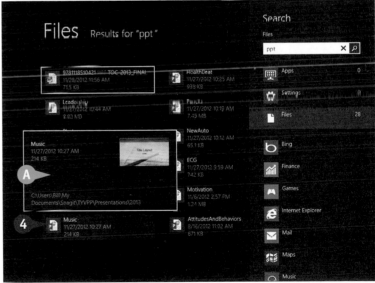

TIP

I remember the date I last saved my presentation, but nothing else. How can I find it?

Repeat Steps **1** to **4** to start the search in the Open dialog box and click the search textbox. The textbox becomes a drop-down list, and on the bottom are two choices under Add a search filter. The two choices are Date modified and Size. If you click Date modified, a calendar appears — click a date on the calendar and you will see only files modified on that date. If you click Size, a list appears with ranges of file sizes — click one of the ranges to see only files of that particular file size.

Open an Existing Presentation

After you save and close a presentation, you must find it and open it the next time you want to use it — you need to open it to design it as well as to present the slide show. You can locate your presentation by using the Open dialog box to browse your computer for it. If you used the presentation recently, the quickest way to open it is to find it in the Recent Presentations list in Backstage view.

Open an Existing Presentation

1 Click the **File** tab to show Backstage view.

2 Click **Open**.

3 Click **Recent Presentations**.

The Recent Presentations list appears.

A You can click the **Pushpin** (📌) to pin a presentation to the list (📌 changes to 📌).

4 If you find your presentation on the list, click it and PowerPoint opens it.

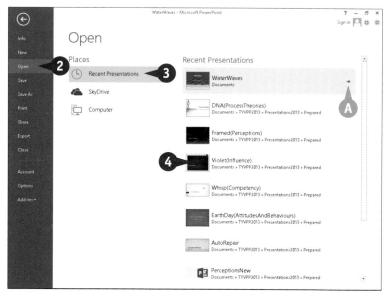

5 If your presentation is not on the Recent Presentations list, Click **Computer**.

B If you find your folder location in the Recent Folders, you can click it there.

6 Click **Browse**.

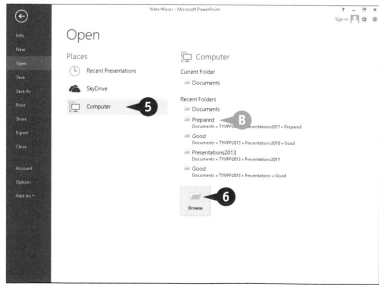

The Open dialog box appears.

7 Click the folder that contains the presentation file you want to open.

This example selects Documents.

8 Click the filename.

This example selects WaterWaves.

9 Click **Open**.

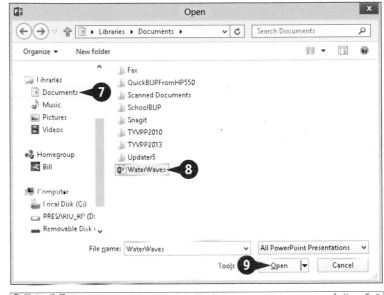

PowerPoint opens the presentation.

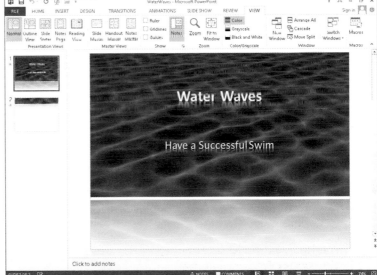

Is there a way to keep my presentation on the Recent Presentations list?

Yes. To pin a presentation to the Recent Presentations list, position the mouse pointer (⌖) over a presentation on the Recent Presentations list and then click the **Pushpin** to the right of the name (⌖ changes to ⌖). To unpin a presentation, click **Unpin** (⌖).

Is there a command for exiting PowerPoint?

No. The PowerPoint application automatically exits when you close your last presentation. If you want to close PowerPoint directly, click the **Close** button (✕) in the upper-right corner of the PowerPoint window.

Close a Presentation

When you finish working with a presentation, you can close it. Closing the presentation gives you a less cluttered workspace on your computer and frees valuable computer memory to process other work that you need to do. If you share the file with others on a network, closing it allows them to access the file without worrying about sharing violations.

When you close a file with unsaved changes, PowerPoint prompts you to save the presentation to avoid accidentally losing your work. For more on saving a presentation, see the section, "Save a Presentation," in this chapter.

Close a Presentation

① Click the **Close** button (✖).

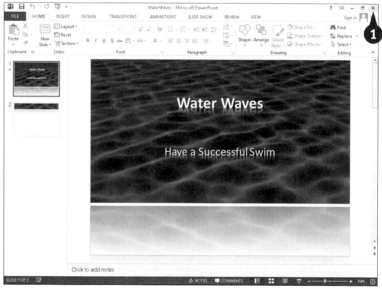

A message may appear, asking if you want to save changes.

② Click **Save**.

Ⓐ If you do not want to save the changes to your presentation, click **Don't Save**.

Ⓑ To abort closing the presentation, click **Cancel**.

The file closes, but PowerPoint remains open.

Note: You can also close the presentation by pressing Alt + F4.

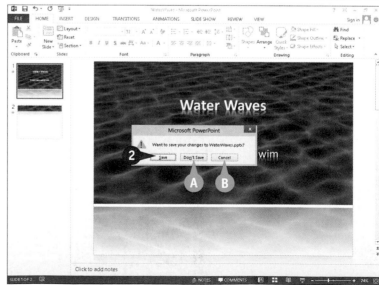

Delete a Presentation

Occasionally you will come across an old file while browsing for a presentation to open. This file may have out-of-date information or may be an unneeded backup copy. You can conveniently delete the file from the Open dialog box.

Deleting old files frees up space on your hard drive. However, you should make sure that the file is backed up somewhere in case you need it in the future.

Delete a Presentation

1 Click the **File** tab to show Backstage view.

2 Click **Open**.

3 Click **Computer**.

4 Click **Browse**.

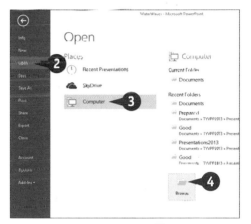

The Open dialog box appears.

5 Right-click the file you want to delete.

This example deletes WaterWaves.

The submenu appears.

6 Click **Delete**.

The Delete File dialog box appears.

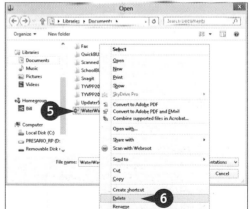

7 Click **Yes**.

PowerPoint deletes the file and puts it in the Recycle Bin.

Note: You also can browse files from Windows Explorer and delete any file.

CHAPTER 2

Navigating PowerPoint

Discover PowerPoint basics such as working in different views and navigating through PowerPoint. Knowing how to navigate through an application can save time, avoid frustration, and help you build a quality presentation. In this chapter, you learn the elements in the PowerPoint screen, and how to get help when you need it.

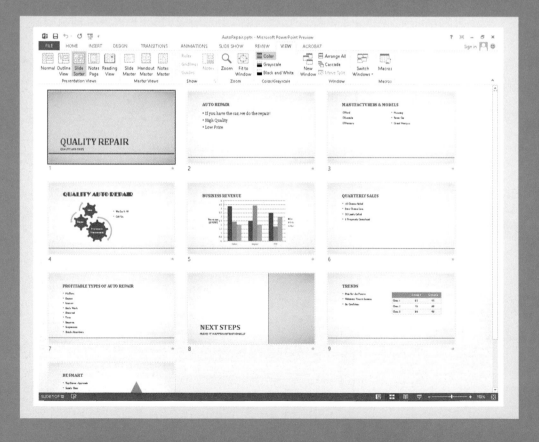

Explore Normal View

Powerpoint offers several views that you can use to work on different aspects of your presentation. Having different views is important because certain views are better for performing certain tasks. For example, arranging slides is easiest in Slide Sorter view.

You will usually work in Normal view, where you can create, position, and format objects on each slide. In Outline view, you can enter presentation text in outline form and the text automatically appears on the slide.

A Navigation Buttons

You can change views using the command buttons on the View tab of the ribbon, or using the command buttons on the status bar. These buttons include *Normal view* (⬜), *Slide Sorter view* (⊞), *Slide Show view* (🖵), and *Reading view* (📖).

B Slides Thumbnail Pane

The Slides Thumbnail pane contains thumbnails of each slide. The thumbnails are numbered by the order in which they appear in the slide show. You can click and drag the thumbnails to change the order of slides and you can delete slides from this pane.

C Slide Pane

The Slide pane is the largest pane in Normal view and shows a slide and all its contents. Here you can create and manipulate slide objects such as graphics and animations, and type text directly on to the slide.

D Notes Pane

The Notes pane appears below the Slide pane. You can enter speaker notes associated with each individual slide into this pane. You can then refer to these notes while presenting a slide show without your audience seeing them.

Navigate PowerPoint Views

In addition to Normal view, you can use Slide Sorter view to organize slides, Notes Page view to create detailed speaker notes, and Slide Show view or Reading view to display your presentation. Each view has certain tasks that are easier to perform in that particular view.

Outline View

Outline view has a pane that enables you to enter text into your slides in a familiar outline format. In this view, the Outline pane replaces the Slides Thumbnail pane. Top-level headings in the outline are slide titles, and entries at the second level appear as bullet points. The outline is a great reference if you need to write a paper to accompany your presentation.

Slide Sorter View

Slide Sorter view is the best view to change the order of slides, delete slides, or duplicate slides. In Slide Sorter view, you can click and drag a slide to move it. If you double-click a slide, PowerPoint changes to Normal view and displays that slide in the Slide pane.

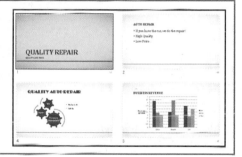

Reading View

You can click Slide Show view (□) to present your show. Slides appear one at a time at full screen size. Reading view (□) is very similar to Slide Show view, but gives you more navigation flexibility because the status bar remains at the bottom of the screen. To exit either view, press Esc.

Notes Page View

In Notes Page view, you can display each slide and the associated speaker notes as one full page. You can also type notes on the page while viewing your slide — this is the most convenient view for typing presentation notes. From the View tab, click Notes Page to work with this view.

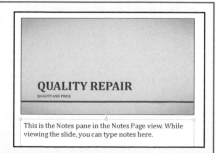

Work with Ribbon Groups, Commands, and Galleries

Y ou can find all the commands that you need to design and present your slide show on the ribbon. The *ribbon* is the user interface at the top of the PowerPoint window. Commands are necessary to design your presentation, and knowing their location allows you to find them quickly so you can work efficiently.

Related commands are grouped on the ribbon tabs. Commands are further arranged into groups on the tab, with the group names shown at the bottom of the group. Some command buttons include down arrows that display menus or galleries of commands when you click them.

Work with Ribbon Groups, Commands, and Galleries

1 Click any tab on the ribbon.

This example selects the View tab.

The commands for the particular tab you clicked appear on the ribbon.

2 Click the button or check box for any command.

This example selects Macro.

The Macro dialog box appears.

3 Click **Cancel** to cancel the command.

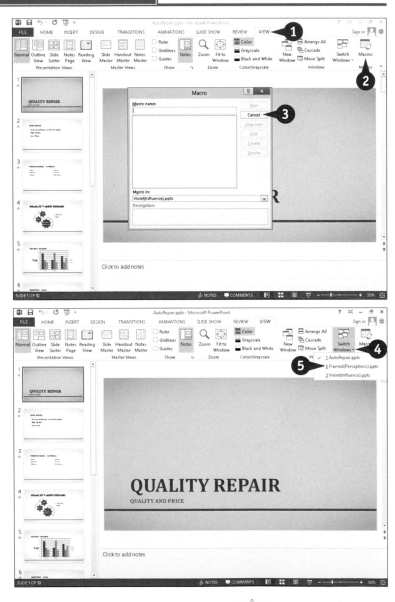

4 Click the down arrow (▼) next to any button to display a gallery.

Note: Clicking a down arrow (▼) displays a menu or menu.

5 Click the desired choice from the menu or gallery that appears.

6 Click a **dialog box launcher** (⬚).

Note: A dialog box launcher (⬚) displays a dialog box when you click it.

In this example, the Grid and Guides dialog box appears.

7 Click **OK** to accept any selections you have made in the dialog box.

The presentation reflects any changes you made.

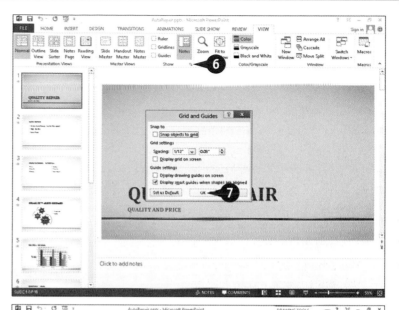

A For some ribbon commands, such as those on a contextual tab, you must first select an object on the slide before choosing a command.

B Note that the Drawing Tools Format tab does not appear until you click an object like a text box.

TIPS

How do I learn what a particular ribbon button does?
Position the mouse pointer (⬚) over the button, and a ScreenTip describing the button appears. You see ScreenTip that lists the button name, any available shortcut key, and a brief description of the button. By default, ScreenTip features are enabled, but you can disable them in the PowerPoint Options dialog box (described in Chapter 3).

What happens if I click the main part of a ribbon button that has a down arrow on it?
If the sole purpose of the button is to open a gallery or menu, PowerPoint does that. If the main part of the button executes a command, PowerPoint applies that command using either the settings you last used or the most commonly used settings for that command.

Arrange Presentation Windows

Sometimes you need to view multiple presentations on-screen at once — for example, when you want to compare their contents or copy a slide from one presentation to another. You can arrange PowerPoint in such a way that you can see multiple open presentations at the same time. This handy feature is found on the View tab.

You should limit the number of open presentations to three or four. Otherwise, you cannot see enough of each presentation to make this feature useful.

Arrange Presentation Windows

1 Open two or more presentations.

2 Click the **View** tab.

3 Click **Cascade** (⌷).

The presentation windows move so they overlap.

Ⓐ You can click **Switch Windows** and then click a presentation in the menu to make that presentation active.

4 Click **Arrange All** (▤).

The presentation windows appear side by side.

Ⓑ You can drag a window's title bar to move the window.

5 Click the **Maximize** button (☐) on one of the windows.

The window appears full screen again.

Find and Use KeyTips

You can use the KeyTips feature to employ keyboard shortcuts to select and execute ribbon commands. You may be more comfortable using your keyboard instead of your mouse or touchpad. For example, you may use a notebook computer with a finicky touchpad. Alternatively, you may have your mouse pointer set up to go fast, which makes it hard to point at something with pinpoint accuracy. KeyTips allows you to run commands quickly without using the mouse or touchpad, making you more proficient in your presentation work.

Find and Use KeyTips

1 Press **Alt**.

A The KeyTips (shortcut keys) for the ribbon tabs and Quick Access Toolbar appear in boxes beside the ribbon tabs.

2 Press the shortcut key for the tab you want to use.

This example presses **S** to display the Slide Show tab.

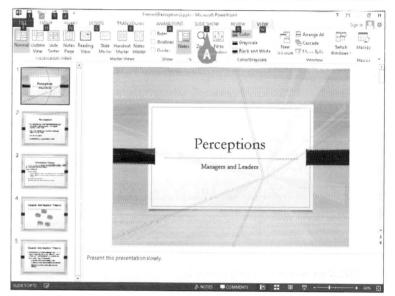

The Slide Show tab appears with KeyTips displayed next to the commands.

Note: To abort using KeyTips, press **Esc**.

3 Press the shortcut key for the command you want to execute.

The command executes, or a menu, gallery, or dialog box appears so you can finish choosing commands.

B This example presses **V** (☑ changes to ☐).

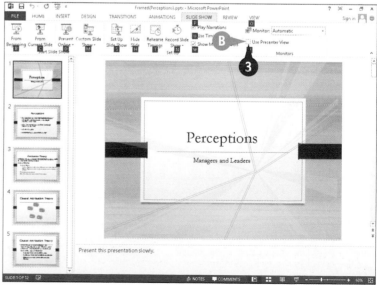

Using the Quick Access Toolbar

The *Quick Access Toolbar* appears above the File tab at the top of the PowerPoint application window. For your convenience, it contains command buttons for the most commonly used PowerPoint commands.

You can click the command buttons on the Quick Access Toolbar to execute these commands quickly. You can also easily add (or remove) some of these commonly used commands to (or from) the Quick Access Toolbar. You can even add your personal favorite commands to it.

Using the Quick Access Toolbar

1 Click the desired button on the Quick Access Toolbar.

PowerPoint executes the command.

Note: Finish executing the command if any menu or dialog box appears.

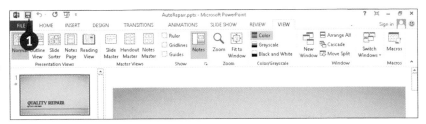

2 Click the down arrow ($\mp$) on the right side of the Quick Access Toolbar to access the menu.

A Note the check mark ($\checkmark$) appearing next to commands on the Quick Access Toolbar.

B Click **More Commands** to see all available commands (see Chapter 3 for more information).

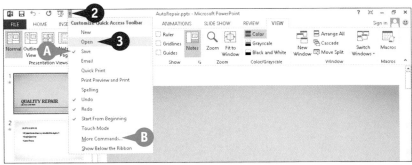

3 Click one of the commands from the menu list.

C The selected command appears as an icon on the Quick Access Toolbar and a check mark ($\checkmark$) appears next to it in the menu.

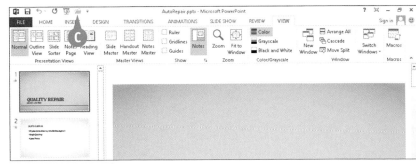

Resize the Notes Pane

It is often handy to have notes associated with slides. You may want to refer to notes while designing a slide or during a slide show presentation. You can enter notes into the Notes pane, which appears under the Slide pane in Normal view. Notes entered into the Notes pane are automatically displayed in Presenter view during a slide show presentation, but your audience cannot see the notes. (See Chapter 15 for more information on Presenter view.) You can resize the Notes pane to make it easier to enter and read the notes.

Resize the Notes Pane

1 Click the **View** tab.

2 Click **Notes**.

Ⓐ The Notes pane appears.

3 Position the mouse pointer (↖) over the pane divider until the mouse splitter pointer (↕) appears.

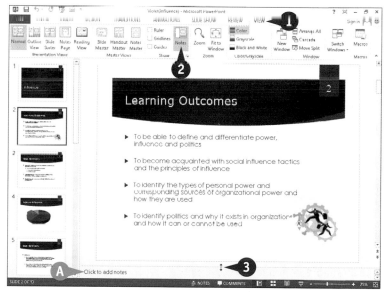

4 Click and drag upward.

The Notes pane resizes and the slide automatically resizes in the Slide pane to compensate.

5 Click **Notes** to hide the Notes pane.

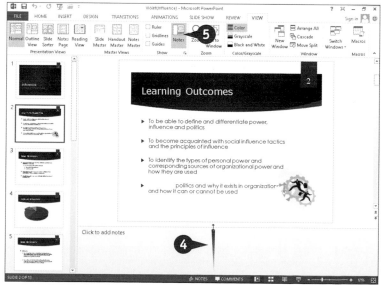

Zoom to Full Screen

There are times when you need maximum space to work on your presentation. For instance, while moving slides in Slide Sorter view, a little more space may allow you to see more slides or allow you to make the slides bigger so you can see them more clearly. You can zoom to full screen in design mode to take advantage of every little bit of space. When you zoom to full screen, the space occupied by the ribbon, status bar, and other elements is used to view the slides. You can zoom to full screen in any view.

Zoom to Full Screen

Hide the Ribbon

1 Click the **View** tab.

2 Click **Slide Sorter**.

Slide Sorter view appears.

3 Click the **Ribbon Display Options** button (⊡) in the upper-right corner of the PowerPoint window.

4 Click **Auto-hide Ribbon**.

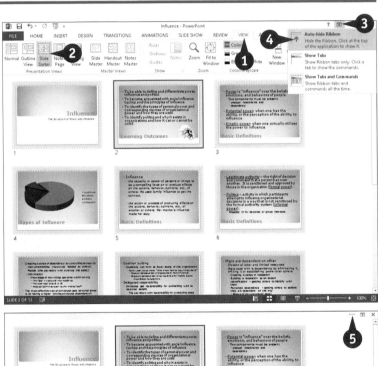

Slide Sorter view zooms to the entire screen.

5 Click the **Ellipsis** button (···) in the upper-right corner of the screen.

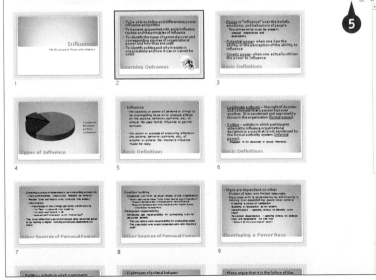

The ribbon appears. You can now access the ribbon commands. The ribbon disappears after executing a command or clicking a slide. Repeat Step **5** each time you want to execute a command.

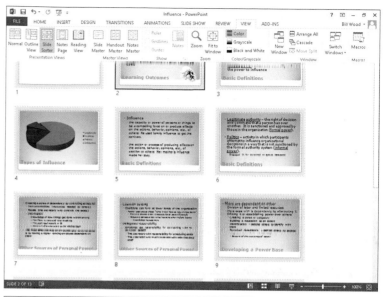

View the Ribbon Continuously

1 Click the **Ribbon Display Options** button ( ).

2 Click **Show Tabs and Commands**.

PowerPoint returns to the window view.

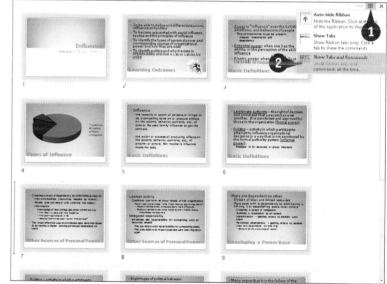

I need more space to work, but I want to use the Quick Access Toolbar. Can I hide the ribbon?

Yes. To hide the ribbon, simply double-click a tab and the ribbon disappears except for the tabs. Click a tab and the ribbon appears temporarily so you can execute a command. Double-click a tab again to show the tab continuously.

Is there an advantage to using the Full Screen feature over using Reading view?

Yes. You cannot design the presentation in Reading view, so if you want to work on your presentation, use the Full Screen feature. If you want to quickly view the slide show and then quickly come back to design mode, use Reading view.

Navigate Slides

Slide show presentations generally contain many slides. As a result, PowerPoint provides different ways to navigate the slides so that you can choose one that is most efficient and effective for what you are doing. The way you work on your project determines the way you choose to navigate. You can use the various scroll bar buttons to navigate slides in Normal view, click a slide in the Slides Thumbnail pane to select a slide, or view slide thumbnails in Slide Sorter view.

Navigate Slides

Navigate Using the Scroll Bar

1 Click the **View** tab.

2 Click **Normal**.

3 Click and drag the scroll bar to scroll through slides.

4 Click the **Next Slide** button (▼) to display the next slide.

5 Click the **Previous Slide** button (▲) to display the previous slide.

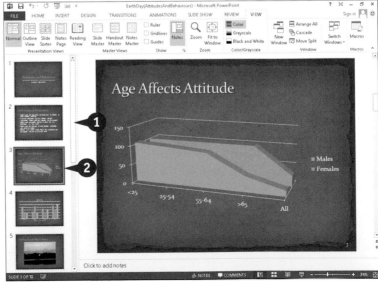

Navigate Using the Slide Thumbnail Pane

1 Click and drag the scroll bar to move through the slides.

2 Click a slide thumbnail.

The selected slide appears in the Slide pane.

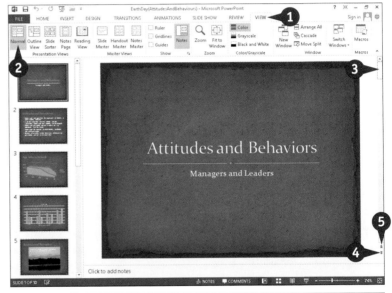

Navigate Using the Outline View

1 Click **Outline View**.

2 Click and drag the scroll bar to move through the slides.

3 Click a slide icon ( ).

The selected slide appears in the Slide pane.

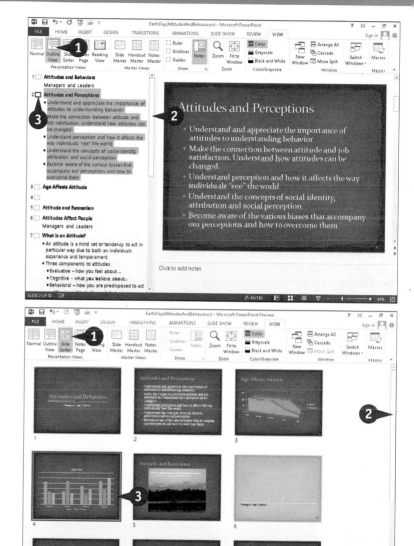

Navigate in Slide Sorter View

1 Click **Slide Sorter**.

Slide Sorter view appears.

2 Click and drag the scroll bar to move through the slides.

3 Click a slide.

PowerPoint selects the slide.

Note: Double-click a slide to view it in Normal view.

TIPS

Why are there no scroll bars in the Slide Thumbnails or Outline View panes?
If PowerPoint can display all slides in the presentation without scrolling down or up, it does not display a scroll bar. The fact that there is not a scroll bar means you are viewing all of the slides in the presentation.

Is there a way to see more slides in Slide Sorter view so I can easily find the one I want to view?
Yes. You can click and drag the Zoom slider in the lower-right corner of the PowerPoint window to make the slides smaller, which shows more slides. You can also click the **Zoom In** ( ) or **Zoom Out** ( ) buttons at each end of the slider.

Using Help

Microsoft Office PowerPoint Help offers two ways to get help. If you are connected to the Internet, it provides help from Microsoft Office Online. If an Internet connection is not available, PowerPoint uses Help files installed on your computer. PowerPoint also allows you to select between searching online and searching on your computer manually. You can find answers to your questions by selecting from a list of popular searches or by searching using keywords. The keyword searches are very similar, whether online or on your computer.

Using Help

1 Click the **Help** button (**?**).

The PowerPoint Help window appears.

2 Type a keyword in the search text box.

A Optionally, you can click in the Popular Searches list.

3 Click the **Search** button (🔍).

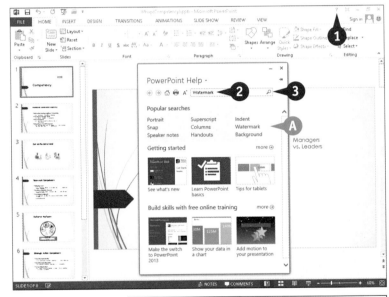

PowerPoint shows a list of online articles.

4 Click the **Home** button (🏠).

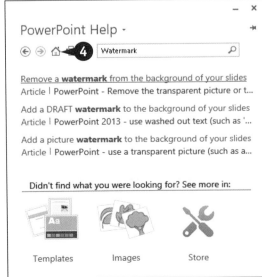

The Help home page appears.

Ⓑ You can click a graphic to show a help article for that topic.

⑤ Click the **PowerPoint Help** down arrow (▼).

The drop box opens.

⑥ Click **PowerPoint Help from your computer**.

The Basic Help home page appears.

Ⓒ Click **Back** (⬅) and **Forward** (➡) to navigate back and forth.

Ⓓ Click **Print** (🖨) to print information.

Ⓔ Click **Use Large Text** (A⁺) to increase font size.

⑦ Type a keyword in the search text box.

⑧ Click the **Search** button (🔍).

PowerPoint displays ribbon commands associated with the keyword you typed.

⑨ Click an item to display detailed information about that item.

⑩ Click **Next** to see more results.

⑪ Click the **Close** button (✖) to exit Help.

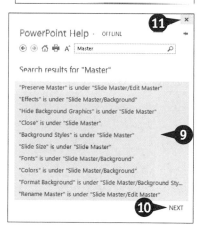

TIP

Is there a fast and easy way to open the Microsoft Office.com Help page from PowerPoint?

Yes. Click **more (Ⓐ)** after executing a search and PowerPoint launches your Internet browser and opens the Microsoft Office.com Help web page. From here, you can click various topics for help. You can even get a training video for PowerPoint 2013 for free!

CHAPTER 3

Changing PowerPoint Options

PowerPoint is a powerful tool that becomes even more powerful when you customize it the way you want it to perform. You can adjust various settings to personalize PowerPoint, so you can use it more efficiently and effectively.

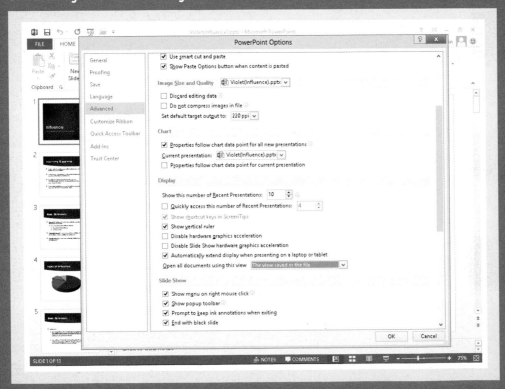

Introducing PowerPoint Options

PowerPoint provides a wide variety of option settings that enable you to customize how it performs. The options are grouped on tabs in the PowerPoint Options dialog box, and then further grouped into categories. You can change these settings to control the behavior of certain features in PowerPoint, and optimize less noticeable settings such as the default save location. Settings that are more visible include customizing the Quick Access Toolbar and the ribbon so that your favorite and most commonly used commands are at your fingertips. Changing PowerPoint options allows you to design presentations as effectively and efficiently as possible.

General Options

In the General options, you can enable or disable the Mini Toolbar and Live Preview. The *Mini Toolbar* is a floating contextual toolbar that gives you quick access to formatting commands when you select text. *Live Preview* shows how a feature affects your slide when you position the mouse pointer (⇖) over a choice in a gallery. You can enable or disable *ScreenTips*, which is the feature that gives you pop-up descriptions of command buttons when you position the mouse pointer (⇖) over a command button on the ribbon. You can also change the username, which appears in the properties of presentations.

Proofing Options

The Proofing tab affects the way that Microsoft Office checks for spelling and grammar errors in PowerPoint. Changes to these settings also affect the settings in the other Microsoft Office programs. You can add words to the custom dictionary and make exceptions to spelling rules. You can customize the powerful AutoCorrect and AutoFormat tools. While you type, *AutoCorrect* detects possible spelling errors and *AutoFormat* adjusts formatting to the surrounding formatting. You can control settings such as whether PowerPoint automatically capitalizes the first words of sentences and whether it checks the spelling of words that are in all uppercase.

Save Options

You can adjust the way PowerPoint saves presentations with the Save options. This tab controls the default file location for saving documents, and allows you to choose the default file format. *AutoRecovery* automatically saves your PowerPoint presentation at regular intervals so that if PowerPoint unexpectedly closes, it can recover your work. You can disable AutoRecovery or adjust how often AutoRecovery automatically saves presentations. You can even save the fonts you use in your presentation so you can guarantee that the presentation looks good even on a computer that does not recognize the fonts you use.

Language Options

The Language tab allows you to choose the language used for the ribbon, tabs, ScreenTips, and Help. You can include additional editing languages, which affect dictionaries, grammar checking, and sorting. This is useful if you use languages other than English in your presentations, such as when your organization has divisions or departments overseas. If you use languages other than English, setting up and using these options can make your experience with PowerPoint 2013 a delightful one.

Advanced Options

Advanced options allow you to customize settings for printing, some editing, and slide show features. Some settings, such as print options, only apply to individual PowerPoint presentations. Advanced options control what you see on the screen during slide show presentations. For example, you can control whether you see the pop-up toolbar during presentations. The *slide show pop-up toolbar* allows you to perform various tasks during a slide show presentation. Cut, copy, and paste options and display options are also found here.

Ribbon and Quick Access Toolbar Options

Although you can add a limited number of commands to the Quick Access Toolbar from the toolbar itself, you can add any command to it from the Quick Access Toolbar tab in the Options dialog box. Along with being able to add commands to the ribbon, you can also add tabs, add groups, and rename existing tabs and groups. An excellent use of this feature is to create a ribbon tab with your most commonly used commands so they are at your fingertips on a single tab, thereby making design work efficient and effective.

Add-ins

Add-ins are small chunks of programming that enhance the functionality of PowerPoint. Add-ins can be developed specifically for PowerPoint, or can be Component Object Model (COM) add-ins that enable you to use the functionality of another program in PowerPoint, such as a PDF writer or screen-capture program. You can get add-ins that give you special tools to design presentations or that add special functionality to your slide shows. Add-ins are available through third parties, or you can create them if you have programming experience.

Trust Center

In the *Trust Center*, you can read the Microsoft privacy statements and learn about security. Malicious programs can be attached to documents in various ways. You can customize settings to control the behavior of safeguards used against these threats. If you open only presentations that you trust, you can minimize security so there is no need to respond to security messages. If you open presentations of unknown origin, you can heighten the security so that malicious programs cannot affect your computer through a PowerPoint presentation.

Modify General Options

PowerPoint provides a wide variety of options that enable you to customize how it works. Options for features such as Live Preview, ScreenTips, and the Mini Toolbar are found in General options. These settings determine whether you see the Start screen when you open PowerPoint and which file extensions PowerPoint will open. You can also change the username, which PowerPoint records in the properties of each presentation to identify who creates it. You can change these options in the General tab of the PowerPoint Options dialog box.

Modify General Options

1 Click the **File** tab to show Backstage view.

2 Click **Options**.

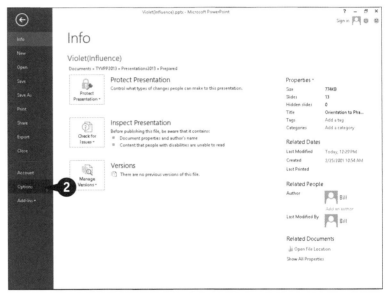

The PowerPoint Options dialog box appears.

3 Click **General**.

4 Click to enable (☑) or disable (☐) options under the User Interface options heading.

Ⓐ You can position your mouse pointer (↖) over the Information icon (ⓘ) to see a brief description of an option.

Ⓑ You can click the **Office Background** down arrow (▼) and select a color scheme for the PowerPoint window.

Ⓒ You can click the **ScreenTip style** down arrow (▼) and select a ScreenTip style to display when you position the mouse pointer (↖) over a command.

5 Click **Default Programs**.

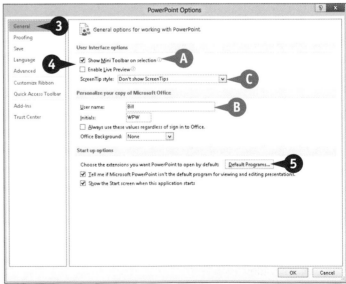

The Set Program Associations dialog box appears.

6 Click to enable (☑) or disable (☐) files whose extensions you want PowerPoint to open by default.

7 Click **Save**.

PowerPoint saves your changes and the dialog box closes.

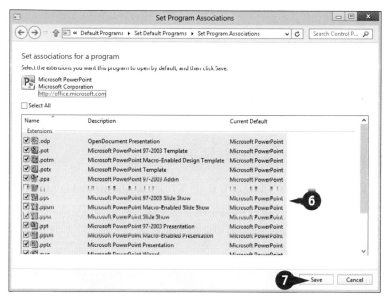

8 Type your username and Initials in the text boxes.

9 Click **Show the Start screen when this application starts** (☑ changes to ☐) to disable the Start screen page when PowerPoint starts.

10 Click **OK**.

PowerPoint applies your new settings and closes the PowerPoint Options dialog box.

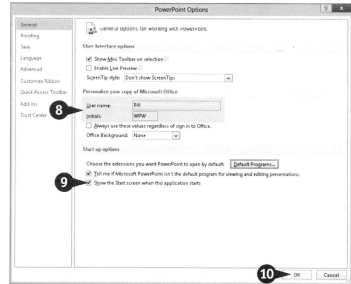

TIP

What is the Mini Toolbar?
The Mini Toolbar is a floating, contextual formatting toolbar that appears when you right-click an object to use the submenu. The Mini Toolbar contains the most commonly used formatting commands for the object that you select. For example, it shows the formatting commands from the Font group of the Home tab when you select text. If you enable the Mini Toolbar in the General options, the Mini Toolbar automatically appears when you click and drag across text in a placeholder.

Change Spelling Options

Misspellings in presentations are never good. The powerful spell-checker in Microsoft Office automatically and continually checks spelling in PowerPoint as you type. The spell-checker identifies possible misspellings by underlining them with a red, wavy line. To review a word, you can simply right-click it. You can use this tool to check spelling as you type text, or you can disable the tool. When you need to check spelling, you can always use the spell-checker manually. You can customize how the spell-checker handles possible misspellings in the PowerPoint Options.

Change Spelling Options

1 Click the **File** tab to show Backstage view.

2 Click **Options**.

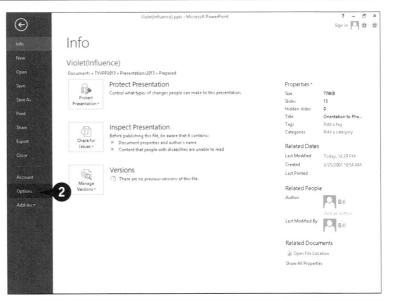

The PowerPoint Options dialog box appears.

3 Click **Proofing**.

4 Click to enable (☑) or disable (☐) options that determine how spell-checker flags certain errors.

Note: Changes that you make here also affect the spell-checker in the other Microsoft Office programs.

5 Click **Custom Dictionaries.**

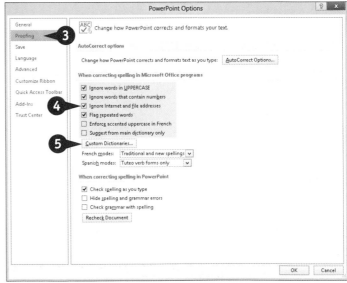

PowerPoint displays the Custom Dictionaries dialog box. PowerPoint automatically creates a custom dictionary (CUSTOM.DIC) when you add words during a spelling check. You can manually add words to your custom dictionary.

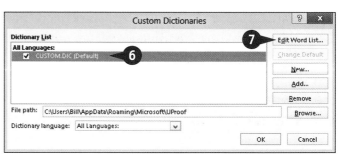

6 Click **CUSTOM.DIC** from the list so it is checked (☑).

7 Click **Edit Word List**.

The CUSTOM.DIC dialog box appears.

8 Type the desired word in the **Word(s):** text box.

9 Click **Add**.

PowerPoint adds the word to the Dictionary list.

10 Click **OK**.

The CUSTOM.DIC dialog box closes.

11 Click to enable (☑) or disable (☐) spell-checker options in PowerPoint.

A If you disable the **Check spelling as you type** option, you can run the spell-checker manually by clicking the **Spelling** command on the Review tab of the ribbon.

12 Click **OK**.

PowerPoint applies your new settings and closes the PowerPoint Options dialog box.

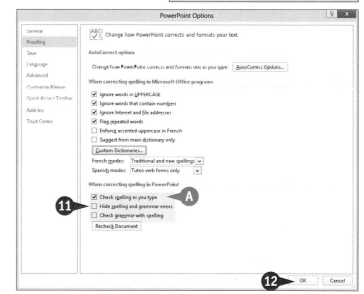

TIP

Can I delete words from the custom dictionary?
Yes. You can delete words from the custom dictionary by following these steps:

1 Follow Steps **1** to **7** in this section.

2 Click the word you want to delete.

3 Click **Delete**.

4 Click **OK** in each of the three open dialog boxes.

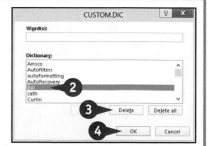

Change AutoCorrect Settings

The AutoCorrect feature automatically corrects common typing and spelling errors as you type. You can add words to a list of common misspellings, empowering AutoCorrect to automatically correct words that you routinely misspell. For example, you can tell it to change "actoin" to the word "action" automatically. You can also delete corrections that already exist on the list. For example, you can delete the automatic correction of changing (c) to ©. You can also make exceptions of words that you do not want to be marked as misspelled.

Change AutoCorrect Settings

1 Click the **File** tab to show Backstage view.

2 Click **Options**.

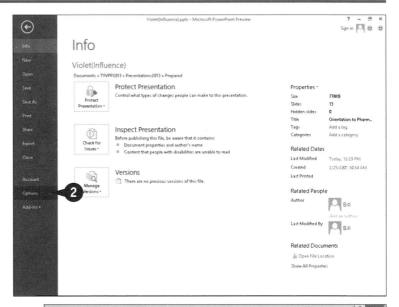

The PowerPoint Options dialog box appears.

3 Click **Proofing**.

4 Click **AutoCorrect Options**.

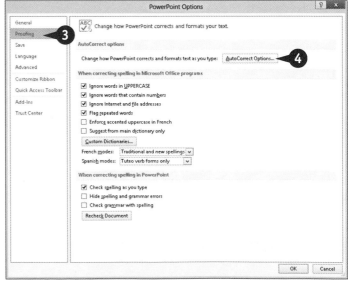

The AutoCorrect dialog box appears.

5 Click the **AutoCorrect** tab.

6 Click to enable (☑) or disable
(☐) any of the standard AutoCorrect options.

A To disable the misspelling correction feature,
click the **Replace text as you type**
option (☑ changes to ☐).

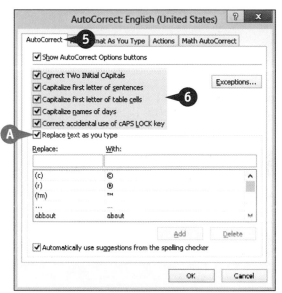

7 To add a word to the list, type the misspelled
version of the word in the **Replace:** text box.

8 Type the correct spelling of the word in the
With: text box.

9 Click **Add**.

B You can delete a word from the list by clicking it
and then clicking **Delete**.

10 Click **OK** in each of the two open dialog boxes.

PowerPoint applies your new settings.

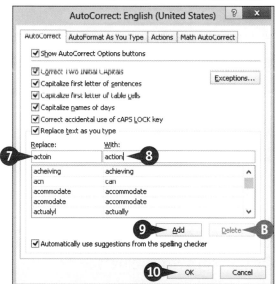

TIP

**AutoCorrect thinks the word "TO." is the end of a sentence and
capitalizes the next letter. How can I prevent this?**
You can add the word to a list of exceptions by following these steps:

1 Follow Steps **1** to **5** in this
section.

2 Click the **Exceptions** button.

3 Click the **First Letter** tab.

4 Type your exception in the
Don't capitalize after: text box.

5 Click **Add**.

6 Click **OK**.

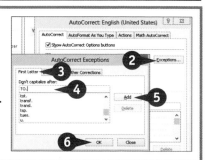

Change AutoFormat Settings

AutoCorrect has a feature called AutoFormat, which speeds up certain formatting that is cumbersome to perform. Examples include changing 1/2 to ½, replacing ordinals (1st) with superscript (1st), and changing Internet paths to hyperlinks (www.test.com). This is a very convenient feature because making these types of formatting changes can be tedious. It also automates bulleted and numbered lists, and automatically fits text to placeholders. You can customize these settings to suit your particular needs to streamline your work.

Change AutoFormat Settings

1 Click the **File** tab to show Backstage view.

2 Click **Options**.

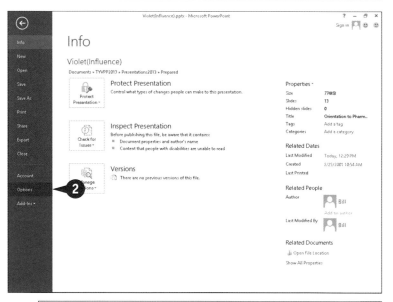

The PowerPoint Options dialog box appears.

3 Click **Proofing**.

4 Click **AutoCorrect Options**.

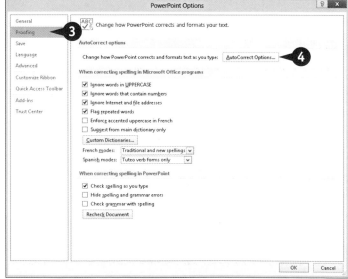

The AutoCorrect dialog box appears.

5 Click the **AutoFormat As You Type** tab.

6 Click to enable (☑) or disable (☐) any of the options under Replace as you type.

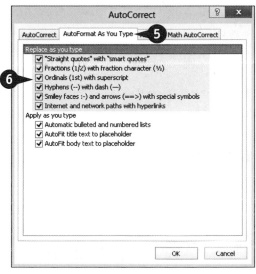

7 Click to enable (☑) or disable (☐) any of the options under Apply as you type.

These settings control whether text automatically sizes in the placeholders.

8 Click **OK** in each of the two open dialog boxes.

PowerPoint applies your new settings and closes both the AutoCorrect and PowerPoint Options dialog boxes.

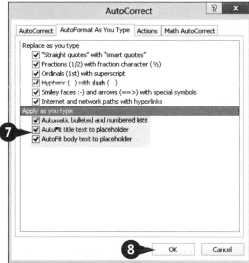

TIP

Why does PowerPoint change words that I type in all caps to lowercase?

AutoCorrect has a setting that corrects the accidental use of the Caps Lock key. To disable this option:

1 Follow Steps **1** to **4** in this section.

2 Click the **Correct accidental use of cAPS LOCK key** option (☑ changes to ☐).

3 Click **OK** to close each of the open dialog boxes.

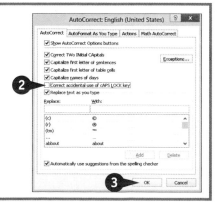

Customize Save Options

By default, PowerPoint saves a presentation in your user Documents folder with the PowerPoint 2013 format. For example, if your username is Bill and you save a presentation for the first time, the Save As dialog box uses the folder c:\Users\Bill\Documents\ as the default. If you share your presentations with colleagues who use an older PowerPoint version, you may want to change the settings so the default file format is the PowerPoint 2003 format because PowerPoint 2003 cannot open a file format later than that. You can also embed fonts in the saved presentation to preserve its look on any computer.

Customize Save Options

1 Click the **File** tab to show Backstage view.

2 Click **Options**.

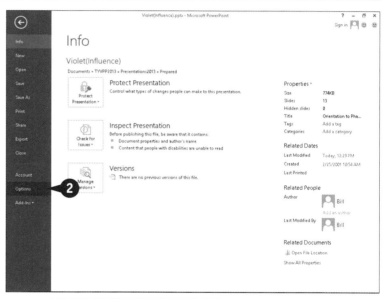

The PowerPoint Options dialog box appears.

3 Click **Save**.

4 Click the **Save files in this format** down arrow (⌄).

5 Click a file format.

Note: The file type for PowerPoint 2013 is PowerPoint Presentation.

The next time you save a new file, the file type you specify here will appear as the file type in the Save As dialog box. You can choose a different file type during the save.

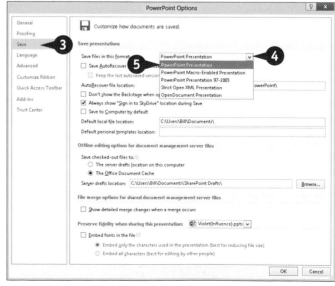

6 Click to enable (☑) or disable (☐) options under the Save presentations heading.

A If desired, click the spinner box (⬍) to change the number of minutes between AutoRecover saves.

B Click to deselect (☐) the **Save AutoRecover information every** option to disable the automatic saving feature.

C AutoRecover files are discarded when you close PowerPoint. Click to enable (☑) this option to retain the last file if you close without saving the file.

D To change the default save location, type a new default location.

7 Click the **Embed fonts in the file** option (☐ changes to ☑).

E The fonts for this particular presentation are saved with it, so it will not appear differently when viewed on a system without those fonts.

F You can further specify whether to embed all characters or only those in use.

8 Click **OK**.

PowerPoint applies your new settings and closes the PowerPoint Options dialog box.

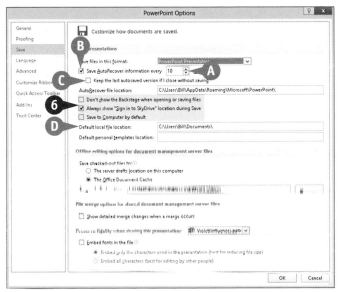

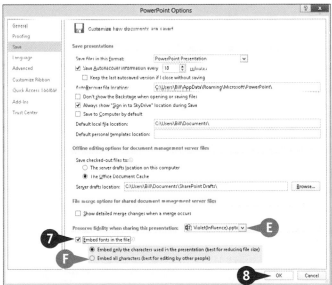

TIPS

What are the pros and cons of having the AutoRecover feature save frequently?

AutoRecover automatically saves your work at regular intervals in case PowerPoint closes unexpectedly. However, the pause you experience during the save might be lengthy if your presentation is large. You can disable AutoRecover if you do not want to be inconvenienced with this pause.

Why would I want to embed fonts in a presentation?

Some fonts are not available on every computer. If you view your presentation on a computer that is missing the fonts you used to design it, PowerPoint replaces the fonts with standard fonts from that computer. Embedded fonts travel with the presentation to ensure they are always in the presentation.

Modify View and Slide Show Options

You can change which features are available in the various PowerPoint views. The availability of these features may be determined by the option settings or by the type of presentation. In the Display and Slide Show options, you can select which view PowerPoint uses by default, such as Normal view or Slide Sorter view. You can also control whether the toolbar appears during the slide show presentation. These choices ensure that your preferred tools are on-screen when you need them.

Modify View and Slide Show Options

1 Click the **File** tab to show Backstage view.

2 Click **Options**.

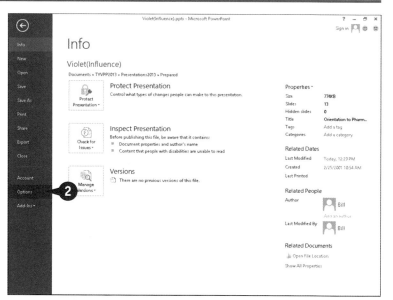

The PowerPoint Options dialog box appears.

3 Click **Advanced**.

4 Click and drag the scroll bar to locate the Display and Slide Show headings.

5 Click to enable (☑) or disable (☐) options under the Display heading.

6 Click the spinner box (⬍) to change the number of files displayed in the Recent list on the File tab.

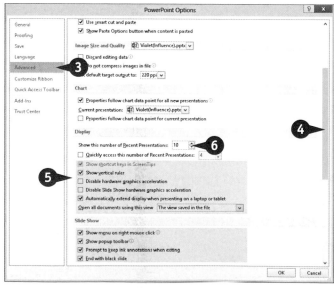

Ⓐ You can position your mouse pointer (⤢) over the information icon (ⓘ) to see a brief description of an option.

7 Click the **Open all documents using this view** down arrow (⌄).

8 Click a viewing choice.

PowerPoint uses the specified view when opening presentations.

9 Click to enable (☑) or disable (☐) options affecting behavior during a slide show.

Ⓑ Determines whether you can use the shortcut menu.

Ⓒ Controls the toolbar that faintly appears at the bottom-left corner of slides.

Ⓓ Determines whether you can save annotations you made on the slides upon exiting the slide show.

Ⓔ Determines whether the slide show ends with a blank, black slide.

10 Click **OK**.

PowerPoint applies your new settings and closes the PowerPoint Options dialog box.

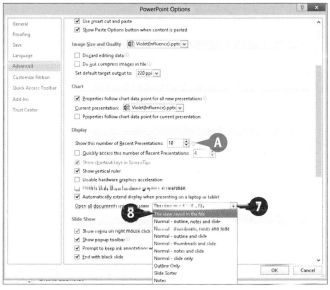

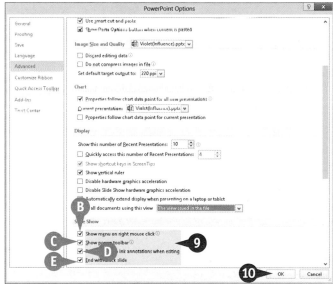

TIPS

What is the benefit of opening the presentation in Outline view?

If you start viewing the outline alone, you can concentrate on building the text for the presentation. This can be particularly helpful when you need a clean slate on which to organize your thoughts. The graphics of a slide can distract you from your outline because you may start thinking about the slide design.

Can I save annotations if I disable the Prompt to keep ink annotations when exiting option?

No. You can only save annotations by using the dialog box that prompts you to save them at the end of the slide show presentation. The prompt does not appear if you disable this option.

Change Editing Settings

You can change how certain editing tools work. For example, you can modify how the cutting and pasting, text selection, and Undo features perform. These features are useful, but can be annoying and cumbersome if not personalized through the settings in the options. You can also control the use of features such as the Paste Options button. This button appears when you paste a cut or copied object or text. It supplies convenient options for pasting, and you can click it to see commands for working with a pasted selection.

Change Editing Settings

1 Click the **File** tab to show Backstage view.

2 Click **Options**.

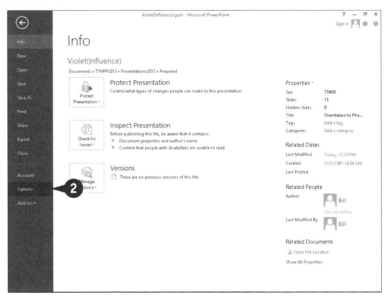

The PowerPoint Options dialog box appears.

3 Click **Advanced**.

4 Click to enable (☑) or disable (☐) options under the Editing options heading.

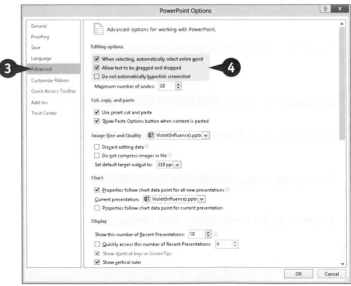

5 Click the spinner box (⬍) to change the number of undo edits you can perform with the Undo button (↶) on the Quick Access Toolbar.

This feature consumes considerable system memory, so if PowerPoint performs slowly, you should lower this number.

Ⓐ Some options apply to only one presentation. You can select which presentation.

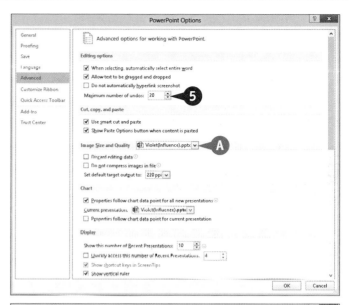

6 Click to enable (☑) or disable (☐) options under the Cut, copy, and paste heading.

Ⓑ Smart cut and paste is a feature where PowerPoint adds missing spacing around pasted text or objects.

Ⓒ Click to disable the **Paste Options** button (📋(Ctrl)▾) that appears when you perform a copy-and-paste operation (☑ changes to ☐).

7 Click **OK**.

PowerPoint applies your new settings and closes the PowerPoint Options dialog box.

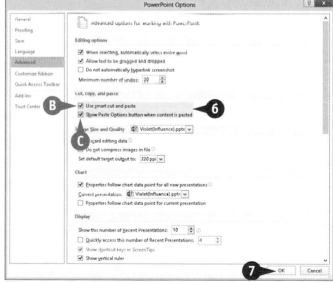

TIPS

What is the difference between the Paste Options button and Smart cut and paste?

The Paste Options button (📋(Ctrl)▾) appears below a pasted object and offers formatting options. Smart cut and paste helps to eliminate errors when you paste. If spacing is not selected around copied text, Smart cut and paste makes sure that spaces are between words.

What number should I use for the maximum number of undos?

The default undo value is 20 and is probably about right. If you need to undo more than 20 actions, it might be faster to reconstruct a slide from scratch. You can also close the file without saving, and then open it again to get back where you started.

Work with Print Options

The PowerPoint Options dialog box offers several print options, making it easy to control presentation printing. For example, you can modify the way your printer handles fonts and the resolution of inserted graphics. You can also specify that a particular presentation always be printed with a particular printer and settings, saving you the trouble of choosing those settings every time you print that particular file. These settings can save time when printing presentations.

Work with Print Options

1 Click the **File** tab to show Backstage view.

2 Click **Options**.

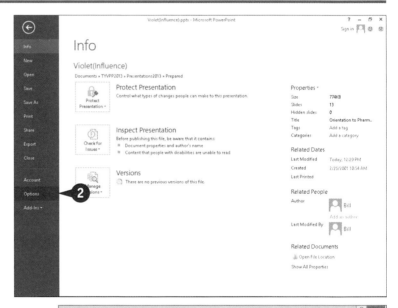

The PowerPoint Options dialog box appears.

3 Click **Advanced**.

4 Click and drag the scroll bar to the bottom of the PowerPoint Options dialog box.

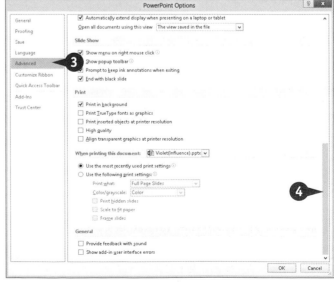

5 Click to enable (☑) or disable (☐) options under the Print heading.

Ⓐ Print in background enables you to work in PowerPoint while printing.

Ⓑ Print TrueType fonts as graphics prevents distortion of fonts.

Ⓒ Enable this setting to use the printer's resolution settings to ensure quality printing of graphics.

Ⓓ High quality increases the resolution of graphics, but can slow printing.

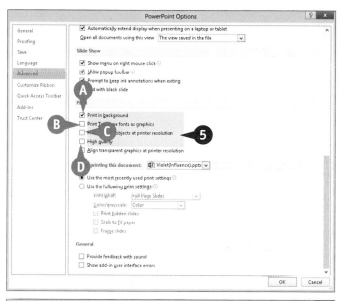

6 The next options apply to a single presentation; click the down arrow (☑) to select which presentation these options will affect.

7 Click the **Use the following print settings** option (○ changes to ◉).

The related settings become available.

8 Click to select print settings.

9 Click **OK**.

PowerPoint applies your new settings and closes the PowerPoint Options dialog box.

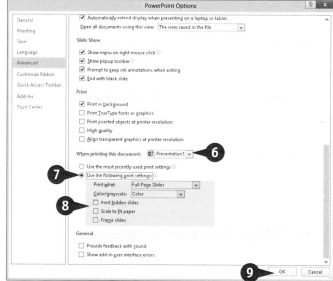

TIPS

How can I change print settings for a presentation that is not on the When printing this document drop-down list?
Only open presentations appear on this list; the current presentation is the default. Click **Cancel** to close the PowerPoint Options dialog box. Open the presentation file, and then reopen the PowerPoint Options dialog box. That presentation now appears in the list.

My printer prints slowly. How can I fix this?
You can try a couple of things. Enabling the **Print in background** option can slow down your printer, so try disabling this feature. Also, disable **Print inserted objects at printer resolution**. This option can slow printing because it may change the resolution of graphics, which can take considerable time.

Customize the Quick Access Toolbar

The Quick Access Toolbar appears above the ribbon in the upper-left corner of the PowerPoint window. You can move it below the ribbon if you like. This toolbar offers buttons for the most frequently used commands, providing even easier access than the ribbon.

You can add buttons to the Quick Access Toolbar to quickly access the commands you use the most, and you can remove buttons that you do not use. This allows you to reduce the number of clicks needed to run commonly used commands, thus streamlining your design work.

Customize the Quick Access Toolbar

1. Click the **Quick Access Toolbar** down arrow (▼).

2. Click **More Commands**.

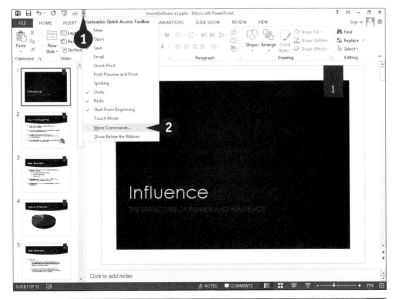

The PowerPoint Options dialog box appears, with Quick Access Toolbar displayed.

3. Click the down arrow (▼) and select the category or tab that holds the command button you want to add to the Quick Access Toolbar.

4. Find your desired command on the list and click it.

Ⓐ To add a command to the toolbar of a particular presentation, click the down arrow (▼) and select that presentation from the Customize Quick Access Toolbar list.

5. Click **Add**.

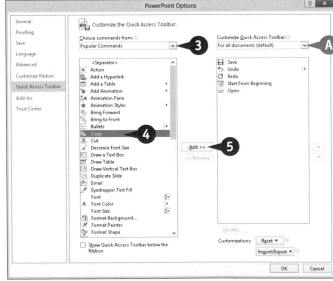

Ⓑ The command appears on the list of commands under Customize Quick Access Toolbar.

Ⓒ Click **Up** (▲) or **Down** (▼) to change a command's position.

Ⓓ Click **Remove** to remove a command from the toolbar.

❻ Click **OK**.

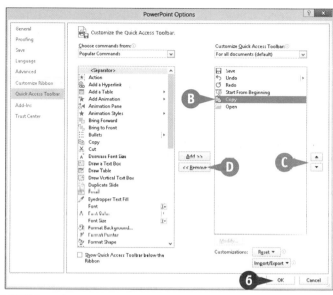

Ⓔ The PowerPoint Options dialog box closes, and the Quick Access Toolbar reflects the changes you made.

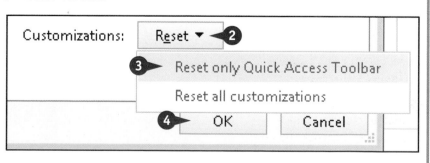

TIP

How do I change the Quick Access Toolbar so it looks like it did when I first installed PowerPoint?
Follow these steps to reset the Quick Access Toolbar:

❶ Follow Steps **1** and **2** in this section.

❷ In the PowerPoint Options dialog box, click the **Reset** button.

❸ Click **Reset only Quick Access Toolbar**.

❹ Click **OK**.

Customize the Ribbon

You can add commands to the PowerPoint ribbon, as well as add tabs and groups. Adding commands to the ribbon adds proficiency to the way you handle tasks and commands. An excellent use of this feature is creating a ribbon tab with your most commonly used commands so they are at your fingertips on a single tab, thereby making design work efficient and effective. You can add commands to existing tabs and rename existing tabs and groups.

Customize the Ribbon

Tour the Ribbon Tab Outline

1 Click the **File** tab to show Backstage view.

2 Click **Options**.

The PowerPoint Options dialog box appears.

3 Click **Customize Ribbon**.

4 Click the **plus sign** (⊞) to expand a level (⊞ changes to ⊟, which is used to collapse a level).

Ⓐ The first level of names on the list shows ribbon tabs.

Ⓑ The second level shows ribbon groups.

Ⓒ The third level shows ribbon commands, or ribbon menus and galleries.

Ⓓ The fourth level shows commands of ribbon menus and galleries that are on the third level.

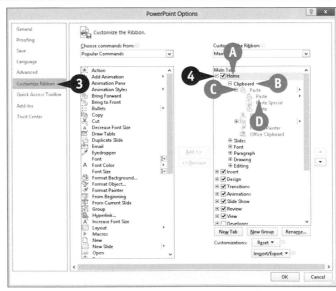

Add a Custom Tab to the Ribbon

1 Click the check box (☑) to disable a tab and remove it from the ribbon (☑ changes to ☐).

2 Click the **plus sign** (⊟) to collapse the Home tab (⊟ changes to ⊞).

3 Click a tab name from the list — your custom tab is inserted below it.

4 Click **New Tab**.

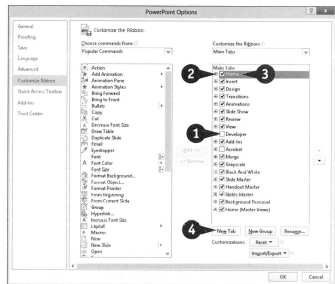

Ⓔ A new tab appears with one new group.

5 Click **New Tab (Custom)**.

Ⓕ You can use the **Up** (▲) and **Down** (▼) buttons to change the position of the tab.

Ⓖ You can remove a custom tab by clicking **Remove**.

6 Click **Rename**.

The Rename dialog box appears.

7 Type a name in the text box.

8 Click **OK**.

How do I make the ribbon look like it did when I first installed PowerPoint?

To reset the ribbon, follow these steps:

1 Follow Steps **1** to **3** in this section.

2 Click the **Reset** button.

3 Click **Reset all customizations**.

4 Click **OK**.

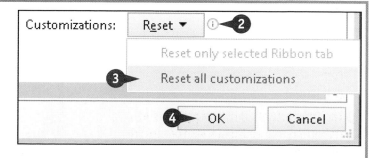

How people use ribbon commands depends upon how they work with PowerPoint. In fact, PowerPoint users often have a group of commands that they frequently use, and so many advanced users create a single tab with all of their favorite commands on it. You can group commonly used commands on a custom tab to make it easier than ever to design your presentation. Creating a presentation takes time, so you can make your design process faster and more effective by creating tabs with your favorite commands on it.

Customize the Ribbon (continued)

Ⓐ The tab name changes to MyTab.

Add a Group

1 Click the **plus sign** (⊞) to expand the Insert tab (⊞ changes to ⊟).

2 Click a group name from the list; your custom group is inserted below it.

3 Click **New Group**.

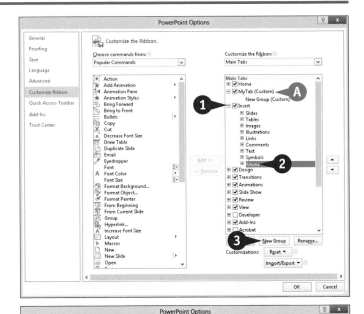

Ⓑ A new group level appears.

Add a Command

1 Click **New Group (Custom)**.

2 Click a command from the list.

3 Click **Add**.

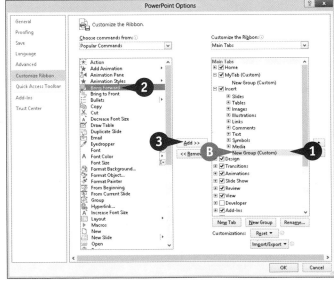

④ Repeat Steps **2** and **3** for any commands you want in any group, including existing groups.

ⓒ PowerPoint adds your commands to New Group (Custom).

⑤ Click **OK**.

The PowerPoint Options dialog box closes, and the ribbon reflects the changes you made.

ⓓ PowerPoint adds MyTab to the ribbon.

ⓔ PowerPoint adds the group, New Group, to MyTab.

ⓕ PowerPoint adds the selected commands to New Group.

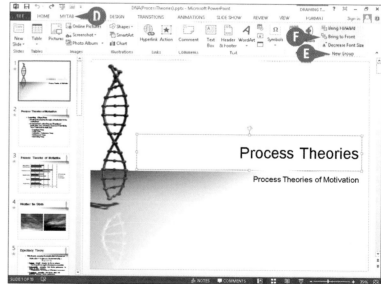

Why do some of the commands that I added to my custom group not work?

Some commands require you to select an object or text before you can use them. Select an object or text, and then try using the commands — they should now be available to use.

On the left side of the Options dialog box, I cannot find the command I want in the selected category. Is there another place to look?

Yes. Click the down arrow (▾) on **Choose commands from**, and then click **All Commands**. If the command is currently available, it appears in the list of all commands. Keep in mind that PowerPoint 2013 may have removed some commands.

CHAPTER 4

Writing and Formatting Text

A professional presentation commands respect and conveys ideas easily. Nice formatting makes text easier to read and helps make your slides more attractive and polished. Changing the formatting can completely change the look, feel, and mood of a presentation.

Understanding Slide Structure

You use PowerPoint to build a presentation slide by slide. Those slides, whether shown as a slide show or printed, make up your presentation. Different types of slides (slide layouts) serve different functions in your presentation. The slide layout controls which objects a slide contains and the placement of those objects on the slide. You can learn more about layouts in Chapter 5. The structure of the presentation affects flow and visual appeal.

Title Slide

The Title slide typically appears first and includes the presentation title or topic, and a subtitle. The subtitle might be the presenter's name or the name of the presenting company, or it might be the date and location of the presentation. There is usually just one title slide in a presentation, though they are sometimes used at the beginning of slide sections.

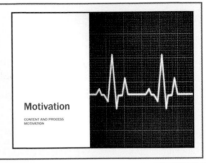

Title and Content Slide

A Title and Content slide is perhaps the most frequently used slide layout. It includes a title plus a placeholder where you can add one of several types of content: a bulleted list, table, chart, clip art, picture, SmartArt graphic (diagram), or media clip (sound or video).

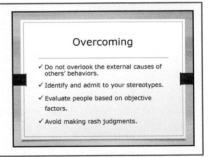

Other Slide Content

PowerPoint provides other slide layouts for your convenience: Two Content, Comparison, Content with Caption, Picture with Caption, and Blank. Each layout includes placeholders to position your information. Choose the layout that best presents your concepts and the associated data or graphics.

Slide Sections

You may need to divide a presentation into logical sections. Section breaks allow your audience to ask questions or for the group to take a break. You can easily change the slide theme of each section, possibly to denote a change in topic. You can introduce a new section with a slide using the Section Header or Title Only layout.

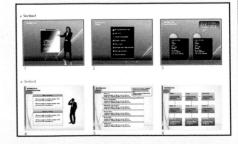

Explore Text Formatting Options

You can use various text formatting tools in PowerPoint to change the appearance of selected text. The Font and Paragraph groups on the Home tab of the ribbon provide most of the tools you need, or you can make formatting changes in the Font or Paragraph dialog boxes. You can also change the formatting of entire placeholders using the Quick Styles command on the Home tab.

Change the Font

When you type text on a slide, it is formatted with a font that is determined by the presentation theme you apply. The font (lettering type) gives a certain look and feel to your presentation, such as formal or informal. Changing the formatting of text can emphasize a certain word or line. You can change the font for selected text or for all text in a title or bulleted list.

Resize Text

Properly sizing presentation text makes the text more readable and attractive. You can modify the text size to reflect the environment where you make the presentation. Smaller text may be readable for a presentation viewed on a kiosk, but larger text may be needed to ensure clarity in a lecture hall. You can also use size to emphasize words.

Change Text Color and Other Attributes

You can use text color for both design and practical purposes. The text color should be appealing to the eye. More importantly, it should provide a good contrast against the slide background so that the text is easy to read. You can also apply attributes such as bold, italic, and underline to slide text. Use colors and attributes to add emphasis to important words or phrases in your presentation.

Selecting Text or Placeholders

You can change the formatting of the text in a placeholder — how you select the placeholder determines which text changes. To select text in a placeholder, simply click the text, click and drag across it, or double-click a word. The placeholder border becomes a dashed line. To select the entire placeholder, click the border. The border becomes solid and your changes affect all of the text in the placeholder.

Add a Slide

When you open a new presentation, PowerPoint creates a blank title slide. To build your presentation, you can add as many slides as you like — just select one from the several slide templates that are available in the slide gallery by default.

Determine the number of slides in your presentation based upon how many topics you want to cover and the time you have available to cover them. Each slide should cover or detail a new topic.

Add a Slide

1 With a presentation open, click the **Home** tab.

2 Click the **New Slide** down arrow (▼).

3 Click the desired slide layout from the gallery.

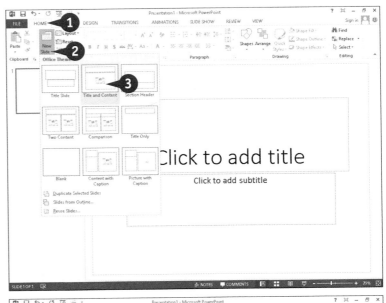

A new blank slide appears with the specified layout.

Note: Depending on circumstances, clicking the top half of the **New Slide** button inserts a slide with either the Title and Content layout or the same layout as the current slide.

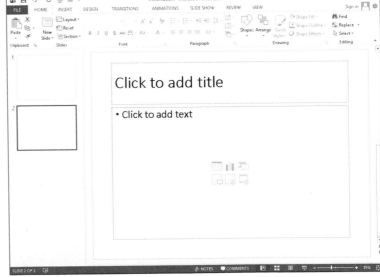

Delete a Slide in Normal View

As you build your presentation, you may decide you do not need a particular slide. In this case, you can simply delete that slide. It is common to use an existing presentation as the basis for other presentations. In that situation, you may need to delete several slides that are irrelevant or out of date. You can either hide or delete slides. If you are confident that you do not need a slide, delete it to keep your presentation uncluttered.

Delete a Slide in Normal View

1 Click the **View** tab.

2 Click **Normal.**

Note: For more on Normal view, see Chapter 2.

3 Right-click the slide you want to delete.

The submenu appears.

4 Click **Delete Slide**.

PowerPoint deletes the slide.

Note: You can also click the slide, and then press Delete.

A Click the **Undo** button (↺) on the Quick Access Toolbar if you decide you need the slide and want it back in the presentation.

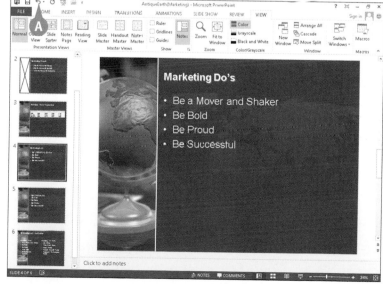

Type and Edit Text on a Slide

You can type text into a placeholder on a slide so you can convey information to the presentation audience through the written word. There are three types of placeholders that can hold text: title, content (bulleted list), and subtitle. You simply click the placeholder and then start typing. You can also go back and edit text you have already typed. Bullet points are discussion points, not detailed sentences. Remember to keep them short.

Type and Edit Text on a Slide

Enter Text

1 With a presentation in Normal view, add a **Title and Content** Slide.

Note: See the section "Add a Slide" in this chapter to learn how to add a slide.

2 Click the title placeholder.

The insertion point appears and the "Click to add title" text disappears.

3 Type your text.

4 Click outside the placeholder.

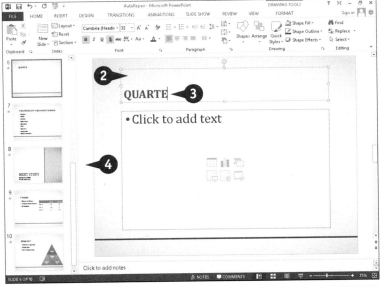

A PowerPoint adds the text.

5 Click the content placeholder.

6 Type your text.

7 Press `Enter`.

B The insertion point moves to the next line.

8 Repeat Steps **6** and **7** for all bullet points for that slide.

9 Click outside the placeholder.

PowerPoint adds the text.

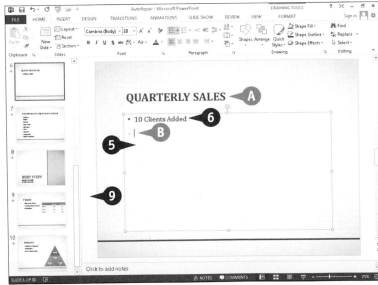

Edit Text

1 Click anywhere within a title, subtitle, or text placeholder.

2 Click the existing text where you want to change it.

The insertion point appears where you clicked. You can press **Backspace** to delete text to the left, or press **Delete** to delete text to the right of the insertion point.

3 Press **Backspace**.

This example deletes the number '2.'

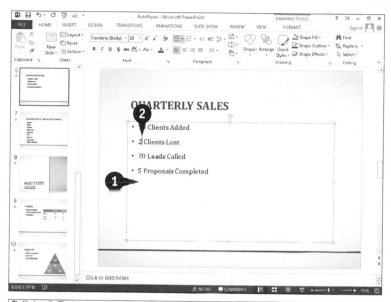

4 Type any text you want to add.

This example types the text 'Two.'

5 Click and drag over one or more words.

6 Press **Delete**.

PowerPoint deletes the selected text.

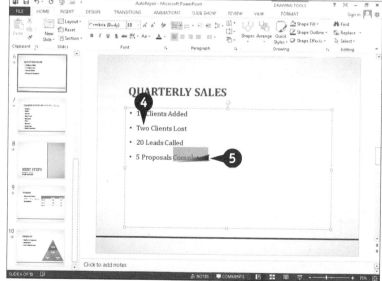

TIPS

Why does my placeholder say, "Click to add text"? Will this appear if I print or run my presentation?

That is simply an instruction to let you know that this placeholder currently has no text entered in it. The words and the placeholder neither print nor appear when you present the slide show. When you click the placeholder to type, it disappears.

When I type text in Outline view, where does it appear?

Text that you type in the Outline tab appears on the currently displayed slide. The top-level heading in a slide corresponds to the title placeholder on the slide. Second-level entries become the bullet items in the text placeholder. Third-level entries are bullet items, and so on.

Format Text Color and Style

Color adds flair to any presentation. You can use text color to make your text more readable and more attractive. Choose text colors that are a good contrast with the background so your audience can easily read the text during the slide show. You can select colors from a standard palette or work with custom colors. Use text colors along with text styles such as bold or shadow to add emphasis to the words in your presentation.

Format Text Color and Style

1 Click a placeholder to select it.

2 Click and drag over one or more words.

3 Click the **Home** tab.

4 Click the **Font Color** down arrow (⏷).

A color palette appears.

5 Select a color from the palette.

A For a custom color, click **More Colors**.

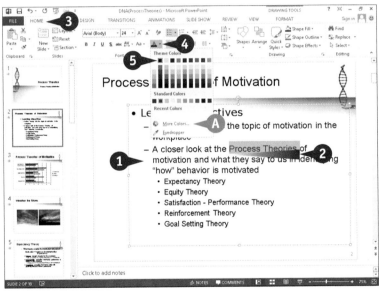

B The text you selected changes to the color you chose.

6 Click and drag over one or more other words.

Note: You can also double-click to select a single word.

7 Click the **dialog box launcher** button (⌐) in the Font group.

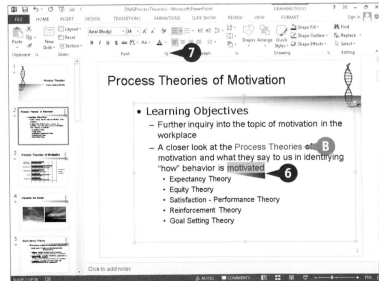

The Font dialog box appears.

8 Click the **Font style** down arrow (⌄).

9 Click a style from the list.

10 Click an effect to apply to your text (☐ changes to ☑).

11 Click **OK**.

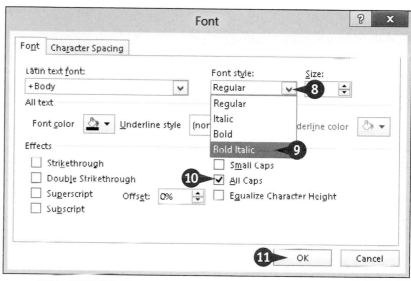

C PowerPoint changes the text to the style that you selected.

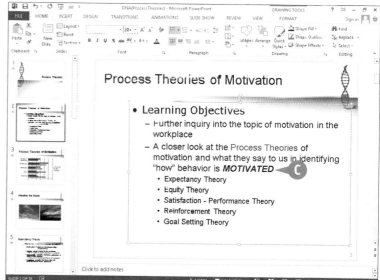

TIPS

What is the difference between applying formats with the Home tab buttons and the Font dialog box?

The Font dialog box enables you to apply several formats at one time from a single location. All possible options are there, including some specialized attributes, such as superscript and subscript, which you do not see in the Font group on the Home tab.

What are superscript and subscript?

These formats either raise (superscript) or lower (subscript) the selected text a set distance from the regular text. Superscript and subscript are often used for footnote or scientific notation, such as 4^2 representing 4 to the second power, or f_x to represent a function of x. Unless you customized the ribbon, these attributes are only found in the Font dialog box.

Format Text Font and Size

The font you choose for text portrays a certain look and feel. Some fonts are playful, and others more formal. Fonts are divided into four main types: serif fonts, with cross strokes on the letter ends; sans serif fonts, which do not have cross strokes on the letter ends; script fonts, which look like handwriting; and decorative fonts such as Algerian, which are heavily stylized. Font size is important because your audience should be able to read all of the text in your presentation without straining their eyes.

Format Text Font and Size

1 Click a placeholder to select it.

2 Click and drag over one or more words.

3 Click the **Home** tab.

4 Click the **dialog box launcher** button (⌐) in the Font group.

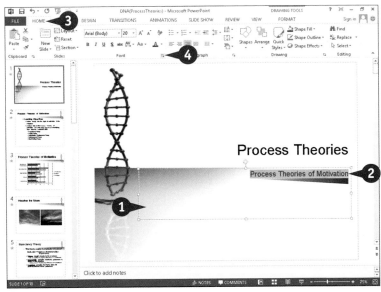

The Font dialog box appears.

5 Click the **Latin text font** down arrow (⌄).

6 Click the desired font.

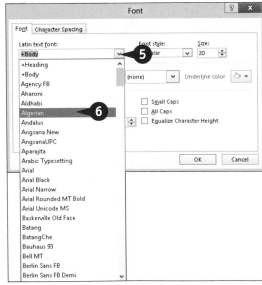

7 Double-click the number in the **Size** text box and type a new font size.

Ⓐ You can also click the spinner (⬍) beside the Size text box to increase or decrease the font size.

8 Click **OK**.

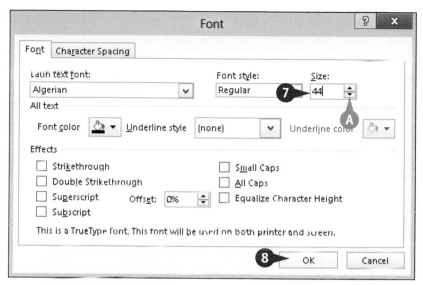

Ⓑ PowerPoint applies the new formatting to the text.

Note: If the placeholder is not wide enough to accommodate the size of the font with the number of characters in one line, then the auto-formatting feature makes the text two lines.

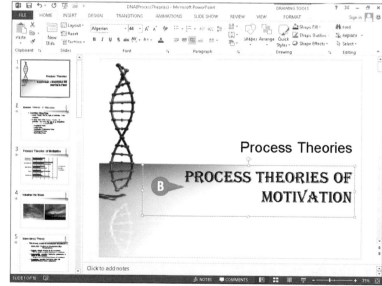

TIPS

There is a Character Spacing tab in the Font dialog box. What does it allow you to do?
The Character Spacing tab allows you to kern the font, or in other words, adjust the character spacing of the text. You can kern the font and specify above which font size you want to start kerning.

Are there limitations on how large or small text can be?
No. You can type whatever font size you like, with the lower limit being 1 and no practical upper limit. However, remember to keep the text readable for the viewer. A very small text size is difficult to see; a huge text size can make text look like a design element.

Cut, Copy, and Paste Text

When you edit your presentation, you can move text by using the Cut, Copy, and Paste features. Using these features assures accuracy and saves time because you avoid typing the text manually. *Cut* removes text from its original location. *Copy* duplicates the text, leaving the original in place. *Paste* places either cut or copied text into another location. You can also cut, copy, and paste objects like placeholders and pictures. If you change your mind or make a mistake, you can use the undo feature to reverse the commands you made.

Cut, Copy, and Paste Text

1 Click the **Home** tab.

2 Click the **dialog box launcher** button (⬚) in the Clipboard group.

The Clipboard task pane appears.

3 Click a text placeholder to select it.

4 Click and drag to select text.

5 Click the **Cut** button (✂).

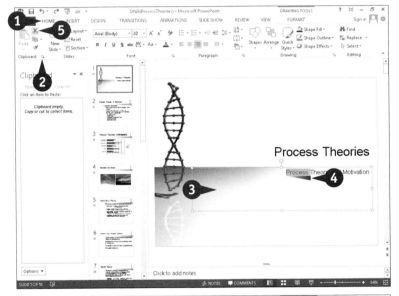

A PowerPoint removes the selected text and places it on the Windows Clipboard.

6 Click and drag to select different text.

7 Click the **Copy** button (📋 ▾).

Note: If you do not open the Clipboard, it holds only your most recent copied or cut text.

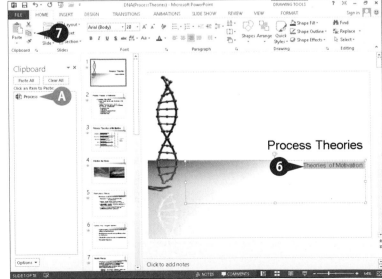

B PowerPoint copies the selected text to the Clipboard.

8 Select the slide where you want to paste the text.

Note: For more information on navigating slides, see Chapter 2.

9 Click within the placeholder to position the insertion point where you want to paste the text.

C The insertion point appears in the placeholder.

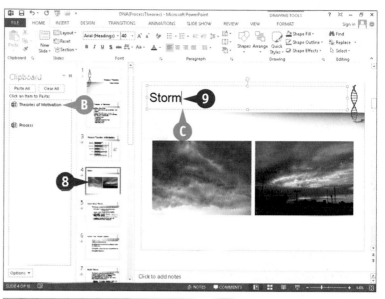

10 To paste an item that you copied, click it in the Clipboard.

D PowerPoint pastes the cut or copied text into the placeholder.

E You can also click **Paste** to paste the most recently copied item, which is always the first item on the Clipboard.

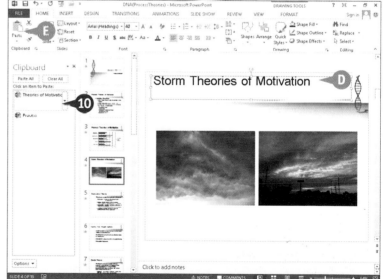

TIPS

Is there an easier and faster way to cut, copy, and paste?
Yes. You can perform these commands by using keystrokes. Press Ctrl+X to cut, Ctrl+C to copy, and Ctrl+V to paste. Use these keystrokes to perform these commands with text, objects, and even files. They work throughout Microsoft Windows.

The text that I copied in Word appears on the Clipboard. Can I delete it?
Yes. Move your mouse pointer (⟍) over the item that you want to delete and then click the down arrow (▾). Click **Delete** on the drop-down list that appears and the item disappears from the Clipboard.

Format Bulleted Lists

Bulleted lists are the heart of any presentation. They summarize key points the presenter wants to make. You can format bulleted lists with different styles of bullets. For example, you can use check marks as bullets in a list of points for a project. You can use pictures and symbols as bullet points and dictate the size of bullet points as well.

If you place the insertion point within the text of a placeholder, only the bullet for that line changes. To change all bullets, click the placeholder border to select the entire placeholder.

Format Bulleted Lists

1. Click the border of a placeholder containing a bulleted list.

2. Click the **Home** tab.

3. Click the **Bullets** down arrow (▼).

4. Click a bullet style from the gallery.

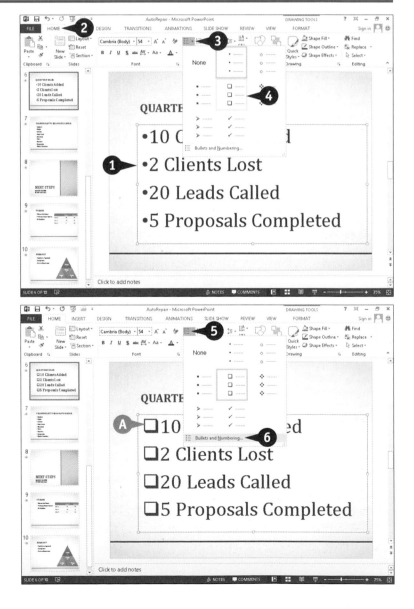

Ⓐ The bullets change to the new style.

5. Click the **Bullets** down arrow (▼).

6. Click **Bullets and Numbering** at the bottom of the gallery.

The Bullets and Numbering dialog box appears.

B You can change the bullet color.

C You can click **Customize** to use a symbol as a bullet.

7 Click **Picture**.

The Insert Pictures dialog box appears.

D You can use a picture from your computer.

8 Type a keyword into the **Office.com Clip Art** text box.

9 Click the **Search** button (🔍).

10 Click a picture from the selection.

11 Click **Insert**.

E The picture appears as a bullet.

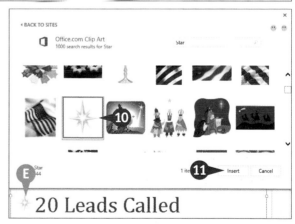

20 Leads Called

TIPS

How can I make the bullets larger?
The Bullets and Numbering dialog box includes a size setting. This setting is expressed in percentage of the text size. If you increase the text size, the bullet size increases proportionally. Double-click in the **Size** text box, type the size you want, and then click **OK** to apply the sizing.

Can I apply a new bullet style to every bullet in the presentation without having to change each individually?
Yes. You can use the master slides to make formatting changes that apply to every slide in the presentation. Chapter 9 covers master slides in detail.

Using the Spelling Check Feature

You should check the contents of your presentation for spelling accuracy because good presentations do not have spelling errors. Not all of us are spelling bee winners, but your audience will definitely notice spelling errors. Fortunately, PowerPoint offers a spelling check feature to improve your spelling accuracy without using a dictionary. You can check the spelling of all the words throughout your presentation so it is as professional as possible.

Using the Spelling Check Feature

1 Click the **Review** tab.

2 Click **Spelling**.

Note: You can also press F7 to start the spelling check.

A The Spelling task pane appears, displaying the first questionable word and suggested spellings.

3 Click a suggestion from the **Suggestions** list.

4 Click **Change** to replace the misspelling.

B You can click **Change All** to replace all instances of the misspelled word.

C You can click **Ignore** to leave the spelling as is.

D You can click **Ignore All** to leave all instances of this spelling as they are.

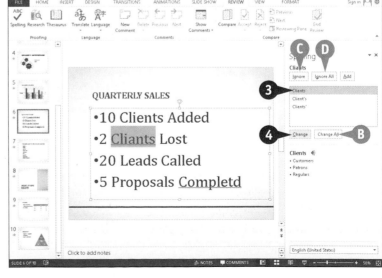

E The spelling check proceeds to the next questionable word.

5 Repeat Steps **3** and **4** until the spell check is complete.

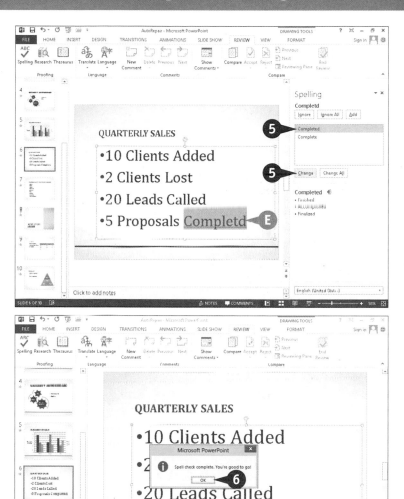

A dialog box appears notifying you when the spelling check is complete.

6 Click **OK**.

The Spelling task pane closes.

Note: If PowerPoint options are set to check spelling as you type, red wavy lines may appear under possibly misspelled words after you type them. You can right-click the word and then click an option in the shortcut menu that appears.

TIPS

Is it possible to check spelling for a specific word?

Yes. Select the word before you run the spelling check. The spelling check starts with the word you select. After taking the appropriate action, simply click the **Close** button (✖) in the Spelling pane.

Is there a way to get PowerPoint to stop flagging a particular word as misspelled?

Yes. In the Spelling pane, click **Add**. This adds the word to your custom dictionary, so it recognizes the spelling as legitimate in the future. Keep in mind that your custom dictionary affects all Microsoft programs, so the word you add will be viewed as a legitimate spelling in all Microsoft programs.

Using the Research Feature

As you type text in a presentation, you may need to check definitions or facts. PowerPoint gives you the convenience of researching a topic without a dictionary, thesaurus, or any other references; you can research the topic without leaving PowerPoint! If your computer has an Internet connection, you can use the Research feature to search reference books and research sites for relevant information on your topic. PowerPoint finds relevant references so you can open them with a click of your mouse button!

Using the Research Feature

① Click the **Review** tab.

② Click and drag across the text you want to research.

③ Click **Research**.

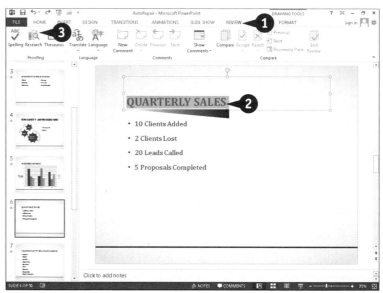

The Research task pane appears with the selected text in the Search for text box.

④ Click the **Search** button (➡ changes to ⏹).

You can click the **Stop** button (⏹) to cancel the search.

Ⓐ The search results appear.

Ⓑ If you want to change the search topic, type it in the **Search for** text box and click the **Search** button (➡).

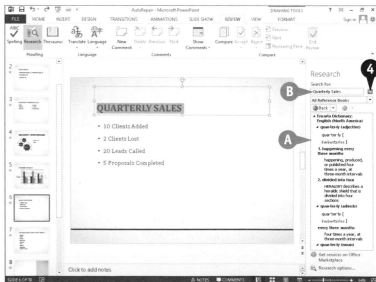

5 Click the **Search for** down arrow (⏷) to change where the Research feature looks for information.

6 Click to select a research site from the drop-down list.

PowerPoint changes the search results to reflect your change.

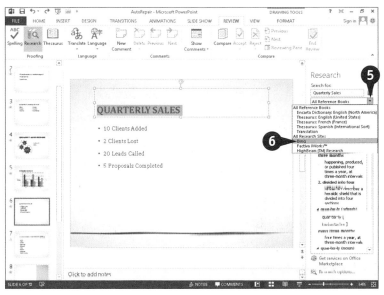

C Click the **Expand** icon (▷) to expand a listing (▷ changes to ◢).

D Click the **Collapse** icon (◢) to collapse a listing (◢ changes to ▷).

E Click **Next** to see the next listings.

7 Click a link.

Additional information appears or a Web site opens, depending on the type of link it is.

8 Click the **Close** button (✖) to close the Research task pane.

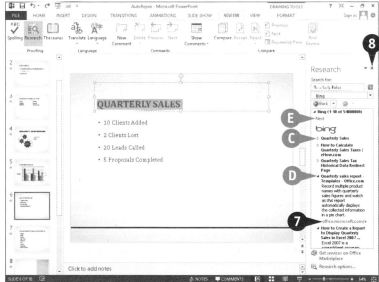

TIPS

Can I specify which research sites PowerPoint will check?

Yes. With the Research task pane displayed, click the **Research options** link at the bottom. A dialog box appears with a list of all resources. Click the check box beside any listed reference, and then click **OK**. The references you selected now appear in the drop-down list.

I followed a link but it did not contain the information I wanted. Is there a way to go back to the original item that was displayed?

Yes. Working within PowerPoint, you can click the **Back** button (◉Back ⏷) in the Research task pane. You can also choose another topic in the Research task pane.

CHAPTER 5

Working with Layouts

Slide layouts are templates that consist of different combinations and arrangements of placeholders. *Placeholders* are rectangular objects on slides that hold text, graphics, charts, tables, SmartArt, and multimedia. Slides may contain one or more placeholders. You use the various slide layouts and place content into placeholders to create your presentation. Slide layouts save you the time and trouble of designing slides from scratch.

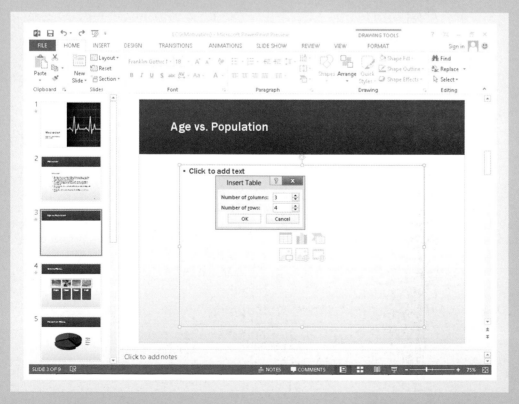

Understanding Layouts and Placeholders

Many presentation slides combine a slide title, graphic elements, and slide text in the form of a bulleted list or table. Your selection of slide layout determines where the title, graphics, and text appear. Slide titles, bullet lists, and other text usually exist in placeholders. Content placeholders can also contain graphic elements, tables, charts, pictures, and SmartArt. The layout of a slide is established by the placement of placeholders on the slide. PowerPoint offers several standard slide layouts. You can use one of these layouts to quickly and easily create a presentation.

Slide Layout Gallery

Clicking the bottom part of the New Slide button opens the Slide Layout gallery. You will find a New Slide button on both the Home and Insert tabs. You can use the gallery to insert a slide with a particular layout. With some exceptions, if you click the top part of the New Slide button, PowerPoint inserts a slide with the same layout as the selected slide.

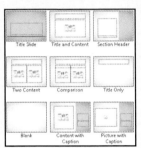

Placeholders

Each slide layout has an arrangement of placeholders. Text placeholders accept only text. Content placeholders accept either text or a graphic element. A content placeholder contains icons that help you insert graphics. You can move placeholders to design slides that suit your particular needs.

Types of Slide Layouts

The Slide Layout gallery enables you to choose a layout for a slide. Some layouts hold only text, such as the Title Slide, Section Header, and Title Only layouts. Other layouts include a title, plus content placeholders. Layouts that feature placeholders include Title and Content, Two Content, Comparison, and Content with Caption.

Slide Layouts Remain Flexible

You can adjust a layout to meet your particular needs. There are handles on the border of the placeholder — dragging any handle resizes the placeholder. To move a placeholder, click its border and then drag it to another location. If a placeholder does not contain any content, it is not visible when you print or show your presentation.

Insert a New Slide with the Selected Layout

To insert a new slide with a particular layout, you can click the bottom part of the New Slide button and choose the desired layout from the Slide Layout gallery. The various slide layouts allow you to give your presentation diversity and to accomplish different objectives such as comparing two lists or showing data in chart form. PowerPoint inserts slides after the currently selected slide. With some exceptions, if you click the main part of the New Slide button, PowerPoint inserts a slide with the same layout as the selected slide.

Insert a New Slide with the Selected Layout

1 Select a slide.

2 Click the **Home** tab.

3 Click the **New Slide** down arrow (▼).

The Layout gallery appears.

4 Click the desired layout.

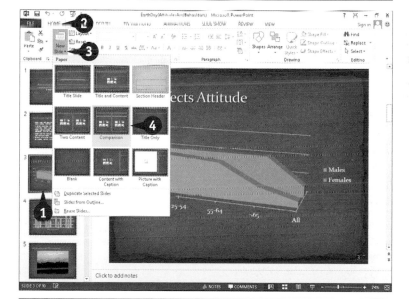

A The new slide with the specified layout appears in the presentation.

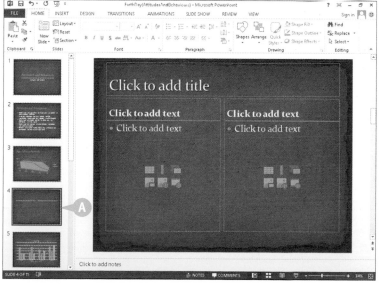

Change a Slide Layout

I f you decide a slide's original layout no longer works, you can apply a different slide layout in Normal view or Slide Sorter view. This allows you to change the layout without designing the slide again. If the configuration of the new layout does not include an element from the original layout — such as a chart that you have set up — PowerPoint keeps that additional element on the slide, even with the new layout.

Change a Slide Layout

1. Select the slide whose layout you want to change.

Note: To learn how to select a slide, see Chapter 2.

2. Click the **Home** tab.

3. Click the **Layout** down arrow (▼).

   The Layout gallery appears.

4. Click a slide layout from the gallery.

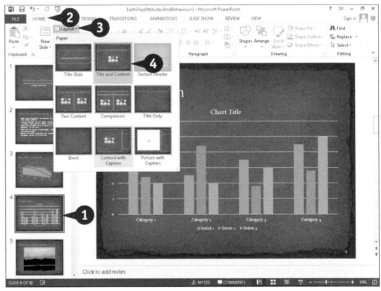

The slide changes to the selected layout.

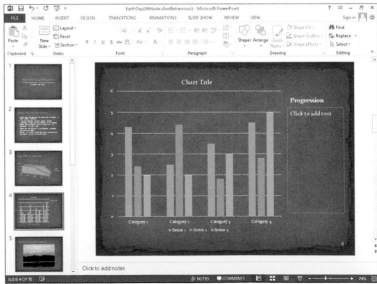

Using Layouts with a Content Placeholder

Content placeholders appear on most of the slide layouts that you will use. You can use content placeholders to build your presentation effectively and efficiently. Content placeholders are convenient containers that allow you to place text or graphics on a slide. They are easy to move and simple to change. Placeholders enable you to insert text, or one of six types of graphical objects onto the slide. You can use text to convey ideas, and graphics to make your presentation more aesthetically dynamic and visually appealing.

Ⓐ Bulleted List

Click the bullet to add text or type a list of items. Press **Enter** at the end of each item.

Ⓑ Tables

Click the **Insert Table** icon (▦) to create a table. You can specify the number of columns and rows in the table.

Ⓒ Charts

Click the **Insert Chart** icon (▮▮) to generate a chart using a chart type that you specify, and data that you type into a spreadsheet.

Ⓓ SmartArt

Click the **Insert a SmartArt Graphic** icon (▦) to insert a diagram using one of the many diagram styles provided by PowerPoint.

Ⓔ Pictures

Click the **Insert Picture** icon (▦) to insert a picture file such as a bitmap or JPEG that you have stored on your computer or other storage media.

Ⓕ Online Pictures

Click the **Insert Online Picture** icon (▦) to select an image from the built-in clip art collection, or import clip art from Microsoft Office Online.

Ⓖ Videos

Click the **Insert Video** icon (▦) to insert a video file that plays during the slide show. You can specify that it plays on command or automatically.

Insert a Table

You can use a table to arrange information in rows and columns for easy data comparison. For example, you might list age groups in the far-left column of a table, and then compare population demographics between males and females in two other columns. Tables are useful for showing important data to your audience. For example, you might use a table to show the data for a chart. You can use a content placeholder to insert a table, and then type data into the table cells.

Insert a Table

Insert a Table

1. Select a slide with a content placeholder.

2. Click the **Insert Table** icon (▦).

   The Insert Table dialog box appears.

3. Click and type the number of columns you want in your table.

4. Click and type the number of rows you want in your table.

Note: Alternatively, you can click the **spinner** (↕) to select the number of columns and rows.

5. Click **OK**.

   The table appears on the slide.

Note: By default, most of the table styles assume that you will enter column headings in the top row of the table.

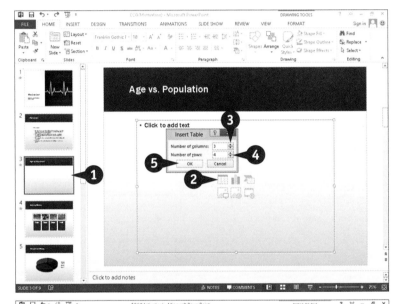

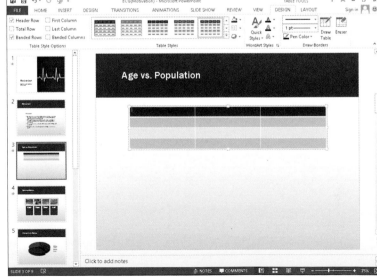

Type Text in a Table

1 Click in the first cell and type a column heading.

This example types Age Group.

2 Press **Tab**.

A The insertion point moves to the next cell.

Note: You can also click in a cell to type data into it.

3 Continue adding column headings and cell entries by repeating Steps **1** and **2**.

4 Click outside the table when finished.

B To change table data, click in the cell, edit your entry, and then click outside the table when finished.

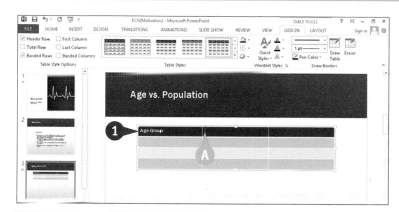

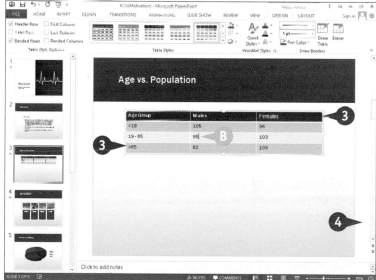

TIP

Can I add and delete rows or columns to tables?

Yes. You can insert and delete rows or columns by following these steps:

1 Click a row or column.

2 Click the **Table Tools Layout** tab.

3 To insert, click an Insert option.

4 To delete, click **Delete**.

5 Select an option from the menu.

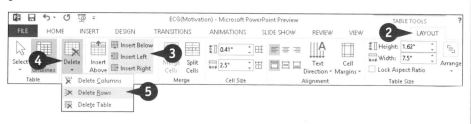

Format a Table

When you insert a table, PowerPoint automatically applies a style to the table based on the theme of the slide. You can add visual impact to your presentation by changing the format of your table. You can add and delete rows and columns, format the text and background, and change the style of the table. There are a variety of ways to select cells, rows, and columns in a table, so experiment with clicking and dragging them!

Format a Table

1 Select a slide with a table.

Note: To learn how to select a slide, see Chapter 2.

2 Click the table.

3 Click the **Table Tools Design** tab.

4 Click the **Table Styles** down arrow (⩢).

5 Click a style from the gallery.

Ⓐ You can click **Clear Table** to remove any previously applied styles.

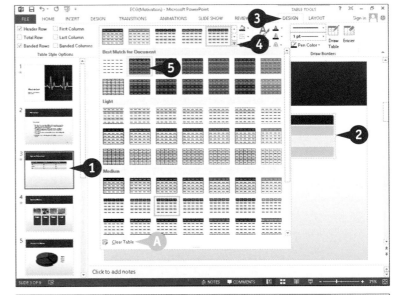

PowerPoint applies the style to the table.

6 Click a row to select it.

You can also click and drag across cells or text.

This example selects the header row.

7 Click the **Quick Styles** down arrow (⩢).

8 Select a style from the gallery.

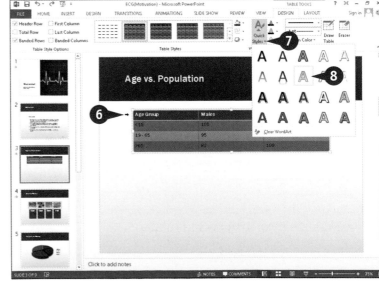

PowerPoint applies the style to the selection.

9 Click and drag across rows to select them.

This example selects all of the rows.

10 Click the **Borders** down arrow (▼).

11 Click a border from the menu.

12 Click the **Home** tab.

13 Click the **Bold** button (B).

14 Click the **Italic** button (I).

15 Click the **Center** button (≡).

PowerPoint applies the formatting changes to the selection.

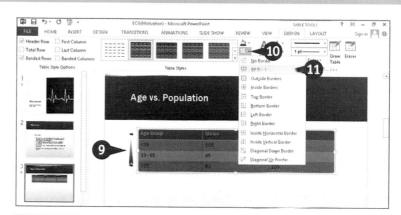

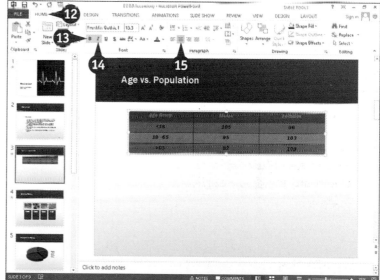

TIP

Can I make size adjustments to the table?

Yes. You can resize your table as follows:

1 Click in the table.

2 Position the mouse pointer (↖) over a handle.

3 Click and drag the handle to size the table.

4 Position the mouse pointer (↖) over a cell border separating rows or columns.

5 Click and drag the border.

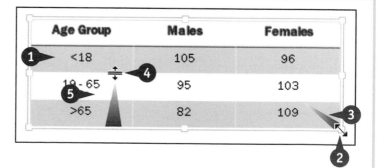

Insert a Chart

Charts present information visually and make a presentation aesthetically pleasing. They give an instant impression of trends, or they compare sets of data, such as sales growth over a several-year span. Charts tell a story with a brief viewing and can convey statistical information quickly. You can add these visual-analysis tools to your presentation to convey summarized information quickly to your audience. PowerPoint allows you to choose the chart type and then type chart data into a spreadsheet.

Insert a Chart

Create a Chart

1 Select a slide with a content placeholder.

Note: To learn how to select a slide, see Chapter 2.

2 Click the **Insert Chart** icon (▮▮).

The Insert Chart dialog box appears.

3 Click a chart type category.

4 Click a specific chart type.

5 Click **OK**.

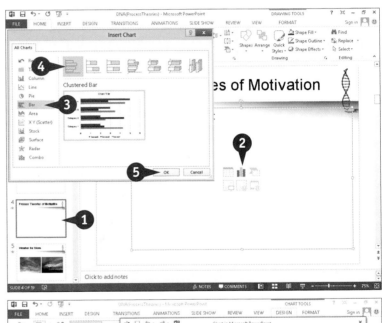

The chart appears, along with sample data in a separate spreadsheet window.

Note: Entering data is similar to entering data into an Excel worksheet.

6 Click in the grid to activate the spreadsheet.

7 Delete any unneeded information in rows or columns.

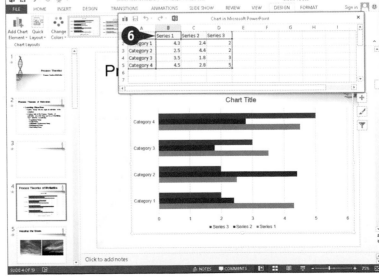

Enter Chart Data

1 Type column headings in Row 1.

2 Type row labels in Column A.

Ⓐ The borders containing the chart data range automatically expand as you enter information.

3 Type your data values in the cells.

Note: You can click a cell and type to enter new data, and double click a cell to edit existing data.

4 Click the **Close** button (×) to close the Excel worksheet.

The spreadsheet window closes and the chart appears on the slide.

5 Click outside the chart when finished.

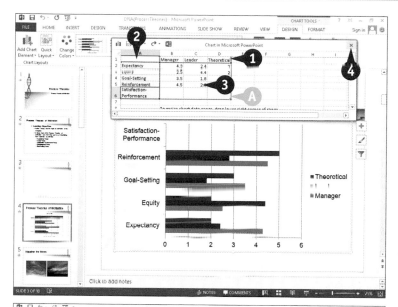

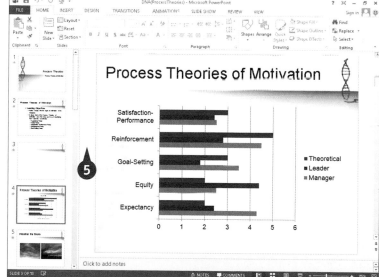

TIP

Can I change the type of a chart?
Yes. Follow these steps:

1 Click anywhere in the chart.

2 Click the **Chart Tools Design** tab.

3 Click **Change Chart Type**.

4 Click a chart type category.

5 Click a specific chart type.

6 Click **OK**.

PowerPoint changes the chart type to the one you selected.

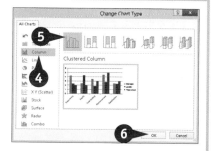

Format a Chart

When you insert a chart, PowerPoint automatically applies a style to the chart based on the theme of the slide. Charts present information visually, so choice of color is important. You can change the formatting of charts to convey a particular mood or to make specific data stand out. To format any object on a chart, you click it and then use the formatting tools on the Chart Tools Design and Home tabs to change it to your liking. Try to keep the chart relatively simple, though — the less complicated and cluttered it is, the easier it is for the audience to understand.

Format a Chart

1 Click anywhere on a chart.

2 Click the **Chart Tools Design** tab.

3 Click the **Chart Styles** down arrow ( ).

4 Click a chart style from the gallery.

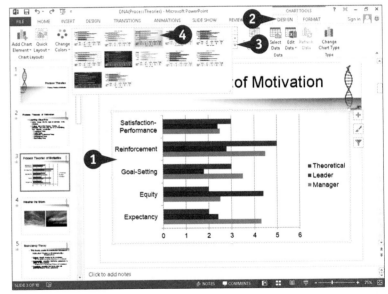

The chart reflects the change in chart style.

5 Click the **Plus** icon ( ).

The Chart Elements box opens. You can add or remove chart elements using this box.

6 Click the **Data Labels** down arrow ( ).

7 Click an item from the selection (changes to).

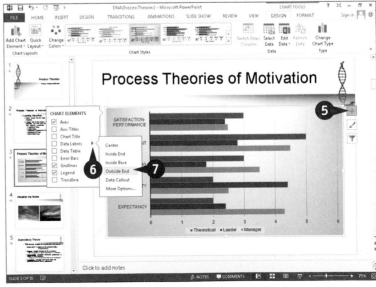

The data labels appear.

8 Click the plot area.

9 Click the **Chart Tools Format** tab.

10 Click **Shape Fill**.

Ⓐ You can alternatively make a selection from the Shape Styles gallery.

Ⓑ You can choose from specialized fill options such as a picture, or different gradients and textures.

11 Click a color from the gallery.

The plot area changes color.

12 Click a data series.

Note: To format a data series (series of bars), click a bar in that series. To format a single bar in the series, click it twice (not a double-click). The same applies to the data labels.

13 Click the **Shape Effects**.

14 Click **Glow**.

15 Click an item from the gallery.

Ⓒ You can change the border color by clicking **Shape Outline**.

PowerPoint applies the formatting to the bars.

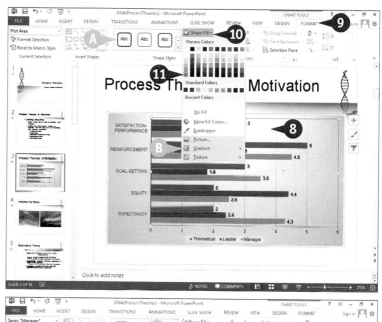

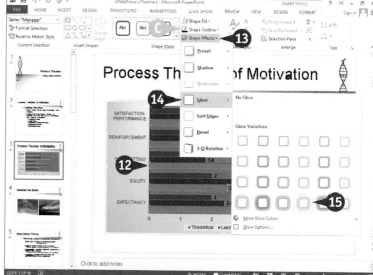

TIP

Can I format the numbers on the axis?
Yes. You can format text in a chart just like other text in PowerPoint by using the Home tab.

1 Click a chart axis.

2 Click the **Home** tab.

3 Click the **Font Size** down arrow (▾).

4 Click a font size from the drop-down list.

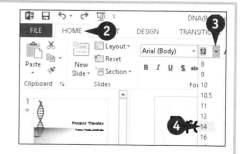

Edit Chart Data

It is not unusual for chart data to change over time. You can update your chart with the most recent information by opening the data spreadsheet and changing the data. You need not show all of the spreadsheet data in the chart. If you decide not to display all of the data, you can remove data elements such as data series or categories from the chart without deleting that information from the spreadsheet. You can later bring removed data back by reversing the process. Alternatively, you can delete the data from the spreadsheet.

Edit Chart Data

1 Click anywhere on a chart.

2 Click the **Filter** icon (▼).

The Chart Filters box opens. You can add (☑) or remove (☐) the data elements with this box.

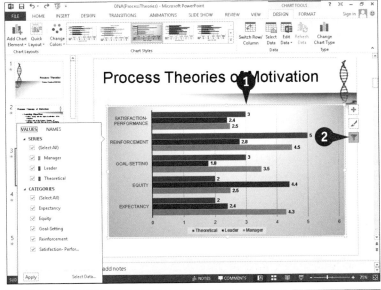

3 Click a series (☑ changes to ☐).

This example hides the Manager series.

4 Click a category (☑ changes to ☐).

This example hides the Satisfaction – Performance category.

5 Click **Apply**.

PowerPoint removes the data elements.

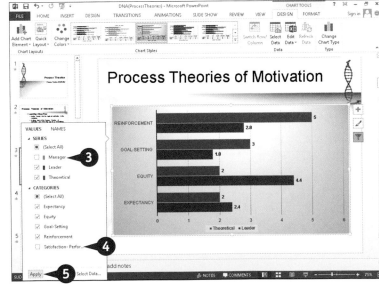

6 Click the **Chart Tools Design** tab.

7 Click **Edit Data**.

The data spreadsheet appears.

8 Double-click a cell to edit the data.

This example is editing Cell A6.

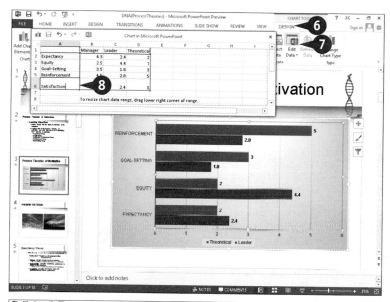

9 Type a column heading and data in Column E.

10 Type a row label and data in Row 7.

Note: The colored borders around the table adjust automatically.

A The chart updates with a new series for the added column.

B The chart updates with a new category for the added row.

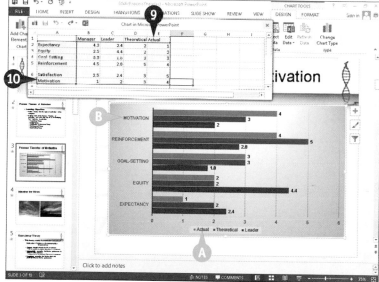

TIP

Are there other ways to show chart data?

Yes. Switching the categories and series gives the data a different, revealing perspective. Follow these steps:

1 Click the **Chart Tools Design** tab, then click Select Data.

2 Click **Switch Row/Column**.

3 Click **OK**.

Insert Pictures

You can illustrate and enhance your slide show presentation using pictures. You can insert various types of pictures into placeholders, including digital camera shots, scanned images, clip art, and bitmaps. These pictures can come from your own collection on your computer, Microsoft Office Online, or a Bing search of the Internet. Bing provides a link to the website that holds the picture and even tells you if the picture is free to use! All pictures found at Microsoft Office Online are royalty-free.

Insert Pictures

1 Select a slide with a content placeholder.

Note: To learn how to select a slide, see Chapter 2.

2 Click the **Insert Picture** icon (⊡).

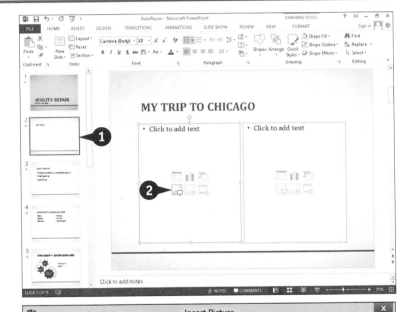

The Insert Picture dialog box appears.

3 Click the folder that contains the picture file you want to insert.

4 Click a picture file.

5 Click **Insert**.

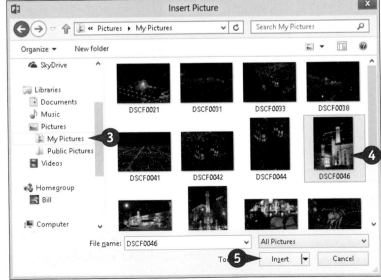

Ⓐ PowerPoint inserts the selected picture into the placeholder.

⑥ Click the **Insert Online Picture** icon (▢).

MY TRIP TO CHICAGO

• Click to add text

The Insert Online Pictures dialog box appears.

⑦ Type a keyword in the Office.com ClipArt text box or Bing Image **Search** text box.

⑧ Click the **Search** icon (🔎).

⑨ Click a picture from the gallery.

⑩ Click **Insert**.

◂ BACK TO SITES

Office.com Clip Art
21 search results for Chicago

Chicago

architecture, buildings, Chicago, Illinois, Midw...
1282 x 1997

Insert   Cancel

Ⓑ PowerPoint inserts the selected picture into the placeholder.

Note: You can resize the pictures as desired. See Chapter 10 to learn how.

MY TRIP TO CHICAGO

TIP

When I click a picture, a Picture Styles group appears on the Picture Tools Format tab. What can I do with this group of tools?

These tools include many ways to make pictures more interesting — several of which involve changing the border. For instance, you can give the picture a reflection such as one you would see in a lake. You can make the picture border glow or give it soft edges. You can frame the picture as though it is hanging from a wall. You can even rotate the picture to give it a three-dimensional look.

Insert Video

Showing instructional videos is a great way to present an information segment in your slide show. You can also show interesting or funny video captures to make your presentation exciting. You can insert videos directly into a placeholder without using an intermediate program to handle the video. Inserting videos directly into PowerPoint saves time and avoids the cost of a program that you otherwise may not use. PowerPoint recognizes videos in a variety of different formats, such as Windows Media Video (WMV) files and Motion Pictures Experts Group (MPEG) files.

Insert Video

1 Select a slide with a content placeholder.

Note: To learn how to select a slide, see Chapter 2.

2 Click the **Insert Video** icon (📹).

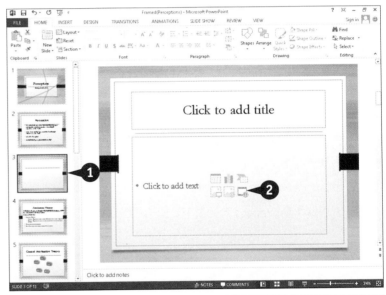

The Insert Video dialog box appears.

A You can search for and insert a video file directly from the Internet.

B You can insert a file from the Internet using the embed code.

3 Click **Browse**.

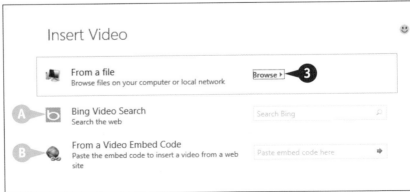

The Insert Video dialog box appears.

④ Click the folder that contains the video file you want to insert.

⑤ Click a video file.

⑥ Click **Insert**.

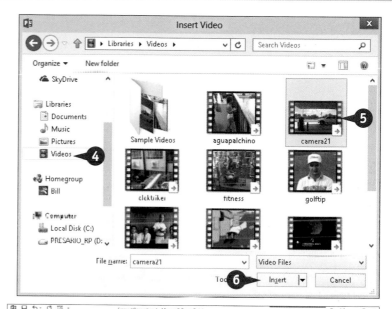

PowerPoint inserts the selected video into the placeholder.

⑦ Click the video.

⑧ Click the **Video Tools Playback** tab.

⑨ Click **Play** (changes to).

The video begins to play.

C You can click the **Forward** (▶) and **Back** (◀) buttons to browse the video.

D You can use the **Volume** button (◀») to adjust the sound.

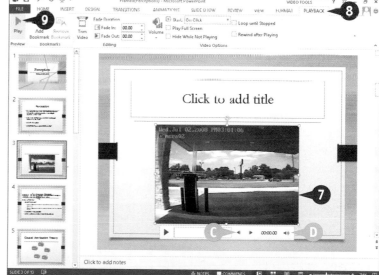

TIP

There is a Hide While Not Playing check mark on the Video Tools Playback tab. What does this option do?
Presenters often do not want a video to be visible when it is not playing. A slide appears uncluttered if the video is hidden, and it can provide a dramatic effect by fading in when it starts playing. If you click to the **Hide While Not Playing** option (□ changes to ✓), the video will not be visible during the slide show if it is not playing. There is a disadvantage, though: To use this feature, you must set the video to play automatically, so you lose some control over when the video plays.

101

Insert a SmartArt Graphic

SmartArt graphics are diagrams that illustrate a process, workflow, or structure. You can use SmartArt graphics or SmartArt diagrams to quickly present concepts in a visually interesting way. For example, a diagram can show the workflow of a procedure or the hierarchy in an organization. Some SmartArt layouts are text only, while others involve text and pictures. You might use a SmartArt picture layout to show the four seasons, and a SmartArt text graphic to describe the steps for starting a race. PowerPoint offers many SmartArt layouts to help you communicate with your audience graphically.

Insert a SmartArt Graphic

1 Select a slide with a content placeholder.

2 Click the **Insert a SmartArt Graphic** icon ( ).

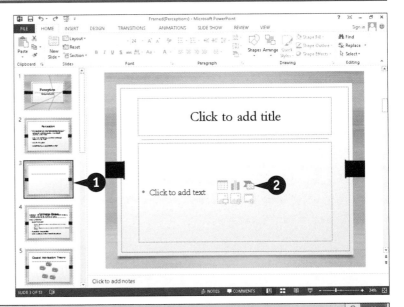

The Choose a SmartArt Graphic dialog box appears.

3 Click a diagram category.

A You can drag the scroll bar to see all of the layouts.

4 Click a specific diagram layout.

5 Click **OK**.

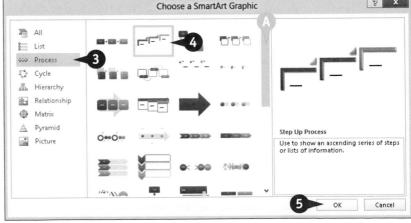

The dialog box closes and the SmartArt graphic diagram appears on the slide.

6 Click the left arrow (<) to open the Text pane (< changes to >).

7 Click **[Text]** next to a bullet.

[Text] disappears and the insertion point takes its place next to the bullet.

Note: You can also edit text directly in the graphical element.

8 Type the text for the element.

9 Repeat Steps **7** and **8** to type text into other graphical elements.

10 Press **Enter** to add a graphical element.

11 Click outside the SmartArt graphic when you are finished.

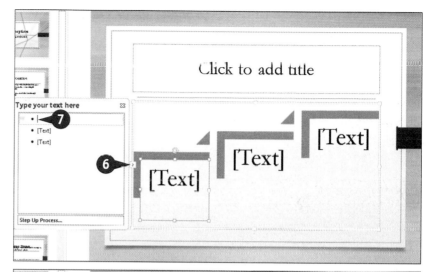

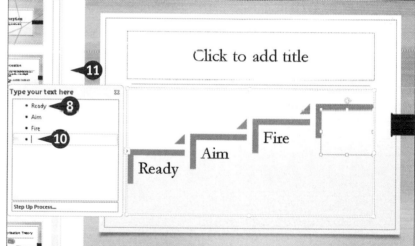

TIPS

Can I add more elements in the SmartArt graphics diagram if I am not using the Text pane?
Yes. Click an element next to where you want the additional element. Click the **Smart Tools Design** tab. Click the **Add Shape** down arrow (▼). The list gives you options about where to place the new element. Click a selection from the list.

How do I add a picture to a SmartArt graphic?
It is just like inserting a picture, as described in this chapter. Make sure the graphic is a picture-specific SmartArt graphic. Click the **Insert Picture** icon in the center of the graphic and follow the same steps as for inserting a picture.

Edit SmartArt

After you create a SmartArt graphic, you can change its look and contents at any time. For example, you can change a SmartArt graphic to a different layout, edit the text, change its color, give it a 3-D effect, or even mix different shapes. You can also format text by changing the font color or style, or by making the font bold or italic. This versatility allows you to create the perfect diagram that sends a specific message to your audience.

Edit SmartArt

1 Click anywhere in the SmartArt graphic to select it.

2 Click the **SmartArt Tools Design** tab.

3 Click the **Expand** button (◁) to open the Text pane (◁ changes to ▷).

4 Click any text in the Text pane or on any element to edit the text.

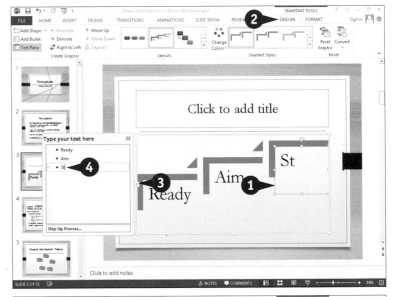

5 Click the **Collapse** button (▷) to close the Text pane (▷ changes to ◁).

6 Click the **SmartArt Styles** down arrow (▼).

The SmartArt Styles gallery appears.

7 Click a style from the gallery.

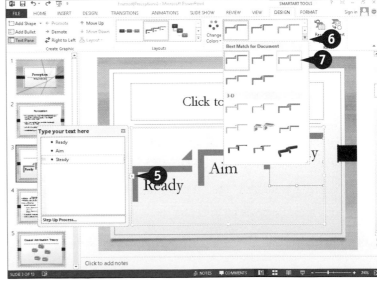

The SmartArt graphic changes style.

8 Click the **SmartArt Layout** down arrow (▼).

The SmartArt Layout gallery appears.

9 Click a layout from the gallery.

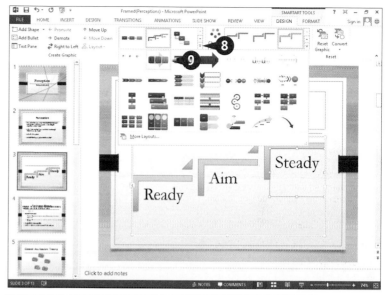

The SmartArt graphic changes layout.

10 Click a single element to select it.

11 Click the **SmartArt Tools Format** tab.

12 Click **Smaller** or **Larger** to change the element's size.

13 Click a Shape Styles command to change the color, border color, or special effect of the shape.

14 Click a WordArt Styles command to change the color, border color, or special effect of the font.

The element reflects the changes you made.

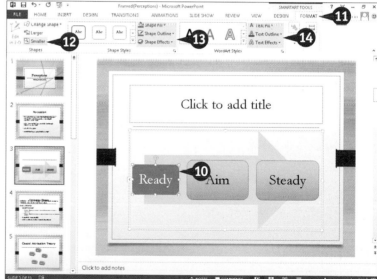

TIP

Are there color themes for the SmartArt graphics?
Yes. Follow these steps to choose from a variety of color themes.

1 Click a SmartArt graphic to select it.

2 Click the **SmartArt Tools Design** tab.

3 Click **Change Colors**.

4 In the Primary Theme Colors gallery, click a color theme.

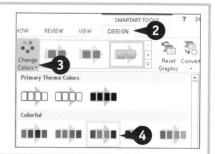

Insert a Slide from Another File

Y ou can insert a slide from one presentation file into another. This can be a great timesaver when you have created a slide with a highly detailed chart, table, or diagram in another presentation. You may want to use a favorite slide in several presentations. For example, a slide showing sales growth may go into a presentation for the sales team, a different one for management, and yet another presentation for potential customers. Importing the slide from the other presentation saves you the trouble of reentering data and reformatting the object on the slide.

Insert a Slide from Another File

1 Select the slide after which you want to insert the new slide.

Note: You can also perform this task in Slide Sorter view. See Chapter 2 to learn how to switch views.

2 Click the **Home** tab.

3 Click the **New Slide** down arrow (▾).

The Layout gallery appears.

4 Click **Reuse Slides**.

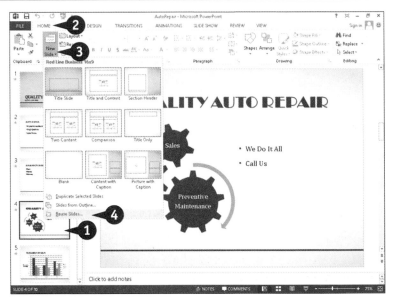

The Reuse Slides task pane appears.

5 Click **Open a PowerPoint File**.

The Browse dialog box opens.

6 Click the folder that contains the presentation file you want to view.

7 Click the presentation file that contains the slide you want to insert.

8 Click **Open**.

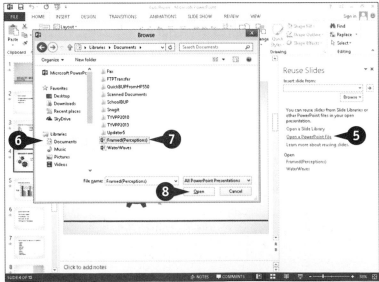

The slides of the selected presentation appear in the Reuse Slides task pane.

9 Drag the scroll bar to find the slide you want to insert.

10 Click the slide.

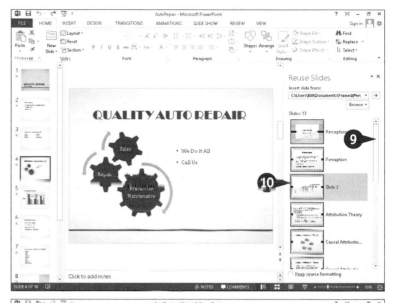

A PowerPoint inserts the slide you clicked after the slide you originally selected.

11 Click the **Close** button (**✖**) to close the Reuse Slides task pane.

Note: If you have two presentations open, you can drag slides from one to another.

TIP

Is there an easy way to import slides from multiple presentations?
Yes. Repeat Steps **1** to **8** and then follow these steps:

1 Click the **Browse** down arrow (▼) in the Reuse Slides task pane.

2 Click **Browse File**.

The Browse dialog box appears so that you can open a different presentation file in the Reuse Slides task pane.

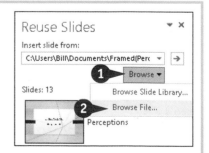

CHAPTER 6

Organizing Slides

After you have created a number of slides, you should check to ensure that the overall flow of your presentation makes sense. A great place to organize your slides is in Slide Sorter view. This view displays a thumbnail (little picture) of each slide. You can use the thumbnails to move, delete, or copy slides with ease.

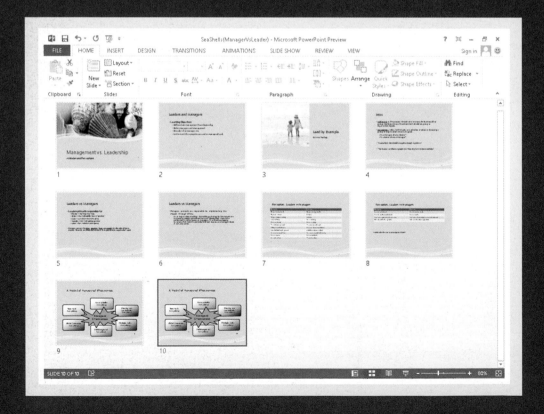

Move a Slide

A good presentation conveys a sequence of ideas in a logical progression. When creating a presentation, you often must reorganize slides to get that sequence right. For example, a presentation on how to build a house would start with building the foundation; continue with rough carpentry, roofing, plumbing, electrical, and drywall; and conclude with finish carpentry and cleanup — all in that order. PowerPoint has the ability to easily move slides so you can quickly order them as necessary.

Move a Slide

1 Click the **View** tab.

2 Click **Slide Sorter**.

Slide Sorter view appears.

3 Click and drag a slide thumbnail to the desired location.

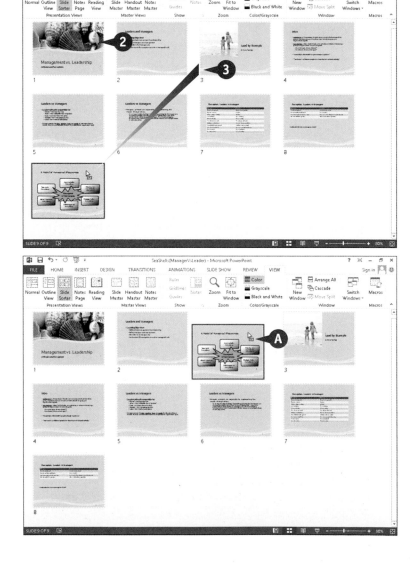

Ⓐ When you release the mouse button, the slide appears in its new position.

Note: Press and hold Ctrl as you drag to create a duplicate slide in the new position.

Copy and Paste a Slide

If you create presentations about similar subjects, you may want to copy a slide from one presentation to another to save time. For example, you may need to copy a slide that contains a table of data. The ability to copy the slide from one presentation to another saves you time because you do not need to re create the slide, you can simply copy and paste it. You can also click and drag a slide from one presentation to another to copy it.

Copy and Paste a Slide

1 Select the slide(s) you want to copy in Slide Sorter view.

Note: You can also perform this task in Normal view.

Note: To select multiple slides, click the first slide, and then press `Ctrl` while clicking additional slides.

2 Click the **Home** tab.

3 Click the **Copy** button (🗐 ▾).

4 Switch to a presentation that is open.

5 In Slide Sorter view, click in between the slides where you want the copied slide to appear.

The insertion point appears.

6 Click the **Home** tab.

7 Click **Paste**.

A The copied slide(s) appear in the presentation.

B You can change the slide back to its original formatting by clicking the **Paste Options** button (🗐 (Ctrl) ▾) and then clicking the **Keep Source Formatting** button.

Delete a Slide in Slide Sorter View

As you build your presentation, you may decide that you do not need particular material. For example, you may need to delete slides if a presentation is outdated or if you decide not to use a slide that you designed. In some cases, you might use a copy of a particular presentation as a template for a presentation that you are designing and you only need certain slides, so you need to delete some of them. When you decide to remove a slide, PowerPoint makes it quick and easy to do so.

Delete a Slide in Slide Sorter View

1 Select the slide(s) you want to delete in Slide Sorter view.

Note: To select multiple slides, click the first slide, and then press **Ctrl** while clicking additional slides.

2 Right-click any selected slide.

The shortcut menu appears.

3 Click **Delete Slide**.

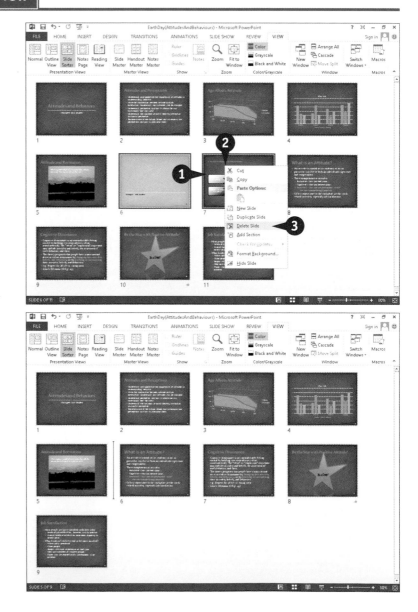

PowerPoint deletes the selected slide(s) from the presentation.

Note: PowerPoint does not prompt you to confirm the deletion. If you want to get the slide back, click the **Undo** icon (↩) on the Quick Access Toolbar.

Note: You can also delete a slide by selecting it and then pressing **Delete** .

Make a Duplicate Slide

If you need to make two slides that are very similar, you can design the first one, duplicate it using the Duplicate Slide feature, and then make minor changes to the new slide. For example, if a slide at the beginning of a presentation lists key topics, you can duplicate it, make minor changes, and use it as a summary. You may want to make a duplicate slide in one presentation, modify it while looking at both slides, and then move it. Duplicating a slide can save time and ensure accuracy of the information on the slide.

Make a Duplicate Slide

1 Select the slide(s) you want to duplicate in Slide Sorter view.

Note: To select multiple slides, click the first slide, and then press **Ctrl** while clicking additional slides.

2 Click the **Home** tab.

3 Click the **New Slide** down arrow (▼).

4 Click **Duplicate Selected Slides**.

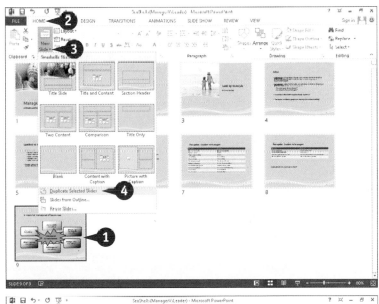

A PowerPoint duplicates the selected slide(s).

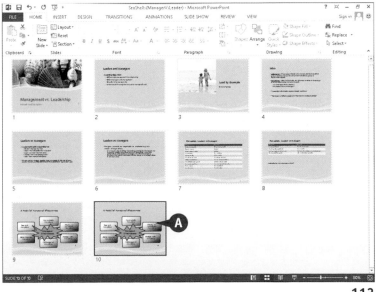

Hide a Slide

Hiding a slide prevents it from appearing during the slide show. By hiding slides, you can create an abbreviated slide show from a presentation without deleting any slides. For example, you may need to give an abbreviated slide show to executives, but a more detailed presentation of the same slide show to managers. You can hide slides, give the presentation, and then unhide them. Hiding slides saves you time by allowing you to prepare only one slide show for two audiences. Hiding slides is also a good way to temporarily remove them to see how your presentation flows without them.

Hide a Slide

1 Select the slide(s) you want to hide in Slide Sorter view.

Note: To select multiple slides, click the first slide, and then press **Ctrl** while clicking additional slides.

2 Click the **Slide Show** tab.

3 Click **Hide Slide**.

A A diagonal line appears through the slide number, indicating that the slide will not appear during the slide show.

Note: To redisplay hidden slide(s), repeat Steps **1** to **3**.

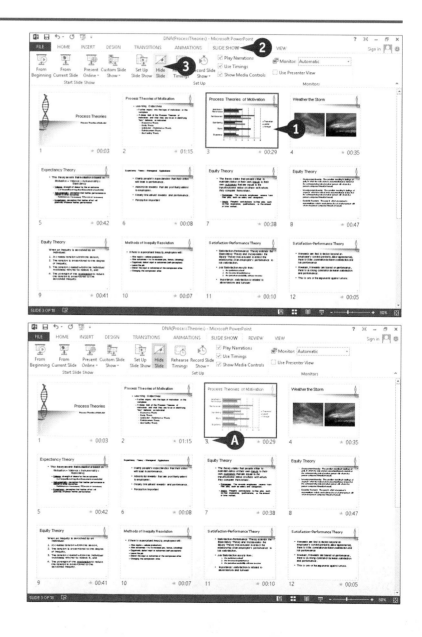

Zoom In the View

In Slide Sorter view, you can view a slide in greater or less detail by changing the zoom level. If you want to view many slides at once, you can select a smaller zoom percentage so that the slides are smaller and more fit in the available space. That approach can help you find a slide more quickly. You can also apply a larger zoom percentage so that you can see fewer slides but in more detail. The appropriate zoom for any particular task can make the task more efficient, thus saving you a lot of time.

Zoom In the View

1 In Slide Sorter view, click the **View** tab.

2 Click **Zoom**.

The Zoom dialog box appears.

3 Double-click the **Percent** text box and enter a number.

Ⓐ You can also click a zoom percentage option.

4 Click **OK**.

Ⓑ You can also click and drag the **Zoom** slider to zoom, or click the **Zoom In** button (➕) or the **Zoom Out** button (➖) at each end of the slider.

PowerPoint displays the slides at the specified zoom level.

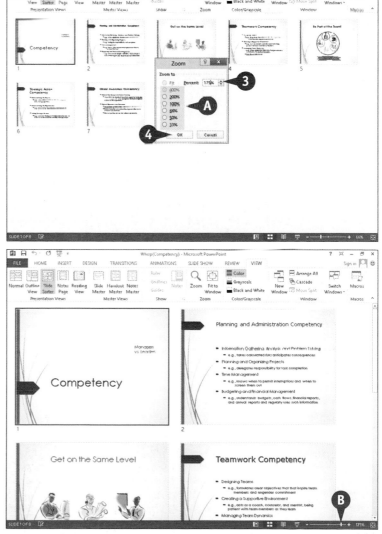

Go to an Individual Slide

When you are working in Slide Sorter view, it is sometimes useful to go to Normal view, where you can view a slide in detail. Sometimes you will see a slide in Slide Sorter view and want to design it. While in Slide Sorter view, you can quickly and easily change to Normal view while keeping the slide selected to see it in detail. Although you can select a slide and then click the Normal view icon, these steps show a faster way to display an individual slide.

Go to an Individual Slide

1 Click the **View** tab.

2 Click **Slide Sorter**.

3 Double-click the slide that you want to see in detail.

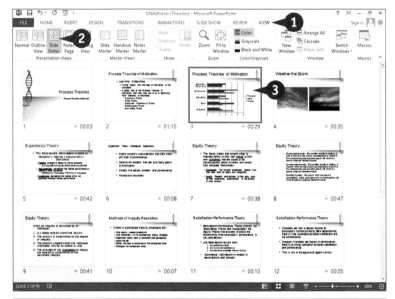

A The slide appears in Normal view.

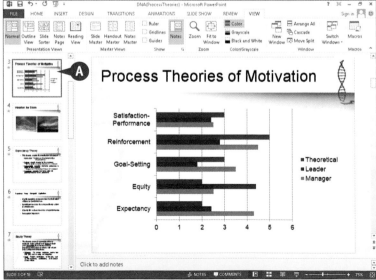

Change Slide Orientation

Typically, slide shows are presented horizontally in the landscape orientation; portrait orientation is vertical, like a business letter. The landscape orientation is made to fit a monitor, widescreen monitor, or projector screen. There are times when you may want your presentation in the portrait orientation — possibly while you print the slide show or to show two slide shows side by side on a screen. You can change the orientation of your presentation, though changing orientation distorts objects on the slides; if you want to show it in the portrait orientation and have it look good, you should change the orientation first, and then design it.

Change Slide Orientation

1 In Slide Sorter view, click the **Design** tab.

2 Click **Slide Size**.

3 Click **Custom Slide Size**.

The Slide Size dialog box appears.

4 Click **Portrait**.

5 Click **OK**.

The scaling dialog box appears.

6 Click **Ensure Fit**.

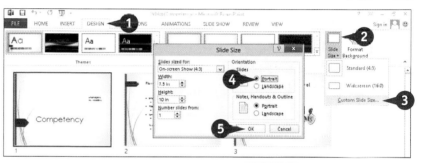

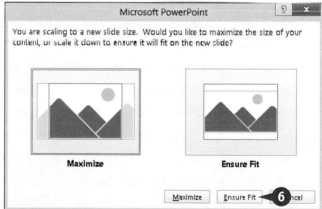

The slides change to the chosen orientation.

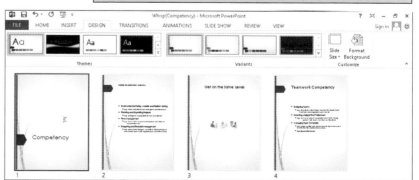

Change Aspect Ratio

You may find yourself presenting a slide show on a variety of screens, such as a widescreen or standard monitor, a notebook monitor, or an LCD or plasma projector. Most of these devices have screens that have one of two aspect ratios: 4:3 (standard) or 16:9 (widescreen). Presentations and templates come in either aspect ratio. You can change the aspect ratio of a presentation so that you can show a slide show on any device and use any template to design a presentation.

Change Aspect Ratio

1 Click the **View** tab.

2 Click **Normal**.

Note: This particular presentation is a 16:9 aspect ratio.

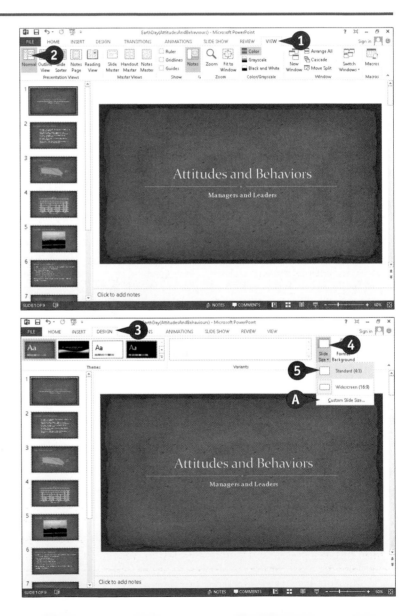

3 Click **Design**.

4 Click **Slide Size**.

5 In the Slide Size menu, click an aspect ratio from the list.

Ⓐ You can also customize an aspect ratio by clicking **Custom Slide Size**.

A sizing dialog box may appear.

6 Click **Maximize** or **Ensure Fit** in the dialog box.

Note: Ensure Fit resizes objects to ensure that they fit on the slide. Maximize does not resize objects, but objects may fall off the edge of the slide as a result.

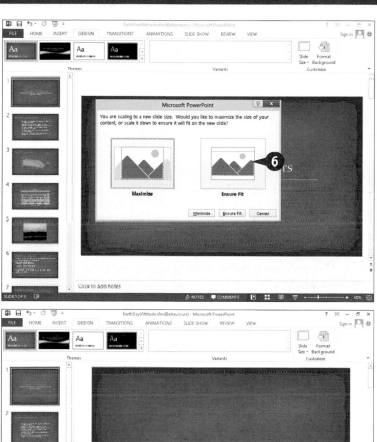

PowerPoint changes the aspect ratio of the presentation.

TIP

The background of my presentation seems a little different after I changed the aspect ratio. Did it change?

Yes, it may have changed — it depends on the circumstances. When you change aspect ratio, AutoFormat may adjust fonts and lines. Changing the aspect ratio in a presentation may skew the slide background and may resize and distort objects. Always inspect your presentation after changing the aspect ratio to see if anything changed. Better still, try to design your presentation in the proper aspect ratio. If you must change the aspect ratio of a template, do it before any design work so that potential distortion only affects the background.

View Slides in Grayscale

There are times when you may want to view your design work in black and white or grayscale. For example, in a presentation with a lot of color in the background, it can be easier to view slide content in grayscale. If you plan to print the slides in grayscale, you may want to switch to grayscale periodically during the design to see how it looks. You can view grayscale slides in Normal, Slide Sorter, or Notes Page view.

Grayscale presents slides in shades of gray. Black and white is extreme because it uses no shading.

View Slides in Grayscale

1 In Normal view, click the **View** tab.

2 Click **Grayscale**.

The presentation appears in grayscale and an additional tab called Grayscale appears.

3 Click the **Grayscale** tab.

4 Click an object in the presentation.

5 Click **Inverse Grayscale**.

Ⓐ The object changes appearance.

6️⃣ Click **Back to Color View**.

The presentation returns to color view.

TIP

Can I print my presentation in grayscale or black and white on a color printer?
Yes. If you use a black-and-white printer, PowerPoint automatically adjusts the presentation to print in grayscale. If you use a color printer, do the following:

1️⃣ Click the **File** tab to go to Backstage view.

2️⃣ Click **Print**.

3️⃣ Click the **Color** down arrow (▼).

4️⃣ Click **Grayscale**.

5️⃣ Click **Print**.

Group Slides into Sections

You may need to present multiple topics in your slide show, calling for a logical separation between topics. For example, you may want to have different themes for morning and afternoon. A presentation on Microsoft Office may need three distinct sections for three different applications, Word, Excel, and PowerPoint. Instead of creating separate presentations, you can easily separate one presentation into sections. The sections exist independently, enabling you to easily apply different themes and color schemes to each section while keeping the sections together in one presentation.

Group Slides into Sections

1 In Slide Sorter view, click the slide that you want to begin your new section.

2 Click the **Home** tab.

3 Click **Section**.

4 Click **Add Section**.

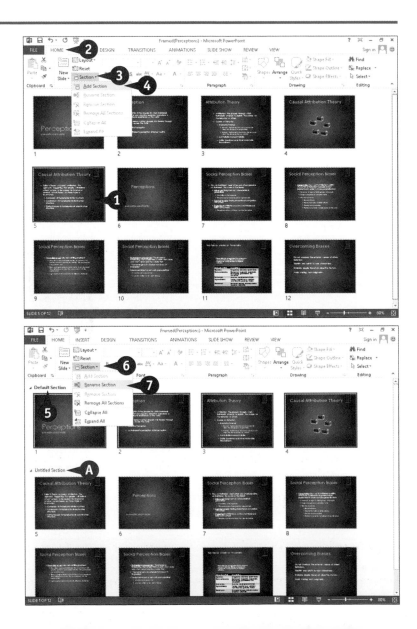

A PowerPoint inserts a section before the slide that you selected.

Note that the beginning part of the presentation becomes a section, too.

5 Click a section you want to rename.

6 Click **Section**.

7 Click **Rename Section**.

The Rename Section dialog
box appears.

8 Type a new name.

9 Click **Rename**.

B PowerPoint renames the
section.

10 Click a **Section**.

11 Click the **Design** tab.

12 Click a variation from the
Variants group.

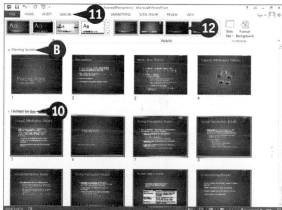

PowerPoint changes the theme
for the section.

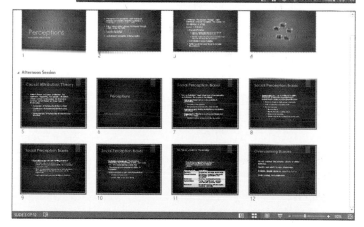

TIP

Can I get rid of a section of my presentation?
Yes. You can remove a section or simply collapse it, depending on your needs.
To remove a section:

1 Click the section.

2 Press Delete.

A To collapse or expand a section, you can click the collapse icon (◢) next
to the section name.

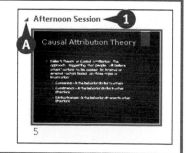

CHAPTER 7

Working with Outlines

Outline view provides the easiest and most convenient way to enter text into your presentation. It helps you organize your thoughts into a simple outline form and hierarchy so that you can focus on the flow of ideas in the presentation. It is a great place to view and make changes to text. If you need to write a paper or report to accompany your presentation, the outline is an excellent resource to write that, too.

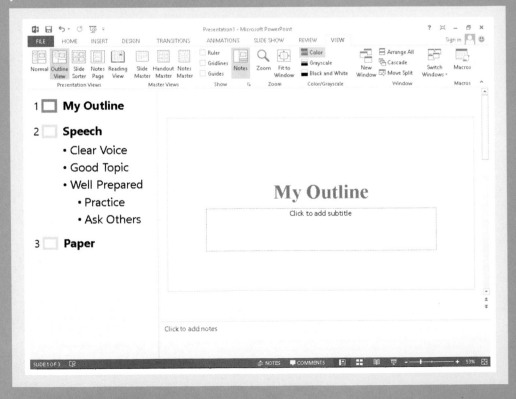

Display Outline View

Outline view is the same as Normal view except the Outline pane replaces the Slides Thumbnail pane. Typing text into a slide in Normal view can be cumbersome — you need to move and manage text and bullets. In Outline view, you simply type text into an outline and PowerPoint adds slides, inserts text into them, and manages bullets. When you finish working with the text, you can switch to Normal view to work on the slide design. You can easily move between Outline view and other views so that you can alternate between typing text and designing the slides.

Display Outline View

1 Click the **View** tab.

2 Click **Outline View**.

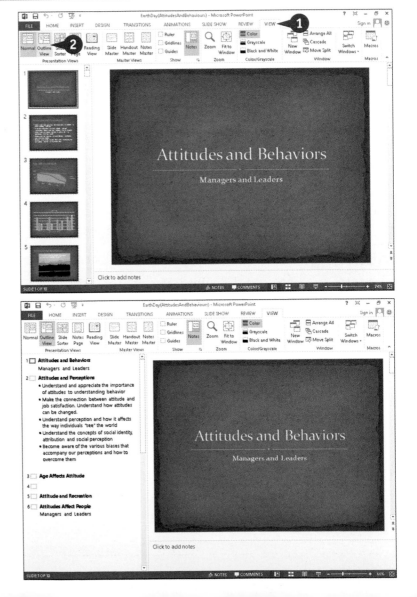

PowerPoint displays Outline view.

Understanding How Outline and Slide Content Relate

You can enter presentation text in Outline view or directly on a slide in Normal view. Typing text into a slide in Normal view can be cumbersome and time consuming — you need to move and manage text and bullets, possibly from slide to slide. In Outline view, you type text in a familiar outline form. To take advantage of Outline view, you must first become familiar with it. You can work more effectively when you understand how the contents of the outline and slides relate to each other.

One Heading, One Slide

Every top-level heading (a heading at level one in the outline) is the title of a slide. When you type text in a title placeholder on a slide, it appears as a level-one heading in the outline. When you type a level-one heading in the outline, PowerPoint adds a slide and the level-one heading appears in the title placeholder on the slide.

Bullet to Bullet

The second level of headings in an outline becomes the bullets in the content placeholder on the corresponding slide. If you have more than one level of bullets in the outline, there will be multiple levels of bullets on the slide, and vice versa. As you type, PowerPoint manages the bullets, but you can change the way they look.

Graphics

Graphics never appear in the outline. You place graphics on slides and you see them in the Slide pane. You can insert graphics in a content placeholder, in a header or footer, or in any available location on the slide. An advantage of Outline view is that graphics do not appear in the outline, so you can concentrate on text.

Special Text

Special text elements include headers, footers, text boxes, tables, charts, and in some cases, WordArt. Many of the graphics have text elements. Text elements such as these are some of the graphics that appear on a slide — they do not appear as part of the outline.

Enter Presentation Content in an Outline

Outline view provides the easiest way to enter text into your presentation. You can build the text for a presentation very quickly with Outline view. You build your outline by typing text and using the Enter and Tab keys, just like any other outline. PowerPoint automatically adds slides for each first-level item in the outline. You can watch the slide develop as you type the text. The first slide in your outline automatically becomes the presentation's Title slide. Additional slides use a Title and Content slide layout automatically, although you can change the layout later.

Enter Presentation Content in an Outline

1 Start a new presentation.

Note: See Chapter 1 to learn how to start a new presentation.

2 Click **View**.

3 Click **Outline View**.

Outline view appears.

4 Click in the Outline pane next to the slide icon (⬜).

5 Type a line of text; the text appears on the slide as you type.

6 Press Enter.

A The insertion point advances to the next line and PowerPoint adds a second slide, a Title and Content slide.

7 Click the **Home** tab.

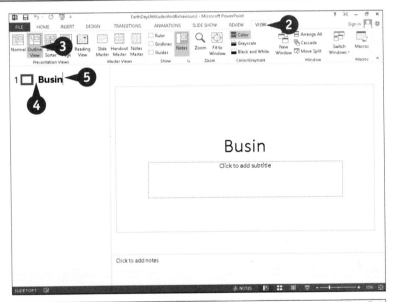

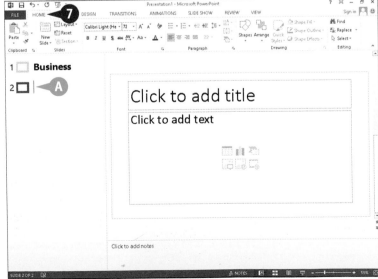

8 Type a second line of text; the text appears on the slide as you type.

9 Press **Enter**.

The insertion point moves to the next line.

10 Press **Tab**.

Ⓑ The insertion point moves one tab to the right, becoming the first bullet on the second slide.

11 Type text for the bullet item.

12 Press **Enter**.

The insertion point moves to the next line.

13 Repeat Steps **11** and **12** to add bullet items as needed.

14 Press **Shift** + **Tab**.

Ⓒ The insertion point moves left, a slide icon appears, and PowerPoint adds a third slide, a Title and Content slide.

TIP

Is there a way to enlarge the Outline pane and make the font bigger to view my outline text?
Yes. Position the mouse pointer (⇱) over the border between the Outline pane and the slide pane until it changes to the mouse splitter (↕). Click and drag the border to the right to enlarge the pane, and click and drag to the left to make it smaller. To increase the font size of the outline, click anywhere in the Outline pane and then click **Zoom** on the View tab. When the Zoom dialog box appears, select a bigger zoom percentage and then click the **OK** button.

Move Slides and Bullet Points in an Outline

As with the content of other types of documents, presentation content evolves. For example, you may review your presentation and decide on a more logical flow for the information. A great advantage of Outline view is the ability to move bullet points easily and text around — even from slide to slide. You can also easily promote and demote bullet points from one level to another. You can even rearrange slides, bullet points, and text in your presentation by dragging and dropping them in the Outline pane.

Move Slides and Bullet Points in an Outline

1 Click the **View** tab.

2 Click **Outline View**.

3 In the Outline pane, click the **Slide** icon (☐) for the slide you want to move.

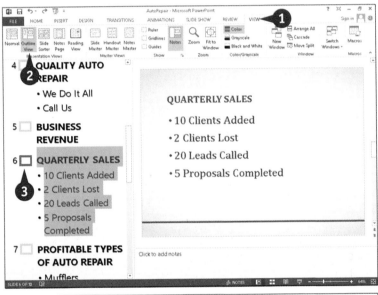

4 Click and drag the **Slide** icon (☐) to the desired position using the horizontal line as a guide.

Note: You can use the **Undo** button (↶) on the Quick Access Toolbar if you make a mistake.

Note: You can also cut, copy, and paste text in the Outline pane.

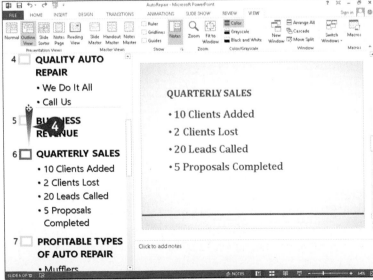

A When you release the mouse button, the slide content moves to where you dragged it.

5 Click the bullet of a bullet point.

6 Click and drag the bullet item to a new location in the bulleted list.

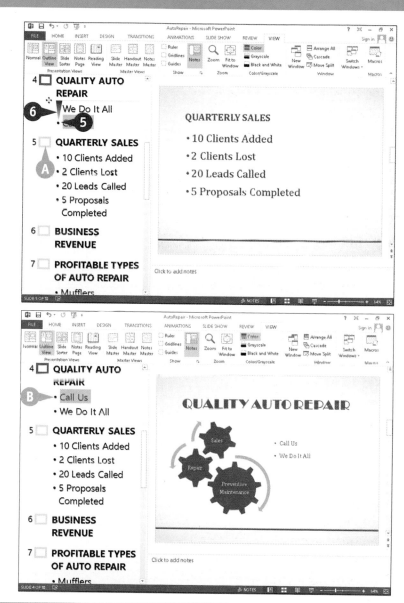

B When you release the mouse button, the bullet item moves to where you dragged it.

Note: You can use this method to move a bullet item from one slide to another.

Note: You can click and drag text to select it and then drag it to another location.

I dragged my slide to another location and now I have more bullet points on the slide. What happened?

You probably dragged the slide to a spot inside another slide. Dragging a slide into a group of bullet points on a second slide breaks the second slide apart and places the bottom bullet points of the second slide on the moved slide.

Are there any other actions I can execute by dragging bullets?

Yes. You can promote and demote bullet points in the outline. Click and drag a bullet left or right until the vertical line representing its outline position reaches the desired outline level. Release the mouse and the bullet point moves.

Promote and Demote Items

As you build and reorganize presentation content, you may need to move bullet points, or possibly slides, in the outline so that they become lower-level bullet points, a method called *demoting*. Conversely, you can move lower-level bullet points to become higher-level bullet points or even slides, which is called *promoting*. Changing the levels of bullet points and slides is cumbersome if you are working on the actual slide. You can save a lot of time and effort using the Outline pane, where you can easily promote and demote items with keystrokes and command button clicks on the ribbon.

Promote and Demote Items

① In Outline View, click the **Home** tab.

Note: See Chapter 2 to learn how to switch views.

② Click anywhere in a bullet point.

③ Click the **Demote** button (
).

Note: Alternatively, you can press `Tab` .

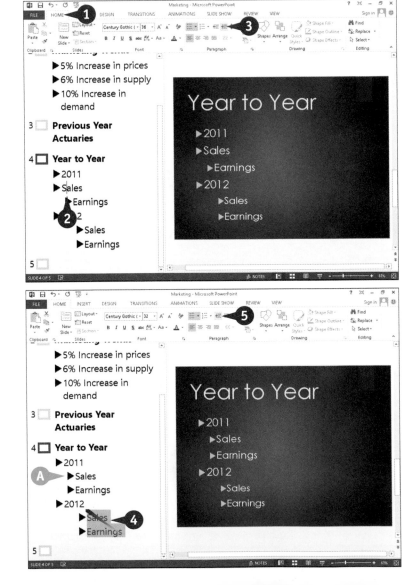

Ⓐ The bullet point moves to the right, down one level in the outline hierarchy.

④ Click and drag across bullet points to select them.

Note: You can click and drag across bullet points at different hierarchy levels to perform this task.

⑤ Click the **Promote** button (
).

Note: Alternatively, you can press `Shift` + `Tab` .

Ⓑ The bullet points move left, up one level in the outline hierarchy.

❻ Click a second level bullet point, one tab to the right of the slide level.

❼ Click the **Promote** button (⬅☰).

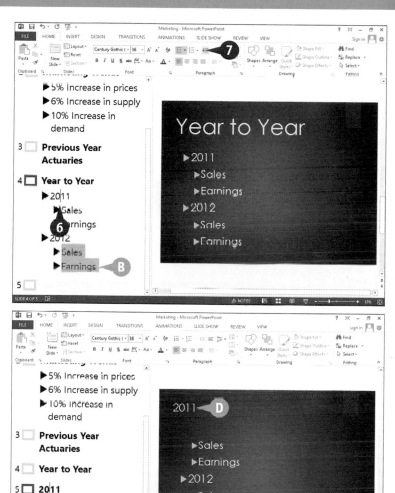

Ⓒ PowerPoint promotes the bullet point to a slide and adds a slide.

Ⓓ The bullet point becomes the title of the new slide.

TIP

Can I promote and demote headings directly on a slide?
Yes. However, you cannot promote or demote a slide title. This is a true advantage of using Outline view. In Normal view, you need to add a slide and then cut and paste bullet points to promote a bullet point to a slide. To change the level of a bullet point on a slide, click the bullet and then click either **Promote** (⬅☰) or **Demote** (☰➡) in the Paragraph group on the Home tab. The change in promotion or demotion occurs both on the slide and in the outline. If you click the bullet point text on the slide, it does not work — you must click the bullet.

Collapse and Expand an Outline

With a lengthy presentation, you can sometimes work more effectively if you collapse an outline so you see only slide titles and expand only certain slides to look at the details on them. Collapsing parts of the outline helps you to easily scroll through the presentation and identify outline items quickly. For example, you may want to collapse the slides that you are finished designing and expand the slides that still need work. You can collapse and expand any part or all of the outline. You can collapse or expand multiple slides. Simply select multiple slides before performing these steps.

Collapse and Expand an Outline

1 Click the **View** tab.

2 Click **Outline View**.

3 Right-click any text within a slide.

The submenu appears.

4 Click **Collapse**.

Ⓐ Click **Collapse All** to collapse all slides in the presentation.

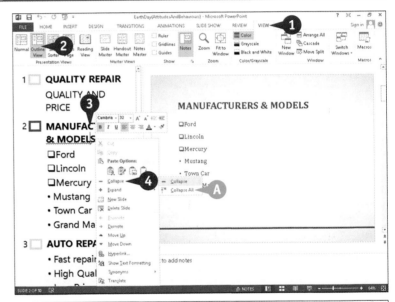

PowerPoint collapses all details and displays a wavy line under the slide title.

5 Right-click a collapsed slide title.

6 Click **Expand**.

Ⓑ Click **Expand All** to expand all slides in the presentation.

The slide details reappear.

Note: You can also double-click the **Slide** icon (▢) to collapse or expand slide details.

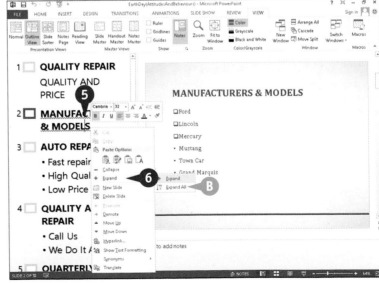

Edit Outline Content

arely does a first draft become a final presentation. You can edit the text in your presentation to make it as professional as possible. You typically want to change your presentation text to polish it, or fix typos and other errors. Many times a second read or proofread produces ideas to improve the wording. For example, maybe you need to update a favorite presentation because it has become outdated. Editing an outline is much like editing text anywhere else in PowerPoint, or in any other application for that matter.

Edit Outline Content

1 Click the **View** tab.

2 Click **Outline View**.

3 Click the point where you want to add or delete text.

4 Type to add text, or press Delete or Backspace to delete the text.

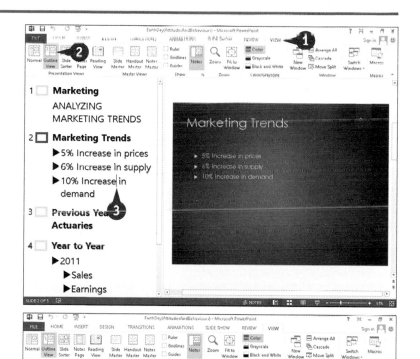

Ⓐ The outline reflects the changes you made.

5 Click the bullet for any bullet point to select the entire bullet point.

Note: You can also click a **Slide** icon (▢) to select an entire slide.

6 Press Delete.

PowerPoint deletes the entire bullet point or slide.

135

Insert Slides from an Outline

If you already have an outline that you want to use as a basis for your presentation, you do not need to retype it in PowerPoint. For example, you may already have an outline that you used to give a speech or to write a paper. To save time, you can import an outline into a new PowerPoint presentation, and then edit and format that content like any other presentation.

PowerPoint imports outlines that are created in Outline view in Microsoft Word. It also imports text file outlines written in text editors such as Notepad.

Insert Slides from an Outline

1 Click the **File** tab to show Backstage view.

2 Click **Open**.

3 Click **Computer**.

4 Click **Browse**.

The Open dialog box appears.

5 Click the down arrow (⌄).

6 Click **All Outlines**.

PowerPoint shows all file types that can hold an outline, such as Word files (.docx), text files (.txt), and rich text files (.rtf).

7 Click the folder that holds the outline file you want to import.

8 Click the outline file.

9 Click **Open**.

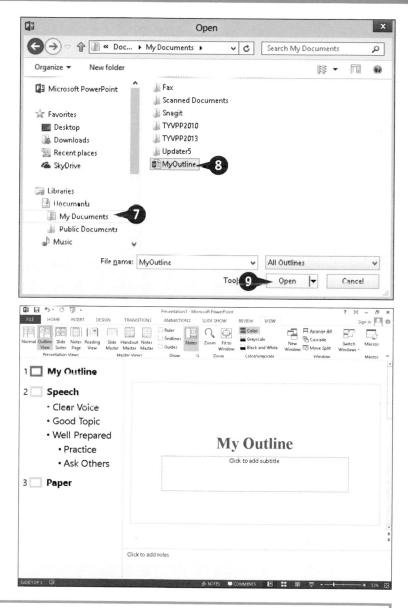

The new presentation appears in Outline view.

All of the content in my Microsoft Word outline became slides. What went wrong?
The outline is not in the proper format. The outline needs to be created with the Outline view in Word, which is very similar to typing an outline in PowerPoint. If you need an outline in both Word and PowerPoint, you can create it in either application and export it to the other application.

How does PowerPoint know where to start each slide?
Each top-level heading in the imported outline becomes the title for a new slide — just like a PowerPoint outline. So, be sure to review the outline before importing it. Make sure each slide title is at the top level in the outline.

CHAPTER 8

Using Themes

You can use the themes that are built into PowerPoint as well as online themes to apply a professional-looking design to your presentation. Although it is possible to design slides by applying slide backgrounds and graphics manually, or by formatting elements on slides or master slides one by one, people most commonly use slide themes to develop their presentations.

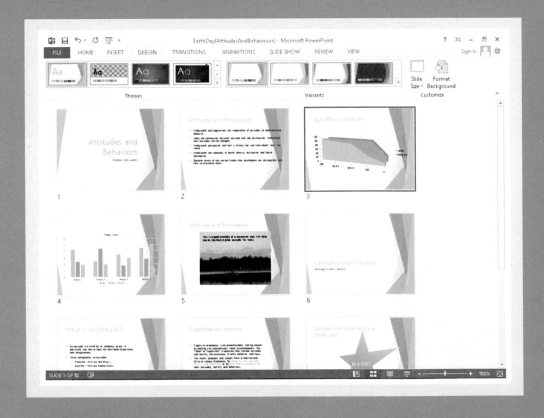

Understanding Themes

A *theme* is the look, color, and graphics that the slides in your presentation have in common. You can use a theme from the PowerPoint program, get one from Microsoft Office Online, or use a theme from an existing presentation. You can also create a blank presentation, and then apply a background and graphics to create your own theme — and then save the theme.

Theme Elements

By default, each new presentation you create uses a blank design theme. When you choose a specific theme, PowerPoint applies a set of colors, fonts, and placeholder positions to the slides. All of these elements vary greatly from theme to theme. The theme can also include a background color, background graphics, and effects for background graphics.

Apply Themes

It is easy to apply a theme to a single slide, a section, or the entire presentation. Generally it is better to use one theme for an entire presentation so that the slides have a consistent look and feel. However, you can also choose to apply a different theme to a particular slide for emphasis.

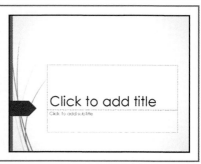

Modify Themes

Although PowerPoint provides professionally designed slide themes, you can tailor existing themes to meet your specific needs. You can change the background, background color, or the color scheme of the entire theme. Once you design a theme you really like, you can save it to the theme gallery to use again.

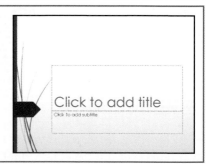

Themes and Masters

Slide masters determine where placeholders and objects appear on each slide layout. Each theme has a master slide for the Title slide, a master slide for the Title and Content Slide, and so on. After you apply a theme, you can modify the masters. Any changes you make to the master slides automatically appear in your presentation slides. You can also change the fonts on the master slides.

140

The Anatomy of a Theme

Themes control several aspects of your slide design. The theme determines the locations of placeholders, the color scheme, the slide background, and any graphics that may be part of the theme. These characteristics vary considerably from theme to theme. For example, the title may be on the top of slides in one theme and on the bottom of slides in another theme. These variations give each theme its own flavor and personality.

Ⓐ Placeholder Position

Placeholder positions vary from theme to theme. Each theme has a set of slide masters that control where placeholders appear on each slide layout.

Ⓑ Graphic Elements

Some themes include graphic elements that are typically part of the background. To avoid accidentally changing them, you can modify them on the slide masters, but not on individual slides.

Ⓒ Color Scheme

Themes control the colors applied to slide text, the background, and objects such as tables, charts, and SmartArt Graphics. You can change colors on individual slides.

Ⓓ Background

Themes specify the background applied to slides. The background might be a solid color, a gradient, or a pattern, and may include graphics.

Ⓔ Effects

Effects give a dimensional appearance to graphics by adding shadows, transparency, 3-D, and more. A theme may apply a particular style of effect to graphics.

Apply a Theme to Selected Slides

You can apply a different theme to a single slide in either Normal or Slide Sorter view. You may want to apply a different theme to a single slide to emphasize the slide or make it stand out. If you apply a different theme to a single slide, you will normally want it to complement the design of the theme used on the other slides in the presentation. As you advance slides, the transition from one theme to another affects your viewers.

Apply a Theme to Selected Slides

1 Click **View**.

2 Click **Slide Sorter**.

3 Select a slide or slides.

Note: To select multiple slides, click the first slide, and then press Ctrl while clicking additional slides.

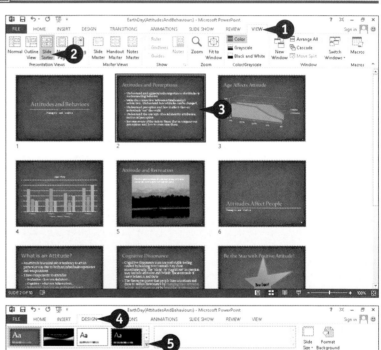

4 Click the **Design** tab.

5 Click the **Themes** down arrow (▼).

The gallery of themes appears.

6 Right-click a theme.

The shortcut menu appears.

7 Click **Apply to Selected Slides**.

A PowerPoint applies the theme to the slide(s) you selected.

TIPS

If I change a few slides to a different theme, can I use the master slide features for those slides?

Yes. When you apply a theme to a presentation, PowerPoint creates a set of master slides for that theme. You get a set of master slides for every theme in your presentation — any of which you can modify. In Chapter 9, you learn about using master slides.

Why does my shortcut menu sometimes have an option called Apply to matching slides?

Apply to matching slides appears on the Themes shortcut menu if you are using more than one theme. You can apply your chosen theme to all slides that have the same theme as the currently selected slide.

Apply a Theme to All Slides

You can apply one theme to all the slides in a presentation. It is important to give your slides a consistent appearance so your presentation looks professional. While the slide layouts may vary, the theme supplies common colors, graphics, and more. This allows you to focus on content rather than design and formatting. You may design a presentation and then decide that the theme you originally chose does not set the proper mood for the presentation. No problem, just apply a different theme for the proper feeling. You can change the theme in either Normal or Slide Sorter view.

Apply a Theme to All Slides

1 In Slide Sorter view, click at least one slide.

2 Click the **Design** tab.

3 Click the **Themes** down arrow ( ).

The gallery of themes appears.

4 Click a theme.

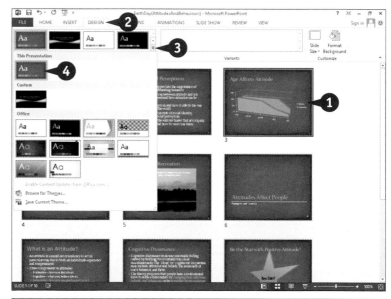

PowerPoint applies the theme to all slides in the presentation.

Note: You can also right-click a thumbnail in the gallery and then click **Apply to All Slides**.

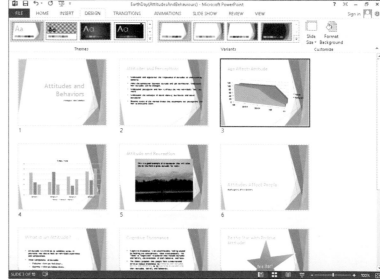

Apply a Theme to a Section

It is common to change topics during a presentation. For example, a person teaching a class about Microsoft Office changes topics when moving from teaching PowerPoint to teaching Excel. If you change topics, you might want to alter the mood to one that is more appropriate for the new topic. You can apply themes to sections of a presentation. Doing so gives each section a look and feel that is consistent with the others, yet makes it obvious that that particular section of your presentation is dedicated to a specific topic. You can change the theme in either Normal or Slide Sorter view.

Apply a Theme to a Section

1 In Slide Sorter view, click a section heading.

2 Click the **Design** tab.

3 Click the **Themes** down arrow ($\equiv$).

The gallery of themes appears.

4 Click a theme.

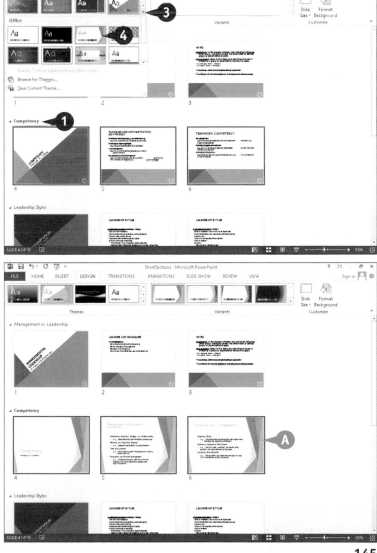

A PowerPoint applies the theme to all slides in the section.

Change Theme Colors

Each theme includes a color scheme. You can add variety or emphasize certain slides by changing the color scheme of only those particular slides. You can also change the color scheme of an entire presentation or a section of a presentation. When you alter the color scheme, the other aspects of the theme, such as placeholder position and background objects, stay the same — only the colors change. You can change the color scheme in Normal view or Slide Sorter view.

Change Theme Colors

1 In Slide Sorter view, click a slide or slides.

Note: To select multiple slides, click the first slide, and then press **Ctrl** while clicking additional slides.

2 Click the **Design** tab.

3 Right-click a color scheme from the Variants gallery.

4 Click **Apply to Selected Slides**.

PowerPoint applies the color scheme to the slides you selected.

5 Select a slide designed with the theme you want to change.

6 Right-click a color scheme from the Variants gallery.

7 Click **Apply to Matching Slides**.

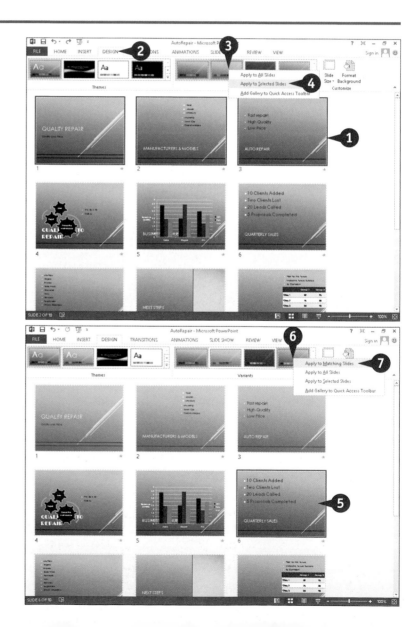

146

PowerPoint applies the color scheme to all slides whose theme matches the selected slide.

8 Right-click a color scheme from the Variants gallery.

9 Click **Apply to All Slides**.

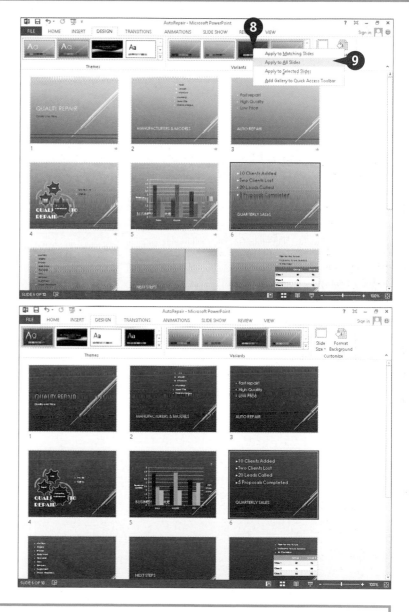

PowerPoint applies the selected color scheme to all slides in the presentation.

Is changing the background color of the theme different than changing the color scheme of the theme?
Yes. When you change the color scheme, it changes the colors of the background plus all of the geometric shapes on the slide, including charts and tables; when you format the background and change its color, it changes only the background and not the geometric shapes. Objects such as pictures and clip art are not affected by either type of change. You can change the background and foreground of objects such as clip art and pictures by formatting them. Some backgrounds are complicated, and changing the color of a complicated background produces a similar effect to changing the color scheme.

Modify the Background

A theme applies a background on which all slide elements sit. You can make the background a color or plain white, or you can even use a texture or digital picture as a background. For example, you can use a digital photo of a new product as a slide background for a presentation introducing the product. You can change the background for one slide, for a theme, or throughout the presentation and you can do this in Normal or Slide Sorter view. Be careful with your choice of background — a complicated background can make a presentation hard to read or distracting.

Modify the Background

1 Select the slide(s) you want to modify in Slide Sorter view.

Note: To select multiple slides, click the first slide, and then press **Ctrl** while clicking additional slides.

2 Click the **Design** tab.

3 Click **Format Background**.

The Format Background pane appears.

4 Click the **Fill** icon ( ).

5 Click **Solid fill** (○ changes to ◉).

6 Click the **Color** button ( ).

7 Click a color.

Ⓐ You can click **Apply to All** to apply the color to all slides.

PowerPoint applies the background color to the selected slides.

8 Click **Gradient fill** (○ changes to ◉).

PowerPoint applies a preset gradient to the background.

B You can adjust gradient options to change the direction and gradient type.

C You fine-tune the gradient by adjusting its characteristics, such as brightness and transparency.

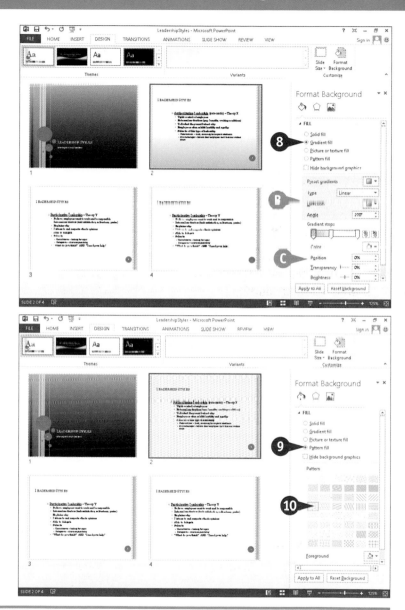

9 Click **Pattern fill** (○ changes to ◉).

10 Click a pattern from the gallery.

PowerPoint applies the background pattern to the selected slides.

In PowerPoint 2010 I could change the font scheme. Can I still do that?

No, you can no longer change the font scheme as part of the theme. In past PowerPoint versions, you could change the font scheme in the theme or the master slides — both accomplished the same result. In PowerPoint 2013, you can only change the font scheme in the master slides.

Why does PowerPoint give me a pattern as soon as I click the Pattern fill option?

PowerPoint applies a preset pattern when you click the **Pattern fill** option. You can either select a different pattern version, or you can click the **Solid fill** option to get rid of the pattern.

Apply a Texture or Picture Background

If you really want to make a slide more dramatic, you can push design limits by using either a texture or a digital picture as a background. For example, you can use a digital photo of a landscape and sunrise for a slide introducing a new idea. Typically, you would not do this for an entire set of slides because a complicated background makes a slide difficult to read and can be hard on the audience's eyes. You can add a picture to the background of a slide in either Slide Sorter or Normal view.

Apply a Texture or Picture Background

1 Select the slide(s) to which you want to add a background in Slide Sorter view.

Note: To select multiple slides, click the first slide, and then press Ctrl while clicking additional slides.

2 Click the **Design** tab.

3 Click **Format Background**.

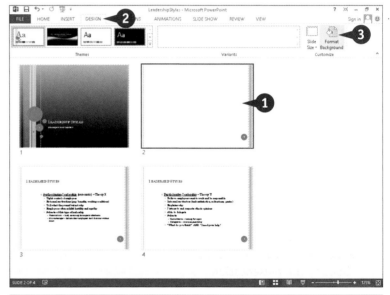

The Format Background pane appears.

4 Click the **Fill** icon (⬧).

5 Click **Picture or texture fill** (○ changes to ◉).

The slide fills with a preset texture.

Ⓐ Click the **Texture** button (⬚▾) to apply a texture to the background.

6 Click **File**.

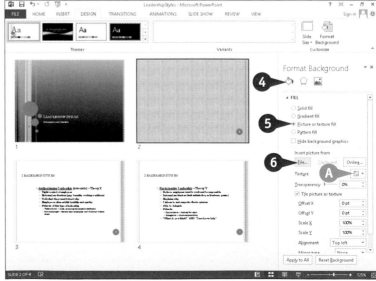

The Insert Picture dialog box appears.

7 Click the folder that contains the picture file you want to insert.

8 Click the picture file.

9 Click **Insert**.

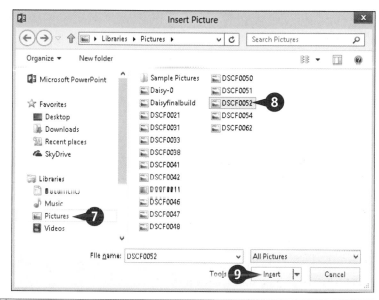

The Insert Picture dialog box closes and the picture becomes the background.

10 Click the **Picture** icon (![icon]) to apply color corrections to the picture.

B You can click **Apply to All** to apply the background to all slides in the presentation.

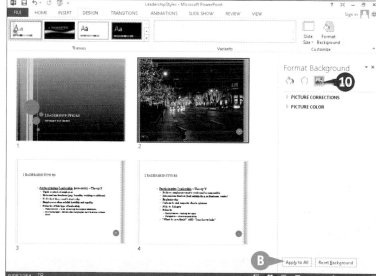

TIP

How can I remove a texture or picture from the background?
With the Format Background pane open, follow these steps:

1 Click the **Fill** icon (![icon]).

2 Click **Solid fill** (○ changes to ◉).

3 Click the **Color** button (![icon]).

4 Click **Automatic**.

PowerPoint removes the background.

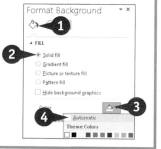

Save Your Own Theme

If you spent a lot of time creating your own theme, you may want to use it again. For example, say you designed a theme from scratch or modified an existing theme, where you applied a color scheme and background that really works, and possibly some graphics. If you do not want to do all this work again, you can save the results as a theme. This enables you to quickly apply that combination of color, background, and graphics to other presentations.

Save Your Own Theme

1 Click the **Design** tab.

2 Click the **Themes** down arrow ( ).

The gallery of themes appears.

A If you save your theme in the PowerPoint theme default folder, it will appear under Custom.

3 Click **Save Current Theme**.

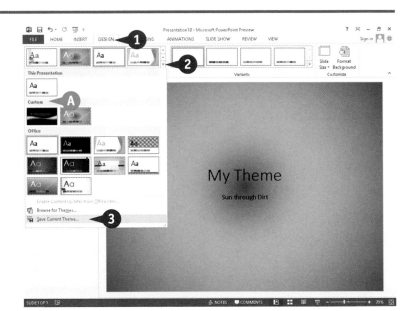

The Save Current Theme dialog box appears.

4 Type a filename.

B This is the default folder location for themes.

Note: Do not change the folder location. Your themes appear in the gallery of themes because they are in this folder location.

5 Click **Save**.

PowerPoint saves the theme and adds it to the Custom section of the gallery.

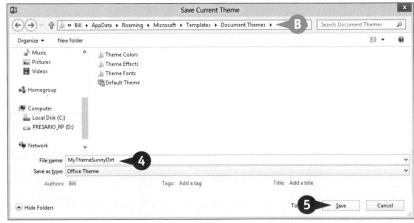

Make a Theme the Default for New Presentations

By default, a new presentation has a blank background and uses the Calibri font in varying sizes and weights for the various placeholders. If you have a theme that you use often, you can make that theme the default for new presentations so it is automatically applied to future blank presentations. This gives you a fast start in designing a new presentation. If the default theme is not right for any particular presentation, you can always change it to one you prefer.

Make a Theme the Default for New Presentations

1 Click the **Design** tab.

2 Click the **Themes** down arrow (▼).

The gallery of themes appears.

3 Right-click the theme you want to set as the default.

4 Click **Set as Default Theme**.

The theme immediately becomes the default theme. Any blank presentation you create uses that theme.

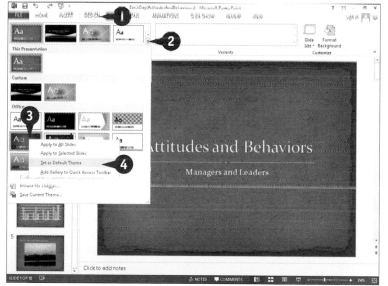

5 Click the **File** tab to show Backstage view.

6 Click **New**.

A The selected theme appears as the default theme.

Save a Template

A *template* is a boilerplate presentation that you use repeatedly but change certain items each time you use it. It includes a presentation design plus reusable content such as slides that you would often use in a particular type of presentation. For example, you may have a template presentation for selling to a purchasing group's clients — content about the purchasing group does not change from client to client, so you would have slides about them in the template along with slides that you would tailor to each client. You can save a lot of time by using templates for repeatable presentations.

Save a Template

1 Click the **File** tab to show Backstage view.

2 Click **Save As**.

3 Click **Computer**.

4 Click **Browse**.

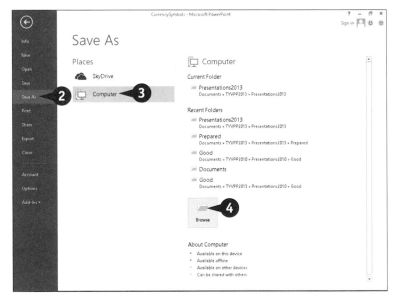

The Save As dialog box appears.

5 Click the **Save as type** down arrow (⌄).

6 Click **PowerPoint Template**.

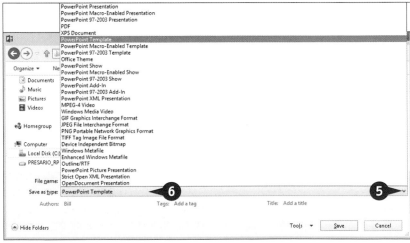

Ⓐ This is the default folder location for themes and templates.

Note: It is best not to change this folder location. Your templates appear in the templates gallery because they are in this folder location, which is the same as the theme folder location.

⑦ Type a filename.

⑧ Click **Save**.

PowerPoint saves the presentation as a template.

⑨ Click the **File** tab to show Backstage view.

⑩ Click **New**.

⑪ Click **Custom**.

Ⓑ Your template appears in the Custom template gallery.

Note: You may need to close and open PowerPoint for the template to appear in the Custom template list.

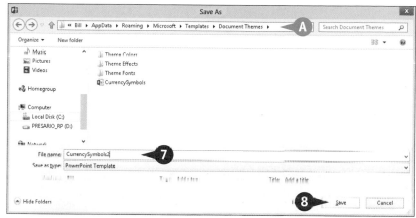

What is the difference between using a template and using a regular presentation as a template?
A PowerPoint presentation has a .pptx file extension and a template has a .potx file extension. If a template (.potx) is in the Template folder, it appears in the template list — you simply click it and PowerPoint creates a new presentation from a copy of the template. If you double-click a presentation (.pptx) in Windows Explorer or on your Desktop, it opens. If you double-click a template (.potx), it creates and opens a copy of itself. The original is protected from unintentional changes because it does not open. To change a template (.potx), you must open it through the Open dialog box.

CHAPTER 9

Using Masters

Masters enable you to make global settings for your slides, such as inserting your company logo or a page number on every slide. When you change a master, all slides based on that master also change.

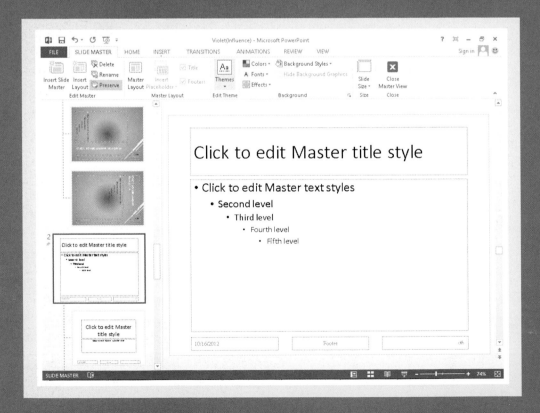

Understanding Masters

PowerPoint offers three master views: the *Slide Master*, which determines how presentation slides look; the *Handout Master*, which controls how a printed version of your presentation looks; and the *Notes Master*, which dictates how a printout of your notes looks. The three master views enable you to set up the basic structure for each slide layout, plus the notes and printed handouts. This saves time because you do not need to design each presentation slide from scratch. For example, the Title and Content slide layout is designed once in the Slide Master view, but you can use it over and over again.

Work with Three Kinds of Masters

The *Master Slides* consist of a set of slides called the *Layout Masters* — there is one Layout Master for each slide layout that you will use to build your presentation. The Master Slides also include a slide called the *Slide Master*, which controls the theme and formatting for the Layout Masters. The Handout Master controls the look and layout of the printed handouts when you print the slides of your presentation. The Notes Master controls how the printout of your presentation notes looks.

Using Masters to Make Global Changes

Any change, including formatting, that you make to a Layout Master is applied to its corresponding presentation slides. For example, if you redesign the Layout Master that controls the Title and Content layout by moving the title from the top of the page to the bottom, every slide in the presentation using the Title and Content layout reflects that change. This saves you time and gives your presentation a consistent look and feel. If you change the formatting of an element on the Slide Master, PowerPoint changes that element on all Layout Masters and all presentation slides.

How Masters Relate to the Theme

Masters are based on themes. When you apply a theme to your presentation, PowerPoint automatically creates a set of Master Slides with that theme. You can alter the theme of your Master Slides and then save it as a new theme. If you apply more than one theme to your presentation, you will have multiple sets of Master Slides — one for each theme. For example, if you have three themes, you will have three Title and Content Layout Masters, one for each theme. You can change the design of the Layout Master of the Title and Content slide in one theme without affecting the Title and Content slides in the other two themes.

Overriding Master Settings

When you make changes to individual presentation slides, those changes take precedence over settings on the corresponding Layout Master or the Slide Master. For example, if you change the font color of the title placeholder of a Title and Content presentation slide in Normal view, a change to the title placeholder font color of the Title and Content Layout Master does not affect it. The change on the individual presentation slide takes precedence. If you place a graphic on a Layout Master, you can omit it from the background of an individual presentation slide in Normal view.

Understanding Slide Master Elements

You can use the Master Slides to create global design settings for your slides. The Slide Master and Layout Masters contain placeholders where you can format text. They also contain various placeholders for footer information, slide numbers, and a date. Any change to a Layout Master is applied to any presentation slide that has its corresponding layout. When you make a formatting change to a placeholder on the Slide Master, PowerPoint applies that change to any corresponding placeholder anywhere in the presentation. One change can affect many slides, but only for the theme associated with the Master Slide you are changing.

Ⓐ Slide Master

The Slide Master is connected to its related Layout Masters with a dotted line. The Slide Thumbnails pane shows one set of Master Slides for each theme.

Ⓑ Layout Masters

Layout Masters represent the various slide layouts that you can insert into a presentation, such as the Title and Content layouts. Changes on a Layout Master affect only those presentation slides with the layout of that particular master.

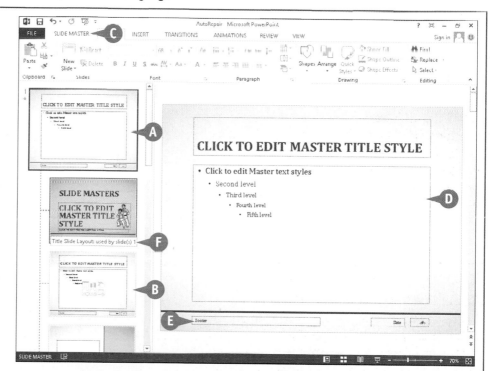

Ⓒ Slide Master Tab

Use the Slide Master tab to change Master Slides — you can design the background of masters, change or insert placeholders, and change theme colors and font schemes.

Ⓓ Placeholders

You can format an entire placeholder, some of its text, or each bullet point individually by selecting a particular bullet point before formatting.

Ⓔ Footer, Date, and Slide Numbers

The Date placeholder positions the date on slides; the Page (#) placeholder provides page numbers on slides; the Footer placeholder provides a footer on the slides.

Ⓕ Dependency on a Master Design

Position the mouse pointer (⌖) over any slide in the Slide Master view and a ScreenTip shows you which presentation slides use that Layout Master design.

Open and Close Slide Master View

You work with the Slide Master and Layout Masters in Slide Master view. Opening Slide Master view automatically displays the Slide Master tab for working with the set of Master Slides. This tab was created to help you design the Master Slides, but you can also use the other tabs on the ribbon. After you make changes to the Master Slides and close Slide Master view, PowerPoint redisplays whatever view you had open previously — Normal view, Slide Sorter view, or Notes Page view. Global changes to presentation slides due to changes in Master Slides are reflected there.

Open and Close Slide Master View

1 Click the **View** tab.

2 Click **Slide Master**.

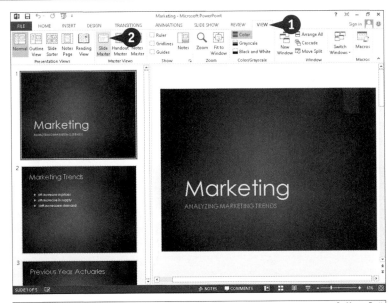

Slide Master view and the Slide Master tab appear.

3 Click the **Slide Master** tab.

4 Click **Close Master View**.

Slide Master view closes and PowerPoint restores the previous presentation design view.

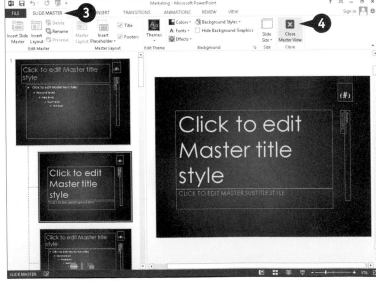

The Layout Masters contain placeholders for the slide title, text or graphic content, date, footer, and slide numbers. If you are not using a particular placeholder, you can remove it from the Layout Masters.

Deleting a placeholder from the Slide Master at the top of the Slides Thumbnail pane does not delete it from the Layout Masters, though formatting changes that you make to placeholders on the Slide Master do affect the formatting of associated presentation slides.

Remove a Placeholder

1 Display Slide Master view.

Note: To display Slide Master view, see the section, "Open and Close Slide Master View."

2 Click the Layout Master that contains the placeholder you want to remove.

3 Click the border of the placeholder to select it.

4 Press Delete.

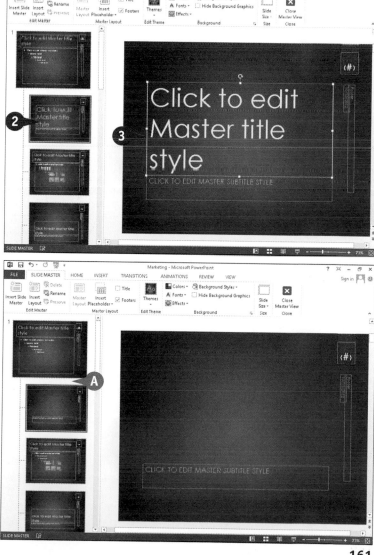

A PowerPoint deletes the placeholder.

Note: If you delete a placeholder from a Layout Master, PowerPoint does not delete the placeholder from *existing* presentation slides. Slides inserted in the presentation *after* you make this deletion from the Layout Master will not contain the placeholder.

Insert a Placeholder

Sometimes the slide layouts that are available to you are not quite right. You may need to add a placeholder to a Layout Master to create a slide layout that suits your needs. You can insert a new placeholder in any Layout Master in Slide Master view. This saves time because you do not have to add the placeholder to every presentation slide that needs one. You can insert placeholders for text or content, plus other types of placeholders like picture or chart placeholders. You can also resize, reposition, or reformat any placeholder at any time.

Insert a Placeholder

1 Display Slide Master view.

Note: To display Slide Master view, see the section, "Open and Close Slide Master View."

2 Click a Layout Master.

3 Click the **Insert Placeholder** down arrow (▼).

4 Click a placeholder type.

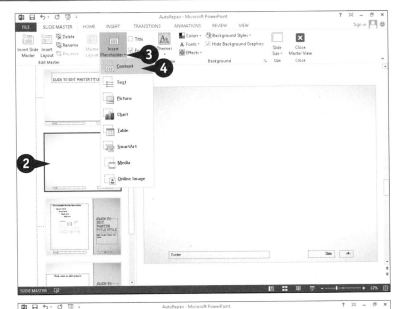

The crosshair pointer (+) appears.

5 Click where you want the upper-left corner of the placeholder and drag across the slide to where you want the lower-right corner of the placeholder.

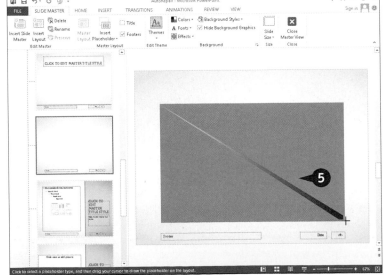

A When you release the mouse button, the placeholder appears.

6 With the new placeholder still selected, click the **Home** tab.

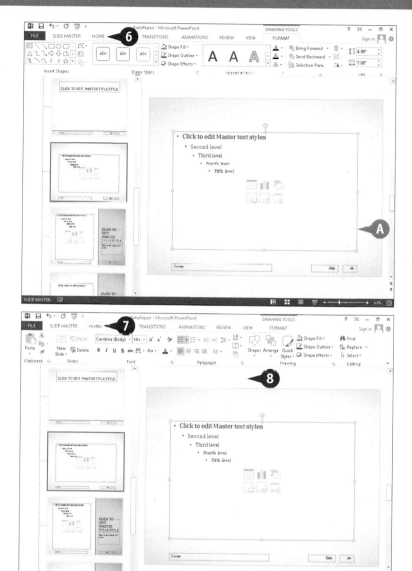

7 Use the tools on the Home tab to format the placeholder.

8 Click outside the placeholder when finished.

TIP

Is there an easy way to reinstate a placeholder that I deleted from the Slide Master?
Yes. Click the Slide Master thumbnail in Slide Master view. The Slide Master is the top slide in the Slide Thumbnails pane — it is the first slide in the set of Master Slides. Click the **Master Layout** button of the Master Layout group on the Slide Master tab. In the Master Layout dialog box, click the check box for the deleted placeholder (☐ changes to ☑) and then click **OK**. PowerPoint reinstates the placeholder. You may notice that you can also control the footer, date, and slide number placeholders in the dialog box.

Add a Footer

The Slide Masters have placeholders for footers that you can use to show information such as your company name on slides. You can move the footer anywhere on the Master Slide. To save time, you can add a footer to a single Master Slide instead of individual presentation slides.

If you add a footer to the Slide Master, it appears on all slides. If you add a footer to a Layout Master, it appears only on presentation slides with that layout. You can also use footers in the Handout Master and Notes Master.

Add a Footer

1. Display Slide Master view.

Note: To display Slide Master view, see the section, "Open and Close Slide Master View."

2. Click the Slide Master or one of the Layout Masters.

3. Click the **Insert** tab.

4. Click **Header & Footer**.

The Header and Footer dialog box appears.

5. Click **Footer** (☐ changes to ☑).

6. Type your information in the text box.

7. Click **Apply**.

Ⓐ You can click **Apply to All** to add the footer to the entire set of Master Slides.

Note: Adding the footer to the entire set of Master Slides also applies the footer to all presentation slides.

Ⓑ The footer appears on the Layout Master and any presentation slides that share its layout.

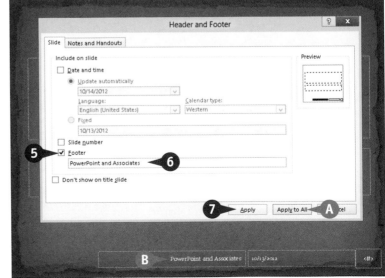

Add a Date

The set of Slide Masters includes a placeholder for a date. You can add a particular date or one that shows the computer's system date. You can move the date anywhere on the Master Slide. To save time, you can add the date to a single Master Slide instead of individual presentation slides.

If you add the date to the Slide Master, it appears on all slides. If you add the date to a Layout Master, it appears only on presentation slides with that layout. You can also use dates in the Handout Master and Notes Master.

Add a Date

1 Display Slide Master view.

Note: To display Slide Master view, see the section, "Open and Close Slide Master View."

2 Click the Slide Master or one of the Layout Masters.

3 Click the **Insert** tab.

4 Click **Header & Footer**.

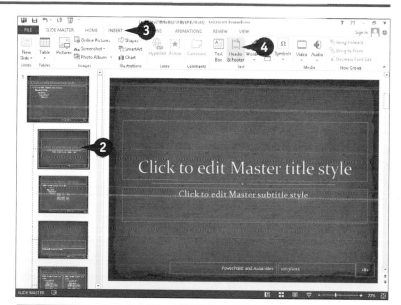

The Header and Footer dialog box appears.

5 Click **Date and time** (☐ changes to ☑).

6 Click the **Update automatically** option (○ changes to ●).

A You can change the format of the date by clicking the down arrow (▾) and selecting a format from the list.

7 Click **Apply**.

B You can click **Apply to All** to add the date to all presentation slides.

C The date appears on the selected slides.

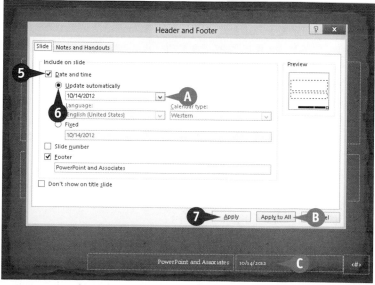

Set Up Slide Numbers

You can have PowerPoint automatically number the presentation slides with the option to not include a slide number on the title slide. You can reposition the slide number placeholder anywhere on the Slide Master or Layout Masters. To save time, you can add the slide number to a single Master Slide instead of numbering presentation slides individually.

You can set up slide numbers on the Slide Master, which affects all slides; Layout Masters, which affect only slides with corresponding layouts; or particular presentation slides in Normal view.

Set Up Slide Numbers

1 Display Slide Master view.

Note: To display Slide Master view, see the section, "Open and Close Slide Master View."

2 Click the Slide Master or one of the Layout Masters.

3 Click the **Insert** tab.

4 Click **Header & Footer**.

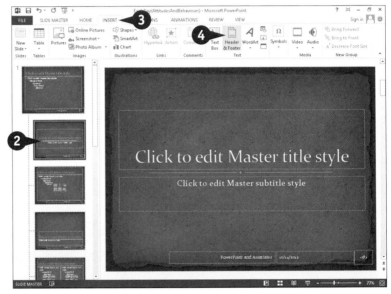

The Header and Footer dialog box appears.

5 Click the **Slide Number** option (☐ changes to ☑).

6 Click the **Don't show on title slide** option (☐ changes to ☑).

7 Click **Apply to All**.

Ⓐ You can click **Apply** to apply slide numbers only to selected slides.

Slide numbers appear on all presentation slides except the title slide.

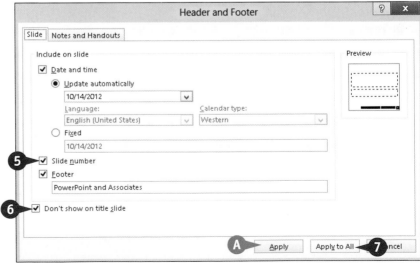

Insert a Graphic in Slide Master View

You can use Slide Master view to insert a graphic or picture that appears on every slide. For example, your organization or company might want its logo on all slides for professionalism and consistency. You can place a graphic or picture on every slide of your presentation by inserting a single graphic in the Slide Master.

If you insert a graphic on the Slide Master, it appears on all slides. If you insert a graphic on a Layout Master, it appears only on presentation slides with that layout.

Insert a Graphic in Slide Master View

1 Display Slide Master view.

Note: To display Slide Master view, see the section, "Open and Close Slide Master View."

2 Click the **Slide Master.**

3 Click the **Insert** tab.

4 Click **Pictures**.

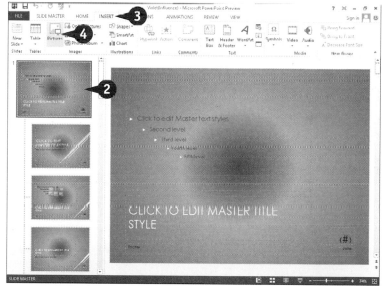

The Insert Picture dialog box appears.

5 Click the folder that contains the image file you want to insert.

6 Click the image file.

7 Click **Insert**.

Ⓐ The dialog box closes and the image appears on the Slide Master, where you can move and resize it as needed. It also appears on all slides.

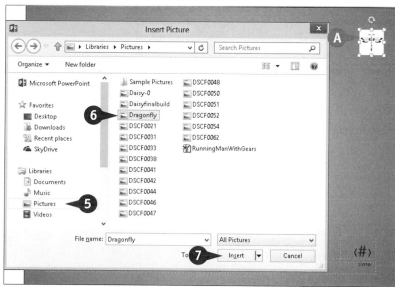

Work with Multiple Masters

You may decide to use a few different looks in your presentation. For example, you may have a theme for your morning session and one for the afternoon session of an all-day presentation. You may decide to use different themes for visual differentiation between sections, yet you want consistency for the slides within each section. When you apply a theme to your presentation, PowerPoint automatically creates a set of Master Slides with that theme. If you apply more than one theme to your presentation, you then have multiple sets of Master Slides — one for each theme.

Occurrence of Multiple Masters

When you apply more than one theme within a single presentation, PowerPoint creates a set of Master Slides for each theme. Each set of Master Slides has a Slide Master, plus one Layout Master for each slide layout that you see in the slide gallery, which you see when you insert a slide. Masters are based on themes, so you cannot switch the theme of a set of Master Slides, though you can create a new blank set of Master Slides and design it from scratch. This enables you to save the theme so you can use it later.

Themes with Multiple Masters

If you use multiple themes (and therefore multiple masters), make sure the themes are complementary. You can do this by selecting slide designs with similar color themes and fonts, plus graphics and backgrounds that work well together. Although you can, you would not typically mix and match themes throughout your presentation; you should apply a theme to a particular section. You can learn how to create sections in a presentation in Chapter 6. When you have sections in your presentation, PowerPoint applies a change in theme to the selected section, not the entire presentation.

Multiple Masters and Slides

If your presentation has multiple masters, you can apply the different master designs to presentation slides by layout and theme. When you insert a slide, you find each theme in the slide gallery. Grouped within each theme, you find the various slide layouts — one for each Layout Master in the Master Slides. For example, if you use three themes in your presentation, you have three Title and Content Layout Masters, one for each theme and all independent of each other. If you change the Title and Content Layout Master of one theme, it does not affect the Title and Content Layout Masters of the other themes.

Masters are Independent

If you change the Layout Master of one set of Master Slides, this change does not affect the same layout on another set of Master Slides. Changes to your Layout Masters are automatically applied and only appear on corresponding presentation slides — those changes only affect the presentation slides with that particular slide layout and theme combination. This means you can change a slide layout for any particular theme without affecting any other Layout Masters with the same layout, but a different theme. To make a universal change for a particular slide layout, you must change each Layout Master for that slide layout in each set of Master Slides.

Insert a New Blank Master

If you cannot find a presentation template that you like, or you need a very specific and unique look, you can create your own set of Master Slides with its own theme. You can insert a blank set of Master Slides and customize it in Slide Master view. You can then format the text in placeholders, change the background, add graphics, and so on. Chapter 4 tells you how to format text, and Chapter 10 provides information on working with graphics. By changing various elements, you can create a unique master design.

Insert a New Blank Master

1 Display Slide Master view.

Note: To display Slide Master view, see the section, "Open and Close Slide Master View."

2 Click **Insert Slide Master**.

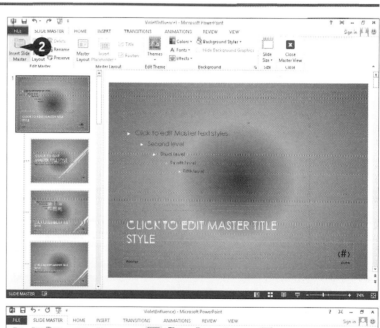

A new set of Master Slides appears.

A PowerPoint numbers each master.

B You can apply an existing theme to the new set of Master Slides by clicking the **Themes** button and selecting a theme from the gallery.

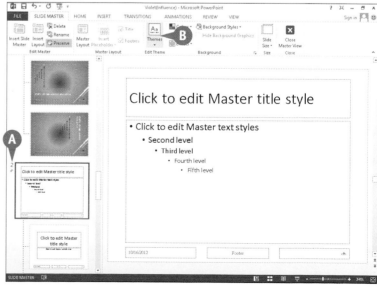

Preserve Master Slides

When you preserve a set of Master Slides, this means that it will not automatically be deleted from a presentation. If you do not preserve it, PowerPoint removes a set of Master Slides if you delete all of the presentation slides that use it. PowerPoint automatically preserves all Master Slides. If a set of Master Slides is not preserved, you can preserve it to avoid its automatic removal. That way, you can use it for future presentation slides. You can also unpreserve a set of Master Slides. You can manually delete a set of Master Slides in Slide Master view even if it is preserved.

Preserve Master Slides

1 Display Slide Master view.

Note: To display Slide Master view, see the section, "Open and Close Slide Master View."

2 Click the Slide Master you want to preserve.

Note: You must click a Slide Master, not a Layout Master.

3 Click **Preserve**.

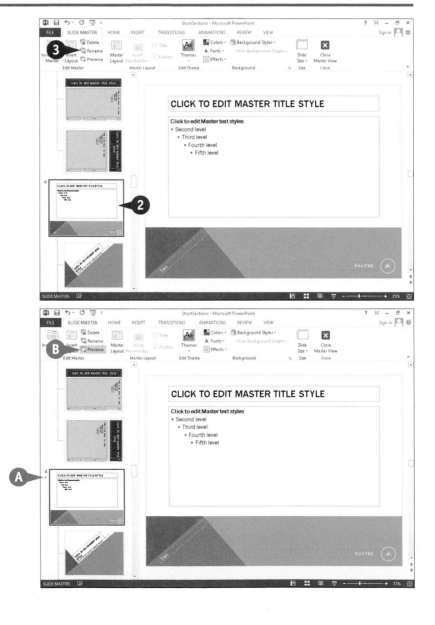

A PowerPoint preserves the master and a Preserve icon (✸) appears on the Slide Master thumbnail.

B The Preserve toggle button becomes highlighted.

Note: To reverse the process, perform Steps **1** to **3** again so the Preserve button is no longer highlighted.

Rename Master Slides

If you insert a blank set of Master Slides, PowerPoint automatically gives it a default name, but you can apply a more descriptive name. For example, if you designed a set of Master Slides with colorful, geometric shapes, you might rename it Deco so the name is easy to remember when you want to refer to it. Giving the Master Slides your own descriptive name makes it easier to select the correct Master Slides when you apply a layout to a slide.

Rename Master Slides

1 Display Slide Master view.

Note: To display Slide Master view, see the section, "Open and Close Slide Master View."

2 Click the Slide Master you want to rename.

Note: You must click a Slide Master, not a Layout Master.

3 Click **Rename**.

The Rename Layout dialog box appears.

4 Type a name.

5 Click **Rename**.

The dialog box closes, and PowerPoint renames the Master Slides.

A You can position the mouse pointer (⟑) over the Slide Master thumbnail to see a ScreenTip with the new name.

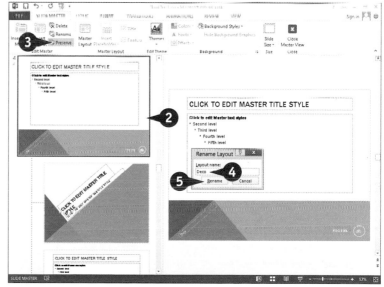

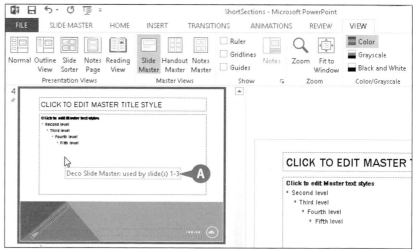

Work with the Notes Master

Changes in the Notes Master affect the Notes Page view and how the Notes Pages print. Notes Page view shows what you will see when you print Notes Pages in Backstage view. The Notes Master has a placeholder for the slide and for the Notes area, as well as placeholders for the header, footer, date, and slide number.

You can modify the format of Notes text, move placeholders around, delete placeholders, and enter headers and footers. See Chapter 14 for information about printing notes.

Work with the Notes Master

1 Click the **View** tab.

2 Click **Notes Master**.

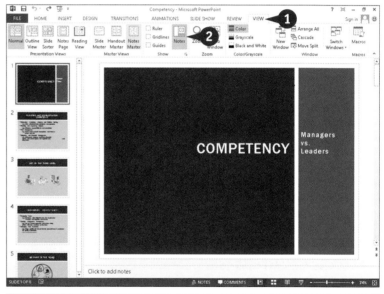

The Notes Master view appears and the Notes Master tab appears on the ribbon.

3 Click any placeholder border and then drag the placeholder to another location.

4 Click any placeholder border and resize it by clicking and dragging one of the handles.

Ⓐ You can click options to add (☑) or remove (☐) placeholders.

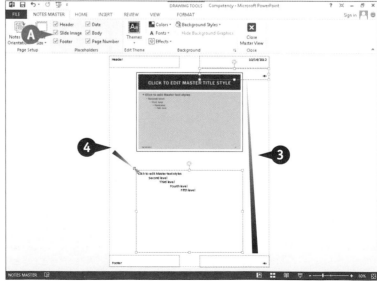

This example resizes the Notes text placeholder, and moves the page number placeholder to the bottom.

5 Click any placeholder border to select it.

6 Click the **Home** tab.

7 Click the **Italic** button (*I*).

8 Type **30** into the **Font Size** text box.

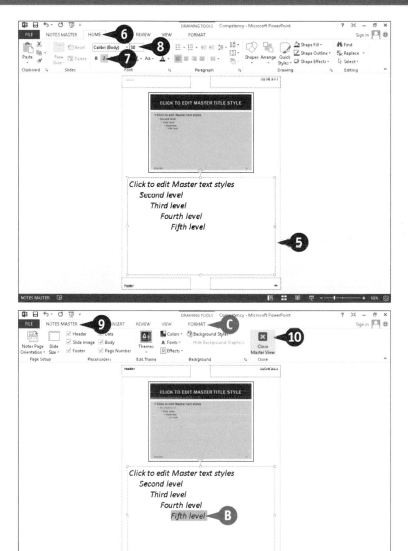

Ⓑ You can select a bullet point to format an individual bullet.

Ⓒ You can click the **Drawing Tools Format** tab to display other formatting options.

9 Click the **Notes Master** tab.

10 Click **Close Master View**.

Notes Master view closes.

TIPS

Is there a way to print just notes, and not slides?
Yes. If you remove the slide placeholder from the Notes Master, the slide images still appear on Notes Page view. You must display Notes Page view, go to each individual page, and delete the slide placeholder. Then the notes print without the slides.

Can I format the font for the header, footer, date, and page number?
Yes. You can format the header, footer, date, and page number placeholders just like any other placeholder. Click the border of the placeholder, and then use commands from the Home tab to format the text or the placeholder.

Work with the Handout Master

Sometimes you may not have notes to print, but you still want to give your audience a handout to take notes. *Handouts* are printouts of the slides in your presentation and they are printed in Backstage view. Handout Master view determines what is printed on the handouts. You cannot move or resize the slide placeholders, but you can move, resize, and format the font of the other placeholders to control the appearance of your printed handouts. Any formatting you do on the Handout Master appears in the Handout printout.

Work with the Handout Master

1 Click the **View** tab.

2 Click **Handout Master**.

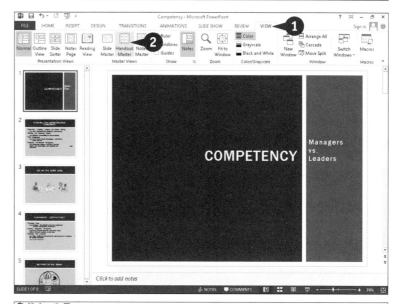

Handout Master view and the Handout Master tab appear.

Ⓐ You can click options to add (☑) or remove (☐) placeholders.

Ⓑ You can click **Fonts** to change the font style of all text placeholders on the page.

Note: You can click commands on the Home tab to format individual placeholders.

3 Click **Close Master View**.

Handout Master view closes.

174

Omit Master Graphics on a Slide

Inserting a graphic on the Slide Master applies that graphic to all presentation slides; inserting a graphic on a Layout Master causes that graphic to appear on corresponding presentation slides. You can prevent a Slide Master graphic from appearing on individual presentation slides. For example, you may need to remove a graphic from a specific presentation slide because the graphic overlaps with other objects, such as a table or chart. You may also need to remove a graphic from certain slides because it simply does not apply to those slides.

Omit Master Graphics on a Slide

1 Select the slide(s) you want to change in Normal or Slide Sorter view.

Note: To select multiple slides, click the first slide, and then press Ctrl while clicking additional slides.

2 Click the **Design** tab.

3 Click **Format Background**.

The Format Background task pane appears.

4 Click **Hide Background Graphics** (☐ changes to ✔).

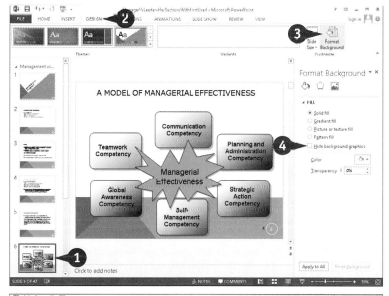

The master graphics disappear from the slide.

5 Click the **Close** button (✖) to close the Format Background task pane.

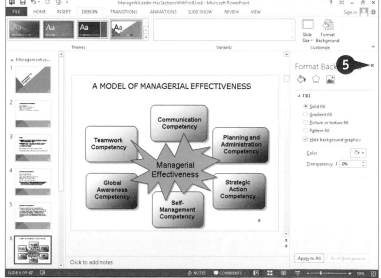

Create a Custom Slide Layout

There may be times when you need a slide with a unique layout. For example, you may want to compare three items, but there is no slide layout with three content placeholders. You can work in Slide Master view to add a new slide layout to the set of Master Slides. This saves time because you do not need to insert additional placeholders into individual slides. You create your custom slide layout with three content placeholders, then insert new slides with the custom layout, or apply the custom layout to existing slides in your presentation.

Create a Custom Slide Layout

1 Display Slide Master view.

Note: To display Slide Master view, see the section, "Open and Close Slide Master View."

2 Click in between the thumbnails where you want to insert the new slide layout.

3 Click **Insert Layout**.

A A new Layout Master appears as a thumbnail.

4 Click **Insert Placeholder**.

5 Click and drag across the slide where you want the placeholder.

Note: See "Insert a Placeholder" earlier in this chapter.

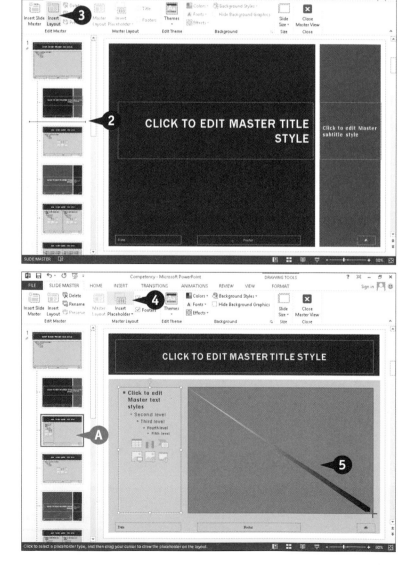

The placeholder appears.

You can move, format, and resize the placeholder as needed.

6 Click **Close Master View** when finished.

Slide Master view closes.

7 Click the **Home** tab.

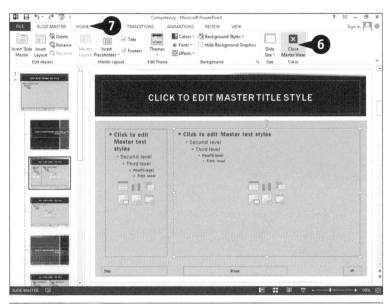

8 Click the **New Slide** down arrow (▼).

The gallery of layouts appears.

B Your custom layout appears in the gallery.

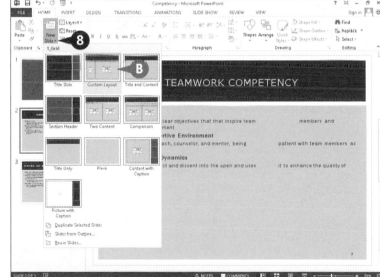

TIPS

Can I assign a unique name to my custom Layout Master?

Yes. Your custom Layout Master works just like any other Layout Master. See "Rename Master Slides" earlier in this chapter to learn how to rename your custom Layout Master. Try to give it a name that uniquely identifies it so you can quickly find it when you insert a slide.

Can I change the background for my custom slide layout?

Yes. You cannot change the theme, but you can change the background. Click your custom Layout Master. You can click commands such as **Colors** and **Effects** in the Background group on the Slide Master tab to make background changes. See Chapter 8 for more on changing backgrounds of slides.

CHAPTER 10

Adding Graphics and Drawings

Adding graphic elements such as photographs, clip art, and shapes to your slides can enhance the attractiveness and effectiveness of your presentation. While you can insert graphics into slide placeholders, you can place graphic elements anywhere on a slide — you are not bound by placeholders. You can also use color and various formatting options to make your presentation picture-perfect.

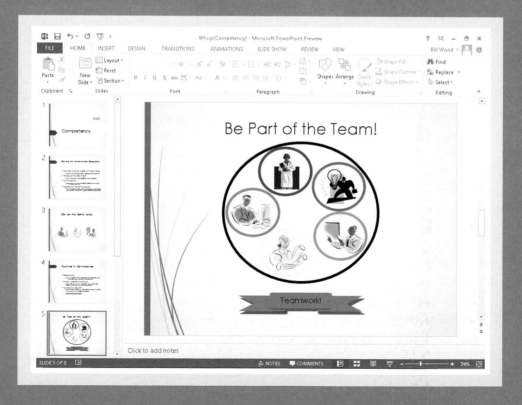

Select Objects

You will often need to format or reposition slide objects such as shapes or pictures. To change an object on a slide, you must first select it. When you click the border of an object to select the entire object, the border becomes solid; when you click the text within an object to select the text, the border becomes a dashed outline. You can also select objects in the Selection pane where you can hide objects, too.

You must select an entire object to format or reposition it. You can format specific text by selecting only that text.

Select Objects

1 Select a slide in Normal view.

Note: To learn how to select a slide, see Chapter 2.

2 Click the text within an object.

The insertion point appears within the text and the border becomes a dashed outline.

Note: You can learn how to select text in Chapter 4.

A The object's contextual tab appears on the ribbon.

3 Click the border of the object.

PowerPoint selects the entire object and the border becomes solid.

4 Press **Ctrl** while you click additional objects (⬚ changes to ⬚).

Note: You can also select multiple objects by clicking and dragging on the slide around them.

5 Click the **Home** tab.

6 Click **Select**.

7 Click **Selection Pane**.

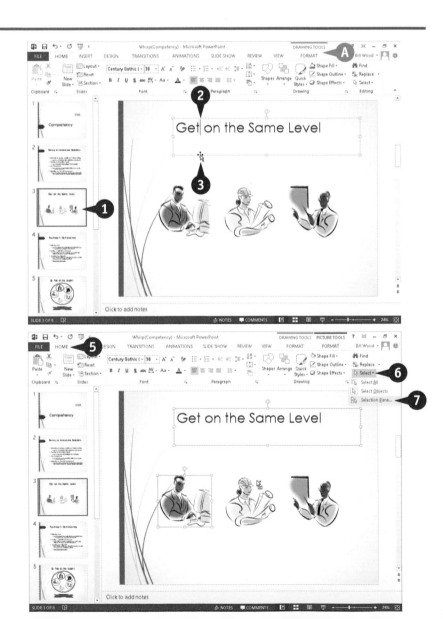

The Selection pane appears.

An item appears in the Selection pane for every shape and placeholder on the slide.

An object is selected or highlighted in the Selection pane if you select it on the slide.

8 Click the **eye** icon (👁 changes to —) to hide an object.

9 Click an item in the list.

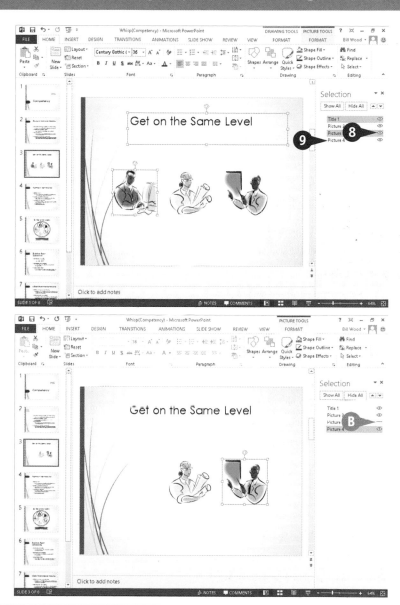

PowerPoint hides and selects the objects.

B You can click the dash icon (—) to expose a hidden object.

Note: You can select multiple objects in the Selection pane by pressing `Ctrl` while clicking them.

TIPS

Can I change the names that PowerPoint gave my shapes?

Yes. You can change their names in the Selection pane. Click the name that you want to change, then double-click it. When the insertion point appears in the text, delete the name that PowerPoint has assigned. Type the name that you want and press `Enter`.

I unintentionally clicked a shape while selecting multiple shapes. Can I deselect it without starting all over?

Yes. That can also happen when you click and drag around a group of objects on a slide — you may get one that you do not want as part of the selected group. Press `Ctrl` while clicking a shape that is part of the selected objects and it becomes deselected.

Move Objects

Details such as the position of the various objects on a slide are very important to the professional appearance of a presentation. When you insert an object, such as a picture, text box, placeholder, or shape, it usually does not appear in the location where you want it. When you insert a slide, you may prefer to position the text and content placeholders in a different location than the standard layout. You can reposition objects on a slide so that you can strategically place them. You move an object by clicking and dragging it.

Move Objects

1 Click an object to select it.

2 Position the mouse pointer (◌) over the border of the object (◌ changes to ✛).

3 Click and drag the object to a new position.

When you release the mouse button, the object appears in its new position.

4 Click anywhere outside the shape when finished.

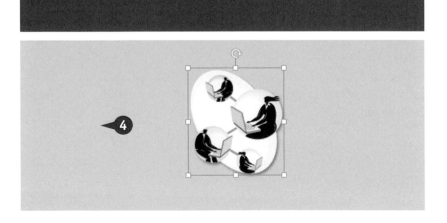

Resize Objects

After placing an object on a slide, you will often want to resize it. For example, when you insert a picture, it may be too small for your audience to see, or it may be bigger than the slide. You can resize objects such as charts, WordArt, pictures, and shapes on your slide to optimize their visual impact.

When you select an object, handles appear on the border. You click and drag a handle to resize the object. Dragging a corner handle while pressing the Shift key retains the object's original proportions.

Resize Objects

1 Click an object to select it.

Ⓐ Handles appear on the border around the object.

2 Position the mouse pointer (↖) over a handle on the border of the object (↖ changes to ⟷).

3 Click and drag outward from the object's center to enlarge it or inward to shrink it (the double-arrow pointer ⟷ changes to a crosshair pointer +).

When you release the mouse button, the object appears at its new size.

4 Click anywhere outside the object when finished.

Change Object Order

When you work with multiple objects, you may want to stack them in layers so that they overlap as objects do in real life; or you may want to overlap them to create a special effect or make them appear three dimensional. For example, if you want to create a shadow effect for an object, the shape that you use as the shadow must be behind that object. Controlling which object appears in front of another object is called *ordering*. PowerPoint includes a feature that makes ordering objects easy and fast.

Change Object Order

1 Click the **Home** tab.

2 Click **Select**.

3 Click **Selection Pane**.

The Selection pane appears.

4 Select an object behind other objects.

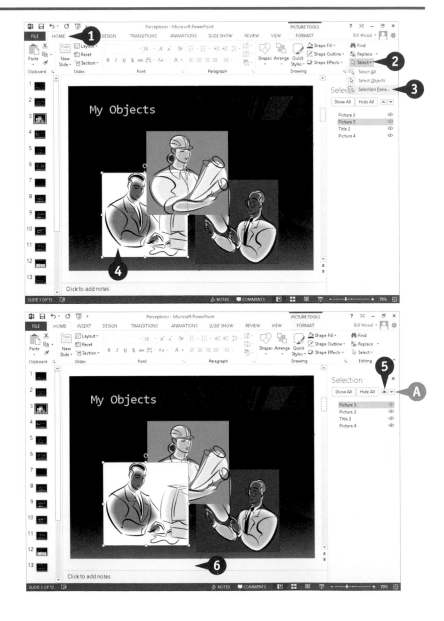

5 Click the **Bring Forward** button (△).

The object moves in front of the other objects.

Ⓐ You can click the **Send Backward** button (▽) to send an object behind the other objects.

6 Click outside the object when finished.

Group and Ungroup Objects

You may create a set of objects that you want to move or format as a unit. For example, you may draw a car using ovals and lines. After assembling the car, you need not move its pieces individually. You can group the objects so that the collection of objects acts as a single object. After grouping objects, changes you make then apply to all the objects in the group, whether you reposition, resize, or format them. Grouping allows you to save time by applying changes to multiple objects.

Group and Ungroup Objects

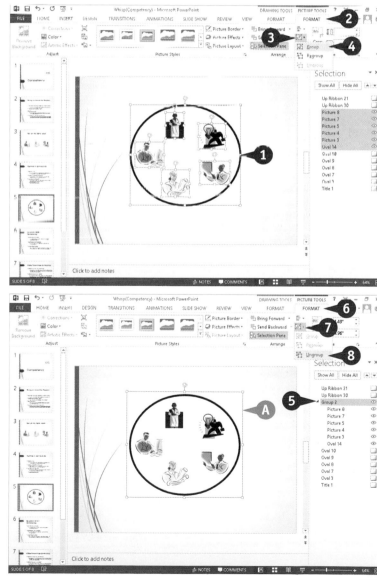

1 Select multiple objects.

Note: See the section, "Select Objects," to learn how to select multiple objects.

2 Click the **Picture Tools Format** tab.

3 Click the **Group** button (⊞ ▾).

4 Click **Group**.

Ⓐ A single selection box appears around the grouped objects.

The group appears in the Selection pane.

5 If not selected, select the grouped objects.

6 Click the **Picture Tools Format** tab.

7 Click the **Group** button (⊞ ▾).

8 Click **Ungroup**.

The objects ungroup.

Merge Shapes

You can make your presentation more interesting by creating and using your own shapes by merging two or more shapes together. For example, you may need a shape that is a circle with a star cut out of the center to frame a person's picture. You can also fragment multiple shapes for a puzzle effect. You can even merge a variety of slide objects — standard geometric shapes, pictures, and clip art. After merging shapes, the new shape works just like any other distinct shape on a slide. You need at least one geometric shape to merge shapes.

Merge Shapes

1 Insert and overlap multiple shapes similar to the example.

Note: To insert a shape, see the section, "Draw a Shape."

Note: Some shapes in the example are transparent so you can see each shape completely.

2 Click two overlapping shapes while pressing **Ctrl**.

3 Click the **Drawing Tools Format** tab.

4 Click the **Merge Shapes** button ( ).

5 Click **Subtract**.

The shapes subtract.

Note: The order in which you select the shapes is important — the first shape that you click remains.

6 Click the picture.

7 Click the shape while pressing **Ctrl**.

8 Click the **Drawing Tools Format** tab.

9 Click the **Merge Shape** button ( ).

10 Click **Intersect**.

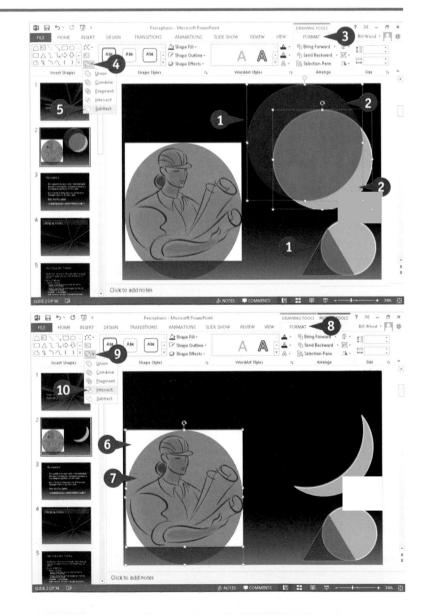

The area where the two shapes intersect remains.

11 Click two overlapping shapes while pressing **Ctrl**.

12 Click the **Drawing Tools Format** tab.

13 Click the **Merge Shape** button (🖉 ▾).

14 Click **Union**.

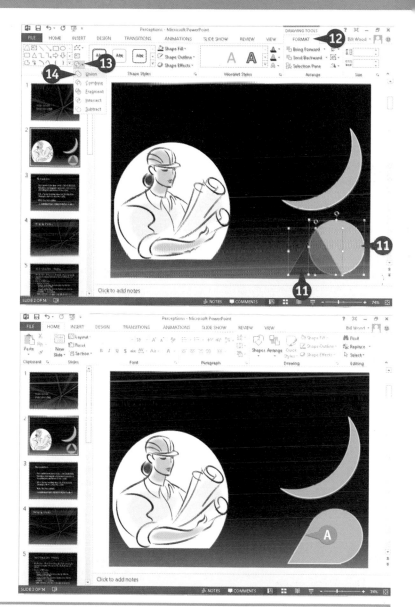

The shapes become a new shape.

A The border extends around the entire shape.

Note: You can click and drag on the slide around multiple shapes to select them.

TIPS

I saw a nice effect where characters were made from a picture. Can I create that?

Yes. Insert your picture and type your characters into a placeholder or WordArt. Place the characters over the picture. Format the characters the way you want them — you cannot format after the merge because the characters become a shape. Click the picture first and then click the words while pressing **Ctrl**. Click the **Merge Shapes** button (🖉 ▾) and then click **Intersect**.

I want everything except where my two shapes overlap. Can I do that?

Yes. You can combine the shapes. Click the **Merge Shapes** button (🖉 ▾) and then click **Combine**. Combine is the opposite of intersect — it removes the intersection from the overlapping shapes.

Insert Clip Art

*C*lip art can be interesting drawings, silhouettes, cartoons, caricatures, and other representations. Photographs are not clip art and the clip art files are usually much smaller than photographs. You can add clip art to slides to make them interesting and engaging. Clip art is usually easier for an audience to see because it lacks the detail of a picture. You can search for clip art by keyword with the online feature in PowerPoint or you can insert your own clip art from your computer. You can insert clip art anywhere on your slide without using a content placeholder, which gives you complete flexibility with how you use it.

Insert Clip Art

1 Select a slide in Normal view.

Note: To learn how to select a slide, see Chapter 2.

2 Click the **Insert** tab.

3 Click **Online Pictures**.

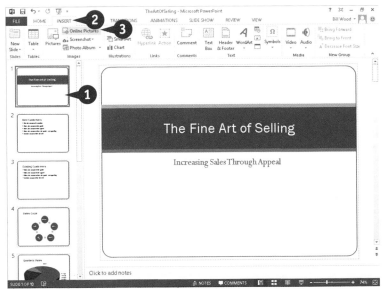

The Insert Pictures dialog box appears.

4 Type a keyword or phrase in the **Office.com Clip Art** text box or the **Bing Image Search** text box.

5 Click the **Search** icon (🔎).

A You can click the **Close** button (✖) to cancel.

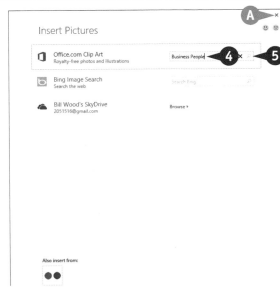

6 Click and drag the scroll bar to scroll through and view the images.

7 Click an image from the gallery.

8 Click **Insert**.

The clip art appears on the slide.

Note: See the sections, "Move Objects" and "Resize Objects," to learn how to position and size the clip art.

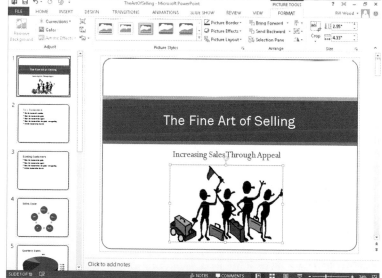

Can I search the entire Internet for clip art?
Yes. First, try the Bing Image search feature. If unsuccessful, Search the web with your browser and save an image to your computer. Then click **Pictures** on the Insert tab and use the Insert Picture dialog box to browse to your saved clip art.

What happens if I insert a sound clip instead of clip art?
When you insert a sound clip on a slide, a small megaphone icon appears on the slide. You can set the sound clip so the sound plays automatically or only when you click the icon. See Chapter 12 for more about inserting sound and movie clips.

Draw a Shape

There are many predefined shapes that you can easily draw on a slide to add visual interest. For example, you might want to put a solid, rectangular background behind a few clip art images. There are many available shapes, from simple geometric shapes to thought bubbles and arrows. You can choose these shapes from a gallery and draw them by simply clicking and dragging. You can type text into many of the shapes, and change the formatting of the shape, the border, and the text. The shape gallery even includes action buttons that run simple actions.

Draw a Shape

1 Select a slide in Normal view.

Note: To learn how to select a slide, see Chapter 2.

2 Click the **Insert** tab.

3 Click **Shapes**.

The gallery of shapes appears.

4 Click the shape you want to draw.

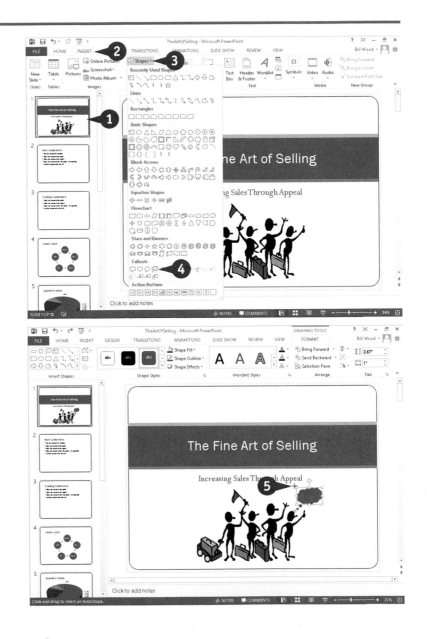

The gallery closes, and the mouse pointer (⬉) changes to the crosshair pointer (+).

5 Click the slide to insert the shape.

When you release the mouse button, the shape appears.

Note: You can also click and drag the crosshair pointer (+) to size the shape while inserting it.

Note: You can use the Rectangle or Oval shape to draw a square or circle. Press **Shift** as you drag to keep the shape perfect.

Add Text to a Shape

I f you think that a plain text box lacks pizzazz, you can create a jazzier text box by adding text to a shape. For example, you can use an arrow with text in it to describe something on your slide. The text appears within the shape, and the shape effectively becomes a fancy text box. You lose a little versatility using shapes with text because shapes lack some of the automation that text boxes have. For example, they do not automatically enlarge or shrink based upon the amount of text you type.

Add Text to a Shape

1 Right-click the shape in which you want to add text.

2 Click **Edit Text**.

The insertion point appears inside the shape.

3 Type your text.

4 Click anywhere outside the shape when finished.

The text appears in the shape.

Note: If the text you type exceeds the width of the shape, PowerPoint continues the text on the next line automatically. You can force a new line by pressing **Enter**.

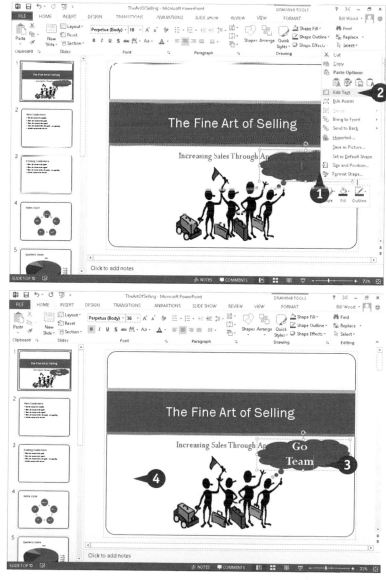

Add WordArt

The WordArt feature enables you to create special effects with text. You can distort WordArt text and apply interesting color styles. For example, if you have a picture of a product, you can use the WordArt feature to bend a phrase over and around the picture. Or, you can emphasize an important word or phrase anywhere on your slide. You can even create a simple logo! WordArt is an object that you can move, resize, or format using techniques discussed earlier in this chapter.

Add WordArt

1 Select a slide in Normal view.

Note: To learn how to select a slide, see Chapter 2.

2 Click the **Insert** tab.

3 Click **WordArt**.

The WordArt gallery appears.

4 Click a WordArt style.

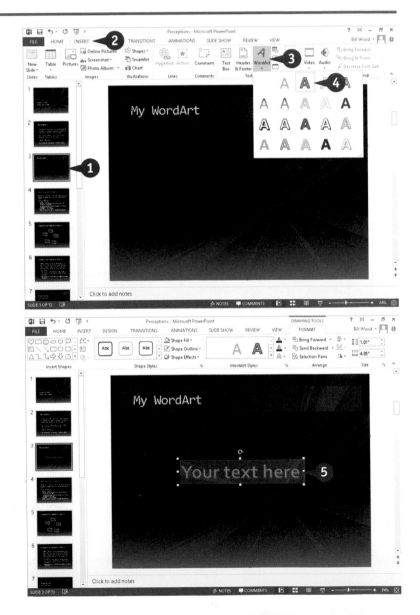

The WordArt appears on the slide ready for you to type a word or phrase.

5 Type your text.

This example creates the text, "Perception is Everything."

As you type, the WordArt automatically sizes itself.

6 Click the **Drawing Tools Format** tab.

7 Click the **Text Effects** button (🄰 ⋅).

8 Click **Transform**.

The Transform gallery appears.

9 Click a variation from the gallery.

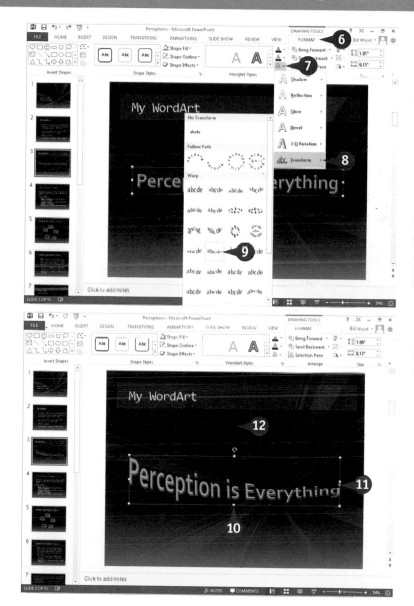

PowerPoint applies the special effect to the WordArt.

10 Resize the WordArt as needed to distort the effect.

11 Drag the pink handles on or inside the WordArt border to change the distortion of the effect.

Note: There may be multiple pink handles.

You can use other tools on the Drawing Tools Format tab to format the WordArt.

12 Click outside the object when finished.

TIPS

I created a WordArt object, but then realized it contains a typo. Is there any way to change it?

Yes. Click the object just like any text box or placeholder. The insertion point appears within the text of the WordArt so that you can make the necessary changes.

How do I change the style and color of the WordArt?

Click the WordArt object, and then click the **Drawing Tools Format** tab when it appears. Click the **WordArt Styles** down arrow (🔻). When the WordArt gallery appears, choose a WordArt style.

Insert a Hyperlink

A hyperlink can perform a variety of actions when you click it during a PowerPoint slide show. It gives you an easy way to go to a different slide in your slide show. You can have a hyperlink open another PowerPoint presentation or open a document from another Office application. A hyperlink also provides you a way to open and create an e-mail message and gives you the convenience of opening a Web page from your slide show. Using hyperlinks to execute these actions during a slide show enables you to run a smooth presentation and impress your audience.

Insert a Hyperlink

Go to a Slide in the Current Presentation

1 Click inside a placeholder where you want to insert the hyperlink.

2 Click the **Insert** tab.

3 Click **Hyperlink**.

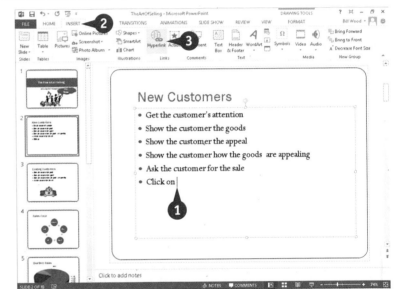

The Insert Hyperlink dialog box appears.

4 Click the **Text to display** text box.

5 Type a name for your hyperlink.

6 Click **Place in This Document**.

7 Click a slide.

8 Click **OK**.

PowerPoint inserts the link to the slide.

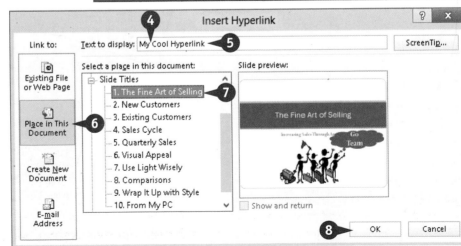

Open a File

1 Repeat Steps **1** to **4**.

2 Click **Current Folder**.

3 Click the **Look in** down arrow ( ).

4 Navigate to and click the folder that contains the file you want to open.

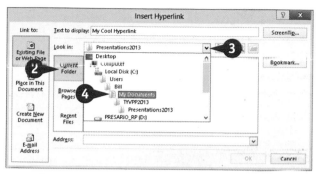

A You can also click the **Browse** button ( ) and find your file with the Browse dialog box.

5 Click the file to open.

6 Click **OK**.

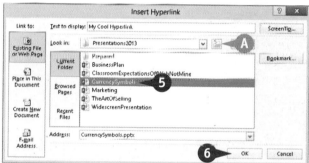

B PowerPoint places the link on your slide.

During the slide show, click the text to follow the link.

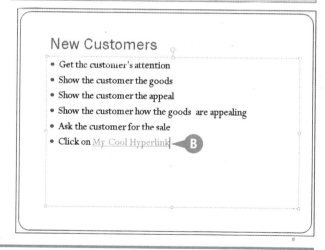

How do I remove a link to a file but leave the link text?
Right-click the hyperlink, and click **Edit Link** on the shortcut menu. When the Edit Hyperlink dialog box opens, click **Remove Link**. The link text remains, but PowerPoint removes the link.

Can I give the hyperlink a longer description?
Yes. You can do this by creating a ScreenTip. Right-click the hyperlink, and click **Edit Link** on the menu. In the Edit Hyperlink dialog box, click the **ScreenTip** button. In the ScreenTip dialog box, type the description and click **OK**. If your ScreenTip feature is enabled, the ScreenTip appears in a little box when you position the mouse pointer ( ) over the link during the slide show.

Add a Text Box

Yyou can add a text box anywhere on a slide, which allows you to have almost unlimited versatility with text. A text box is more flexible than a placeholder because it does not automatically produce a bulleted list and it does not become part of the outline in Outline view. A text box is great for freeform text and automatically enlarges, shrinks, and wraps text, depending on the amount of text you type. Keep in mind that text box contents do not appear in Outline view.

Add a Text Box

1 Select a slide in Normal view.

Note: To learn how to select a slide, see Chapter 2.

2 Click the **Insert** tab.

3 Click **Text Box**.

The mouse pointer (⬚) changes to the Text box insertion (↓).

4 Click where you want to place the upper-left corner of the text.

The text box appears with an insertion point inside.

5 Type your text.

6 Click anywhere outside the text box when finished.

Note: You can adjust the text box width; the height adjusts automatically based on the amount of text you type. You can also move the text box anywhere. For more information, see the sections, "Resize Objects" and "Move Objects."

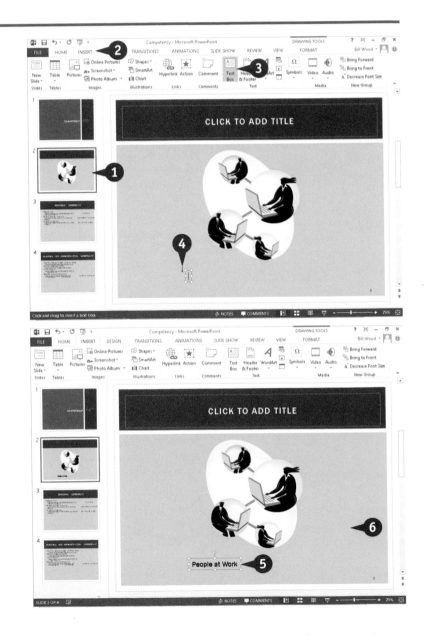

Apply a New Effect

Occasionally, you may want to give an object a special effect to make the object vivid or dramatic. You can use shape effects to add dimension and realism to the object's appearance. For example, you can apply a reflection effect that gives the appearance of the object reflecting in a lake. You can also give an object a soft, blurred border, or give it a shadow or glow. When you select an object, the contextual Format tab that appears on the ribbon provides you with many tools to apply effects and formatting to the object.

Apply a New Effect

1 Click an object to select it.

2 Click the **Picture Tools Format** tab.

3 Click **Picture Effects**.

Note: For a shape, you would click **Shape Effects**.

4 Click a Picture Effect.

This example selects the Reflection effect.

5 Click a variation of the effect.

This example selects a reflection variation.

A PowerPoint applies the special effect to the object.

6 Click anywhere outside the object when finished.

Note: You can also apply special effects from the Home tab.

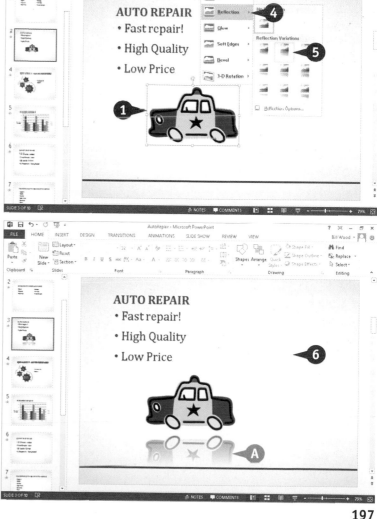

Format Objects

Y ou can adjust the formatting of an object to make it more visually appealing or easier to see against a slide background. For example, you can add a fill color, modify the font, change the thickness or color of lines, and modify arrow styles. Details and fine-tuning such as object formatting make your presentation pop — you can produce objects very specific to your needs and adjust the colors of objects to look good against the background of the slide and other objects on the slide.

Format Objects

1 Click the object to format.

The object's contextual tab appears.

Note: You can learn how to select and format text in Chapter 4.

2 Click the **Drawing Tools Format** tab.

3 Click the **Shape Styles** down arrow (▼).

4 Click a color scheme from the gallery.

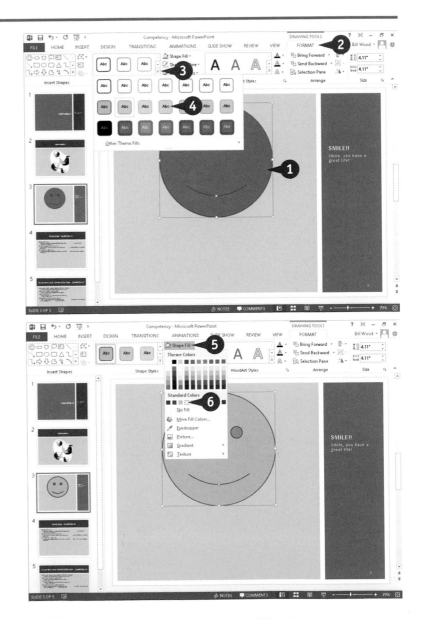

The color scheme changes.

5 Click **Shape Fill** to change the color of the object.

6 Click a color from the color palette.

The shape changes color.

7 Click **Shape Outline**.

8 Click **Weight**.

A You can change the border color.

B You can change the border style.

9 Click a weight from the menu.

This example changes the weight of the shape's border.

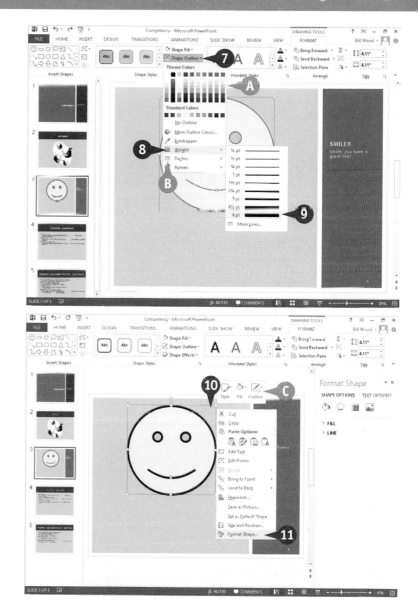

PowerPoint applies your changes.

10 Right-click the object.

The shortcut menu appears.

C You can also use the Mini Toolbar to apply formatting.

11 Click **Format Shape**.

The Format Shape task pane appears; you can use the task pane to perform any formatting.

TIPS

I want every shape that I draw to appear with a blue fill color. Is there a quick way to do that?

Yes. Draw any shape and then click **Shape Fill** on the Drawing Tools Format tab. Click the blue fill color you want to use. Right-click your shape and click **Set as Default Shape**. Shapes you insert will now appear in blue.

Can I make an object transparent?

Yes. Open the Format Shape task pane, and then click the **Fill** icon (⬥). Click **Fill** if that section is not expanded. If not selected, click **Solid Fill** (○ changes to ◉). Type a percentage into the **Transparency** text box or use the **Transparency slider** or **spinner** (🔼) to adjust the transparency.

Color with the Eyedropper

You can match colors by sampling a color from anything on your slide and then applying it to anything on the slide that you select. Matching colors is important because color is essential to the look and feel of your presentation. Determining the color of something in PowerPoint is a cumbersome task, and if the color is not a standard color, it becomes difficult. The eyedropper allows you to match colors with a couple of clicks, saving you time. You can sample from anything on your slide such as the background, text, objects, and even pictures!

Color with the Eyedropper

1 Select the object whose color you want to change.

2 Click the **Drawing Tools Format** tab.

3 Click **Shape Fill**.

4 Click **Eyedropper**.

The Eyedropper pointer (🖊) appears.

5 Position the Eyedropper pointer (🖊) over the color you want to sample.

6 Click the object.

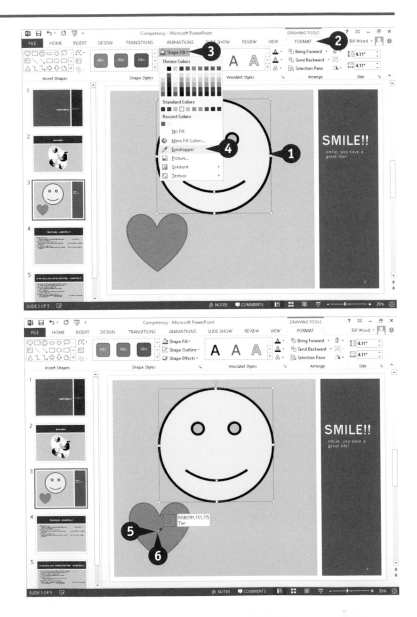

The object now matches the color of the sampled color.

7 Click the border of an object that contains text.

Note: Optionally, you can change the color of specific text by selecting only that text within the object.

8 Click the **Home** tab.

9 Click the **Font Color** button (△ ▾).

10 Click **Eyedropper**.

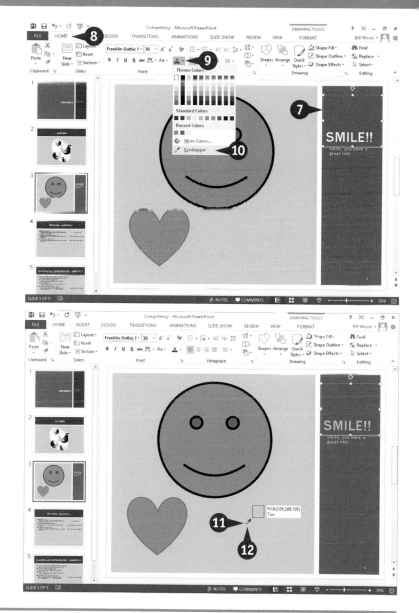

The Eyedropper pointer (🖊) appears.

11 Position the Eyedropper pointer (🖊) over the color you want to sample.

12 Click the object.

The text now matches the color of the sampled color.

TIPS

Can I sample a color from a different slide than the slide that holds the object whose color I want to match?

No. As soon as you click on a slide in the Slide Thumbnails pane, you lose the Eyedropper pointer (🖊). You can cut and paste the object onto the slide with the sample color, match the color, and then cut and paste the object back to the original slide.

Why does the Eyedropper feature not seem to work when I click a placeholder containing text?

The insertion point is between characters. You must either click the placeholder border to select the entire placeholder or click and drag across text to select specific text.

Arrange Objects with Smart Guides

Symmetry on a slide is important for its look and is pleasant for the audience to view. For example, you may want similar objects on a slide to be proportionate to and equidistant from each other. PowerPoint 2013 introduces a new feature called Smart Guides. Smart Guides allow you to align objects, center objects, resize multiple objects to the same proportions, and arrange objects equidistant from each other — all in real time. You can use Smart Guides to save time while designing an outstanding presentation.

Arrange Objects with Smart Guides

1 Insert three similar objects, such as clip art or pictures, onto a slide that contains a placeholder.

Note: See the section, "Insert Clip Art," for more information.

2 Resize an object so it is a different size from the others.

Note: See the sections, "Move Objects" and "Resize Objects," for more information.

3 Click and drag an object until the left edge aligns with a placeholder.

A red, dashed line appears, indicating that the object is aligned with the placeholder.

4 Release the mouse button.

5 Click and drag the object until the top edge is aligned with another object.

6 Click and drag the object until it is equidistant from the other objects.

Red, dashed lines and arrows appear, indicating that the object is aligned with the other objects.

7 Release the mouse button.

8 Click and drag the resized object so the top is aligned with and equidistant from the others.

Red, dashed lines and arrows appear, indicating that the object is aligned with the other objects.

9 Release the mouse button.

10 Resize the object to be the same size as the others.

Red, dashed lines and arrows appear, indicating that the object is aligned with the other objects.

11 Release the mouse button.

PowerPoint aligns the objects.

Get on the Same Level

Get on the Same Level

Get on the Same Level

TIP

How are Smart Guides different from gridlines and guidelines?
Smart Guides change as you move and resize objects. They are particularly helpful in making objects equidistant from each other. Smart Guides appear and disappear as you move objects around. You need to be very close to an aligned position for them to appear, and so they can be challenging to use. Gridlines and guidelines are continuously visible while they are enabled. Gridlines can help you plot objects on a slide, while guidelines are movable and are particularly useful for lining up objects with background features. All of these tools have similar uses, but some are more helpful than others with certain tasks.

Use the Grid and Guides

There are times when you may need a guide to help you line up objects on a slide. PowerPoint offers a feature that helps you position and align objects with precision. The grid looks like graph paper lines on your slide; guides run across the entire slide and can help you line objects up with details on the slide background. You can also adjust the granularity of the grid. If you need to make small, fine positioning, you can make the distance between gridline points small, or make the distance large for easier alignment. You can also have objects snap to the gridline for easy and fast alignment.

Use the Grid and Guides

1 In Normal view, click the **View** tab.

2 Click the check box to enable (☑) **Gridlines**.

3 Click the check box to enable (☑) **Guides**.

4 Position the mouse pointer (⇦) over the Guide until it changes to the mouse splitter (↕).

5 Click and drag the Guide to move it in a position to align two objects.

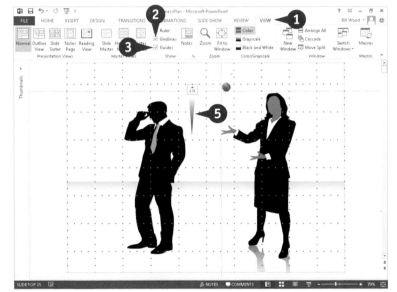

6 Click the **dialog box launcher** (⌐₁).

The Grid and Guides dialog box appears.

7 Click the check box to enable (☑) **Snap objects to grid**.

Ⓐ You can change the spacing of the Gridlines.

Ⓑ You can click the check box to disable (☐) Smart Guides.

8 Click **OK**.

Objects will now snap to the Gridlines as you move them.

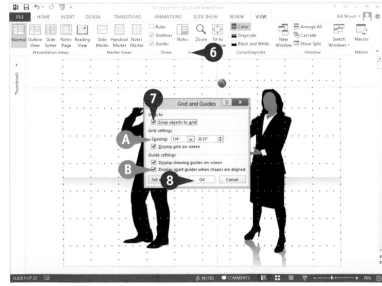

Nudge Objects

You may want to move an object by very small increments. For example, you may want two objects to touch, but not overlap. Using the mouse to perform delicate and precise movements can be tricky, yet these small details can be important to a presentation. Nudging is a feature that moves objects by small increments using keystrokes. The nudge feature enables you to move a selected object incrementally to the right, left, up, or down on the slide. You can use nudging together with the gridlines and guidelines feature to align objects perfectly.

Nudge Objects

1 In Normal view, select an object.

2 Press ⬆, ⬇, ⬅, or ➡ as many times as needed to nudge the object in the desired direction.

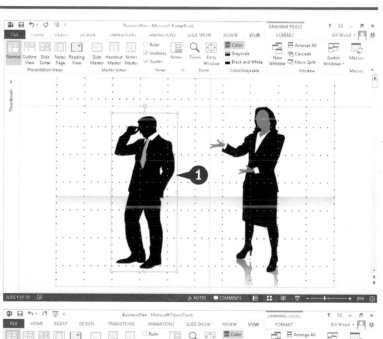

This example presses the Up arrow 20 times to move the object up one gridline, a distance of one-quarter inch.

3 Click outside the object to deselect it.

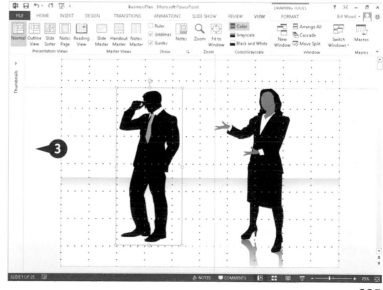

Align Objects

You can align objects relative to each other quickly and easily for a picture-perfect look. For example, you can align several objects at the same position as the leftmost object, or you can distribute objects evenly relative to one another. With the advent of Smart Guides, this feature may seem antiquated, but it is not. It allows you to align many objects perfectly with a couple of clicks, as opposed to the Smart Guides feature, which performs alignment in a very convenient way, but only one object at a time.

Align Objects

1 Select multiple objects.

Note: See the section, "Select Objects," to learn how to select multiple objects.

2 Click the **Picture Tools Format** tab.

3 Click the **Align** button (≣ ▾).

4 Click **Align Bottom**.

The bottoms of all the selected objects align with the bottom-most object.

5 Click **Distribute Horizontally**.

The objects distribute evenly horizontally.

A You can click **Align to Slide** (✓ appears on the menu) to make the objects align with the edges and center of the slide as a reference.

B You can click **Align Selected Objects** (✓ appears on the menu) to make the objects align with each other.

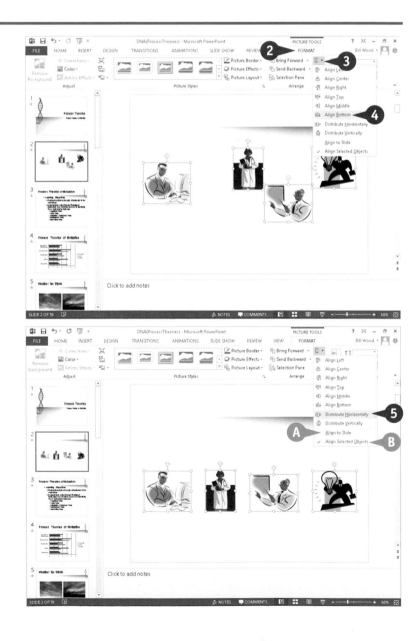

Flip and Rotate Objects

Sometimes when you combine several shapes to create a more complex graphic or you want a picture to appear more dramatic, you can rotate it. For example, you may have a triangle shape as a hill with a clip art car going up the hill. PowerPoint enables you to rotate an object 360 degrees or quickly flip it horizontally or vertically to accomplish that dramatic effect. The Picture Tools Format tab offers all of the flip and rotation tools, but you can also click and drag to rotate the object.

Flip and Rotate Objects

Flip Objects

1️⃣ Click an object to select it.

2️⃣ Click the **Picture Tools Format** tab.

3️⃣ Click the **Rotate** button ( ).

Note: For SmartArt, you must first click **Arrange** after clicking the SmartArt graphic and before clicking **Rotate**.

4️⃣ Click **Flip Horizontal**.

The object flips horizontally.

Rotate Objects

1️⃣ Click an object to select it.

2️⃣ Position the mouse pointer ( ) over the rotation handle ( ) (changes to).

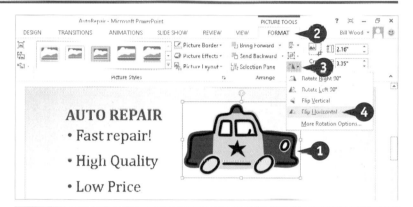

3️⃣ Click the handle.

The rotation pointer ( ) changes to the rotation movement arrows ( ).

4️⃣ Drag clockwise or counterclockwise.

When you release the mouse, the object stays at the new angle.

CHAPTER 11

Enhancing Slides with Action

Animations and transitions create action in your slide show presentations. Animations give movement to text and objects so a slide show does more than display static bullet points. Transitions add an interesting effect when the slide show advances from one slide to another.

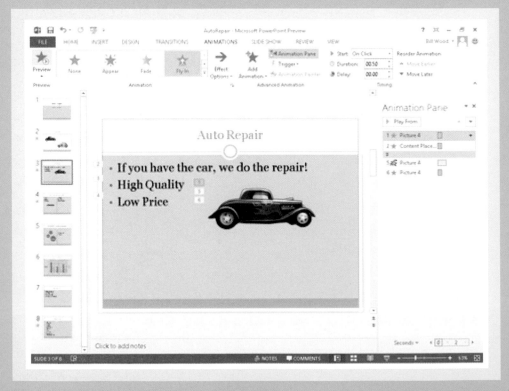

Understanding Animations and Action Buttons

Animations help you add emphasis to text or an object on a slide. Adding animation to slide objects causes them to appear on the slide at different times and with special motion. For example, you might animate a set of bullet points to move onto the screen one at a time. Animations keep your audience engaged with the presentation, but you should use them sparingly — overusing animations can make your presentation seem too busy. Action buttons perform an action when you click them during a slide show. This action might be moving to a particular slide or opening a different application or file.

What Is Animation?

In PowerPoint, *animation* refers to object motion on slides. There are many animations from which to choose and you can apply several animations to one object. For example, you can have a ball bounce onto the slide and then have it spin. There are three types of animation: An entrance animation brings an object onto the slide; an exit animation takes an object off the slide; an emphasis animation does something to an object while it is on the slide, such as rotate or spin — it does not move the object on or off the slide.

How Animations Work

You apply animations to objects one at a time and one after another. You determine when they run. You can have them run automatically when the slide advances, set them to be triggered by the previous animation, or trigger them manually by clicking the slide. You can also run the animation for a particular object by clicking that object. An animation can be set up to run after a delay, and it has a duration time that you can change. You can also arrange the sequence order of animations. This can all be controlled through the Animation pane. Let your imagination come alive with animation!

How Action Buttons Work

Action buttons provide interaction, not just action. You can draw an action button on a slide and then select the action that occurs when you click the button during the slide show. For example, clicking the action button might open a web page or an external document such as a proposal. The action button may take you to a different slide or update a chart with the most recent data. There are various standard actions that you can assign to an action button, and if you are advanced enough to use macros, action buttons can also trigger them.

Preview Animations and Action Buttons

To create a professional presentation, choose appropriate effects and always make sure they run properly. Both the Animation pane and the Animations tab on the ribbon offer a Play button so you can easily observe the animation at the click of a command. Previewing the behavior of an action button is not as easy; you must run the slide show and click the button to verify its behavior. Animations and action buttons add complexity to your slide show, so use them sparingly and always thoroughly review them before showing your slide show to an audience.

Designing and running animations can be a complicated business, and it is nice to have a central place from which to do it. PowerPoint provides you with a handy tool called the Animation pane to help you manage animations. The Animation pane allows you to reorder the animations, see what objects they move, view and set the duration of the animations, and set the trigger for each animation. You can also perform these tasks on the Animations tab of the ribbon. Click the Animation Pane button on the Animations tab to show the Animation pane.

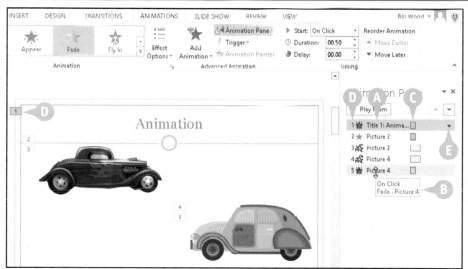

Ⓐ Animation List

PowerPoint lists each animation in the order that it runs; each animation is attached to an object, which is also listed. Green items are entrance animations, yellow items are emphasis animations, and red items are exit animations.

Ⓑ Animation Description

Position the mouse pointer (↖) over the animation to view its trigger and name.

Ⓒ Duration Bars

These bars show the timing and duration of each animation. Position the mouse pointer (↖) over the bar to view the duration time.

Ⓓ Sequence Numbers

These numbers correlate with the sequence numbers attached to the objects. Click either number to select the animation.

Ⓔ Animation Settings

Click the down arrow (▼) on any animation to change its settings.

Apply an Animation

Add some excitement and creativity to your presentation by designing it with some animation! You can have your bullet points fly onto the slide point by point to keep your audience focused on one point at a time. You may decide to have SmartArt appear one piece at a time, or have a picture zoom into the slide and then do a turn! You can use the Animations tab on the ribbon to apply an animation to any slide object.

Apply an Animation

Apply to Clip Art or a Picture

1 Select an object to animate.

You can apply the same animation to multiple objects by selecting them all at the same time.

Note: See Chapter 10 to learn how to select objects.

2 Click the **Animations** tab.

3 Click the down arrow (⤓) in the Animations group.

The gallery of animations appears.

4 Click an animation.

A PowerPoint applies the animation to the object and assigns it a sequence number.

B PowerPoint places an animation icon (✦) next to the slide thumbnail.

Note: You can apply multiple animations to one object.

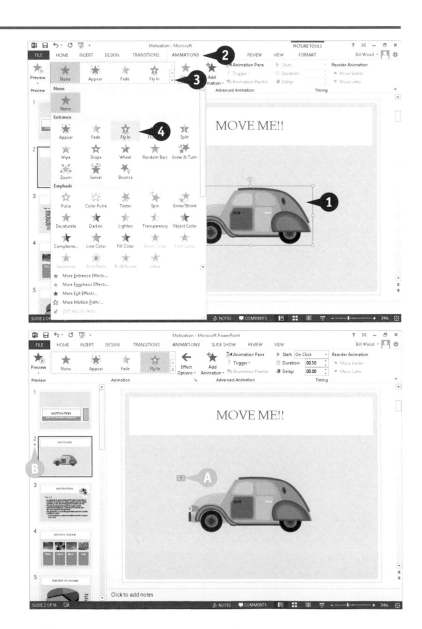

Apply to Bullets

1 Select a placeholder with bullet points, or click the border to select the entire placeholder.

Note: See Chapter 10 to learn how to select objects.

2 Click the **Animations** tab.

3 Click the down arrow (⤓) in the Animations group.

4 Click an entrance transition.

This example chooses Fly In.

C You can click these menu items to see more animations.

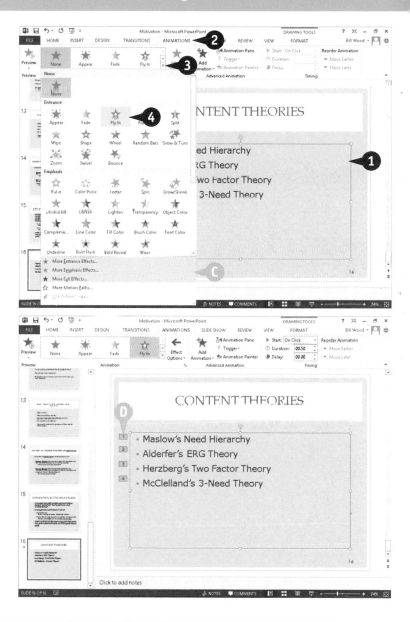

D PowerPoint applies a sequence number to each bullet on the placeholder.

During the slide show, one bullet point will fly onto the slide every time you click the mouse button.

TIP

How do I use the different types of animations?

Typically, you would not use multiple entrance or exit animations on the same object, or even a single entrance and exit on the same object. For example, if you want to substitute a new car for an old car, you would start with the old car on the slide. Maybe next, you would use some entrance animations to fly in some bullet points explaining that you are swapping cars, and drive the new car onto the slide. Then you would use emphasis animations to make the new car glow and the old car teeter. After that, an exit animation could make the old car fade off the slide.

Preview an Animation

You can see each and every animation in your presentation simply by running the slide show, but if you are working on the animation for a slide, previewing animations in Slide Show view is not very convenient. To be efficient and effective, you need a way to look at the animation while on the slide you are designing. You can see the animation on individual slides in Normal or Slide Sorter view. Previewing the animation of a slide enables you to verify that the animation works as expected and is appropriate for the slide's content.

Preview an Animation

1 Select a slide with animation in Normal view.

Note: You can also preview animations in Slide Sorter view.

2 Click the **Animations** tab.

All of the animation sequence numbers appear.

3 Click **Preview**.

PowerPoint runs all animations on the slide.

A In this example, the car flies in from the right.

Note: You can also preview animations by running the entire slide show. See Chapter 15 to learn how to run a slide show.

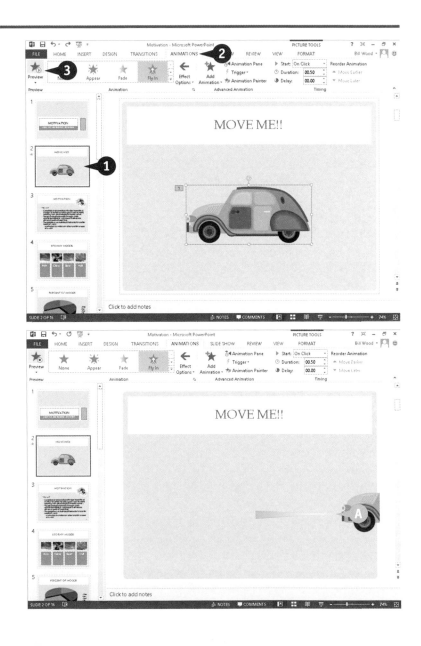

Add an Animation

You can apply different animations to different objects on a slide, and you can also apply multiple animations to one object. This enables you to make an object perform a variety of movements, creating a complex special effect. For example, you can have a ball bounce onto the slide, grow larger, do a spin, and then glow or pulse. Simple is usually best, so try not to create too much complexity. Impress your audience with your showmanship and your design abilities!

Add an Animation

1 Select an object that already has an animation.

2 Click the **Animations** tab.

3 Click **Add Animation**.

The gallery of animations appears.

A Use the scroll bar to see more animations.

4 Click an animation.

B An additional sequence number appears.

In this example, the object has two animations that will run sequentially. The Teeter animation will run second because its sequence number is 2.

Change Animation Effects

PowerPoint gives you the flexibility to choose the motion of an animation. For example, the Fly In animation can bring the object onto the screen from any direction. For complex objects made from multiple parts such as SmartArt, the animation can appear on the screen as one piece, in pieces simultaneously, or in pieces at separate times. You can move a shape and its text separately. You have complete control over the animations, which gives you almost unlimited possibilities.

Change Animation Effects

1. Select a slide with animation in Normal view.

2. Click the sequence number of the animation you want to change.

3. Click the **Animations** tab.

4. Click **Effect Options**.

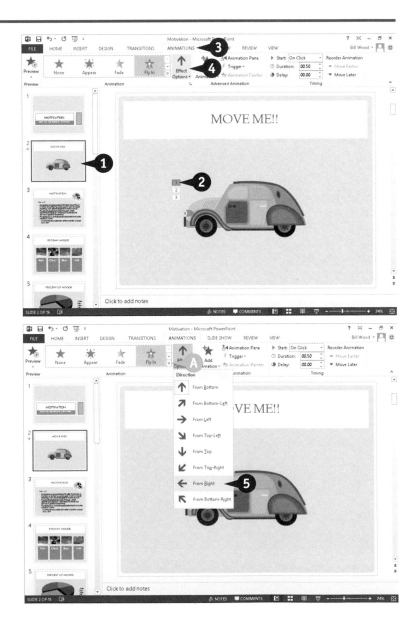

The gallery of effects appears.

5. Click an effect from the gallery.

Note: For objects with multiple pieces, there are two additional options: All at Once and By Paragraph. Click **All at Once** to have multiple pieces move independently but at the same time. Click **By Paragraph** to have multiple pieces appear separately.

PowerPoint changes the effects for the animation.

Ⓐ To change the actual animation, select a different animation from the Animation gallery.

Change the Animation Trigger

Something must trigger an animation to run, and you can determine what that trigger is. The trigger can be the appearance of the slide on the screen, it can be you clicking anywhere on the slide, or it can be you clicking a particular object on the slide. You can also trigger the animation to run with or after another animation. The default trigger is clicking the slide, but you can change it to any of the other triggers. Clicking the slide or an object on the slide gives you complete control over when the animation runs.

Change the Animation Trigger

Standard Trigger

1 Click the **Animations** tab.

2 Click an animation.

3 Click the **Start** down arrow (▾).

4 Click a start option.

This example chooses After Previous, which means that the animation will automatically run after the previous animation ends.

Ⓐ On Click runs the animation when you click the slide.

Ⓑ With Previous runs the animation simultaneously with the previous animation.

Note: To run the first animation automatically when the slide first appears, set its trigger to With Previous.

Ⓒ The sequence number becomes the same as the animation that triggers it.

Ⓓ Note the timing change.

Trigger with Click of Object

1 Click **Trigger**.

2 Click **On Click of**.

3 Click an object name.

The animation will now run when you click that object during your slide show.

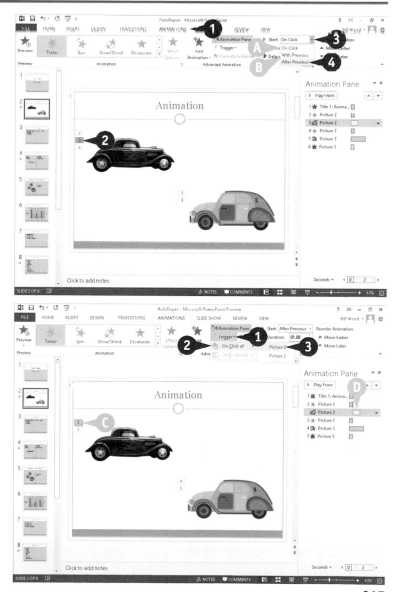

Modify Animation Timing

Sometimes you want things to happen quickly, while other times slow is better. You can modify the duration of your animation — *duration* is the amount of time the animation runs from beginning to end. You can also change the delay time between the animation's trigger and its start. For example, if you set an animation's trigger to Previous Animation and the Delay to one second, the animation will start one second after the previous animation ends. This flexibility enables you to be very exact while creating an effect that will have maximum impact on your audience.

Modify Animation Timing

1 Click the **Animations** tab.

2 Click **Animation Pane** to open the Animation pane if it is not open.

3 Click an animation.

The trigger of the selected animation is After Previous.

A This animation's sequence number is the same as the previous animation because its trigger is set to After Previous, which means the previous animation triggers it.

4 Click the **Duration** spinner (⬍) or type a number into the text box to adjust the length of time that the animation runs.

5 Click the **Delay** spinner (⬍) or type a number into the text box to adjust the delay between the trigger and when the animation starts.

6 Click **Preview**.

This example sets the duration to 2.00, and the delay to 1.00. The third animation will now start after a 1-second delay and last for 2 seconds.

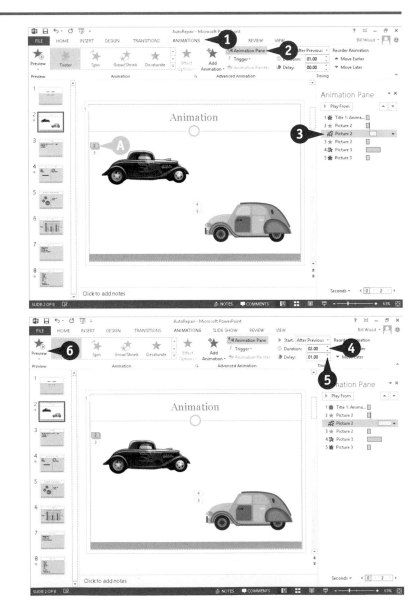

Reorder Animations

After applying multiple animations on a slide, you can change the order in which the animations play on the slide during your presentation. You can arrange the order of the animations in many ways. You can even run an animation of one object, then an animation of another object, and then more animations of the first object. Each bullet on a placeholder can be animated, and you can treat them as a group or individually when reordering animations. When you run the slide show, each bullet appears on the slide individually.

Reorder Animations

1 Select a slide with multiple animations.

2 Click the **Animations** tab.

3 Click **Animation Pane** if it is not open.

4 Click an animation.

5 Click an order option for the animation.

This example selects Move Earlier.

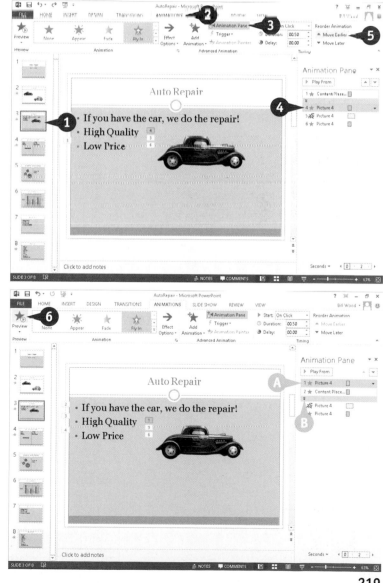

Ⓐ The animation moves in the list.

This example moves the animation earlier in the list.

Ⓑ Note that the bullets are grouped, so the animation moved ahead of the entire group. You can move the animation in between bullets by clicking the chevron (⋎) to ungroup the bullets, and then clicking the Move Earlier or Move Later buttons.

6 Click **Preview**.

Add a Motion Path

When you animate an object bouncing onto the slide, the shape and length of the bounce are determined by the animation. If you want more versatility than that, you can use a motion path, which is another kind of animation. With a motion path, you determine the object's location on the slide, the starting point of the animated movement, and the ending point of the movement. The object's location on the slide and the starting location of the motion path do not need to be the same.

Add a Motion Path

1. Click an object.

2. Click the **Animations** tab.

3. Click the **Animation** down arrow (⤓).

4. Click and drag the scroll bar to the bottom to see the motion paths.

   Ⓐ Click **More Motion Paths** to see all motion paths.

5. Click a motion path.

   The motion path appears.

   Ⓑ The green and red markers indicate the beginning and end of the motion.

6. Click the motion path if it is not selected.

7. Click **Effect Options**.

8. Click **Edit Points**.

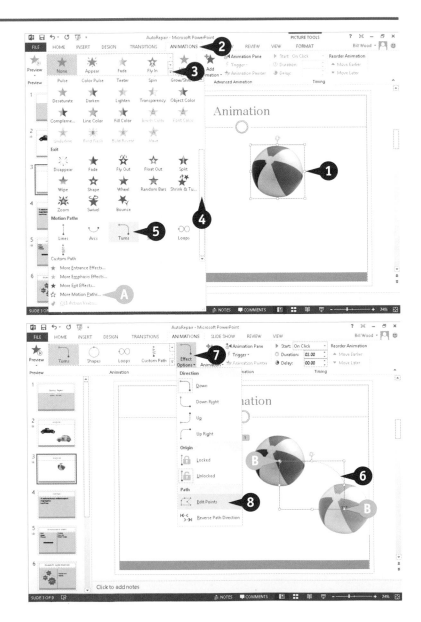

The motion path enters edit mode.

9 Click and drag anywhere on the line to change the shape of the motion path.

10 Click and drag the handle on the blue line to distort the motion path.

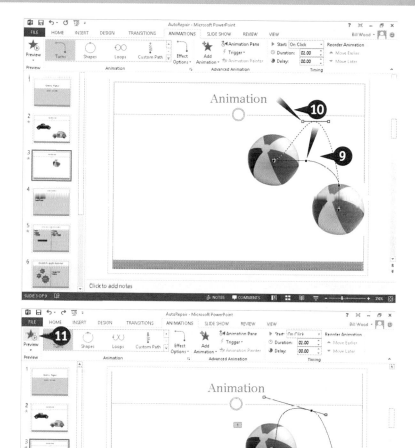

11 Click **Preview** to see the movement of the motion path.

TIP

Is there a way to change the size of the motion path without changing the shape of the line?
Yes. Click and drag a handle on the border to change the size of the motion path without changing its shape.

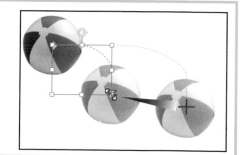

Remove an Animation

As you experiment with various animations, it is useful to know how to add them, as well as how to remove them. Too many animations on a slide can be distracting for your audience, so if you apply animations to a slide and decide they make it too complex, PowerPoint makes it quick and easy for you to remove some of them. The most convenient way to remove an animation is in the Animation pane.

Remove an Animation

1 Click the **Animations** tab.

2 Click **Animation Pane** if it is not open.

3 Click an animation.

4 Press Delete.

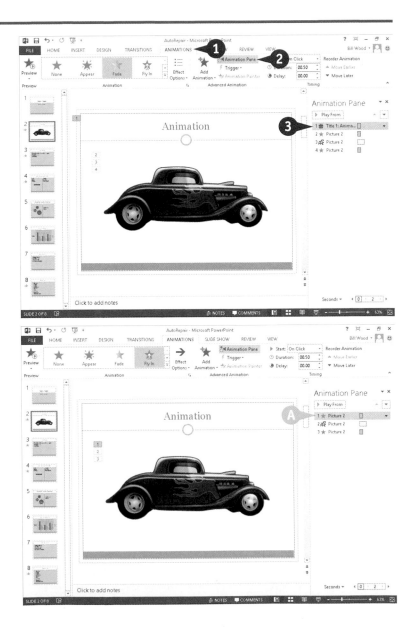

Ⓐ PowerPoint removes the animation from the object.

Apply a Transition

A transition is the act of going from one slide to another, and it offers yet another opportunity to add variety to your presentation. With transitions, you can vary the way a slide appears, such as fading from one slide to the next. You can apply a transition in Normal or Slide Sorter view to a single slide, multiple slides, or all slides. You may want to use the same transition throughout your presentation, or mix it up and use various transitions on different slides. Applying the Random transition tells PowerPoint to randomly apply a different transition to each slide in your presentation.

Apply a Transition

1 In Normal view, select the slides to which you want to apply a transition.

Note: See Chapter 10 to learn how to select objects.

2 Click the **Transitions** tab.

3 Click the **Transitions** down arrow ( ).

The gallery of transitions appears.

4 Click a transition.

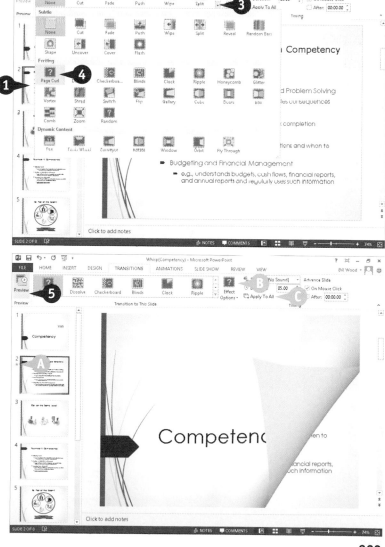

PowerPoint applies the transition to the selected slides.

Ⓐ The transition icon ( ) appears beside the slide's thumbnail.

Ⓑ You can click **Effect Options** to change the direction of the transition movement.

Ⓒ You can click **Apply To All** to apply the transition to all slides.

5 Click **Preview** to see the transition.

Remove a Transition

Sometimes while designing a presentation, you may apply a transition and then decide that it just does not work. As you experiment with various transitions, you need to know how to apply them, as well as how to remove them. Using too many transitions in a presentation can be distracting for your audience, so if you decide your presentation is too complex, you may want to remove some of the transitions. PowerPoint enables you to remove any transition in your presentation easily and quickly.

Remove a Transition

1 Select a slide with a transition in Normal or Slide Sorter view.

Note: See Chapter 10 to learn how to select objects.

2 Click the **Transitions** tab.

3 Click the **Transitions** down arrow (⤓).

The gallery of transitions appears.

4 Click **None**.

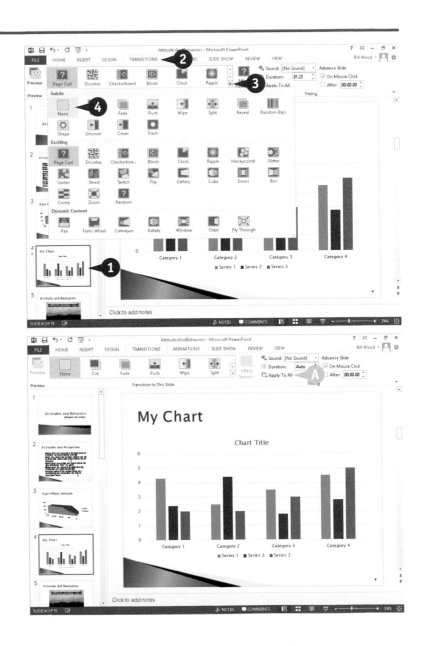

PowerPoint removes the transition and the transition icon disappears from the slide.

Ⓐ You can click **Apply To All** to remove transitions from all slides in the presentation.

Advance a Slide after a Set Time Interval

When you run a slide show, you can use one of two methods to advance from slide to slide. You can advance slides manually by clicking the slide, or you can set a timer that automatically advances to the next slide after a set amount of time. For example, if you are showing a presentation with pictures of a house, you may want to advance the slides automatically every ten seconds while you talk about the house. You can change these settings in Normal view, but Slide Sorter view is preferable.

Advance a Slide after a Set Time Interval

1 Select a slide with a transition in Slide Sorter view.

Note: See Chapter 10 to learn how to select objects.

2 Click the **Transitions** tab.

3 Click the **After** check box (☐ changes to ☑); this makes the slide automatically advance.

4 Click and hold the spinner (⯅⯆) to set a time interval.

Ⓐ The time interval appears under the slide.

Ⓑ If you leave the On Mouse Click check box selected (☑), you can also advance the slide by clicking your mouse.

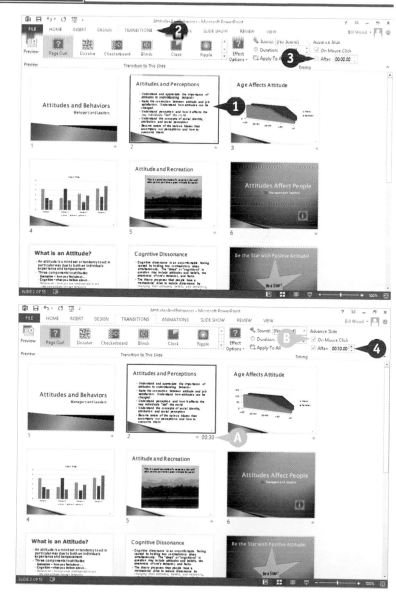

Add a Transition Sound

You can apply a sound to one or more slides in a presentation to accent important points. When used appropriately, transition sounds highlight important information during a slide show. For example, you may want applause when the slide that shows the top three sales representatives appears. Use transition sounds sparingly because the sounds will have greater impact, drawing attention to the most important information. Using transition sounds on too many slides can ruin the impact of using sounds. Using the same sound repeatedly also reduces its impact. You can apply a sound without using a visual transition.

Add a Transition Sound

1 Select a slide with a transition in Normal or Slide Sorter view.

Note: See Chapter 10 to learn how to select objects.

2 Click the **Transitions** tab.

3 Click the **Sound** down arrow (▼).

4 Click a sound.

Note: You can select [No Sound] from the menu to remove a sound from a transition.

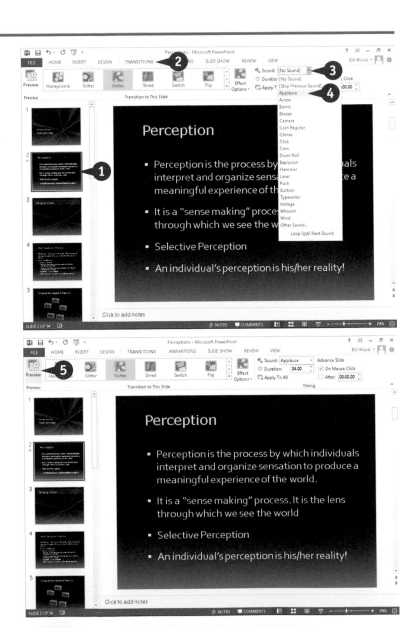

PowerPoint applies the sound to the transition.

5 Click **Preview** to hear the sound.

Note: Preview is available only if you apply a visual transition to the slide, not just a sound.

Set a Transition Speed

You can further customize a transition by changing the transition speed. The transition speed controls the rate at which the transition effect plays. Transitions are set with a default run speed that seems to be the right speed for each particular transition, but you may need a faster or slower transition speed. For fade-and-dissolve transitions, you might prefer a slow transition speed so the audience gets the full effect. For transitions such as wipes, you might prefer a faster speed that keeps the slide show moving.

Set a Transition Speed

1 Select a slide with a transition in Normal or Slide Sorter view.

Note: See Chapter 10 to learn how to select objects.

2 Click the **Transitions** tab.

3 Click the **Duration** spinner (⬍) to change the transition speed.

4 Click **Preview** to view the transition at the speed you specified.

The transition plays.

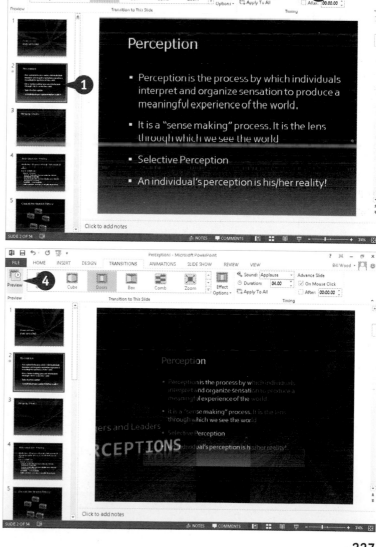

Insert an Action Button

Action buttons enable you to jump quickly and easily to a slide during a slide show. You can also use them to open a web page, another presentation, or a document from another application such as Excel. There are various standard actions that you can assign to an action button, and if you are advanced enough to use macros, action buttons can also trigger them.

Jumping to a web page requires an Internet connection. Any document that opens via an action button must be available on your computer.

Insert an Action Button

1. Select a slide in Normal view.

2. Click the **Insert** tab.

3. Click **Shapes**.

4. Click an action button style.

   The mouse pointer (⊣) turns into a crosshair (+).

5. Click where you want the button.

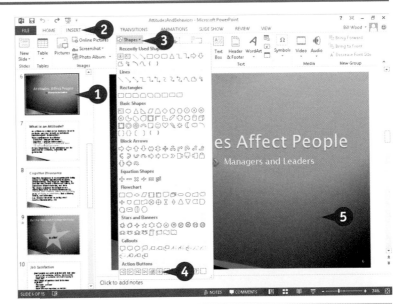

A. The action button appears and the Action Settings dialog box opens.

6. Click **Hyperlink to** (○ changes to ◉).

7. Click the **Hyperlink to** down arrow (⌄).

8. Click **URL**.

The Hyperlink to URL dialog box appears.

9 Type **http://www.microsoft.com** in the text box.

10 Click **OK**.

B You can click the **Play sound** check box and select a sound from the list. The sound will play when you click the action button during the slide show.

11 Click **OK**.

12 Click the button during the slide show.

C The default browser opens the Microsoft web page.

TIPS

My web page address is long. Is there a better way to enter it in the text box besides typing it?

Yes. Open your web browser and browse to the web page that you want to open during the slide show. Select the URL and press Ctrl+C to copy the address. Edit the action button and then press Ctrl+V to paste the URL into the text box.

What if I want to change what an action button does?

Right-click the action button and then click **Edit Hyperlink**. This displays the Action Settings dialog box, where you can make your changes.

CHAPTER 12

Incorporating Media

PowerPoint enables you to build exciting visual and sound effects into your presentations. You can place photographs, videos, and audio clips anywhere on your slides to enhance presentations. You can add dramatic artistic effects to your photographs or remove the background from them. Finally, you can edit photos and videos directly in PowerPoint, saving time and money because you do not need an editing program.

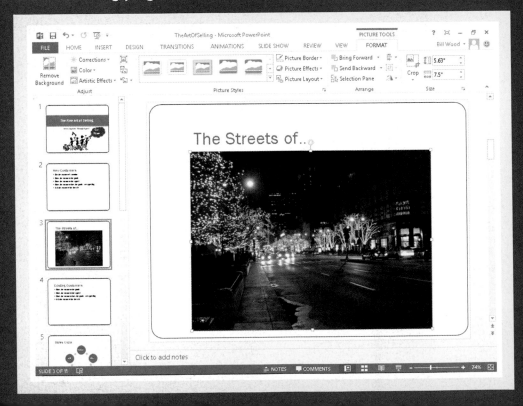

Insert a Picture

If you have an image file stored on your computer, such as your company logo or a picture of your product, you can insert the image into a PowerPoint slide. It is common for PowerPoint presentations to have pictures in them. You can insert pictures into a placeholder using the Insert Picture icon in the placeholder, or you can insert a picture directly on a slide to give you more versatility when you work with it. After you insert an image file, it becomes an object on your slide. To learn how to move, resize, and format objects, see Chapter 10.

Insert a Picture

1 Select a slide in Normal view.

2 Click the **Insert** tab.

3 Click **Pictures**.

The Insert Picture dialog box appears.

4 Select the folder containing the file you want to insert.

5 Click the file.

6 Click **Insert**.

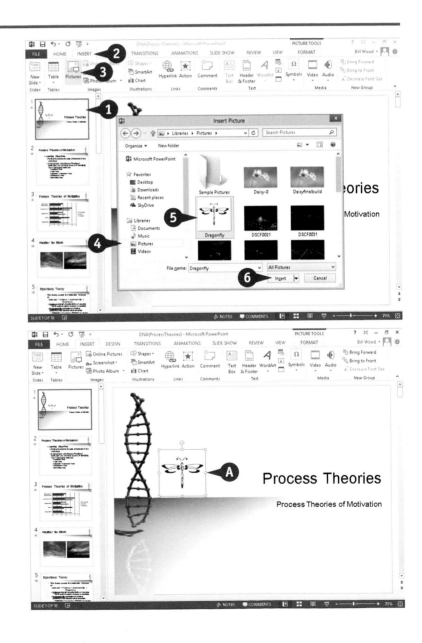

Ⓐ The image appears on your slide. Size and position the image as needed.

Note: To learn how to position and resize objects, see Chapter 10.

232

Add a Border

S ome clip art has transparent backgrounds, but sometimes the background of the picture or clip art does not blend with the background of the slide. After you insert a picture, you may want to set it apart from the rest of the slide by adding a border to it. A border makes the picture crisp, and also helps it stand out from other items on the slide and makes a clear break from the background of the slide. You can format the border by changing the thickness, making it something other than solid, or converting it to a different color.

Add a Border

1 Click a picture.

2 Click the **Picture Tools Format** tab.

3 Click **Picture Border**.

The gallery of borders appears.

4 Click a border color.

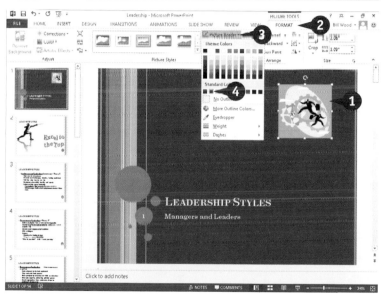

A The border appears around your picture.

5 Click **Picture Border**.

6 Click **Weight**.

7 Click a border thickness.

The border thickness changes.

B You can click **Dashes** to change the border to something other than solid such as dashes or dots.

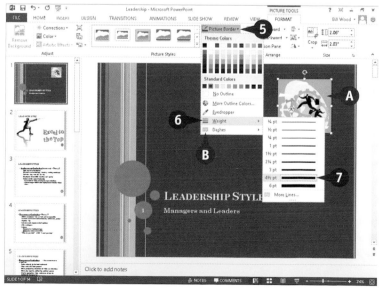

Adjust Brightness and Contrast

You can adjust the brightness and contrast of a picture in PowerPoint to maximize its visual impact. Many times, a picture is not perfect when you take it, or it does not show well on a screen. Brightness indicates how bright or dark the entire picture is. Contrast indicates how well you can see shades and colors against each other in the picture. Typically you want the picture to be bright and have high contrast because then it is easy for the audience to see. Adjusting the brightness and contrast may be all the picture needs to look good.

Adjust Brightness and Contrast

1 Click a picture.

2 Click the **Picture Tools Format** tab.

3 Click **Corrections**.

The gallery of corrections appears.

4 Click a **Brightness/Contrast** option from the gallery.

Ⓐ You can also apply a **Sharpen/ Soften** effect.

Ⓑ You can click **Picture Correction Options** for more detailed options.

PowerPoint adjusts the brightness and contrast.

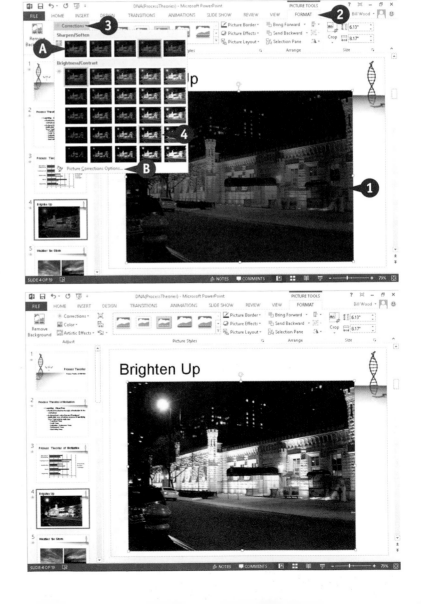

Adjust Color

Conditions outside of your control can affect a picture that you take with your camera. PowerPoint saves you the time and effort of performing color corrections in another program because you can do it right in PowerPoint! You can adjust the color of your pictures to make them pleasing to the eye, or recolor them for interesting effects. For example, you may want a picture that is monochrome in a color that matches the color scheme of your presentation. Standard color variations are determined by the theme of the presentation, but many other variations are also available.

Adjust Color

1 Click a picture.

2 Click the **Picture Tools Format** tab.

3 Click **Color**.

The gallery of colors appears.

4 Click your choice of **Color Saturation**, **Color Tone**, or **Recolor** options.

This example selects a recolor option.

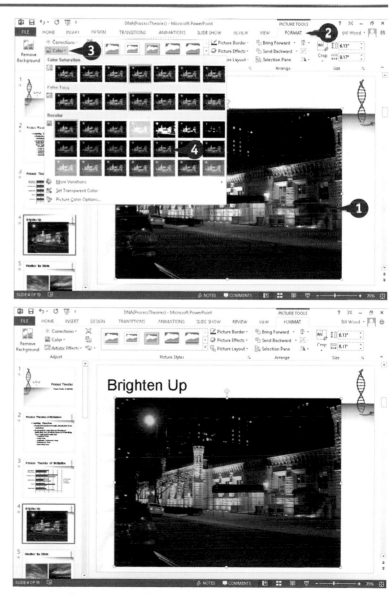

PowerPoint adjusts the color.

Note: Color Saturation determines how much color is in the picture and varies anywhere from black and white to a lot of color.

Note: Color tone affects the actual color — for example, a change in color tone may give the white items in your picture a slightly yellow hue.

Crop a Picture

A picture often contains things that you would rather not have in the image. For example, you may have a picture of a few friends, but only want the face of one particular friend in the picture. You can crop a picture so that the main subject of the picture fills the entire image. When you resize a picture, the objects in the picture change size accordingly and proportionately — you simply change the size of the picture. Cropping trims the edges from a picture in the same way as cutting them with a pair of scissors.

Crop a Picture

1. Select a picture.

2. Click the **Picture Tools Format** tab.

3. Click **Crop**.

   Black crop marks appear around the picture.

4. Position the mouse pointer ($\mathbb{k}$) over a crop mark ($\mathbb{k}$ changes to ∟).

5. Click the crop mark (∟ changes to $+$).

6. Drag the crop mark inward to remove a part of the picture.

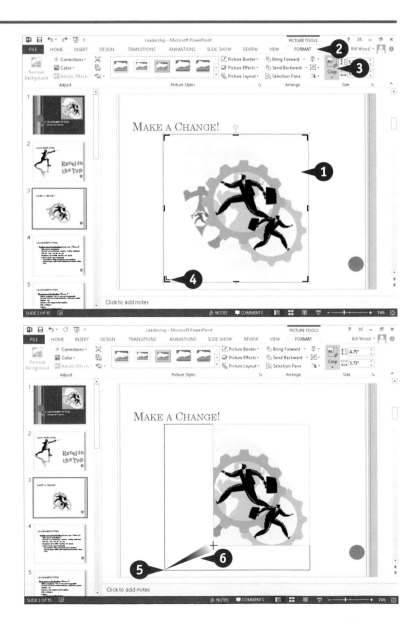

When you release the mouse button, you can see both the original picture and the cropped picture.

7 Click **Crop**.

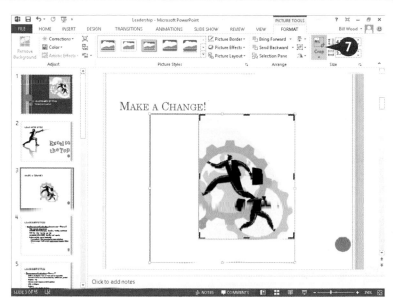

PowerPoint crops the picture.

8 Move and resize the picture if needed.

Note: See Chapter 10 to learn how to move and resize objects.

TIP

Can I crop a picture to an interesting shape?
Yes. There are two ways to crop to a shape. The first way is to click a picture and then click the **Picture Tools Format** tab. Click the **Picture Styles** drop-down arrow (⟱), and then click an option from the gallery. This method also includes a picture effect such as a picture frame. The second way is to crop to a shape without a picture effect, click the **Picture Tools Format** tab and then click the **Crop** drop-down arrow (⟱). Click **Crop to Shape** and then click one of the myriad options from the shapes gallery; the picture crops to that shape.

Remove the Background from a Picture

You may want to remove the background of a picture so you can work with just the main subject of the picture. Using the Remove Background feature in PowerPoint, you can remove the background from a picture easily and simply, and superimpose the remaining image onto a slide background or possibly another picture. This automated feature helps you avoid the inconvenience of importing the picture into PowerPoint after using a separate program to remove the background.

Remove the Background from a Picture

1 Select a picture.

2 Click the **Picture Tools Format** tab.

3 Click **Remove Background**.

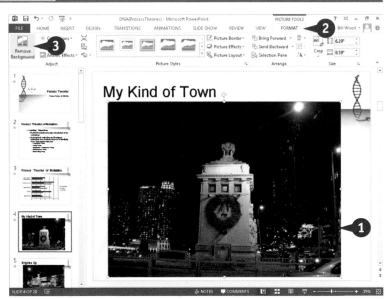

The background becomes magenta and PowerPoint automatically attempts to detect the object in the foreground. A marquee with handles appears.

4 Position the mouse pointer over a marquee handle (ℝ changes to ⟺).

5 Click and drag the marquee handle (⟺ changes to +) to resize the marquee.

6 Repeat Steps **4** and **5** with the various marquee handles until PowerPoint detects the foreground object that you want.

Note: Very small adjustments to the marquee help PowerPoint determine the object that you want in the foreground.

7 Click **Keep Changes**.

A To escape without saving changes, you can click **Discard All Changes**.

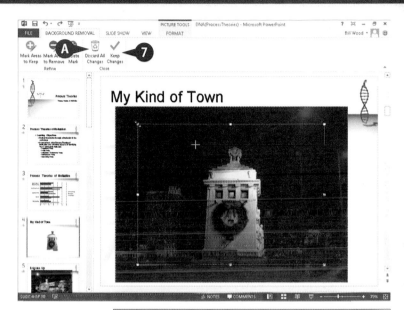

PowerPoint removes the background and only the foreground subject remains.

TIP

How can I include or exclude an image detail?

You can fine-tune the detected object. To add an area for inclusion:

1 Click the **Mark Areas to Keep** button in the Refine group.

2 Click and drag across the magenta area that includes your detail.

A PowerPoint includes the detail and marks it with a plus sign.

To erase the mark so that the detail is excluded, click the **Delete Mark** button, and then click the mark.

Using Artistic Effects

You may want to apply an interesting effect to a photo to add spice to your slide show. For example, you can make a picture look as if an artist sketched it. Many of these common special effects are available at the click of a button in graphics programs. Several artistic effects are also available in PowerPoint, so there is no need to use a separate program to give your picture a special effect. You can apply effects such as pixelation, blurring, and pencil sketch without leaving PowerPoint.

Using Artistic Effects

1 Select a picture.

2 Click the **Picture Tools Format** tab.

3 Click **Artistic Effects**.

The gallery of artistic effects appears.

4 Click an artistic effect.

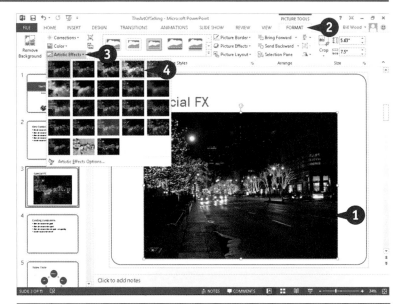

PowerPoint applies the artistic effect.

Compress Pictures

I mage and picture files can be very large. When you insert them into your presentation, your PowerPoint file also becomes large. This can slow the performance of your slide show presentation as well as performance while designing your presentation. You can improve performance by compressing image files, which has little impact on their quality. PowerPoint gives you the ability to determine how much compression occurs, thereby determining how much the compression affects the quality of the image. Compressing pictures permanently changes the images — you cannot reverse those changes.

Compress Pictures

1. Select a picture.

2. Click the **Picture Tools Format** tab.

3. Click the **Compress Pictures** icon (⬚).

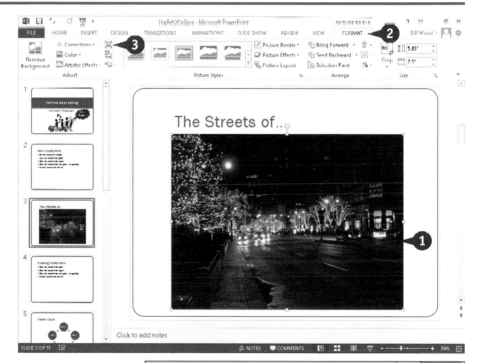

The Compress Pictures dialog box appears.

4. Click to disable (☐) **Apply only to this picture** so all pictures in your presentation are compressed.

5. Click **Screen** (○ changes to ⦿) for a resolution you can show to an audience with a projector.

6. Click **OK**.

PowerPoint compresses the pictures.

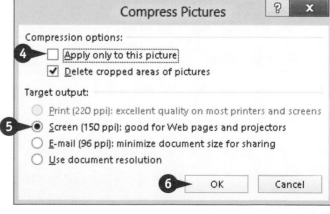

Using Layout Effects

You may want to organize and compare several pictures on one slide. You can make pictures look sharp by combining them with SmartArt Graphics, which is much more attractive than arranging the pictures on the slide with a list of bullet points. SmartArt Graphics enable you to combine pictures in many interesting groupings, and then apply text to the individual pictures or the entire group. You can also apply a workflow or hierarchy to pictures using SmartArt Graphics — using pictures in this way can give the audience an immediate impression without you saying a word.

Using Layout Effects

Apply a Layout

1 Select pictures in Normal view.

Note: To select multiple pictures, click the first picture, and then press **Ctrl** while clicking additional pictures.

2 Click the **Picture Tools Format** tab.

3 Click **Picture Layout**.

The gallery of picture layouts appears.

4 Click a picture layout.

PowerPoint applies the SmartArt Graphics picture layout to the pictures.

Note: See Chapter 5 to learn how to edit and change SmartArt Graphics and how to enter text into SmartArt Graphics.

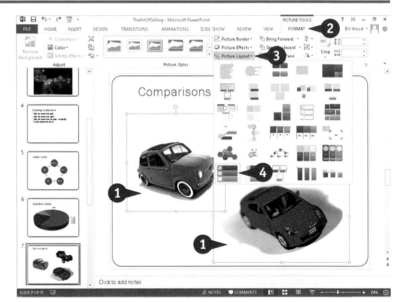

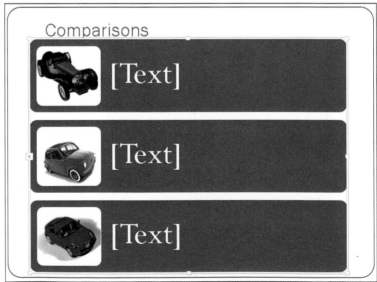

Change a Picture

1 Click a picture.

2 Click the **Picture Tools Format** tab.

3 Click the **Change Pictures** icon (🖳).

The Insert Pictures dialog box appears.

4 Click **From a file**.

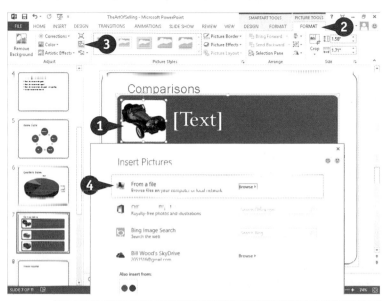

The Insert Picture dialog box appears.

5 Click the folder containing the picture file.

6 Click the picture.

7 Click **Open**.

Ⓐ PowerPoint changes the picture to the image you selected.

TIPS

Can I change the order of the pictures?
Yes. Click a picture in the SmartArt layout, and then click the **SmartArt Tools Design** tab. Click either **Move Up** or **Move Down** and the order of the picture changes accordingly.

Can I add another picture holder?
Yes. Click the SmartArt layout, click the **SmartArt Tools Design** tab, and then click **Add Shape**. You can also move a picture from one side of SmartArt to the other; click the SmartArt, click the **SmartArt Tools Design** tab, and then click **Right to Left**.

Insert Media from the Internet

When you try to use only your own resources to design a presentation, you severely limit yourself while designing it. The Internet has an unlimited amount of clip art, pictures, video clips, and audio clips. Much of this media is royalty-free, as is the case with the media from the Microsoft Office.com website. Searching the Internet for this type of content can be cumbersome, but PowerPoint has a search feature for just this purpose so you can save time and effort. You can insert the perfect video or picture directly into your presentation with just one or two keywords.

Insert Media from the Internet

1 Select a slide in Normal view.

2 Click the **Insert** tab.

3 Click **Online Picture**.

The Insert Pictures dialog box appears.

4 Click the **Office.com Clip Art** text box and type a keyword.

5 Click the **Search** icon (🔎).

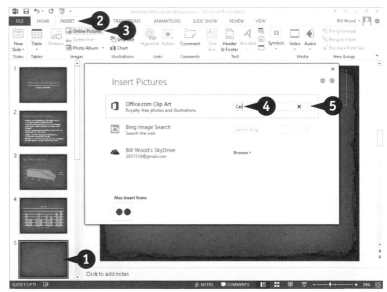

The Office.com results appear.

A You can click the **Close** button (✖) to cancel.

B Note the picture description and picture size.

6 Click **Back to Sites**.

7 Repeat Steps **4** and **5** using the Bing Image Search.

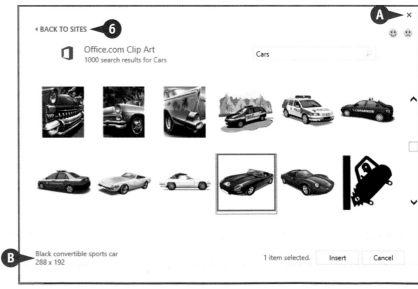

The Bing Image Search results appear.

C Note the picture description, picture size, and the hyperlink to the website where the picture originates.

D Some of these pictures are not royalty-free.

8 Click **Show all web results** for even more results.

9 Click an image.

10 Click **Insert**.

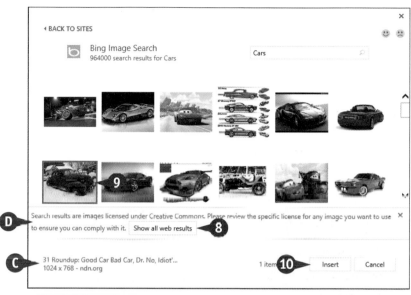

The image you selected appears on the slide.

Note: PowerPoint filters its search to the choice you make. For example, if you click the **Video** button on the Insert tab, PowerPoint only searches for videos.

TIPS

What is the SkyDrive search option in the Insert Pictures dialog box?

Microsoft has a convenient, free service called SkyDrive where you can store and share files in your own space. For example, you can load pictures to SkyDrive and give your friends access to it so they can download your pictures to their computer. PowerPoint accesses your SkyDrive directly to search and download pictures into your presentation.

Can I also download video and sound clips from the Internet?

Yes. This procedure also works for downloading video and audio clips from the Internet. Instead of clicking **Online Pictures** on the Insert tab, you click **Video** or **Audio**, and PowerPoint looks for only video or audio clips depending on your choice.

Insert Video and Audio Clips

You can enhance your slide show by inserting video or audio on a slide. A video clip can provide endorsements, testimonials, or instructional pieces that can be helpful during a presentation, or you may want to include something interesting or funny. An audio clip can play interesting sounds, such as applause, during a slide, or you can play an audio clip as background audio during several slides or even the entire slide show.

Both audio and video clips use this same procedure, except when you insert audio, a megaphone icon appears on the slide instead of a video.

Insert Video and Audio Clips

1 Select a slide in Normal view.

2 Click the **Insert** tab.

3 Click **Video** or **Audio**.

4 Click an option in the drop-down menu.

This example chooses **Video on My PC**.

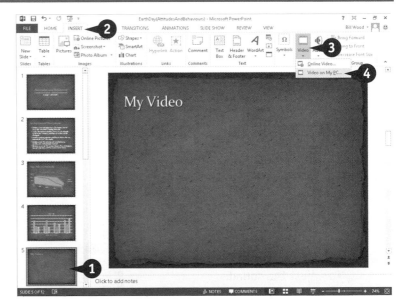

The Insert Video or Insert Audio dialog box appears.

5 Select the folder containing the file.

6 Click the file.

7 Click **Insert**.

The video or audio appears on your slide.

Note: You can size and position a video as needed. To learn how to position and resize objects, see Chapter 10.

Ⓐ The Control bar appears when you position the mouse pointer (◌) over the clip.

⑧ Click the **Playback** tab.

⑨ Click **Play** (▶ changes to ▮▮).

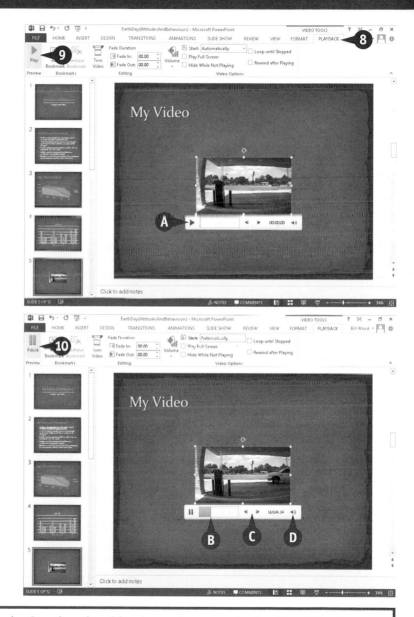

Ⓑ You can click anywhere on the slide to jump to any part of the clip.

Ⓒ You can click the **Forward** (▶) and **Back** (◀) buttons to jump forward or backward 0.25 seconds.

Ⓓ You can use the **Volume** button (◀») to adjust the sound.

⑩ Click **Pause** (▮▮ changes to ▶).

The video or audio stops playing.

TIPS

Can I play the video in full screen during the slide show?

Yes. To make the video play full screen, click the video, click the **Video Tools Playback** tab, and then click the **Play Full Screen** check box (☐ changes to ☑) in the Video Options group.

Starting the video is cumbersome during the slide show. Can I make it smoother?

Yes. On the Video Tools Playback tab, click to enable (☑) **Hide While Not Playing**, click to enable (☑) **Play Full Screen**, and then click the **Start** down arrow (▼) and select **Automatically**. Now the video plays full screen and starts automatically when the slide appears, plus you do not see it when it is not playing.

Record an Audio Clip

You can bring interesting sound effects into your presentation with audio clips. You can draw your audience into your slide show by playing audio at just the right time during the show. For example, you may want applause when a slide with sales figures appears. You can also use a longer audio to play sound for several slides, or maybe background music for the entire slide show. You can record an audio clip in PowerPoint and insert it directly to a slide without using different software to record it first. Bring excitement to your slide show by recording your own audio directly to a slide.

Record an Audio Clip

1 Select a slide in Normal view.

2 Click the **Insert** tab.

3 Click **Audio**.

4 Click **Record Audio**.

Note: You need a microphone attached to your computer to perform this task.

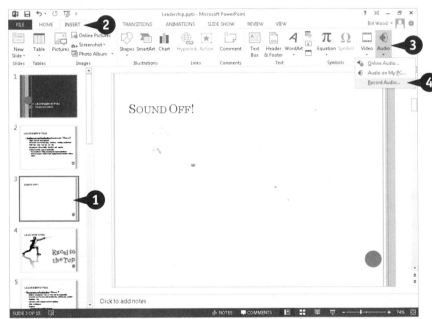

The Record Sound dialog box appears.

Ⓐ Click **Cancel** to abort the recording and discontinue insertion of the audio.

5 Click the **Name** text box.

6 Type a name for your recording.

7 Click the **Record** button (⏺).

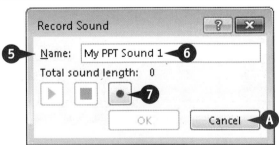

8 Record your audio into the microphone.

9 When you are finished, click the **Stop** button (■).

10 Click the **Play** button (▶) to listen to your recording.

D You can click the **Record** button (●) to continue recording additional audio.

11 Click **OK** when you complete your recording.

12 Click the **Audio Tools Playback** tab.

13 Click **Play** (⏸ changes to ⏸).

The audio plays.

C You can use the **Volume** button (◀») to adjust the sound.

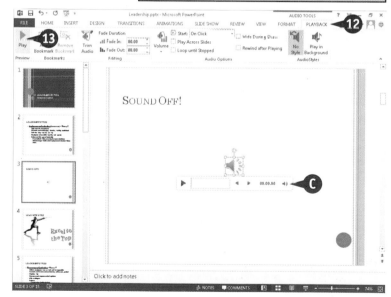

TIPS

Can I change the megaphone icon to something else?

Yes. Click the megaphone icon and then click the **Audio Tools Format** tab. Click the **Change Pictures** button (🖼) in the Adjust group and use the Insert Pictures dialog box to insert a picture as described in this chapter.

What is the Play in Background button?

The Play in Background button enables the audio clip to start automatically when the slide appears. The audio does not stop — it plays across multiple slides, looping until you stop it or the show ends. These settings appear as check boxes on the Audio Tools Format tab.

Trim Video Clips

Videos are usually not the length you want for your presentation, and so you will probably want to trim them. You may want to only play a snippet of a video during a slide show to show a little information about something, or you may have a leader or trailer in the video that you do not need your audience to see. PowerPoint gives you the convenience to trim the video right on the slide so you need not leave PowerPoint to use other software to do it.

Trim Video Clips

1. Click a video clip.

2. Click the **Video Tools Playback** tab.

3. Click **Trim Video**.

The Trim Video dialog box appears.

4. Click and drag the green marker where you want the video to begin.

The video frame that plays at that time appears in the window.

5 Click and drag the red marker where you want the video to end.

The video frame that plays at that time appears in the window.

6 Click **OK**.

The dialog box closes and PowerPoint trims the video to your specifications.

7 Click the **Video Tools Playback** tab.

8 Click **Play** (⏵ changes to ⏸) to view the trimmed video.

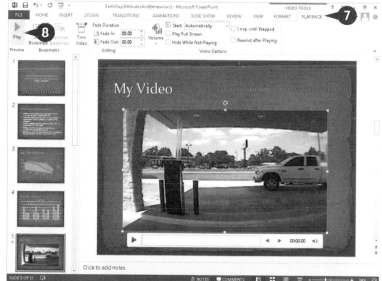

TIPS

What is the Fade Duration?
The Fade Duration fades the beginning or end of the video; you can use it only when you trim the video. The length of time the fade effect lasts is determined by the time you set in the **Fade In** and **Fade Out** text boxes. The effect gives your video a soft feel.

What is the Hide While Not Playing feature?
The Hide While Not Playing feature hides the video if it is not playing. You need to start the video automatically, because you cannot manually start the video when it is hidden. This feature is convenient because the video clip hides after it is done playing, so you can show the rest of the slide.

Trim Audio Clips

You may have an interesting part of a song to play for your audience, or a clip from an interview to share with them, but you do not want to play an entire audio clip for them. You might have an audio clip that you recorded and inserted directly onto a PowerPoint slide, but it needs to be shorter. In any of these cases, you can trim an audio clip directly in PowerPoint to make it the perfect length for your purpose. This handy feature saves you the inconvenience of trimming the audio clip in a different program and then importing it into PowerPoint.

Trim Audio Clips

1 Click an audio clip.

2 Click the **Audio Tools Playback** tab.

3 Click **Trim Audio**.

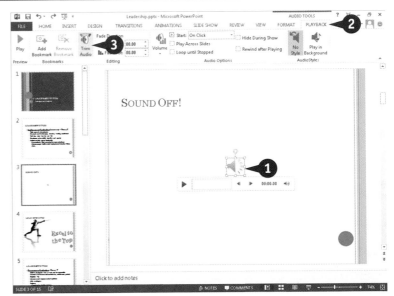

The Trim Audio dialog box appears.

4 Click the slide where you want to listen to the audio.

Note: Do not click the slide if you want to start listening from the beginning.

5 Click the **Play** button (▶ changes to ❚❚).

6 Listen and find where you want to trim the beginning and end of your audio.

7 Click the **Pause** button (🔲 changes to ▶) to stop the audio.

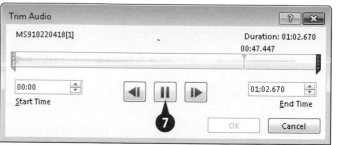

8 Click and drag the green marker where you want to trim the beginning of the audio.

9 Click and drag the red marker where you want to trim the end of the audio.

10 Click **OK**.

The dialog box closes and PowerPoint trims the audio to the length that you specified.

11 Click **Play** (🔳 changes to 🔳) to listen to the trimmed audio.

Note: Trimming an audio clip is reversible. Repeat this process to reverse it.

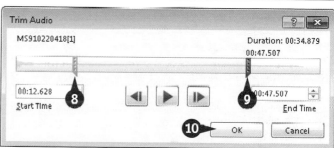

TIPS

What happens when I set the Start setting to Automatically?

You can start both audio and video clips in two ways. You can start them when you click them, or they can start automatically when the slide appears when you set **Start** to **Automatically**.

How does the Play across Slides option work?

When you enable (☑) **Play across Slides**, an audio clip plays until it ends, even if you advance to other slides. If you do not want the audio to end, enable (☑) **Loop until Stopped**.

Insert a Screenshot

You may want to show something from your computer in a slide show. For example, you may want to take a screenshot of an SAP data entry screen to show why users are having difficulty entering information into a data entry form. You can take a screenshot of an open window or a section of the computer display and insert it onto a slide without leaving PowerPoint. The screenshot feature is a fast and convenient way to take a snapshot of something on your computer and put it into a presentation.

Insert a Screenshot

Choose an Open Window

1. Select a slide in Normal view.

2. Click the **Insert** tab.

3. Click **Screenshot**.

   The Available Windows gallery appears. Windows that are open, but not minimized, appear in this gallery.

4. Click a window in the gallery.

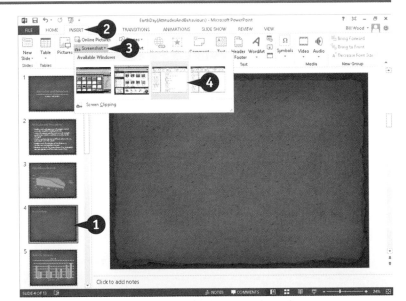

   PowerPoint inserts the window screenshot onto the slide.

Note: Only windows that are not minimized appear in the Available Windows gallery. If you want to take a screenshot of a window, it must be restored or maximized.

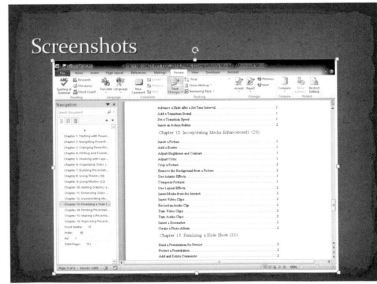

Choose a Section of the Screen

1 Repeat Steps **1** to **3** in the previous steps.

The Available Windows gallery appears.

2 Click **Screen Clipping**.

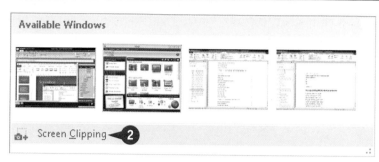

The PowerPoint window disappears, showing whatever is under it. The mouse pointer (⇖) changes to the crosshair pointer (+).

3 Click and drag across the section of screen that you want in your screenshot.

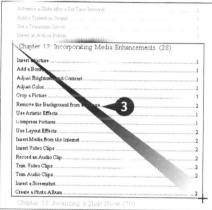

The PowerPoint window reappears and the screenshot appears on the slide. You can size and position the screenshot as needed.

Note: To learn how to position and resize objects, see Chapter 10.

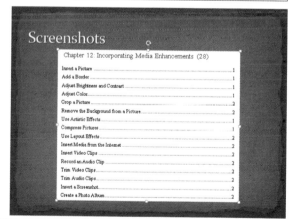

TIPS

When I use the Screen Clipping option, how do I get the correct screen?

PowerPoint shows you what is directly under it when it minimizes. Minimize all active windows on your computer and then use the Windows taskbar to restore the window of interest — if you want your Desktop, restore nothing. Now restore PowerPoint and perform the Screen Clipping process.

How do I take a screenshot of two or more windows?

Minimize all windows. Restore and arrange the windows you want in the screenshot. Restore the PowerPoint window and click the **Insert** tab. Click **Screenshot**, and then click **Screen Clipping**. Click and drag across the windows with the crosshair pointer (+).

Create a Photo Album

You can set up slides so that they advance automatically, and you can also play an audio clip across slides and have it loop indefinitely. This is a perfect scenario to show a photo album. You can create a photo album and then show it like any other slide show or set it up to flip through the pictures automatically, complete with background music! You can create an especially nice photo album to share pictures with family and friends with the professionalism that PowerPoint affords you. The procedure described here creates a new presentation.

Create a Photo Album

1 Click **Insert**.

2 Click the **Photo Album** drop-down arrow (▼).

3 Click **New Photo Album**.

The Photo Album dialog box appears.

4 Click **File/Disk**.

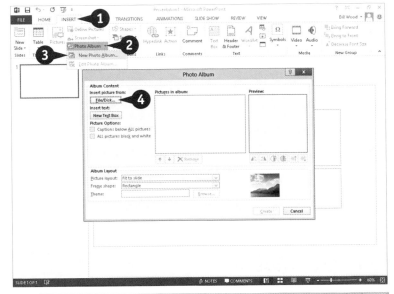

The Insert New Pictures dialog box appears.

5 Click the folder that holds your picture files.

6 Click pictures that you want in your photo album while pressing Ctrl to select multiple files. All selected pictures appear in the photo album.

7 Click **Insert**.

The Insert New Pictures dialog box closes.

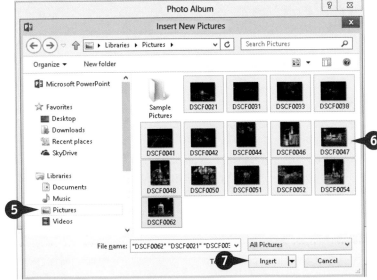

The Photo Album dialog box reappears.

8 Click a picture to view it.

9 Click the **Picture layout** drop-down arrow (⌄) and select a layout.

🅐 You can use these picture correction features if you select only one picture.

🅑 You can click to select one or more pictures to move or remove them.

🅒 This option is available only when the layout has multiple pictures.

10 Click **Create**.

PowerPoint creates the photo album.

Note: You can design a photo album like any other presentation.

Note: Click **Edit Photo Album** from the Photo Album drop-down menu on the Insert tab to change the pictures in the slide show.

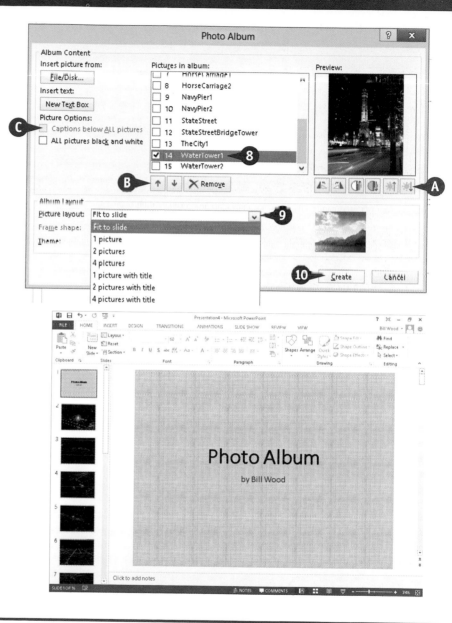

What is the New Text Box button in the Photo Album dialog box?
You may want to include an explanation or comments about your photographs on a slide. You can click the New Text Box button and PowerPoint inserts a text box in the Pictures in album list. You can move the text box or a photograph within the list by clicking it and then clicking the **Move Up** (⬆) or **Move Down** (⬇) buttons. After you create the photo album, you can click the text box on the slide and type your text. You can insert multiple text boxes into your photo album or even into a slide.

CHAPTER 13

Finalizing a Slide Show

After you add all of your slide content, tweak your slide design, and add graphics, animations, and transitions, you are almost done. Now, you perform the final tasks to complete your presentation. You review it, comment on it, set the show parameters, rehearse, and possibly record a narration. Finally, you can run your slide show!

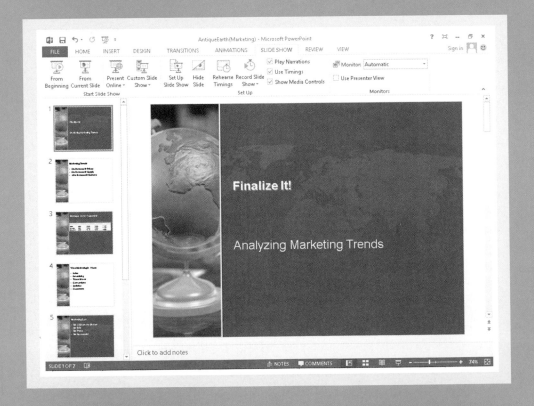

Send a Presentation for Review

You may want to seek feedback on your presentation before you give a slide show. A second opinion helps because another viewer can spot errors you missed or suggest improvements. You may want another person to check your facts, validate technical advice, or verify procedures. You can e-mail your presentation to others for review and the reviewers can add comments to the presentation and then e-mail it back to you. You then have the information you need to make your presentation as good as it can possibly get.

Send a Presentation for Review

Send the e-mail

Note: These steps assume that your e-mail program is properly configured to work with other applications.

1. Click the **File** tab to show Backstage view.

2. Click **Share**.

3. Click **Email**.

4. Click **Send as Attachment**.

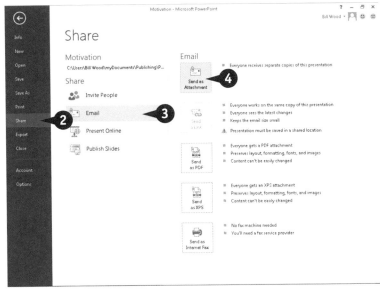

An e-mail message window appears.

5. Click the **To** text box and type the recipient's e-mail address.

6. Click the message pane and type text for the message.

7. Click **Send**.

The application sends the e-mail with the presentation attached.

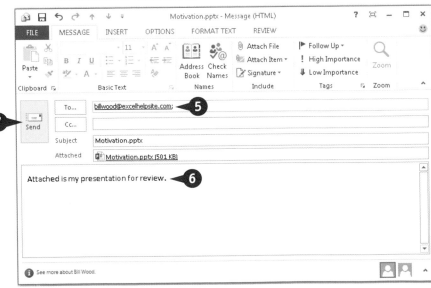

260

Receive the e-mail

1 After you receive a file back from a reviewer, open the e-mail.

2 Right-click the PowerPoint attachment.

3 Click **Save As**.

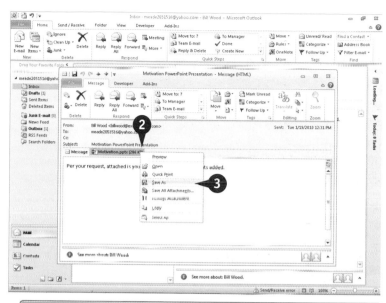

The Save Attachment dialog box appears.

4 Click the folder that you want to contain the file.

5 Click the **File Name** text box.

6 Type a name.

7 Click **Save**.

The e-mail application saves the PowerPoint presentation. You can now open and review the presentation.

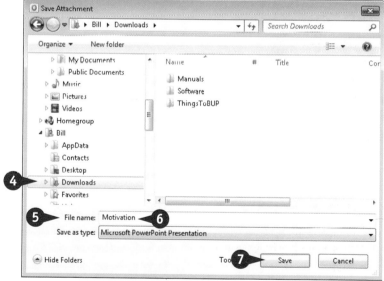

TIPS

When I e-mail a presentation for review, what does the recipient need to do?

The recipient needs to open the presentation in PowerPoint in order to review it. That person can click the **Review** tab, and then click the **New Comment** command to add comments. PowerPoint adds the reviewer's initials and a number to each comment.

What can I do if my recipient cannot open my PowerPoint 2013 file?

Try saving the file in a compatible format with older PowerPoint versions. To save in a compatible format, click the **File** tab, and then click **Export**. Click **Change File Type**, and then click **PowerPoint 97-2003 Presentation** in the Presentation File Types list. Continue to save the file as you normally would.

Protect a Presentation

You may not want anybody else to present your slide show, or you may not want others to see how you designed it. Your presentation may have sensitive information that you want to protect in case it falls into the wrong hands. PowerPoint allows you to protect your presentation. You can password-protect your presentation so that only those with the proper credentials can open it. Remember to record the password, though — you will want to open it yourself!

Protect a Presentation

1 Click the **File** tab to show Backstage view.

2 Click **Info**.

3 Click **Protect Presentation**.

4 Click **Encrypt with Password**.

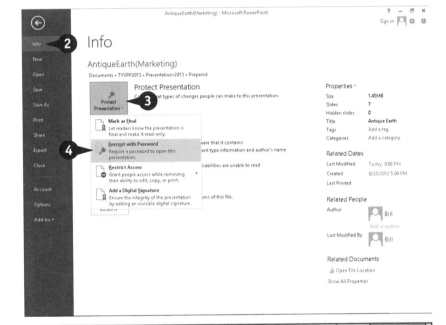

The Encrypt Document dialog box appears.

5 Click the **Password** text box.

6 Type a password.

7 Click **OK**.

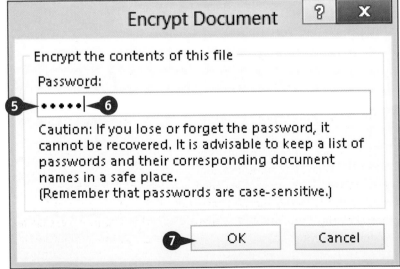

The Confirm Password dialog box appears.

8 Click the **Reenter password** text box.

9 Type the password.

10 Click **OK**.

Confirm Password

Encrypt the contents of this file

Reenter password:

8 ••••• **9**

Caution: If you lose or forget the password, it cannot be recovered. It is advisable to keep a list of passwords and their corresponding document names in a safe place.
(Remember that passwords are case-sensitive.)

10 ► OK   Cancel

A PowerPoint protects the presentation.

11 Click **Close**.

12 Open the presentation.

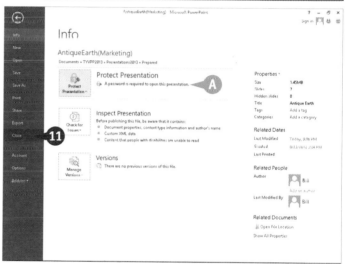

Info

AntiqueEarth(Marketing)
Documents » TYVPP2013 » Presentations2013 » Prepared

Protect Presentation
A password is required to open this presentation. **A**

Inspect Presentation
Before publishing this file, be aware that it contains:
- Document properties, content type information and author's name
- Custom XML data
- Content that people with disabilities are unable to read

11

Versions
There are no previous versions of this file.

Properties
Size   1.45MB
Slides   7
Hidden slides 0
Title   Antique Earth
Tags   Add a tag
Categories   Add a category

Related Dates
Last Modified Today, 9:06 PM
Created   8/13/2012 2:06 PM
Last Printed

Related People
Author   Bill
               Add an author
Last Modified By   Bill

Related Documents
Open File Location
Show All Properties

PowerPoint asks for the password.

Password

Enter password to open file
AntiqueEarth(Marketing).pptx
Password:

OK   Cancel

TIPS

How can I remove the password?
You go through the same process as when you add a password. However, when the Encrypt Document dialog box appears, it displays an encoded password. Delete the encoded password and click **OK**. The presentation then becomes unprotected.

What is the Mark as Final item on the Protect Presentation menu?
The Marked as Final feature shows you and others that the presentation is finished and ready for presenting. The Save command is no longer available and PowerPoint places an icon in the status bar indicating the final status. When you open a presentation with this status, a message appears, informing you of the status. You are given the option to edit and save the presentation.

Add and Delete Comments

If you have been asked to review a presentation or you want to mark up your own presentation, you can use the comments feature to document your notations. PowerPoint identifies each comment with a marker, making it easy for the presentation designer to find and consider each comment. Each comment contains the name of the person making the comment and the date, and the comment can be attached to a slide or an object on the slide. After you add your comments, save the file and the presentation comments are ready for review.

Add and Delete Comments

1. Select a slide in Normal view.
2. Click the **Review** tab.
3. Click **New Comment**.

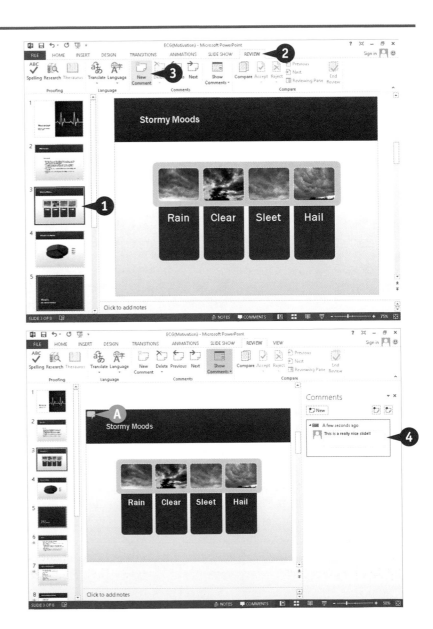

The Comments task pane appears.

A. A comment marker appears on the slide.

4. Type the comment text.
5. Press **Enter**.

Note: You can click and drag the comments marker to move it.

6 Click an object on the slide.

7 Click **New**.

8 Type the comment text

9 Press Enter.

B A comment marker appears on the object.

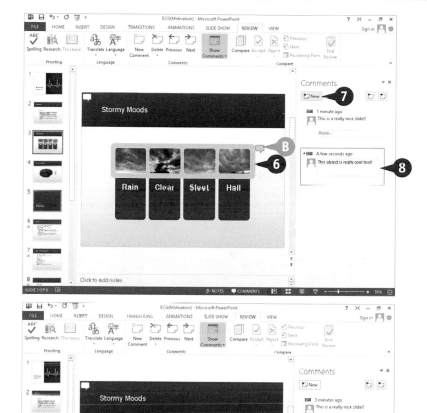

10 Position the mouse pointer (↖) over a comment.

The Delete icon (✕) appears.

11 Click the **Delete** icon (✕).

PowerPoint deletes the comment.

TIPS

I noticed some misspellings in the comments. How do I change them?

Select a comment by clicking either the comment marker or the comment in the Comments pane. Click the text once to select all of the text, and click again to insert the insertion point in the text. Edit the text and press Enter.

Why do some comment markers overlap a little and others overlap almost completely?

Comment markers that overlap almost completely are comments and their replies, which are grouped tightly, and when you click these markers, they are all selected. Comment markers that are grouped loosely and barely overlap are different comments on the same slide or object — you can select them individually.

Review Comments

Apresentation with comments in it is like a printout with sticky notes on it. You can page through the presentation file, read the individual notes, and decide whether to make any changes based on them. You can then delete (throw away) individual comments as you review them or delete all comments on a slide or in the presentation. You can also show or hide comments — that way, you can design your presentation without distractions, but come back to comments at a later time if needed.

Review Comments

1. Select a slide with a comment in Normal view.

2. Click the **Review** tab.

3. Click **Show Comments**.

4. Click **Show Markup**.

5. Click **Show Comments**.

6. Click **Comments Pane**.

   The Comments pane and all comments appear.

7. Click a comment marker.

   The comment appears selected in the Comments pane.

8. Click a **Reply** text box.

9. Type a reply.

10. Press **Enter**.

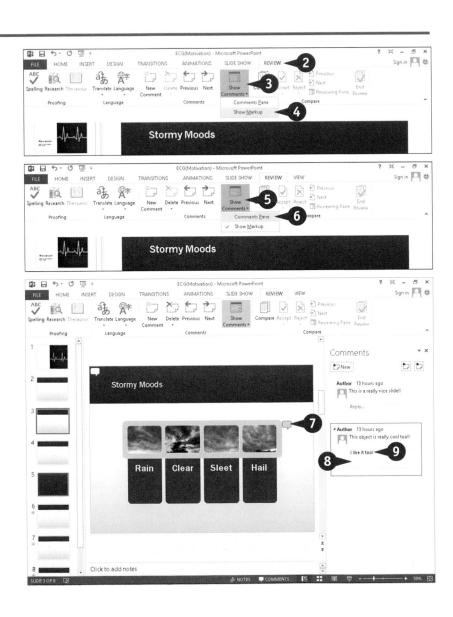

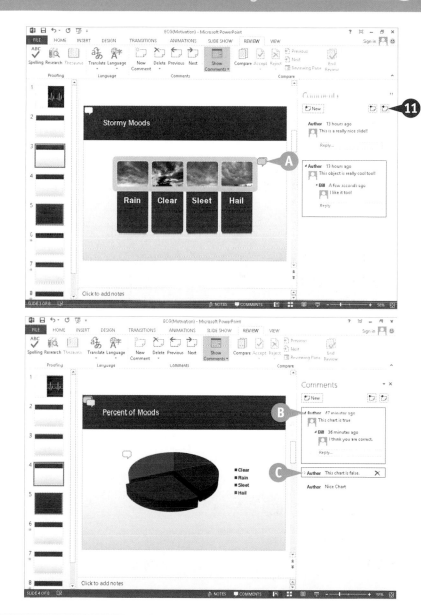

🅐 Note that the comment and its reply are grouped together.

⑪ Click the **Next Comment** button (🔁).

Note: You can use the Next Comment (🔁) and Previous Comment (🔁) buttons to move from one comment to another, as well as from slide to slide.

PowerPoint moves to the next comment on the next slide.

🅑 You can click the **Collapse** icon (◢) to collapse a comment.

🅒 You can click the **Expand** icon (▷) to see a collapsed comment.

TIPS

I noticed that some of my comments say Author on them. Why is that?

If you view comments on the same computer where you created the comments, PowerPoint uses the word *Author* to denote who made the comment, thereby avoiding any confusion with names.

Can I print comments along with my handouts?

Yes. Comments and comment markers print by default when you print slides. However, there is an option to hide them during printing if you do not want to print them. This option is in the drop-down list where you select the slide layout for the printout in Backstage view.

Select a Show Type and Show Options

You should have no surprises during your slide show, so before you run it for an audience, you should check the settings so you know exactly what will happen when you run it. These settings include the type of slide show, whether the slide show repeats continuously, whether you want to use narration and animations, and the pen color for annotations made on the screen during the slide show. These settings allow you to configure the slide show to your particular needs so you are as comfortable as possible during the slide show.

Select a Show Type and Show Options

1 In Normal view, click the **Slide Show** tab.

2 Click **Set Up Slide Show**.

The Set Up Show dialog box appears.

3 Click an option to select whether you want a speaker to present your slide show, a person to view it on a computer, or many people to view it at a kiosk (○ changes to ◉).

4 Click either the **Manually** option (slides advance with a mouse click) or click the **Using timings, if present** option (○ changes to ◉).

Note: This setting only has an effect if you set any slide timings. Timings, such as setting a slide to advance automatically or after you rehearse timing the show, do not work if you set this option to Manually.

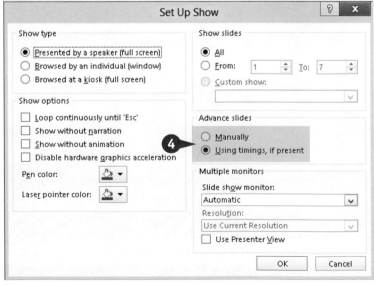

268

⑤ Click one or more options to select whether you want your show to loop continuously, run without narration, or run without animation (☐ changes to ☑).

⑥ Click the **Pen color** button (🖌▾) and select a color from the palette.

⑦ Click the **Laser pointer color** button (🖌▾) and select a color from the palette.

Note: See Chapter 15 to learn about Pen annotations and the Laser Pointer.

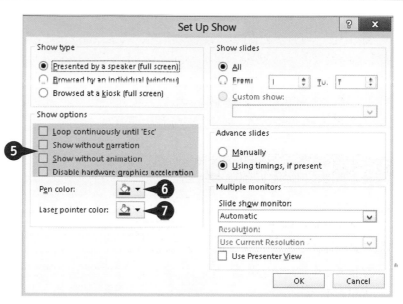

⑧ Click **OK**.

PowerPoint applies your new settings and closes the dialog box.

⑨ Click the **Save** icon (🖫) to save the settings.

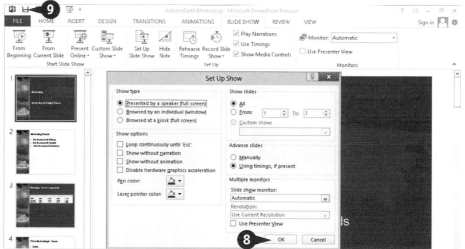

TIPS

Why would I want to show my presentation without animation?

Animations are fun, but on computers lacking adequate resources, they may run slowly and delay your show. If you are using an older computer to present your show, preview it to be sure that animations run smoothly. If they do not, change this setting to avoid any problems.

What is a loop and why would I use it?

Looping is a term for running media, such as songs or videos, over and over again from beginning to end. If you plan to show your presentation at an informational booth or kiosk, where people may stop, watch a bit, and then move on, you probably want the presentation to loop.

Specify Slides to Include

You may create a larger presentation, but decide that you want to show only some of the slides to a particular audience. For example, you may want to show the beginning, summary, and conclusion of a slide show to executives, but present the entire slide show to an audience that needs to see details, such as middle management. To limit the slides that display, you can create a custom slide show that you can quickly and easily access and play. When it is time to present your slide show, you can find and begin the custom show with a few clicks of your mouse.

Specify Slides to Include

1 In Normal view, click the **Slide Show** tab.

2 Click **Custom Slide Show**.

3 Click **Custom Shows**.

The Custom Shows dialog box appears.

4 Click **New**.

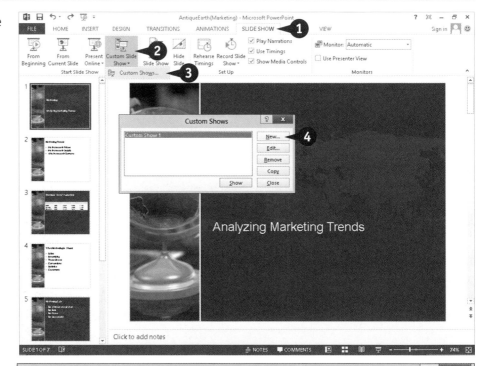

The Define Custom Show dialog box appears.

5 Click the **Slide show name** text box.

6 Type a name.

7 Click the slides that you want in your custom slide show (☐ changes to ☑).

8 Click **Add**.

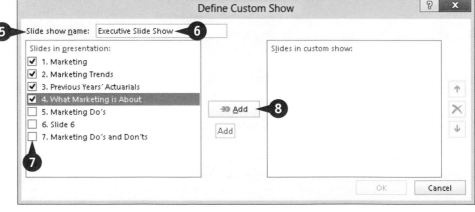

A PowerPoint adds the slides to the Slides in custom show list.

9 Click **OK**.

B PowerPoint adds the custom show to the list.

10 Click **Close**.

11 Click **Custom Slide Show**.

The menu lists all custom slide shows for this particular presentation.

12 Click the custom show you want to present.

PowerPoint starts your custom slide show.

TIPS

Can I show a range of slides quickly without creating a custom slide show?

Yes. Click **Set Up Slide Show** on the Slide Show tab. Under the Show Slides heading of the dialog box, click the **From** option. Type the beginning and ending slide numbers and then click **OK**. When you present the slide show, only that range of slides are shown.

What if I do not want to show a slide located in the middle of my presentation?

With a large presentation, it may be inconvenient to build a custom show that excludes only one slide. In this case, just hide the slide. Change to Slide Sorter view, right-click the slide, and then click **Hide Slide** on the shortcut menu.

Rehearse Timing

Completing your presentation in the allotted time is considered courteous. You can use the Rehearse Timings feature to time a practice run of your slide show to ensure that it takes the proper amount of time to deliver. This helps you arrange your presentation so it fits into the time allotted for it. You can also use the Rehearse Timings feature to time slides when you set up slides to advance automatically during your slide show and when the slide show is programmed to play continuously.

Rehearse Timing

1 Click the **Slide Show** tab.

2 Click **Rehearse Timings**.

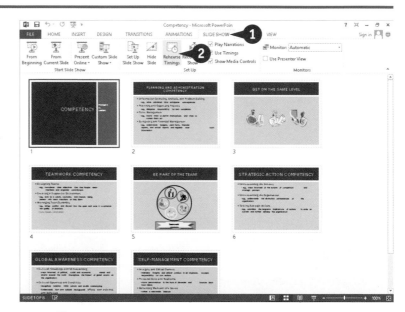

The slide show begins and the Recording toolbar appears.

3 Rehearse the slide narrative, clicking the **Next** button (→) to advance the slide.

Ⓐ This shows the elapsed time of the current slide.

Ⓑ This shows the elapsed time of the entire show.

Ⓒ Click **Repeat** (↺) to start the timing over for the current slide.

Ⓓ Click the **Close** button (✖) to exit the slide show early.

④ Click the **Pause** button (❙❙) to suspend the timing.

The Recording Paused dialog box appears.

⑤ Click **Resume Recording**.

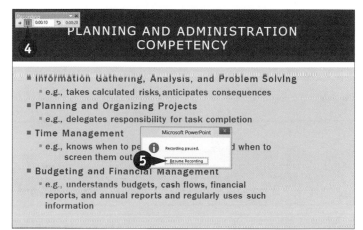

After the last slide, a message box asks if you want to save the timings.

⑥ Click **Yes** to save the timings, or click **No** to exit the rehearsal without saving the timings.

The presentation appears in Design view.

Ⓔ The timing applied to each slide appears below its thumbnail.

⑦ Click the **Save** icon (🖫) to save the timings.

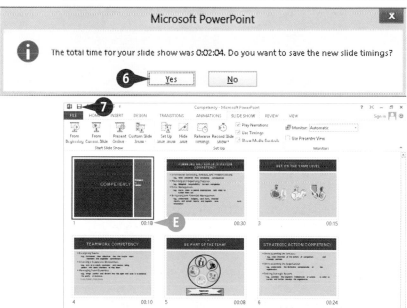

Rehearsing timings and recording a slide show seem to be the same thing. Are they?
They are very similar. You can have slides advance automatically through a slide show if you either rehearse timing or record a show. The significant difference is that you can record a narrative and the movements of the laser pointer when you record the show. Considering you usually record a show because you are absent when the slide show is running, this is a pretty important difference. If the slide show runs on a kiosk or on someone's computer, you probably want to record a narration and the movements of the laser pointer.

Record a Narration

If you do not intend to present your PowerPoint show live — for example, if you are showing your presentation at a kiosk — you can record a narration that talks the viewer through your key points. Recording a slide show also sets up your presentation to advance automatically at the end of each slide's narration. This nice feature gives you the option to give the presentation in person, or to personalize a presentation where you are not physically present. You do not necessarily need to record the entire presentation; you can record just a few slides if you choose.

Record a Narration

1 Plug a microphone into your computer.

2 Click the **Slide Show** tab.

3 Click **Record Slide Show**.

The Record Slide Show dialog box appears.

4 Click to enable (☑) both options.

5 Click **Start Recording**.

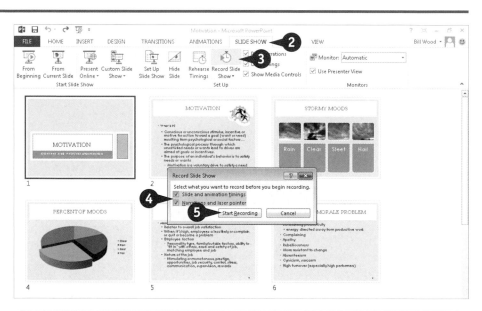

The slide show begins and the Recording toolbar appears.

6 Narrate the slide, speaking clearly into the microphone.

7 Click the **Next** button (➡) to advance the slide.

Note: See the section, "Rehearse Timing," to learn more about the Recording toolbar.

8 Press **Ctrl** while clicking the primary mouse button to display the laser pointer, and then drag it across the screen to show items of interest.

When the slide show ends, Design view reappears.

A The timing applied to each slide appears below its thumbnail.

B Slides with narration display a speaker icon.

9 Click to enable (☑) both **Play Narrations** and **Use Timings**.

10 Click the **Save** icon (🖫) to save the narration.

11 Click **From Beginning**, sit back, and watch the automated slide show.

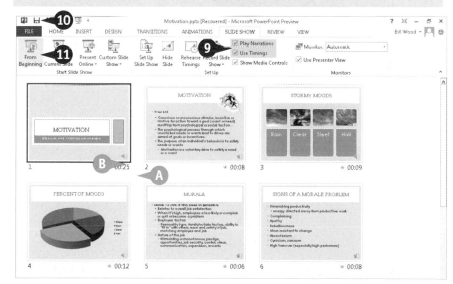

TIP

Can I clear timings and narrations?
Yes. Follow these steps:

1 Click the **Slide Show** tab.

2 Click the **Record Slide Show** down arrow (▾).

3 Click **Clear**.

4 Click an item from the menu.

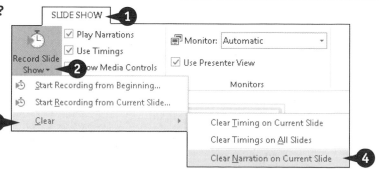

Package a Presentation

You can save a presentation in a format that includes a PowerPoint viewer, plus any files needed to view your presentation. This viewer enables the presentation to be viewed on a computer that does not have PowerPoint installed on it, thereby allowing anyone to view your presentation. This may also be a good time to personalize your presentation by recording a narrative. If any media is linked to the presentation instead of embedded in it, the package includes those files, as well as embedding fonts into the presentation.

Package a Presentation

1 Click the **File** tab to show Backstage view.

2 Click **Export**.

3 Click **Package Presentation for CD**.

4 Click **Package for CD**.

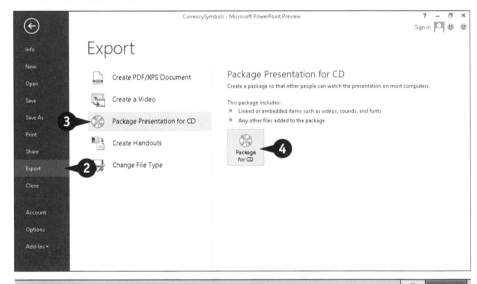

The Package for CD dialog box appears.

5 Click **Copy to Folder**.

Ⓐ You can also insert a CD in your CD drive and then click **Copy to CD** — PowerPoint burns the presentation files directly to the CD.

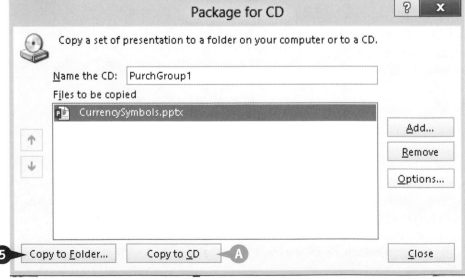

The Copy to Folder dialog box appears.

6 Click in the **Folder name** text box, and then type a name.

B Note the folder location where the presentation package will be saved. You can click **Browse** to change the location.

7 Click **OK**.

8 Click **Yes** in reply to the message that asks, "Do you want to include linked files in your package?"

C PowerPoint creates a presentation package and saves it in the folder location that you specified.

9 Send the entire folder to your intended viewers. In this example, the PurchGroup1 folder is sent to intended viewers.

D To view the slide show, double-click the presentation.

Note: If the computer does not have PowerPoint, this action opens a web page to download the PowerPoint viewer.

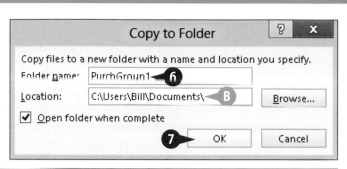

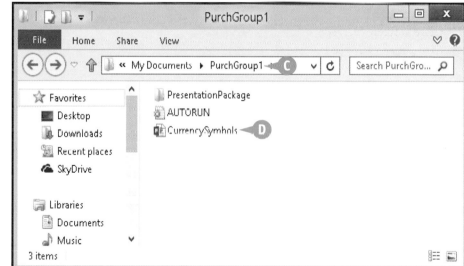

TIPS

What is the purpose of the Options button?
You can click the **Options** button to open the Options dialog box. This displays the options Linked files and Embedded TrueType Fonts — always keep these enabled (☑). This ensures that your presentation looks the way you intended. You can also set a password to open the presentation and check for personal data that may be in the presentation.

What is the Add button for?
You can include more than one presentation in a package. Click the **Add** button and the Add File dialog box appears — use it to browse to another presentation. When you find the presentation file you want to add, click it and then click **OK**. PowerPoint adds it to the list.

CHAPTER 14

Printing Presentations

There are several reasons to print a presentation. You may want a hard copy of your slides to review away from your computer, or you might want to print slide handouts for your audience to follow during your live presentation. You might also want to print a copy of your outline or notes to give to your audience.

Using Print Preview

It is a good practice to see what your slides look like before you use resources for printing. Slides with colorful or dark backgrounds can use a lot of printer ink, and color printers are expensive to operate. You can use the Print Preview feature to see what your printout looks like before printing so you do not waste these resources. Print Preview has options that allow you to see what your printout will look like: slides, black-and-white slides, notes, outline, and so on. You can preview any of these options before printing.

Using Print Preview

1 Click the **File** tab to show Backstage view.

2 Click **Print**.

PowerPoint displays the slide show in the Print Preview view.

A You can navigate through the pages.

B You can zoom in and out.

3 Click **Edit Header & Footer**.

The Header and Footer dialog box appears.

4 Click the **Date and time**, **Slide number,** and **Footer** options to enable settings (☐ changes to ☑).

Note: See Chapter 9 to learn more about header and footer settings.

5 Click **Apply to All**.

C Alternatively, you can click **Apply** to apply the setting to only the currently visible page.

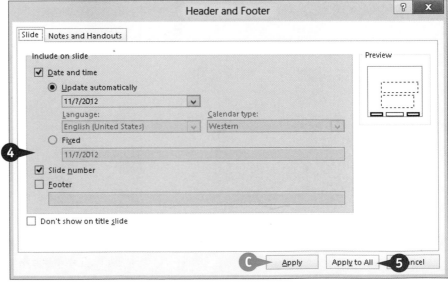

PowerPoint applies your new settings and closes the Header and Footer dialog box.

D The date and slide number appear in the Print Preview.

6 To change printers, click the **Printer** down arrow (⌄).

7 Click a printer.

PowerPoint changes the printer.

8 Click the **Copies** spinner (⬍) or type a number into the text box to change the number of copies to print.

9 Click **Print**.

PowerPoint prints the presentation.

Why is my Print Preview black and white when I have it set up for color?

PowerPoint knows if a black-and-white printer is selected for printing, so it automatically shows the Print Preview in black and white. Select your color printer from the Printer list, and the Print Preview changes to color.

How can I quickly tell how many pages will print if I choose to print multiple slides per page?

Look at the lower-left corner of the Print Preview screen. The status area indicates the total number of pages that will print and which page you currently have displayed in Print Preview. For example, if you have 11 slides and you want to print two slides per page, it will say 2 of 6.

Print Slides

Y ou can create a printout of your slides if you want to review them on paper or if you want to give your audience a handout. You can print a single slide, your entire presentation, or selected slides. You can print slides in black and white, grayscale, or in color if you have a color printer available. There are other options, too. You can print multiple slides per page, print your notes with slides, or even frame slides so you can see white slides against the white, printed pages.

Print Slides

1 Click the **File** tab to show Backstage view.

2 Click **Print**.

PowerPoint displays the slide show in Print Preview view.

3 Click the **Slides** down arrow (▼).

4 Click **Custom Range**.

A You can click **Print Current Slide** to print the visible slide.

B You can click **Print Selection** to print the slides currently selected in Normal view.

C You can print custom shows by selecting them here.

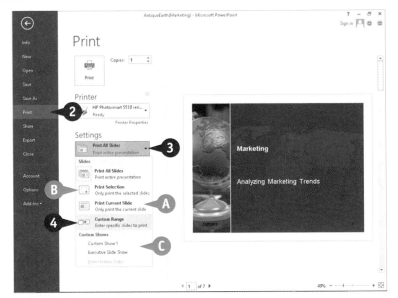

5 Type the slide numbers you want to print in the **Slides** text box, separated by commas.

D Click the **Information** icon (ⓘ) for more information.

This example types 1, 3-5, which will print slide numbers 1, 3, 4, and 5.

6 Click **Print**.

PowerPoint prints your selection of slides.

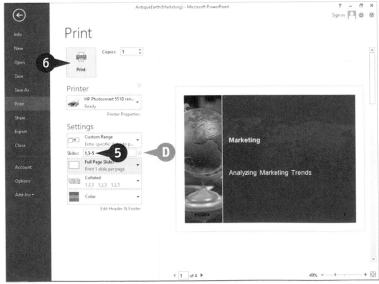

Print Hidden Slides

You may decide not to show every slide in a presentation, but you want to print the entire presentation for someone to review. For example, you may want to hide information concerning managers while presenting a slide show to workers, but you want Human Resources to review a hard copy of the presentation. You can quickly switch between printing or not printing hidden slides with a few clicks of the mouse button. By default, PowerPoint prints hidden slides, but you can easily adjust print settings to exclude hidden slides from printing.

Print Hidden Slides

1 Click the **File** tab to show Backstage view.

2 Click **Print**.

The Print Preview appears.

A In this example, 26 pages are scheduled to print.

3 Click the **Slides** down arrow (▼).

4 Click **Print Hidden Slides** (✓ disappears from the menu).

B You can also click to print a presentation section.

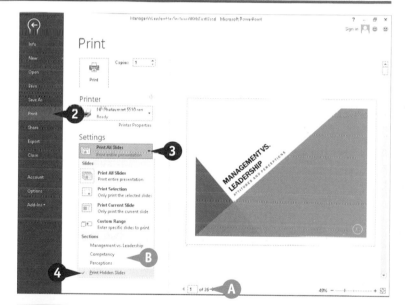

C PowerPoint changes the number of pages now scheduled to print.

5 Click **Print**.

PowerPoint prints the presentation without the hidden slides.

Note: The Print Hidden Slides option is disabled if there are no hidden slides in the presentation.

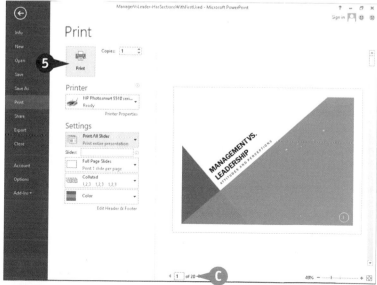

Print Handouts

A presentation handout helps audience members follow along and gives them a place where they can write notes for future reference. You can view presentation handouts in Print Preview and easily print them from that view. You can print anywhere from one to nine slides on a handout page, in landscape or portrait orientation. Printing several slides per page can save paper when you want to print handouts for a lengthy presentation, but make sure your audience can read the slides when there are several per page.

Print Handouts

1 Click the **File** tab to show Backstage view.

2 Click **Print**.

PowerPoint displays the slide show in Print Preview view.

3 Click the **Print Layout** down arrow (⌄).

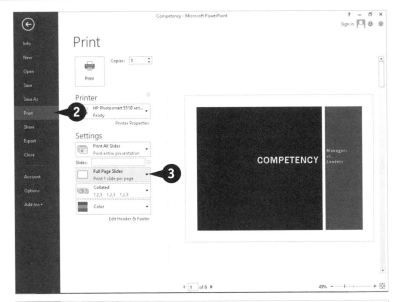

The gallery of print layouts appears.

4 Click a layout under the Handouts heading.

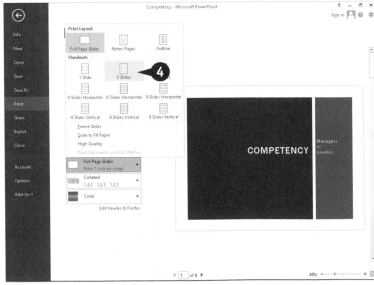

The slide layout changes in Print Preview, and the orientation drop-down list appears under the Settings heading.

5 Click the **Orientation** down arrow (▼).

6 Click an orientation.

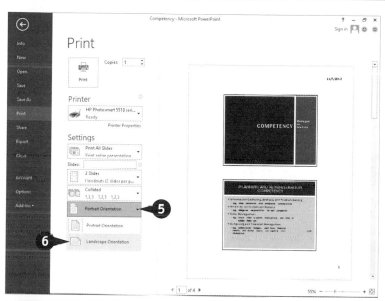

The page orientation changes in Print Preview.

7 Click **Print**.

PowerPoint prints the presentation in the layout you specified.

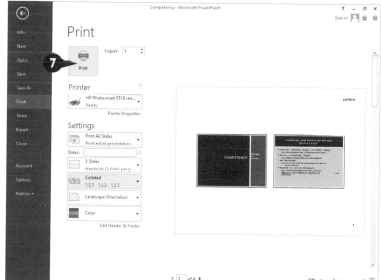

TIPS

Can I add a background color to the actual handout page, or hide information like the page number?

Yes. Click the **View** tab and then click **Handout Master** (see Chapter 9). You can enable (☑) or disable (☐) page information by clicking the check boxes in the Placeholders group on the Handout Master tab. Click **Background Styles** and click a background from the gallery. Click **Close Master View** when you finish.

How many slides should I include per page in a handout?

Two slides per page ensures that your audience can read the handout and leaves plenty of space for notes. If you have only a few bullet points per slide, you may be able to read the handout with four slides per page.

Print Handouts with Microsoft Word

Handouts in PowerPoint are structured and somewhat limited. For example, you cannot change the size of slides on the handout printout and you cannot edit notes in Print Preview. PowerPoint gives you more versatility by letting you export printouts to Microsoft Word. After exporting to Word, you can do anything to your handouts. For example, you can build a report from your presentation. Exporting to Word gives you versatility because you can now take advantage of all the capabilities of Word. Keep in mind that the Word document is not automatically saved. Remember to save it.

Print Handouts with Microsoft Word

1 Click the **File** tab to show Backstage view.

2 Click **Export**.

3 Click **Create Handouts**.

4 Click **Create Handouts**.

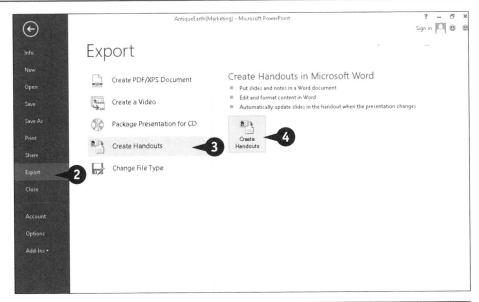

The Send to Microsoft Word dialog box appears.

5 Click an option under the Page layout in Microsoft Word heading (○ changes to ◉).

6 Click an option to paste or link the slide images in Word (○ changes to ◉).

7 Click **OK**.

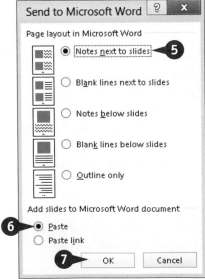

A document with the layout you chose appears in Microsoft Word.

Note: The Word document may appear only as a blinking task on the Windows taskbar. Click the icon to see the Word document.

Note: Word does not save the document automatically. If you are keeping the handouts, save it now.

8 Edit the Word document just like any other Word document.

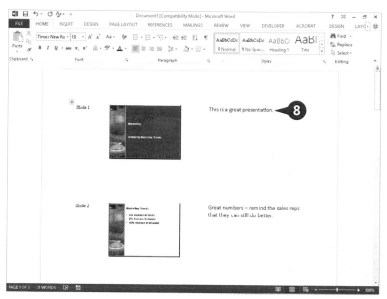

A You can add, edit, and format any text.

B You can delete slides and add graphics.

9 Click the **Save** icon (🖫) to save the Word document.

10 Click the **Close** button (✖) to close the Word document.

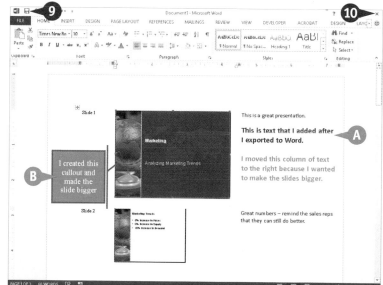

TIPS

Why does my computer seem to lock up when I create handouts with Microsoft Word?

The process takes a while, so you must be patient. The Word document may open minimized, which means it only appears on the Windows taskbar. Go to the Windows taskbar and click the Word document (it should be blinking) to make it appear.

What is the difference between Paste and Paste link?

If you choose **Paste**, PowerPoint pastes images into the Word document. If you select **Paste link**, the images in Word are linked to the presentation, and you can double-click the images to edit the presentation slides. Choosing **Paste link** creates a smaller Word document, but the presentation must accompany it. Choosing **Paste** makes the Word document independent, but bigger.

Print the Outline Only

Sometimes you want to focus only on the presentation text and not the graphics. For example, you may want to give a copy of the outline to audience members as a reference. It may also be convenient for you to have only the bullet points on paper so you can look down at the podium instead of looking at the projector screen during the slide show. You can print the presentation outline to do just that. The printed outline includes titles, subtitles, and bullet points, but does not include any text entered in footers or inserted text boxes.

Print the Outline Only

1 Click the **File** tab to show Backstage view.

2 Click **Print**.

PowerPoint displays the slide show in Print Preview view.

3 Click the **Print Layout** down arrow (▼).

The gallery of print layouts appears.

4 Click **Outline**.

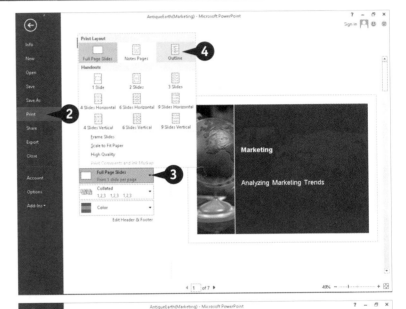

Print Preview changes to Outline view, and the orientation drop-down list appears under the Settings heading.

A You can click here to change the orientation of the page.

5 Click **Print**.

PowerPoint prints the outline.

Print Notes

If you are presenting a slide show, you may want a cheat sheet with additional facts or answers to possible audience questions. You can print each slide with its associated notes — the notes that were typed in the Notes pane of Normal view. The Notes printout shows one slide per page and includes the notes under the slide. You can resize and move the slide and format the notes font in the Notes Master view. You can refer to the Notes pages during the presentation, or give them to audience members as a reference.

Print Notes

1 Click the **File** tab to show Backstage view.

2 Click **Print**.

PowerPoint displays the slide show in Print Preview view.

3 Click the **Print Layout** down arrow (▼).

The gallery of print layouts appears.

4 Click **Notes Pages**.

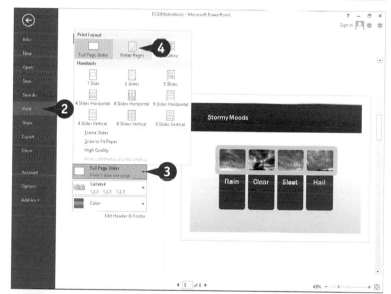

Print Preview changes to Notes Pages view, and the orientation drop-down list appears under the Settings heading.

Ⓐ You can click here to change the orientation of the page.

5 Click **Print**.

PowerPoint prints the Notes pages.

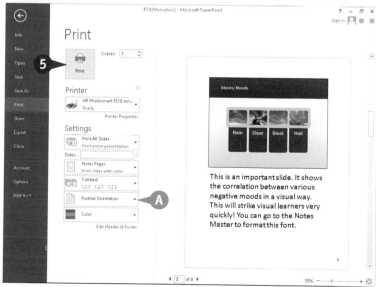

Print in Black and White or Grayscale

You can print a presentation in color, black and white, or grayscale. Grayscale provides some shading to help you see graphics and background elements. Black and white removes all shading, and this can significantly reduce your ability to see background and graphics details. Printing in color is expensive compared to black-and-white printing and it can also be slower, depending on the printer. Many times your audience does not need color printouts and printout drafts need not be in color, so you can save resources and money by printing on a black-and-white printer.

Print in Black and White or Grayscale

1 Click the **File** tab to show Backstage view.

2 Click **Print**.

PowerPoint displays the slide show in Print Preview view.

3 Click the **Color** down arrow (▾).

4 Click **Grayscale**.

Ⓐ You can click **Pure Black and White** to print in black and white with no shading.

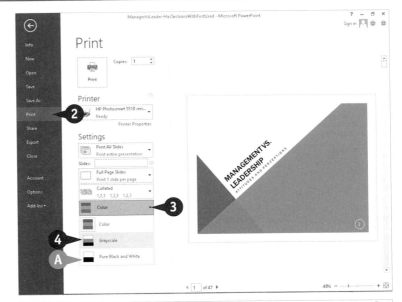

Print Preview appears in grayscale.

5 Click **Print**.

PowerPoint prints the presentation in grayscale.

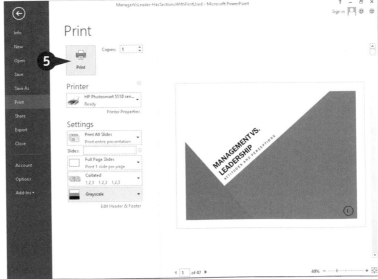

Frame Slides

You can make your presentation handouts really sharp by framing the slides. When you print slides with a frame, PowerPoint places a neat borderline around the edge of the slides and defines them on the printed page. Having a frame around slides in a printout is particularly nice when the slides of your presentation are white or a light color. The frame sets the slides apart from the white, printed page, and improves the appearance of the printout by defining the edge of the slides.

Frame Slides

1 Click the **File** tab to show Backstage view.

2 Click **Print**.

PowerPoint displays the slide show in Print Preview view.

3 Click the **Slide Layout** down arrow (▾).

The gallery of print layouts appears.

4 Click **Frame Slides**.

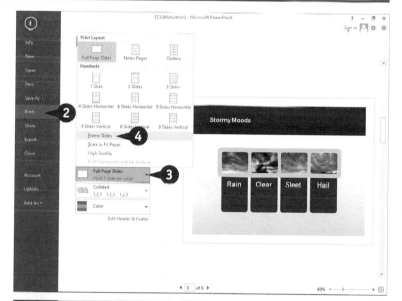

Ⓐ Print Preview shows a border around the slides.

5 Click **Print**.

PowerPoint prints the presentation.

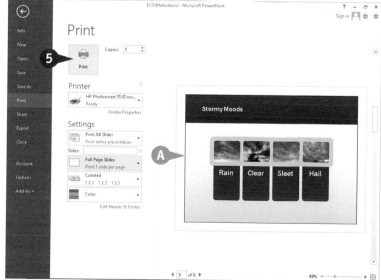

CHAPTER 15

Presenting a Slide Show

Before you present your PowerPoint slide show, be sure you understand the tools that are available to you during the show. These tools were designed to help you give a flawless presentation. Familiarity with them will enable you to present the slide show smoothly.

Game Day!

Get Ready to Present

A successful live presentation requires solid content, good design, and a prepared presenter. Preparing to make a presentation involves double-checking your presentation for problems and getting comfortable with your material and presentation environment. Many times, the person presenting a slide show is not only assessed on the quality of the ideas that they are trying to convey, but also on the professionalism of the presentation, the quality of the slide show, and salesmanship. Become familiar with your presentation, the tools, and your surroundings so you can give the best show possible.

Check Your Presentation for Errors

Checking your slides for details such as spelling, grammar, and typos can save you a lot of embarrassment at show time. Use the presentation outline to review the text so you are not distracted by design elements. A person should not proofread his or her own work. Have a third party review the presentation. That person may catch errors that you miss. Use the PowerPoint tools that are available to help you; PowerPoint contains a spelling and grammar checker, a thesaurus, a research tool, and a word counter. Use these valuable tools to your fullest advantage to build the best presentation possible.

Rehearse the Slide Show

Practice your presentation several times before you present it to an audience. Rehearse in front of a mirror or with a friend, or record yourself. You may discover undesirable mannerisms or expressions that you want to avoid. Know your material so you can anticipate each slide and each bullet point — know what comes next. Avoid looking at and reading from the slide show. Finishing your presentation in the allotted time is considered courteous. Use the Rehearse Timings feature in PowerPoint to check your timing, and then change your presentation accordingly. You want the slide show to move along, but not be rushed.

Know Your Presentation Space

To avoid problems during your presentation, visit the site before the presentation if you can. Knowing the size of the room, the acoustics, and the layout of the stage and audience seating can help you prepare. If the space is large, you may need a microphone. Close the blinds if the space is too bright. Try to meet your audience before the slide show. This makes you more comfortable with them, gives them a chance to ask preliminary questions, and allows you to identify people who need extra attention. Too many questions and comments during a presentation can bog it down.

Set Up Your Show

Be sure to check those all-important slide show settings. (For more information, see Chapter 13.) Before the slide show, you should set up the format for the presentation, such as a live presentation versus one shown at a kiosk, which slides to include, monitors and resolution, and how you will control the advancement of the slides. Even if you are using your own laptop, it could crash, so bring a backup of your presentation. Package it with the PowerPoint viewer in case you find yourself on a computer without PowerPoint. Package any files that are linked to the presentation as well.

Start and End a Show

You typed a lot of text, inserted graphics, and worked with design settings. Finally, your hard work pays off and you get to present your slide show. All you need is to start the slide show and navigate through it. You can end the show at any time or view all of the slides. For the most professional presentation possible, you probably want to start the show and have the first slide or a black screen visible before the audience arrives. You can start the show from any view.

Start and End a Show

1 Click the **Slide Show** tab.

2 Click **From Beginning**.

Note: You can also press F5 to begin the show.

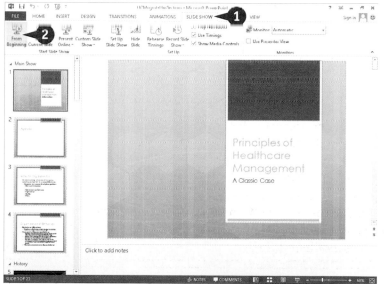

The slide show begins.

When you move the mouse pointer ( ), the on-screen toolbar appears faintly in the lower-left corner.

3 To end the show before you reach the last slide, click the **Options** icon ( ) on the on-screen toolbar.

4 Click **End Show**.

Note: You can also end the slide show by pressing Esc.

The slide show closes.

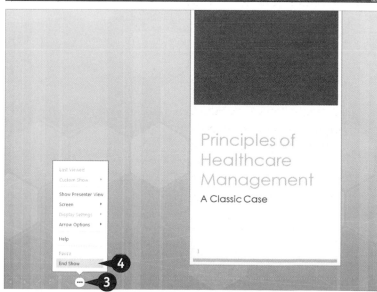

Navigate Among Slides

No slide show would be any good without the ability to move through the slides. You can use the shortcut menu or the Slide Show on-screen toolbar, or click the screen to move through a slide show. You can move back or forward one slide at a time or you can pick a specific slide to show. You can also press the keyboard arrows to move forward and backward through the slide show. All of these options are also available in Presenter view, which is covered later in this chapter.

Navigate Among Slides

1 With your presentation in Slide Show view, click the **Next** icon (⊚) to advance the slide.

Note: You can also click the slide or press ⬇ to advance the slide. Keep in mind clicking the slide also runs animations.

2 Click the **Previous** icon (⊚) to move to the previous slide.

Note: You can also press ⬆ to move to the previous slide.

The slides advance.

3 Click the **All Slides** icon (⊕).

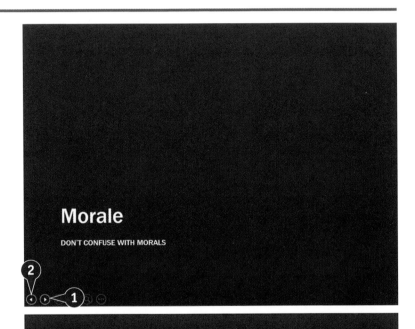

All slides appear.

④ Click the slide you want to show.

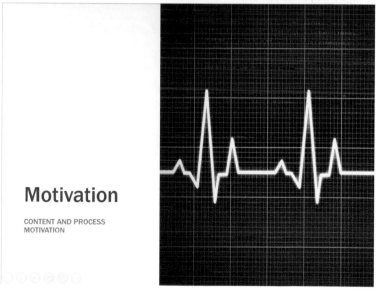

The selected slide appears.

Motivation

CONTENT AND PROCESS
MOTIVATION

TIPS

I clicked the All Slides icon and I am now in All Slides view. Can I return to the slide show without switching slides?

Yes. In the upper-left corner of the screen is a back button (⬅). Click that button and the slide show returns to the current slide.

The slide thumbnails in the All Slides view are too small. Can I make them bigger?

Yes. In the lower-right corner of the All Slides view is a zoom slider. You can click and drag the slider or click anywhere on the zoom slider to zoom in or zoom out, which resizes the slide thumbnails. You can also use the plus and minus signs at either end of the zoom slider to zoom in and out.

Zoom In

Ideally, you want all the text and objects on a slide to be easily visible to your audience without them straining to see. You may have something on your screen, though, that is unavoidably hard to see. If your audience has trouble seeing something on a slide, you can zoom in on the slide with a click of the on-screen toolbar during the slide show. After zooming, you can move the zoom area to any region of the slide with a simple click and drag of the mouse.

Zoom In

1 With your presentation in Slide Show view, click the **Zoom** icon ( ) on the on-screen toolbar.

A A marquee appears, showing the zoom area. The mouse pointer ( ) changes to a zoom magnifying glass ( ).

2 Drag the marquee with the zoom magnifying glass ( ) to the area of interest.

3 Click the screen.

B PowerPoint zooms in on the marquee area. The zoom magnifying glass (🔍) changes to the zoom hand (✋).

4 Click and drag the zoom hand (✋) to any area of the slide, and the zoom area moves.

Press **Esc** to return to the full screen view.

TIPS

The slides seem to advance properly when I use the Forward icon on the on-screen toolbar, but not when I click the slide. Why not?
You may have some animations on the slide that run when you click the slide instead of advancing the slide. Also make sure that you enable (☑) **On Mouse Click** on the Transitions tab.

I set up the slide show to advance slides automatically, but sometimes I want to advance faster. Can I?
Yes. Enable (☑) the **On Mouse Click** option on the Transitions tab. The slide will advance automatically and also when you click either the slide or the **Next** icon (◉) on the on-screen toolbar.

Use the Pointer

You have options regarding how you use the mouse pointer during the slide show, such as showing or hiding it. The laser pointer is also a great way to draw your audience's attention to a particular spot on a slide. The laser pointer is an on-screen tool that gives the illusion that you are pointing at the screen with a hand-held laser pointer. You can quickly and easily enable and use the laser pointer during your slide show to point something out with flair and style, or you can stick with the faithful standard mouse pointer.

Use the Pointer

1 With your presentation in Slide Show view, click the **Options** icon (☉) on the on-screen toolbar.

2 Click **Arrow Options**.

3 Click a setting from the menu.

Automatic shows the mouse pointer (↖), but hides it when inactive; **Visible** shows the mouse pointer continuously; **Hidden** hides the mouse pointer continuously.

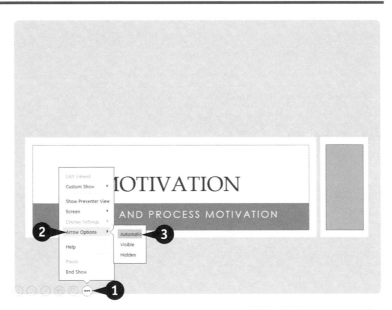

4 Click the **Pen** icon (⊘) on the on-screen toolbar.

5 Click **Laser Pointer**.

The mouse pointer (⤢) changes to the laser pointer (●), and the laser pointer appears continuously.

6 Drag the mouse around the area you want to identify on-screen.

7 Position the pointer over the on-screen toolbar.

The pointer temporarily changes back to the mouse pointer (⤢).

8 Click the **Next** icon (◉).

A The slide advances and the pointer changes back to the laser pointer (●).

9 Press **Esc**.

The laser pointer (●) changes to the mouse pointer (⤢).

MOTIVATION

CONTENT AND PROCESS MOTIVATION

MOTIVATION

• What is it?

  • Conscious or unconscious stimulus, incentive, or motive for action toward a goal (want or need), resulting from psychological or social factors...

  • The psychological process through which unsatisfied needs or wants lead to drives.

  • The purpose of an individual's behavior is to satisfy needs or wants.

    • Motivation is a voluntary drive to satisfy a need or a want.

2

TIPS

Is there an easier way to turn on the laser pointer?
Yes. Constantly going to the on-screen toolbar is inconvenient and strains the audience. To use the laser pointer briefly, press **Ctrl** then press the primary mouse button, and then drag the mouse to move it. When you release the mouse button or the **Ctrl** key, the mouse pointer (⤢) comes back.

Can I change the color of the laser pointer?
No, but the laser pointer is designed in such a way that it is clearly visible, even on a red slide background, or a red graphic or table. It actually shows well on any color because it is red with a white corona.

Mark Up with Pen and Highlighter

PowerPoint enables you to draw freehand on your screen during a slide show with a pen tool. You can use it to highlight or annotate important points in the slide show. You can choose Pen for a thin, opaque line, or Highlighter, which gives you a much thicker, translucent line. You can also choose a color for both. You can save annotations so they appear the next time you present your slide show — PowerPoint asks if you want to save annotations when you exit the show, but only if that option is enabled in PowerPoint Options (see Chapter 3).

Mark Up with Pen and Highlighter

1 With your presentation in Slide Show view, click the **Pen** icon (⊘) on the on-screen toolbar.

2 Click **Pen**.

The pointer changes to a point of color on the screen.

A You can click to change the color of the Pen or Highlighter.

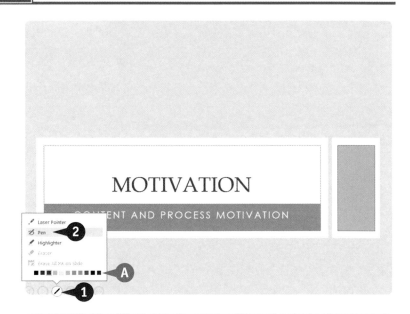

3 Click and drag on the screen around the area you want to identify.

A line appears where you dragged the mouse.

4 Press Esc to turn off the Pen.

5 Click the **Pen** icon (⊘) on the on-screen toolbar.

6 Click **Highlighter**.

The pointer changes to a rectangular patch of color on the screen.

7 Click and drag on the screen over the area you want to highlight.

A thick, translucent line appears where you dragged the mouse.

8 Press Esc to turn off the Highlighter.

9 Press Esc to exit the slide show.

PowerPoint asks if you want to save your annotations.

10 Click **Keep** or **Discard**.

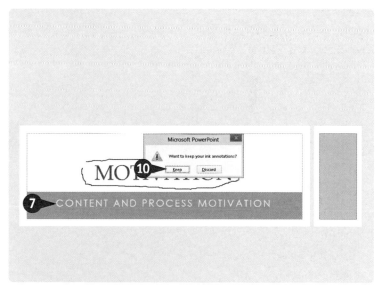

TIPS

Why can I not seem to erase my annotations?
You can only erase annotations during the current session of your slide show. If you exited the slide show and saved the annotations when prompted, they are permanent and you cannot erase them the next time you view the slide show.

Why does PowerPoint exit the slide show when I press the Escape key to clear the Pen?
You may have pressed Esc a second time, which exits the slide show. Be patient, it sometimes takes a few seconds for the Pen or Highlighter to change back to the mouse pointer (⇖). You may need to move the mouse to see the pointer if your on-screen arrow option is set to Automatic, which hides the pointer when inactive.

Erase Annotations

When you work with the Pen and Highlighter tools to mark up a slide, in essence, the slide becomes a whiteboard or blackboard. These tools allow you to circle or highlight many things in your slide show. However, you may want to remove some markings from a slide if you marked the wrong thing or if you need more room on a slide where there are too many markings. You can remove annotations from the slide using a tool in the on-screen toolbar.

Erase Annotations

1 With your presentation in Slide Show view, click the **Pen** icon (⊘) on the on-screen toolbar.

2 Click **Eraser**.

The mouse pointer (⬚) changes to an eraser (✎).

A You can click **Erase All Ink on Slide** to remove all annotations from the current slide.

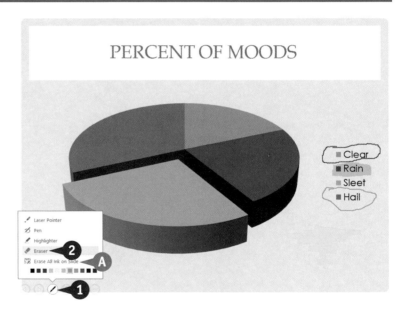

3 Position the eraser (✎) over an annotation and click the annotation.

The annotation disappears.

4 Press `Esc` to clear the eraser.

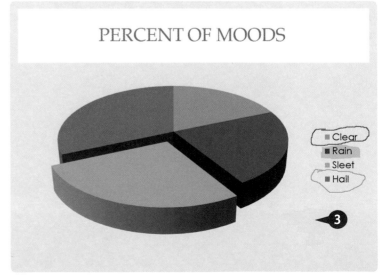

Display Slide Show Help

Y ou probably do not know everything about PowerPoint, so you may need help during the slide show. If you need help running your show after starting it, you do not need to stop the show to open PowerPoint Help. The slide show on-screen help shows shortcuts for running the show and managing presentation features such as pointer options. If you are using Presenter view, you can open the on-screen help for the slide show without the audience seeing it because it opens on the Presenter view screen on your laptop.

Display Slide Show Help

① With your presentation in Slide Show view, click the **Options** icon (☺) on the toolbar.

Note: You can also right-click the screen to display the shortcut menu.

② Click **Help**.

Note: You can also press **F1** during the slide show to see Help.

The Slide Show Help window appears.

Ⓐ PowerPoint categorizes the shortcuts with a tab for each category.

③ Look up the shortcut to perform the procedure you want.

The shortcut is in the left column and the description is in the right column.

④ When you finish, click **OK**.

The Help window closes.

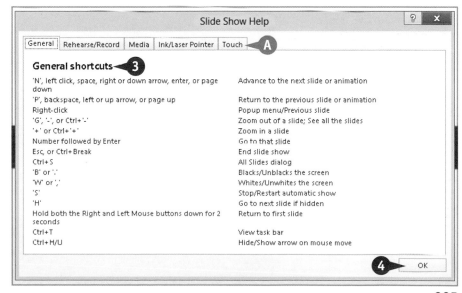

Enable Presenter View

You can give a smooth presentation by using Presenter view. You can view your presentation complete with speaker notes on your computer, while the audience views only the slide show on the main screen. With Presenter view, you can see your notes, the slide show controls are continuously visible and accessible, and PowerPoint Help shows only on your monitor. If you need to go to the All Slides view to go to a particular slide, only you see it. A timer shows the elapsed time, and you can see both the current and the next slide.

Enable Presenter View

1 Click the **Slide Show** tab.

2 Click **Use Presenter View**
(☐ changes to ☑).

3 Begin the slide show.

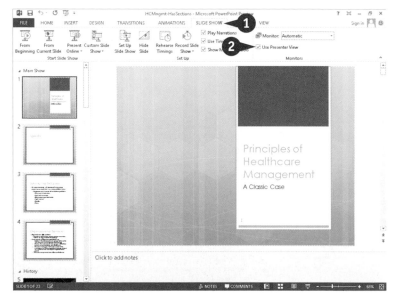

Your laptop shows Presenter view.

Ⓐ You can click **Display Settings** to specify which screen shows the main show and which screen shows Presenter view.

Ⓑ You can click **Show Taskbar** to switch to a different program.

Ⓒ You can click **Black Screen** (⬛) to display a black screen.

4 Click **End Slide Show**.

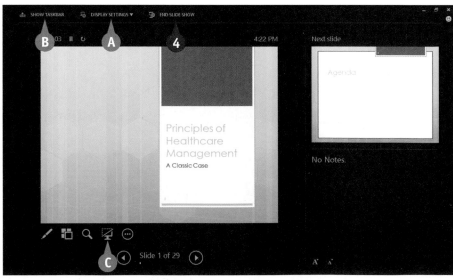

Use Presenter View

During a live presentation, you want to give the audience your full attention, which means not looking at the projector screen. If you are presenting on a projector screen or monitor, you can use Presenter view on your laptop. With Presenter view, you see the slide currently being viewed by the audience, the next slide, any notes you made, and a suite of tools specifically designed to help you give a professional presentation. There is no need to search for tools on the main screen or have the audience watch you search for another slide. Everything is visible and available in Presenter view.

Ⓐ Toolbar

The toolbar is nearly identical to the on-screen toolbar and is always visible in Presenter view.

Ⓑ Command Buttons

These commands are conveniently visible in Presenter view, but hidden on the main screen.

Ⓒ Timer

The timer shows the elapsed time of the show, and you can pause and restart it.

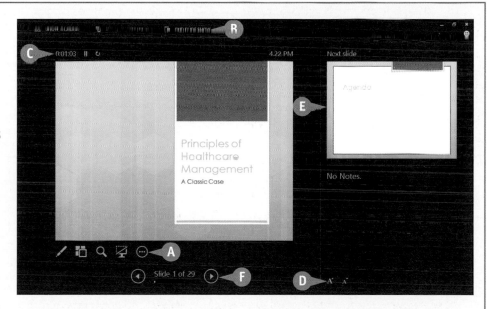

Ⓓ Notes

Notes are visible and you can change their font size.

Ⓔ Slide Preview

You can see the next slide and collect your thoughts in preparation.

Ⓕ Advance Slides

You can advance slides with confidence by clicking buttons instead of slides.

Switch to a Different Program

You can switch to a different program and work with it during a slide show. For example, if you are giving a presentation on Microsoft Word, you may need to go to Word to demonstrate a feature that you are showing in your slide show. Perhaps someone asks to see the data for a chart and you want to show it during the slide show. You can quickly and easily switch to that other program, work with it, and then return to your slide show. To return to your slide show, you can minimize or close the other program.

Switch to a Different Program

1 With your presentation in Slide Show view, click the **Options** icon ( ).

2 Click **Screen**.

3 Click **Show Taskbar**.

The Windows taskbar appears.

4 Click an open program on the taskbar.

This example clicks Excel.

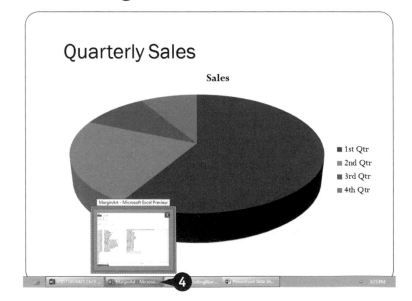

The program you clicked appears on the screen.

5 To return to your slide show, find the slide show on the taskbar and click it.

Ⓐ You can also click the **Close** button (✖) to close the program, Excel in this example, or the **Minimize** button (▬) to minimize the program.

The slide show reappears.

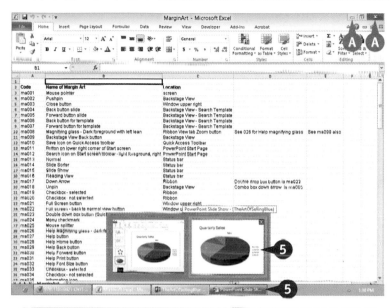

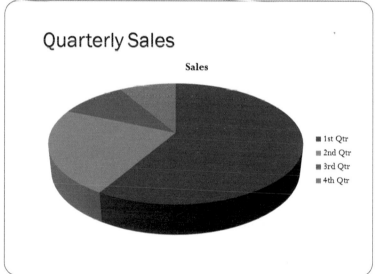

TIPS

Can I open a program during a slide show?
Yes. When the taskbar appears, you can use it in any way that you normally would, including to go to the Windows 8 Start screen to open a program. You can also press ⊞ to switch between the Windows 8 Start screen and the slide show.

Is there another way to switch to a different program?
Yes. If you are using a laptop and the audience is watching on a projector screen or monitor, you can use Presenter view. Presenter view has a command button for this very purpose. You can switch to another program with one click of the mouse.

CHAPTER 16

Publishing a Presentation

PowerPoint enables you to share your presentation in many different ways. You can save your slide show in different file formats, such as a PDF, Word document, or video file. You can also publish slides as JPEG or TIFF graphics.

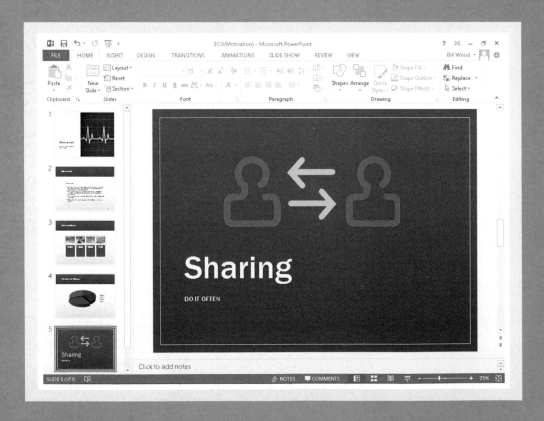

Compare Presentations

If you have someone review your presentation and make changes, PowerPoint enables you to compare the presentation with the original. You can send a copy of your presentation to peers, possibly through e-mail, and allow them to review and edit it — no need to do anything special, just send it. After everyone makes changes, you can compare them all to the original. This feature makes it unnecessary to read the entire presentation thoroughly in order to check for changes that others have made — PowerPoint points out the changes for you. Then, you can accept or reject their changes.

Compare Presentations

1 Open the original presentation that you sent to others for review.

Note: In this example, the username of the presentation copy was changed to Art in PowerPoint Options.

2 Click the **Review** tab while in Normal view.

3 Click **Compare**.

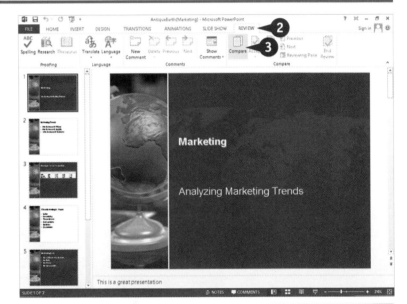

The Choose File to Merge with Current Presentation dialog box appears.

4 Click the folder that contains the edited presentation.

5 Click the presentation that others have edited.

Note: The name of the edited presentation does not need to be the same as the original.

6 Click **Merge**.

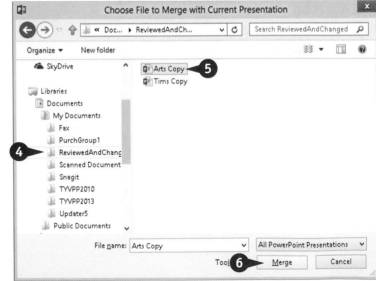

The Reviewing pane (also called the Revisions pane) appears.

7 Click a slide with changes, or click **Next** to go to the first change.

A Changes are marked with an icon (🖉).

B Changes to slides appear in the Slide Changes box.

C Changes to the presentation, such as slide deletions, appear in the Presentation Changes box.

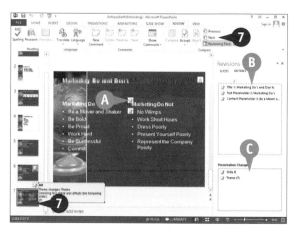

8 Click a marker (🖉).

When you position the mouse pointer (🖑) over a marker, the details of the change appear.

9 Click **Accept**.

D Accepted changes display check marks.

10 Click **Previous** or **Next** to go to other changes.

11 Click **End Review**.

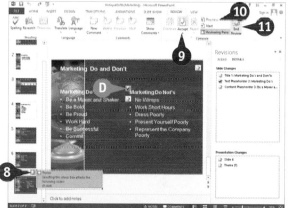

A dialog box appears, asking if you want to end the review.

12 Click **Yes**.

Note: PowerPoint rejects any unaccepted changes.

Microsoft PowerPoint

Are you sure you want to end the review for 'AntiqueEarth(Marketing).pptx'? This will end the review, and any unapplied changes will be discarded.

12 Yes   No

Was this information helpful?

TIPS

Can I see the slides from the edited presentation?

Yes. The Reviewing pane automatically appears with the Details tab displayed. Click the **Slides** tab in the Reviewing pane, and PowerPoint shows you the slide from the edited presentation that correlates to the slide that you have selected in your presentation.

Can I reverse accepting a change?

Yes. Accepted changes display check marks. Click an accepted change and then click the **Reject** command button on the Review tab. Any changes that are not accepted are automatically rejected when you end the review; however, you can always run the comparison again.

Make a PDF Document from a Presentation

You can make a PDF (portable document format) file from your presentation so that anyone with a PDF reader can view your presentation. A PDF file can be viewed on virtually any computer because PDF readers are free. This feature allows you the convenience of creating a PDF file without the expense of buying a PDF writer! Another benefit of a PDF file is that you can view it on a computer monitor or print it on paper. By saving a presentation as a PDF file, you preserve your presentation's fonts, formatting, and images.

Make a PDF Document from a Presentation

1 Click the **File** tab to show Backstage view.

2 Click **Export**.

3 Click **Create PDF/XPS Document**.

4 Click **Create PDF/XPS**.

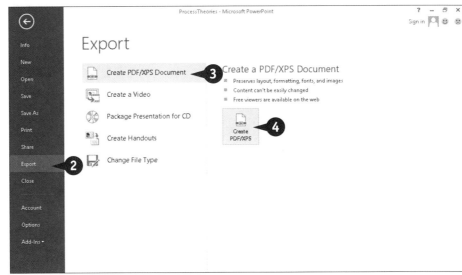

The Publish as PDF or XPS dialog box appears.

5 Click the folder where you want to save your file.

6 Click the **File Name** text box.

7 Type a name.

8 Click **Options**.

Ⓐ You can output any of the four types of printouts (see Chapter 14).

Ⓑ If you choose **Handouts**, you can specify the number of slides per page.

Ⓒ You can select a range of slides to print.

⑨ Click **OK**.

⑩ Click **Publish**.

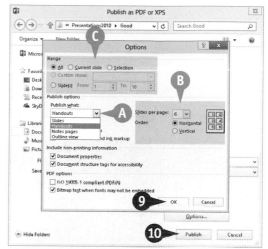

PowerPoint creates the PDF file in the specified folder and shows the status.

PowerPoint opens the file with your PDF reader.

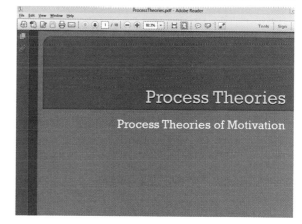

TIPS

I do not have a PDF reader on my computer. Where can I find one?

PDF viewers are free, and most computers already have a PDF reader installed at the time of purchase. However, if you do not have one, you can go to the Adobe website, www.adobe.com, and download their Acrobat Reader.

What is the advantage to preserving the fonts, formatting, and images of my presentation?

Computers can have different sets of fonts loaded with their software. It is possible that a computer viewing your presentation does not have the font you used. Preserving the fonts, formatting, and images carries that information along with the presentation so it looks the same on any computer.

Create a Video of a Presentation

You can create a video of your presentation, which gives you complete control over how people can show and distribute it. Almost anybody can view it because PowerPoint saves it in either a Windows Media Video (WMV) or MPEG-4 format, which can be viewed on most computers. A video that you make from a presentation is secure because no one can change it once it is a video — nobody can see hidden chart data or your design secrets. A video is a great way to present a slide show from a kiosk — start it, let it continually loop, and forget it!

Create a Video of a Presentation

1 Click the **File** tab to show Backstage view.

2 Click **Export**.

3 Click **Create a Video**.

4 Click the **Resolution** down arrow (▼).

5 Click a resolution suited to your needs.

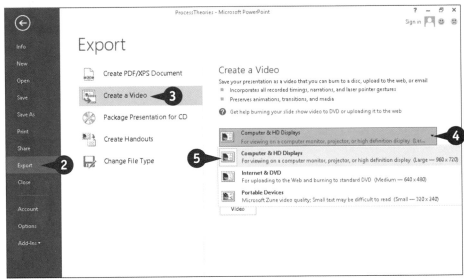

6 Click the **Timings and Narrations** down arrow (▼):

Ⓐ You can click **Don't Use Recorded Timings and Narrations** if you recorded them, but do not want to use them.

Ⓑ You can click **Use Recorded Timings and Narrations** if you recorded them and want to use them.

Ⓒ You can click **Record Timings and Narrations** if you want to record them at this time.

Note: See Chapter 13 to learn about recording timings and narrations.

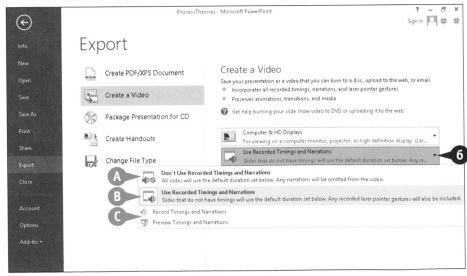

7 Click the text box and type a default time.

The default time refers to how long a slide appears if it has no timings associated with it or you chose not to use timings.

D You can click **Help** for online help.

8 Click **Create Video**.

The Save As dialog box appears.

9 Click the folder where you want to save the video.

10 Click the **File name** text box to select it, and then type a filename.

E You can click here to change the file type.

11 Click **Save**.

The dialog box closes and PowerPoint creates the video in the specified folder.

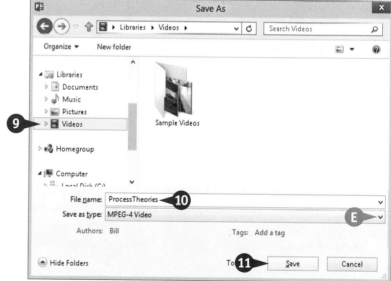

TIPS

Why does nothing seem to happen when I click Save?

It takes a long time for PowerPoint to make the video. Curiously enough, it does not notify you when it is done. However, while it is working, you see a status meter and Cancel button at the bottom in the status bar. When the status meter disappears, the video is done.

Why would I want to change the resolution?

The higher the resolution of your video, the bigger the file, and the more memory it takes to run it. This affects load times and sometimes the quality of playback if computer resources are limited. The Resolution drop-down list has settings for the Internet and for portable devices. You can change the resolution for your target audience.

Save a Presentation as a Slide Show

You can make it easy on your audience and yourself by viewing your presentation through a PowerPoint Show. You can save the presentation so that it opens automatically in Slide Show view. To open it, you navigate to it with Windows Explorer, double-click it, and it opens as a slide show. This is particularly convenient if you are not familiar with PowerPoint but want to do a slide show. Not having to open the file through the PowerPoint program also prevents your audience from seeing your design copy.

Save a Presentation as a Slide Show

1 Click the **File** tab to show Backstage view.

2 Click **Export**.

3 Click **Change File Type**.

4 Click **PowerPoint Show**.

5 Click and drag the scroll bar to scroll to the bottom of the screen to show the Save As button.

6 Click **Save As**.

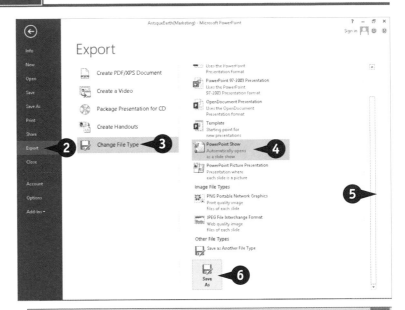

The Save As dialog box appears.

7 Click the folder where you want to save your file.

8 Click the **File name** text box.

9 Type a filename.

10 Click **Save**.

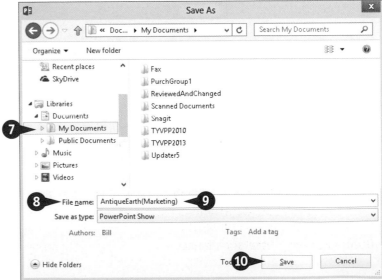

The dialog box closes and PowerPoint creates the PowerPoint Show file in the specified folder.

11 Open Windows Explorer, find the file in the specified folder, and then double-click it.

The file opens as a slide show.

Marketing

Analyzing Marketing Trends

TIPS

What do the different PowerPoint extensions mean?
PPSX is the extension for a PowerPoint Show file. PPTX is the extension for a PowerPoint presentation. PPTM is the extension for a presentation that contains macros, and POTX is the extension for a PowerPoint Template. PPT is the extension for a presentation in the 97-2003 format, and ODP is the extension for the Open Document Presentation format.

Are there other advantages to sending a PowerPoint Show (PPSX) to someone instead of a standard presentation (PPTX)?
Yes. If you send this format to others instead of the standard presentation format, they will not be able to see or change the details of your design. They will also not be able to copy any part of your presentation.

Publish Slides as Graphics

You can create a graphic of each slide in your presentation so that you can use them for different purposes. You may want to post them on a website, make high-quality prints, or make them part of a database. You can create either PNG images or JPEG images. PNG are print quality and JPEG are Internet or database quality. There is no need to create a new folder to hold the graphic files, because PowerPoint creates a new folder during this process.

Publish Slides as Graphics

1 Click the **File** tab to show Backstage view.

2 Click **Export**.

3 Click **Change File Type**.

4 Click an image file type.

This example selects **PNG Portable Network Graphics**.

5 Click and drag the scroll bar to scroll to the bottom of the screen so you can see the Save As button.

6 Click **Save As**.

The Save As dialog box appears.

7 Click the folder where you want to save your file.

8 Click the **File name** text box.

9 Type a filename.

This example uses the filename, ECG(Motivation).

10 Click **Save**.

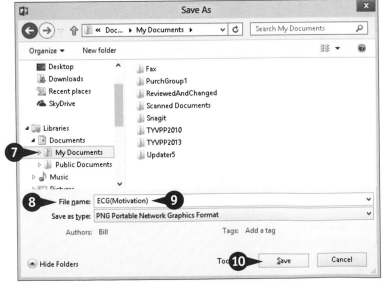

A dialog box appears.

11 Click **All Slides**, or click **Just This One** to save only the current slide.

A dialog box appears.

12 Click **OK**.

PowerPoint creates the graphics for each slide in the folder you specified.

In this example, PowerPoint created a folder called ECG(Motivation) in the specified folder, and it contains the PNG graphics.

13 Navigate to the folder with Windows Explorer.

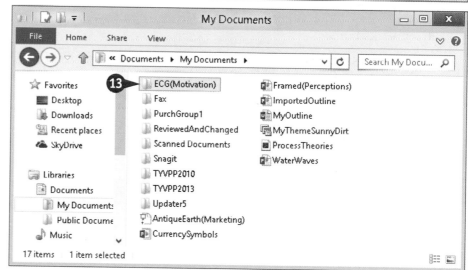

TIPS

How does the Image File Type PNG differ from JPEG?

A JPEG is a picture type that is compressed and trades image quality for smaller file size. The PNG format uses a compression format that does not trade image quality for file size. PNG produces better results for certain applications such as printing.

I saved the graphics to the My Documents folder, but I cannot find them. Where are the files?

PowerPoint creates a folder for you, and places all the graphics in it. You will find this folder in the folder you specified (My Documents, in this case) and it is named whatever you typed into the File name text box.

Broadcast a Presentation

In today's business world, it is common for people to communicate using the Internet. Many business people now join a meeting remotely instead of flying or driving to the meeting. You can broadcast your slide show so anyone who has an Internet connection can watch the show live, and without the expense of a webcast service! PowerPoint creates a link to the broadcast to share with audience members. All your audience needs is a web browser and the link to join the slide show! You must have a Microsoft account, which is free, to broadcast a slide show.

Broadcast a Presentation

1 Click the **File** tab to show Backstage view.

2 Click **Share**.

3 Click **Present Online**.

4 Click **Present Online**.

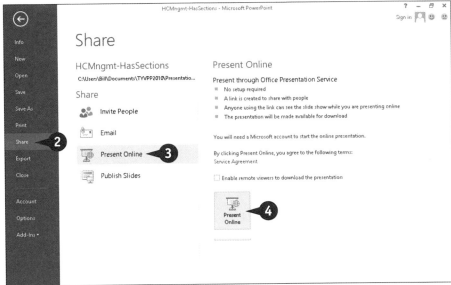

The Sign in dialog box appears. If you are already signed into your Microsoft Live account, you do not receive this dialog box.

5 Type your username.

6 Type your password.

7 Click **Sign in**.

8 Click this link if you do not have a Microsoft account.

The Present Online dialog box appears. You are connected and can start presenting at any time.

9 Click **Copy Link**.

10 Paste the link into an e-mail and send it to your audience.

Audience members can copy and paste the link from their e-mail into a web browser.

11 Click **Start Presentation**.

Note: You may need to wait for all audience members to join the slide show. If the slide show has begun when they join the web session, it appears in their web browser. If the slide show has not yet started, a message appears, telling them to wait for it to begin.

12 Present the slide show.

13 When the slide show ends, click **End Online Presentation**.

14 In the dialog box that appears, click **End Online Presentation**.

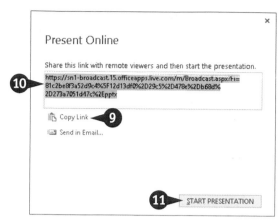

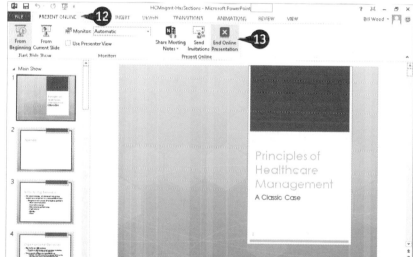

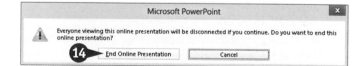

TIPS

What is the Send in Email link in the Present Online dialog box?

If you use Microsoft Outlook as your e-mail program, you can click **Send in Email**. Outlook then composes a new message and automatically pastes the link into the e-mail, so all you need to do is to add e-mail addresses to the e-mail.

Can I send more invitations after closing the Present Online dialog box or after starting the show?

Yes. If you started the slide show, press Esc to stop it and display Normal view. Click the **Present Online** tab, and then click **Send Invitations**. The Present Online dialog box appears and you can send more invitations to join the show. Click **From Beginning** to restart the show.

Save the Presentation to SkyDrive

You can post a presentation to SkyDrive and give permission to people to access it and work with it. SkyDrive is a storage location that is available to anybody who has a Microsoft Live account, and most computers with an Internet connection can access the account. SkyDrive is a service provided by Microsoft free. Storing files to SkyDrive is convenient for two reasons: it gives you an off-site place to back up important files, and you can give permission to people to access your presentation on SkyDrive.

Save the Presentation to SkyDrive

Create a SkyDrive

1 Click the **File** tab to show Backstage view.

2 Click **Save As**.

3 Click **Add a place**.

4 Click **SkyDrive**.

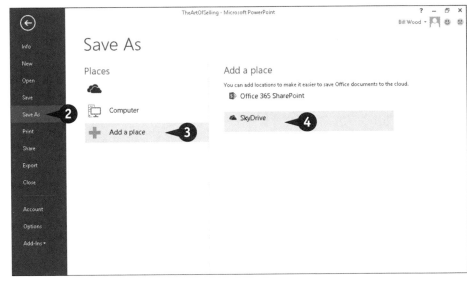

The Microsoft account Sign in dialog box appears.

Ⓐ If you do not have a Microsoft account, click the **Sign up** link.

5 Click the text box and type your username.

6 Click the text box and type your password.

7 Click **Sign in**.

Microsoft creates a SkyDrive for you.

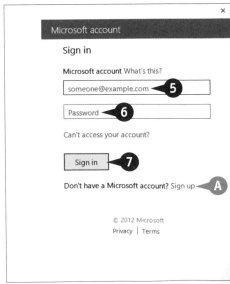

Save to SkyDrive

1. Click the **File** tab to show Backstage view.

2. Click **Save As**.

3. Click your **SkyDrive**.

4. Click **Browse**.

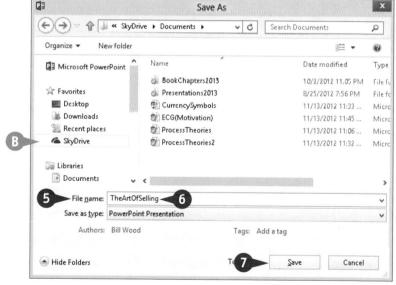

Ⓑ The Save As dialog box appears with the Documents folder in SkyDrive selected.

5. Click the **File name** text box.

6. Type a name.

7. Click **Save**.

PowerPoint saves your presentation to SkyDrive.

I previously saved my presentation to my computer. Where is it now?

Just like any other Save As operation, you now have a presentation in both the original save location on your computer and SkyDrive. If you want people to see changes that you make, you need to make the changes to the presentation in the SkyDrive location.

Now that I saved the presentation to SkyDrive, how do I get to it?

Double-click your user folder icon on your Desktop, and then look in your user folder (the user folder in the example in this section is named Bill Wood). The folder is named SkyDrive and the icon looks like two clouds. You can also click **SkyDrive** on your Windows 8 Start screen.

Share the Presentation with SkyDrive

People with permission to access your presentation on SkyDrive can edit or view the presentation with the PowerPoint application on their computer. They can also access the presentation with the PowerPoint Web App if they do not have Office 2013 on their computer. Sharing a presentation with SkyDrive sends an e-mail and link to people, and enables permission in SkyDrive for those people to access the file. You can also create a link to the presentation manually so you can copy and paste the link.

Share the Presentation with SkyDrive

Share via E-mail

Note: You must save the presentation to SkyDrive before sharing it.

1. Click the **File** tab to show Backstage view.

2. Click **Share**.

3. Click **Invite People**.

4. Click the text box and type recipients' e-mail addresses.

5. Click the **Permissions** down arrow (▾).

6. Click **Can edit** or **Can view**.

7. Click the text box and type a message to the recipients.

8. Click **Share**.

A PowerPoint adds the recipients to the Shared list and sends them an e-mail with a link to SkyDrive.

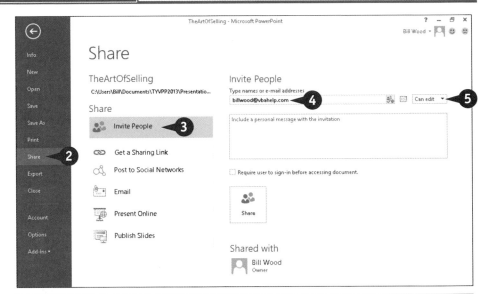

Share via a Link

Note: You must save the presentation to SkyDrive before creating a link.

1 Click the **File** tab to show Backstage view.

2 Click **Share**.

3 Click **Get a Sharing Link**.

4 Click **Create Link**.

B PowerPoint creates a link to the presentation on SkyDrive. You can copy and paste this link into a web browser to access the presentation. Note that there is a link for editing and a link for viewing.

Note: You can paste this link to a Word or Notepad document and put it on a network drive for people to access, or you can send it to someone in an instant message.

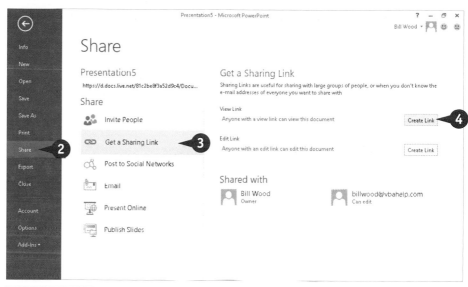

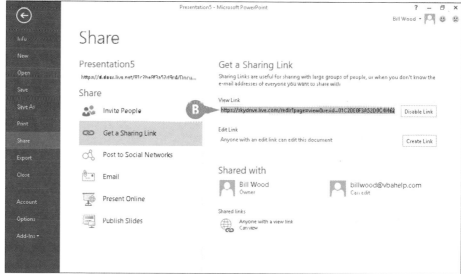

TIPS

When I click Invite People, a button appears that says Save to Cloud. What does this mean?

You have not yet saved the presentation to SkyDrive. Click **Save to Cloud** and the Save As screen appears. Then save the presentation to SkyDrive (for more information, see the section, "Save the Presentation to SkyDrive").

I want to give permission to edit to some people, and permission to view to others. Can I do that?

You can repeat Steps **2** to **8** for each person; in this case, you would need to do it twice. Repeat the process, but change the recipients, the message, and the choice in Step **6** from *Can edit* to **Can view**. Click **Share**, and PowerPoint adds those people with viewing permission.

Index

Index